THE DAIRY BOOK OF HOME MANAGEMENT

Published by Wolfe Publishing Ltd.
10 Earlham Street, London WC2
for the Dairy Industry.

Contributors

JOHN ALBION
ALBERT ALLEN
LAURIE ANDERS
DR. ROBERT ANDREW
PETER CAVE
JOHN GASELEE
MARION HARRIS
AMBROSE HEATH
RONALD HOGG
B. J. HURREN
MARIE JENNINGS
JOANNA MACDONALD
VIOLET SIMONS
ANNE TURNER
F. R. UNDY
JOHN VINCENT
LORNA WALKER
RONALD WARRING
ERNA WRIGHT

Line drawings by
STEPHEN PRITCHARD, F.R.S.A.
and DAVID HUNTER

Also in this series: **THE DAIRY BOOK OF HOME COOKERY**

SBN 72340142 X

© Milk Marketing Board of England and Wales 1969

******

2

Contents

CONTENTS

COLOUR PAGES

COVER PHOTOGRAPHS : Melvin Grey

New Money, Weights & Measures

Decimalisation means the changeover of our highly individual system of £ s. d. (sterling) to a system based on tens and multiples of ten. **Metrication** is an invented word which implies the changeover from our even more individual system of measurement.

MONEY

Our old monetary system uses three separate units—the Pound, the Shilling and the Penny. The new system uses only two, the Pound and the New Penny.

Symbols for the new currency are £ for the Pound and P for the New Penny. The Pound is divided into 100 New Pennies, so that each New Penny is worth 2.4 times the old one.

We have used seven coins—2s. 6d., 2s., 1s., 6d., 3d., 1d., ½d. Under the new system we have only six. These will be:

NEW		OLD
½p.	(bronze)	1.2d.
1p.	(bronze)	2.4d.
2p.	(bronze)	4.8d.
5p.	(cupro-nickel)	1s.
10p.	(cupro-nickel)	2s.
50p.	(cupro-nickel)	10s.

'D' day—the day when banks and most government departments change over to decimal working is 15th February 1971.

There is no exact equivalent in the new coins for some amounts under 1s. Here is the approximate conversion table:

£ s. d.	Decimal	£ s. d.	Decimal
1d.	½p.	7d.	3p.
2d.	1p.	8d.	3½p.
3d.	1p.	9d.	4p.
4d.	1½p.	10d.	4p.
5d.	2p.	11d.	4½p.
6d.	2½p.	1s.	5p.

● *Note that only the 6d. and 1s. values convert exactly to the new values of 2½p. and 5p. All the others are approximations.*

CONVERSION

The table shown here enables you quickly to convert old amounts under 10s. into New Pennies. The old amounts run across the top and down the side of the table, and the answer you are looking for is where the two columns cross expressed in New Pennies. Thus 6s. 4d. becomes 31½p. and 9s. 2d. becomes 46p.

	1d	2d	3d	4d	5d	6d	7d	8d	9d	10d	11d
0	½	1	1	1½	2	2½	3	3½	4	4	4½
1/-	5	5½	6	6	6½	7	7½	8	8½	9	9	9½
2/-	10	10½	11	11	11½	12	12½	13	13½	14	14	14½
3/-	15	15½	16	16	16½	17	17½	18	18½	19	19	19½
4/-	20	20½	21	21	21½	22	22½	23	23½	24	24	24½
5/-	25	25½	26	26	26½	27	27½	28	28½	29	29	29½
6/-	30	30½	31	31	31½	32	32½	33	33½	34	34	34½
7/-	35	35½	36	36	36½	37	37½	38	38½	39	39	39½
8/-	40	40½	41	41	41½	42	42½	43	43½	44	44	44½
9/-	45	45½	46	46	46½	47	47½	48	48½	49	49	49½

10/- = 50p

METRICATION

The most important of the old measures in domestic use are:

WEIGHT (AVOIRDUPOIS)
16 ounces	=1 pound (lb.)
14 pounds	=1 stone
28 pounds (2 stone)	=1 quarter
112 pounds (4 quarters)	=1 hundredweight (cwt)
20 hundredweight	=1 ton

LENGTH
12 inches	=1 foot (ft.)
3 feet	=1 yard
1,760 yards	=1 mile
5,280 feet	=1 mile

AREA (SQUARE MEASURES)
144 sq. inches	=1 sq. ft.
9 sq. ft.	=1 sq. yard
4,840 sq. yards	=1 acre
640 acres	=1 sq. mile

VOLUME
5 fluid ounces	=1 gill
4 gills	=1 pint
2 pints	=1 quart
4 quarts	=1 imperial gallon

Compare this complicated system with the metric system:

WEIGHT
10 decigrammes	=1 gramme (g.)
10 grammes	=1 decagramme (dag.)
10 decagrammes	=1 hectogramme (hg.)
10 hectogrammes	=1 kilogramme (kg.)

● *The only weights in common use are the gramme and the kilogramme.*

LENGTH
10 millimetres	=1 centimetre (cm.)
10 centimetres	=1 decimetre (dm.)
10 decimetres	=1 metre (m.)
10 metres	=1 decametre (dam.)
10 decametres	=1 hectometre (hm.)
10 hectometres	=1 kilometre (km.)

● *The only lengths in common use are the centimetre, the metre and the kilometre.*

AREA

These are the same as for length, except that the word 'square' is inserted before each measurement, as in:

1 sq. hectometre	=10,000 sq. metres (a hectare)
1 sq. kilometre	=1,000,000 sq. metres

VOLUME
10 centilitres	=1 decilitre (dl.)
10 decilitres	=1 litre (l.)
10 litres	=1 decalitre (dal.)
10 decalitres	=1 hectolitre (hl.)

Comparison

WEIGHT
1 gramme	=0.035 ounces
1 kilogramme	=2.2 pounds

LENGTH
1 millimetre	=0.039 inches
25.4 millimetres	=1 inch
1 metre	=39.37 inches
	=3.28 feet
	=1.09 yards
1 kilometre	=3,281 feet
	=0.62 miles (about ⅝)

AREA
1 sq. metre	=10.764 sq. ft.
1 sq. hectometre	=2.5 acres
1 sq. kilometre	=0.386 sq. miles

VOLUME
1 litre	=1.76 pints
	=0.22 gallons
1 cubic metre	=1.3 cubic yards
	=220 gallons

RULE-OF-THUMB GUIDE
28 grammes (roughly 30 grammes)	=1 oz.
50 grammes	=1¾ oz.
100 grammes	=3½ oz.
250 grammes	=8¾ oz.
500 grammes (½ kilo)	=1 lb. 1½ oz.
750 grammes (¾ kilo)	=1 lb. 10 oz.
1000 grammes (1 kilo)	=2 lb. 3 oz.
1 Litre	=1¾ pints
½ Litre	=17½ fld. oz.

(These figures are approximate)

TEMPERATURE

The conversion of Fahrenheit temperatures into Centigrade has been in use for some time, but still causes confusion. Here is the table:

● *0 °C is the freezing point of water.*
● *15 °C is the temperature on a warm spring day.*
● *36.8 °C is the normal body temperature.*
● *100 °C is the boiling point of water.*
● *The arithmetic involved to convert Fahrenheit to Centigrade is: subtract 32, multiply by five and divide by nine.*

Kitchen Planning

It isn't easy to lay down hard and fast rules for planning a kitchen—so much depends on what you have available, in terms of space, equipment and money. There are, though, some priorities which should be observed if you are to have a pleasant, easy-to-work-in kitchen.

KITCHEN LAYOUT

Kitchen planning really means using the space available. Briefly, the following is considered as essential equipment for the kitchen:

● *A kitchen sink. For general use—to include a certain amount of clothes-washing—this should be not less than 10 in. deep with 15 in. between the spout of the taps and the bottom of the sink, to allow for the easy removal of full buckets.*
● *Working surfaces. Free-standing or built-in, if possible with washable tops.*
● *Cooker.*
● *Refrigerator.*
● *Larder.*
● *Laundry equipment—washing machine, spin dryer, electric iron and ironing board and airing facilities.*
● *Storage-room for dry goods, vegetables, bread, cooking utensils.*
● *Rubbish-disposal facilities.*

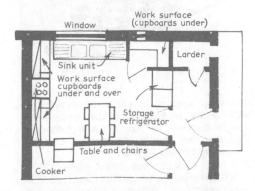

A kitchen plan showing the principles of good design as promoted by the Council of Scientific Management in the Home.

The correct sequence of kitchen layout (as recommended by the Council of Scientific Management in the Home) should be:

Work-surface/cooker/work-surface/sink/work-surface

As you will see from our illustrations, this sequence can be obtained in many permutations.

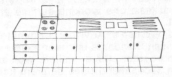

1.   All along one wall of the kitchen

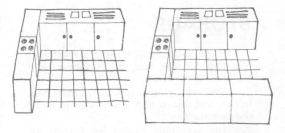

2.   In an L-shape   3.   In a U-shape

Stick as closely to this plan as you can. Your kitchen will be an easier, more pleasant place to work in as a result. Here are some additional tips:

Cooker, sink and working surfaces. These should be as close together as possible. Under the window or at right angles to it are the best positions. Because of plumbing requirements, the sink should be placed first. The housewife should not have to work in her own light.

Storage requirements. It helps to have storage places as near the kitchen door to the rest of the house as possible. Access to the working surfaces is also important, and remember that condiments and flavourings should be near the cooker. Vegetable racks should be in a well-ventilated area.

Utensils and kitchen cutlery. These are best kept near the sink, and/or near the cooker.

Cleaning materials. Many need to be near the sink, where they will be used. Mops, brushes, cleaners, etc. should be kept away from food.

HEIGHTS FOR WORKING SURFACES

Recent research indicates that the standard height of three feet for working surfaces is not always convenient. For certain types of work, 2 ft. 9 in. is right. Have at least one working surface at this height.

The Women's Advisory Committee of the British Standards Institution representing more than three million women in Britain, recommend three different heights for the working surfaces in any one kitchen.

STORAGE

Storage should not be just a matter of reaching for the nearest cupboard and stuffing things away.

1. Store the most-used items from two to five feet above floor level. This reduces the need to stretch.

2. The maximum height for a shelf for comfortable reach is 5 ft. 10 in., or 5 ft. 6 in. if it is over a working surface which has to be leant across. Do not put things you need frequently above this height.

3. Adjustable shelving is most economical on space. Open-plan shelving is sensible if you have no dust problems.

4. Narrow shelves (2 to 12 in. wide) are most useful, because you can see everything clearly.

DO-IT-YOURSELF KITCHEN PLANNING

Assuming that a housewife is faced with replanning her kitchen, how should she set about it? Here is a step-by-step plan.

1. Examine the area in the kitchen. Is it large enough for your needs? If it isn't,

A simple conversion of an old kitchen. Above: the original layout. Below: The kitchen after conversion, the main points of which are: provision of new cupboards and working surfaces, boxing-in of protruding pipes, etc., replacement of the old cooker, cutting-in of a window, tiling of the floor and better lighting.

can you 'stretch' it, either by moving a wall or by re-organising the equipment you will need to have in the kitchen? Perhaps the laundry equipment can be placed elsewhere in the home.

2. Next look at these three points:

Ventilation. Adequate ventilation is very important. Windows alone are not enough. You have to consider the condensation created by cooking. Make sure you have adequate air-changes for comfort.

Lighting. Inadequate lighting, apart from being dangerous, can have bad psychological effects on the family.

Heating. Very often the kitchen is left unheated because the assumption is that the cooking and laundry processes will provide the necessary heat. There are many jobs done in the kitchen, however, that do not generate heat, and so you should consider some other form of background heating for the kitchen.

3. The next areas for attention are the walls and the floor.

Walls. It is considered that a pound of grease is vapourised on to the kitchen surfaces every day. This means that enamel, plastics, chrome, tiles and paintwork gradually become dulled with a film of grease and dirt, and this applies particularly to white and pastel shades. So choose sturdy gloss paint for kitchen walls, or specially-marketed kitchen wallpapers and kitchen wall-coverings.

Also, unless you can afford very frequent redecoration, choose colours which will look fresh as long as possible. Remember that walls and ceilings should be easy to clean, and should not reflect glare.

Colour schemes are a matter for personal choice, but remember that the kitchen can be a hot, steamy place, and so cool and fresh colours (pale blue, lemon) can be welcomingly refreshing during a hectic 'cook-in'.

Floors. Kitchen floors should be easy to clean, quiet and resilient. Basic choice lies

COMFORT IN YOUR KITCHEN

It is possible that when you are in your kitchen you are straining your back reaching up to cupboards which are too high, or bending over sinks or working surfaces which are too low. Here are some simple guidelines to help you get maximum comfort.

1. The standard height of 3 ft. is not always convenient as a working height, an alternative height of 2 ft. 9 in. is desirable for one of the work-surfaces.

2. Most accessible storage area is from 2 ft. to 5 ft. from floor. . . use for most used items.

3. Maximum height of shelf for comfortable reach is 5 ft. 10 in.

4. Maximum height of shelf for comfortable reach across bench or over work-surface is 5 ft. 6 in.

5. Adjustable shelving is more economical of space. Open shelves are convenient for much used items but if you live in town where they can collect too much dust the advantage can be lost. It is possible though to fit roller or other 'front'.

6. Narrow shelves are most useful (up to 12 in. wide) as everything can be seen easily. Generally deep shelves do not save much wall space because they have to be more widely spaced.

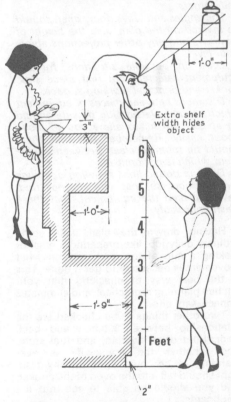

Extra shelf width hides object

Feet

7. Where the vertical spacing in a bank of shelves is not equal it is better to allow for storing the tallest items on the topmost shelf rather than on the bottom shelf.

between linoleum, plastic tiles, thermo-plastic tiles, vinyl thermoplastic tiles, polyvinyl chloride sheeting, clay quarry tiles and terrazo and mosaic.

4. You may not be able to do much about the outlook, but where there is more than one window try to have the sink by the one with the most attractive view.

5. List the equipment you have. Add a list of non-essential equipment you would like, and try to arrange this in a pencilled plan so that you can get the sequence recommended by the Council of Scientific Management in the Home. When drawing the plan note the following points:

● *All fitments and appliances should be measured accurately. So should the room itself, taking into account all projections and corners.*
● *The angles and ways doors open should be marked on the plan, also the height of windows and any other projections above floor level.*
● *Draw in possible situations for the equipment selected, but first place sink, cooker and principal working surface.*
● *Distances between pieces of equipment which are not placed side by side should be at least 30 in. to allow you to move about easily. Remember too that there should be room to clean between equip-ment which is not built-in.*
● *Draw in dotted lines showing openings for all doors so that you do not find, having placed the equipment, that these clash impossibly.*

Having drawn the plan, take some ordinary daily job, like preparing a meal or making a cup of tea, and trace in what movement is necessary to get it done. This is the best way of checking that your kitchen planning is practical, and eliminates unnecessary effort.

Two other things to be checked are the relationship between kitchen and back door, front door, dustbin, and fuel store, and whether the housewife is ever standing in her own light. Ideally also, light should fall into the oven of the cooker, and you should be able to see into the cupboards.

Pay attention to all these things, and your kitchen should be an easy and pleasant place to work in.

MODERN KITCHENS

New trends in the kitchen are emerging every day. They include:

1. Kitchens are getting larger, say 100 sq. ft. to 120 sq. ft. with dining space.

2. Correct arrangement of equipment within the kitchen is becoming even more important.

3. More eating in the kitchen, and more interest in cooking by men. Hence the introduction of cooker hoods (eliminating smoky, greasy kitchens), and the growing popularity of gadgets like the electric frying pan and other electrical cooking aids which appeal to men.

4. New types of equipment will be introduced to help the housewife make more use of storage space. 'Furniture' for shelves and drawers increases.

5. Major appliances becoming more sophisticated. Dishwashers, freezers and waste-disposal units are more widely used.

6. More and more convenience foods.

7. More disposable paperware—kitchen towels, napkins, plates and cutlery.

8. Rethinking of functions of major appliances such as cookers. More split-level cooking, and independent ovens with adjustable height for cooking and cleaning.

9. Microwave cooking to save still more time.

10. Two-sink kitchens and other sophisti-cated equipment designed to give gourmets more enjoyment from working in the kitchen.

11. Widespread use of the new non-stick, easy-to-clean surfaces—on saucepans, frying pans, rolling-pins, ovens.

12. International Standards for important equipment.

Buying Food

Between a quarter and a third of most people's incomes is spent on buying food and drink. It is the largest single item in the budget, and the more money we have the more we spend on it. We spend it on better quality, more 'convenience 'foods, more eating out.

Daily minimum food requirements are:
- *2–3 oz. meat or 4–6 oz. fish*
- *1 egg, or 1 oz. cheese, or 1 rasher of bacon*
- *½ pint of milk (1 pint for children)*
- *1 serving of fresh fruit*
- *1 serving potatoes or other root vegetables*
- *1 oz. butter*

Only after this has been provided should you think in terms of starchy foods, such as bread, cake and biscuits.

BUYING MEAT

Meat is expensive. It is a particularly important food because of the protein it contains. When you are buying meat, remember:

1. As yet there is no grading of meat, so learn to recognise good meat.

2. Choose your regular butcher with care, and ask his advice on the type and cut of meat to buy (newspapers and radio also give information).

3. Choose meat in its best season when it is most economical.

4. Meat has to be sold by either net weight or gross weight whether or not it is pre-packed.

5. Cheaper cuts of meat are as nourishing as dearer ones.

6. Carefully examine meat you buy in a supermarket. Some supermarkets have specially-tinted lights which make the meat look more attractive.

7. Although home-killed meat is considered best for flavour, frozen imported meat, carefully cooked, can be delicious.

GOOD BEEF HAS:
- *A 'bloom'*
- *A bright, light red colour*
- *Soft, creamy-coloured fat*
- *Flecks of fat in the lean, called 'marbling'*
- *A pink hue in the bone*

GOOD LAMB HAS:
- *Pink coloured flesh in very young lamb, darkening to cherry red by age, feeding and breed*
- *Fat which is almost white in home-produced, whiter and more brittle in imported lamb*
- *Bluish tinge to the bone at the knuckle end of legs and shoulders*

GOOD PORK HAS:
- *Lean, slightly pinkish colour*
- *Smooth velvety skin, firm not oily*
- *Milk-coloured fat, clean-cut edges*
- *Square joints*

GOOD VEAL HAS:
- *External layer of thin, creamy-white fat. This is home-produced dairy-fed veal*
- *Pink colour (the butcher will call it 'white')*

POULTRY

Chicken. Describes any bird you can roast, sauté, grill or fry with good results. It generally means a chicken reared for table use up to 20 weeks old, and weighing from 2½ lb. to 5 lb. 'Broilers' are chickens between 2½ lb. and 3½ lb., and aged up to 10 weeks.

Spring chicken. Used to be the description applied to a bird from eight weeks to four months old, and this is the range in which the products of the broiler industry are to be found.

Fowl. Means poultry not specifically reared for table use, and refers specially to birds at the end of their first or second laying season. If you are sold what is called a 'roasting fowl', it means one of the larger 5-to-7 lb. birds, and it probably needs careful, long cooking.

Capon. Used to mean a young cockerel, castrated, specially reared and fattened to increase quality and quantity of flesh, but today 'caponisation' may be achieved by the injection of hormone capsules into the neck of the bird. Average weight of a capon is 5-to-7 lb.

Poussin. Used to mean a small bird, between four and eight weeks old, suitable for serving one person. With the development of the broiler industry, it has come to mean a chicken weighing up to 1 lb.

A GOOD CHICKEN HAS:
● *A soft-breastbone when thawed-out, with gristle at one end only*
● *Smooth legs*
● *Smooth feet, with small scales and short spurs. If the chicken has coarse-scaled legs, hard feet and long spurs, it is old, and not suitable for roasting*

The above general signs apply to all poultry.

Turkey. Turkeys can weigh from 6 lb. to over 30 lb. All weights are dressed weights.

Ducks. 'Ducklings' are most popular, and are up to nine months old. After this age, ducks get thinner and tougher. Weight is between 3 lb. and 8 lb., and the bigger the duckling the better value for money. **Aylesbury ducks.** Means one strain of ducks reared for the table. **Norfolk ducks.** Should come from Norfolk, but often do not.

Game. The season varies with the type of game, but generally it covers August, September, October to December, February, March. Frozen game is available but expensive.

GOOD GAME HAS:
● *Feathers still on. The plumage is a good guide to age. Young birds have softer, more even feathers.*
● *Plump, pliable legs, short spurs and a firm plump breast*

MEAT PRODUCTS AND SAUSAGES

Here are some important points to remember:

1. It is more difficult to be sure of what you are getting with these products, so study the available information very carefully.

2. 'Meat paste, chicken', 'Chicken paste' and 'Chicken paté' are descriptions of different products containing different quantities of chicken, and this example is one of many. Try to know what you are buying. 'Luncheon meat' has to have at least 80% meat, while 'Meat loaf', which may look similar, needs to have no more than 65%.

With sausages, 'Frankfurters', 'Vienna sausages' or 'salami' must have 80% meat—unless they are canned, when they need have only 63%.

3. Shop around and ask questions if you are in doubt.

FISH

As a general rule, fish is cheaper than meat. It is also a most valuable source of protein, and we in this country are lucky to have a good source of many delicious varieties of fish.

Fish, frozen or fresh, must be sold by net or gross weight, like meat. You should be told the weight when you are buying. This also applies to fish products, but there are exceptions—fried fish, shellfish in the shell, jellied and pickled fish.

Fish products are as confusing to the consumer as meat products. 'Canned salmon', for example, can cover a species of fish that has no relationship to salmon.

GOOD FISH HAS:
● *Firm flesh*
● *Bright eyes*
● *Red gills, bright clear markings and scales that adhere closely to the skin*

Two further points worth remembering when you are buying fish:
● *Medium-size fish are frequently better than large ones.*
● *Cheaper varieties not to be despised. Often have higher food value than more expensive kinds*

Seawater Fish

This is divided broadly into two main groups:

White fish—fish with white flesh, such as sole, plaice, haddock, cod and whiting.

Oily fish—with richer and less easily digested flesh, such as herring and mackerel. This has considerably higher food value.

Freshwater Fish

Trout and other freshwater fish are available at some seasons, but freshwater fish is available in very small quantities by comparison with saltwater fish.

Shellfish

Make sure that shellfish are absolutely fresh.
● *Choose fish that feel heavy for their size*
● *Choose fish with shells free from incrustations—these indicate old age*
● *Oysters and mussels should have their shells tightly closed*

FRUIT AND VEGETABLES

The fruit and vegetable trades are becoming more sophisticated. Much grading is done these days, although this may not be apparent to you at the point of sale. Ask for your fruit and vegetables by grade. The grades are 1 to 3 according to quality. The weight must be known to you before you buy. Countable produce may be sold by count, and visible packs, if containing no more than eight objects, need not be marked with numbers.

How to Choose Fresh Vegetables and Fruit

1. Take a pea out of a pea pod. It should disintegrate under gentle pressure. Or a bean in the hand. If it snaps easily when bent it is fresh, if it only bends the chances are it is stale.

2. Yellower outer leaves on cabbage, savoys or brussels sprouts indicates that they are stale.

3. If the outside leaves of vegetables are missing, it could mean that they have been removed because the vegetables are stale.

4. Any shrinking and softening of root vegetables means they could be stale, or have been stored badly. They should be smooth-skinned and firm to the touch.

5. Choose fruit that feels heavy for size, is firm and not flabby.

6. You can usually judge the quality of strawberries and other soft fruit by sight. They should not be pappy or mouldy.

7. Do not buy apples with bruised or shrunken skins.

MILK

All fresh milk sold to the public is from tuberculin-tested cows. Grades of milk (explained in our section on page 59) are controlled, and government standards regulate hygiene on farms and all stages of production and distribution. The price is also controlled.

Milk must be sold by capacity measurement or by net weight. The standard pack for milk is the one-pint bottle, but smaller pack sizes are available for vending machines and other special uses. Milk sold in a vending machine must have the quantity marked on the container and on the outside of the machine.

Dried milk can be sold in any quantity or capacity, but this must be marked on the label, which must also indicate the equivalent number of pints of liquid milk if the gross weight of the container is under 10 lb.

CREAM

Cream is not price-controlled. It is usually sold in quarter-pint and half-pint quantities, but as there is no legal requirement that it should be sold in specified quantities, you may also find four fluid ounce and eight fluid ounce cartons. The container must be marked with the net weight or capacity measurement.

CHEESE

Many different kinds of cheese are made in the British Isles, and it is worth remembering that there is as much energy in 2 oz. of cheese as in ¼ lb. of steak or 6 oz. of fish.

BUTTER

Butter varies with each manufacturer but quality control ensures each brand maintains a constant flavour. Butter contains at least 80% butterfat and no more than 16% water. It also contains vitamins A and D, together with small amounts of protein, milk sugar and minerals. Pre-packed butter must be marked with the net weight, and packed in quantities of 2, 4, 8 or 12 oz., 1 lb. and 1½ lb. and multiples of 1 lb.

OTHER FATS

SUET
Block suet should be rendered beef suet free from fibrous tissue. It must contain not less than 99% beef fat. Shredded suet must not contain less than 83% beef fat, and must also be free from fibrous tissue.

LARD
Natural fat from pigs. Weights or quantities are as for butter.

EGGS

Eggs are sold by count, not weight. They are normally graded by weight into Large, Standard, Medium and Small.

Brown eggs are usually sold at 1d. or 2d. a dozen more than white-shell eggs. There is no extra food value, but many people prefer their looks.

Other varieties of eggs on sale include duck's, plover's and gull's eggs.

BREAD AND FLOUR

There are strict standards of quality of bread and flour, and also of weight of bread. Regulations control both composition and description. Because the outside part of the wheat grain, which contains some of the nutrients, is removed during the making of all flour except wholemeal flour, flour is required by law to have nutrients added to bring it back to the level of wholemeal flour.

Bread is marketed under the following broad classifications:
● *White bread. Many varieties and brand names*
● *Brown or wheatmeal bread*
● *Wheatgerm bread (e.g. Hovis)*
● *Wholemeal bread. Made from wholemeal flour only*
● *Soda bread. Contains sodium bicarbonate*
● *Milk bread. Contains not less than 6% milk solids and state 'skimmed' milk*
● *Butter bread. Contains not less than 6% butter fat*
● *Protein bread (e.g. Procea). Contains not less than 22% protein*
● *Rusks, starch-reduced breads, biscuits or breakfast cereals. Cannot be called starch-reduced unless they contain less than 50% carbohydrates (a normal loaf of bread contains 83% carbohydrates)*

How to Choose Bread

1. The crustiest bread is baked on the oven-bottom. Look for loaves with crusty bottoms.

2. A good crust can be achieved on a tin loaf if it is baked longer.

Basic Cookery

COOKING METHODS AND TERMS

Aspic. A clear savoury jelly made from stock which sets by itself or with the aid of gelatine.

Bake. To cook by dry heat in the oven.
Baste. To moisten food while it is cooking with spoonfuls of melted fat or gravy.
Beat. To stir food with a brisk whipping motion using a wooden spoon or fork.
Blanch. To plunge food in boiling water or fat for a few minutes.
Blend. Carefully to mix different foods together until they form a whole and lose their separate identities.
Boil. To heat until boiling point is reached, or cook in boiling water.
Bouquet Garni. A bouquet of herbs either tied together or wrapped in a piece of muslin, usually consisting of a bayleaf, a sprig of thyme and a piece of parsley. Used to flavour soups, sauces, casseroles, etc.
Braise. To brown foods in hot fat, then to cook them slowly in a small amount of liquid in a covered container.

Canapé. A small piece of toasted or fried bread covered with a savoury mixture.
Chop. To cut food into small pieces. For fine chopping (particularly parsley and

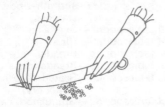

mint) use a sharp knife, holding the tip down on the board and chopping with the middle and heel of the blade.
Clarify. To clean or purify fat by bringing a mixture of fat and some water to the boil, then leaving it in a cool place. The fat settles on top of the water, and the sediment sinks to the bottom. The cleansed fat may be lifted off the water, and dried with a paper towel ready for use.

Coat. To dip food in a batter or other liquid, (usually milk or beaten egg) and breadcrumbs, or to pour sauce over a food so that it is covered.
Consistency. The texture and general appearance of a mixture.
Coating consistency. A sauce or other liquid is at coating consistency when it coats (covers) the back of a spoon dipped into it.
Croûte. A small round of fried bread used for serving steaks or savouries.
Cream. To combine foods by beating them together with a wooden spoon or fork until they are smooth, soft and fluffy.
Croûton. Small cubes of bread fried until crisp and golden. Used for garnishing soups.

Dredge. To sprinkle. Usually applied to flour, caster or icing sugar.

Escalope. A thin slice of meat.

Flambé. Food 'flamed' with brandy or fortified wine, which improves flavour and removes excess fat. Heat brandy, set it alight, quickly pour it flaming over the food.
Fold in. To mix a very light food with a heavier one by lightly turning and folding one food into the other until they are combined.
Frosting. Soft icing with a crisp surface, made from granulated sugar and used to decorate cakes.
Frying. Cooking food in hot fat. **Shallow** frying is cooking food in a shallow layer of melted fat which will cover the bottom of the pan. **Deep** frying involves immersing the food in deeper hot fat.

Garnish. Small pieces of food used to decorate and add colour to a dish.
Gill. Quarter of a pint.
Glaze. To coat with a liquid to give a shiny appearance.
Grill. To cook food quickly under a high heat.

Knead. To press, stretch and fold food with the hand to combine ingredients to a dough, and break down trapped air.

Lard. To increase the amount of fat in foods that have little of their own.

Marinade. A mixture usually of vinegar or wine, oil and seasoning. Used for steeping food to improve its flavour and make it more tender. This process is known as **marinating.**

Parboil. To cook partially by boiling before completing the cooking by some other method.

Pestle and mortar. A mortar is a bowl-shaped container made of either stone or

wood, in which foods can be pounded to a powder or purée with a pestle.

Poach. A method of cooking food by immersing in water that has been brought to boiling point then reduced to a slow simmer.

Pot roast. To cook with a little fat in a tightly-covered heavy saucepan. Particularly good for meat which may be a little tough or dry.

Pressure cook. To cook food in a specially-designed heavy saucepan which can steam the food under pressure at a very high temperature so the food cooks quickly.

Purée. To reduce cooked foods to a smooth pulp by passing them through a sieve with a wooden spoon. A similar effect may be achieved by using a liquidiser.

Reduce. To cook a liquid quickly in order to decrease the quantity, and make it more concentrated and thicker.

Roast. To cook food in an oven with fat.

Roux. Melted butter mixed with an equal quantity of flour. Used to thicken sauce and gravies.

Sauté. To cook and brown food by turning it frequently in a little very hot fat.

Score. To slit the top surface of food to allow for expansion in cooking.

Simmer. To cook food in a liquid at a temperature just below boiling point.

Souse. A method most often used for cooking fish—in mixture of vinegar and water. Not to be confused with the pickling of fish.

Steam. To cook foods in the steam from boiling liquid. A specially-designed steamer can be used, or the food may be cooked between two plates over boiling water, or in a covered basin resting in boiling water.

Stew. To cook food slowly in liquid in a covered container.

Stock. Liquid in which vegetables or the bones of fish, meat or poultry have been cooked. Used for soups, sauces, gravies, etc.

Sweat. To cook food gently in fat until it is soft and 'sweats'.

Tournedos. Thick portions of steak cut from the beef fillet.

Whip. Light, swift introduction of air by beating with a fork or hand-whisk.

Whisk. Light, swift introduction of air into a mixture by using a whisk, rotary beater or electric mixer.

Zest. Thin, coloured layer of orange or lemon peel used for flavouring. Take care not to include the bitter white pith.

MEASURES

SPOON MEASURES

The following are all approximately 1 oz.:

2 level tablespoons—Flour, custard powder, cornflour and other powdery starches

2 level tablespoons—Semolina

1 level tablespoon —Rice

5 level tablespoons—Breadcrumbs (fresh)

3 level tablespoons—Breadcrumbs (dry)

4 level tablespoons—Grated cheese (fairly dry)

1 level tablespoon —Granulated, caster and brown sugar

3 level tablespoons—Icing sugar (sifted)

2 level tablespoons—Desiccated coconut

1 level tablespoon —Syrup, honey treacle and jam

2 level tablespoons—Ground almonds, hazelnuts and walnuts

2 level tablespoons—Dried fruits (currants, sultanas and raisins)

2 level tablespoons—Cocoa powder

16

OTHER HANDY MEASURES

All cup measures shown are for British Standard Institute cups, which hold ½ pint or 10 fluid oz.

See also Weights & Measures Section

¼ cup firm packed soft brown sugar	—2 oz.
1 cup granulated sugar	—8 oz.
1 cup caster sugar	—8 oz.
1 cup flour	—5 oz.
½ cup tomato ketchup	—5 oz.
1 cup dessicated coconut	—4 oz.
1 cup grated cheese	—4 oz.
1 cup cooked lamb	—8 oz.

1 cup cooked chicken	—8 oz.
1 cup mixed dried fruit	—6 oz.
½ cup chopped mixed nuts	—4 oz.
¼ cup chopped dates	—2 oz.
½ cup seeded raisins	—6 oz.
1 cup blackberries	—8 oz.
1 cup butter or margarine	—4 oz.
3 cups rhubarb	—1 ½ lb.

OVEN SETTINGS

Description	Gas Mark	Electric Setting
Very Cool	Less than ¼	200 °F
	¼	225 °F
Cool	½	250 °F
Fairly Warm	1	275 °F
Warm	2	300 °F
Fairly Moderate	3	325 °F
Moderate	4	350 °F
Fairly Hot	5	375 °F
	6	400 °F
Hot	7	425 °F
	8	450 °F
Very Hot	9	475 °F
	More than 9	500 °F

● *This chart should be used only as a rough guide, because oven temperatures and settings vary slightly. Check with the manufacturer's temperature chart.*

VEGETABLES

Artichokes (Globe)

Season: April–September

Cut off stalk, and remove outer leaves. Wash in cold water. Plunge in boiling salted water and cook for 30–50 min. (depending on size) until soft. Serve hot with melted butter, or cold with French dressing.

● *Select artichokes that have crisp, green, fleshy leaves. They are more usually* served as a separate course. To eat, pull off the leaves, dip in melted butter, then suck off tender flesh. Heart of a globe artichoke is considered a delicacy.

Artichokes (Jerusalem)

Season: October–July

Scrub and peel very thinly. Cook in

boiling salted water to which a little vinegar or lemon juice has been added (this keeps them white) for 30–40 min. Serve hot with melted butter, or coated with white or cheese sauce.

Asparagus

Season: May–July

Cut away a little of the white, woody base of stalk. Wash asparagus carefully, tie lightly into bundles (as illustration) and either steam or boil gently for 15–30 min., time depending on thickness. Serve hot with melted butter.

● *Usually served as a separate course. Green asparagus more tender, and all stalk may be eaten. White asparagus has better flavour, but only tips are tender.*

Aubergine (Egg Plant)

Season: July–February

Wash, remove stalk, slice aubergine. Sprinkle with salt and leave for ½ hour to take away strong flavour. Rinse well. Fry slices in plenty of hot butter.

● *Aubergine may also be cut in half and baked. Good to slice and add to meat casseroles.*

Avocado Pear

Season: all year

Cut avocado in half lengthways, remove stone and fill cavity with French dressing. Serve as 'starter'.

● *Fruit should be very ripe, when it will feel soft if gently pressed.*

Broad Beans

Season: April–August

Remove beans from shells, and cook in boiling salted water for 10–15 min. until soft. Serve tossed in butter, or coated in white parsley sauce.

● *Best eaten young.*

French Beans

Season: July–September

Cut off ends, and cook whole in boiling salted water for 10–15 min. Serve tossed in butter.

● *Select fresh, crisp, unwrinkled beans.*

Haricot Beans

Season: dried, so available all year

Soak beans overnight in cold water.

Place in a pan, cover with cold salted water, bring to boil, then simmer for 2–3 hours. Serve tossed in butter, or in a white sauce.
● *Haricot beans can be put on top of pastry to prevent it rising during cooking.*

Runner Beans

Season: July–September
Cut off ends and slice thinly and diagonally. Cook in boiling salted water for 10–15 min.

Beetroot

Season: all year
Scrub and cook whole in boiling salted water, and simmer with lid on, until quite tender (2 hours or longer) peel off skin, dice and serve hot in white sauce, or leave to cool and serve sliced in vinegar.
● *Frequently sold as cooked beetroot.*

Broccoli (Head)

Season: March–May
Cut into sprigs, discarding any very thick stem. Cook in boiling salted water for 10–15 min.

Broccoli (Sprouting)

Season: March–May
Wash well and cook in boiling salted water for 10–15 min.

Brussels Sprouts

Season: September–April
Remove outer leaves, trim stalks, cut any large sprouts in half so they are all a similar size. Cook in boiling salted water for 5–10 min.
● *Do not overcook, or flavour and nourishment will be lost.*

Cabbage

Season: There are spring, summer and winter varieties
Remove outer leaves, cut into quarters and shred fairly finely. Cook in boiling salted water for 5–10 min.
● *Do not overcook. It is good shredded finely and served raw for winter salad.*

Red Cabbage

Season: October–March
May be cooked as ordinary cabbage (as above). Alternatively, wash and shred cabbage, fry some sliced onion in butter until soft, add cabbage, sliced cooking apple, few cloves, sugar, little vinegar and salt and pepper. Cover and cook very slowly for about 2 hours. May be necessary to add a little stock or water.
● *Red cabbage is a classic accompaniment to braised game or pork.*

Carrots

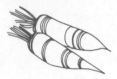

Season: all year
Scrape young carrots and leave them whole. Peel older carrots, and either cut into sticks lengthways or cut into slices. Cook in boiling salted water until tender (20–30 min. depending on age). They are good served mashed by themselves, or with other vegetables.
● *New carrots are delicious served glazed. Cook in sufficient slightly salted water just to cover, and add 1 oz. butter to every pound of carrots. Cook until liquid has nearly evaporated. Toss and serve.*

Cauliflower

Season: May–March
Cut into sprigs, discarding any thick stalk. Cook in boiling salted water for 10–15 min. May be served coated in white sauce.

Celeriac

Season: September–March
Peel off outside skin, and cut into small pieces. Cook in boiling salted water for 20–30 min. Serve tossed in butter or coated in white sauce.
● *Variety of celery with a turnip-shaped root.*

Celery

Season: August–February
May be eaten raw as salad. Alternatively, cut off green leaves, divide celery into sticks, wash thoroughly, cut into pieces and cook in boiling salted water for 20–30 min. Serve coated in white sauce.

Chicory

Season: October–March
May be eaten raw as salad, or cooked whole (or cut in quarters) in a little boiling salted water for 15–20 min. Serve with melted butter, or coated in white sauce.
● *In France, this vegetable is known as endive. To avoid discolouration when*

preparing chicory for a salad, use a stainless steel knife.

Chilli (See RED OR GREEN PEPPERS)

Corn on the Cob

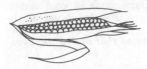

Season: July–September
Strip off leaves and 'silk' threads, trim stalk. Cook in slow-boiling salted water for 20–30 min. Serve with plenty of melted butter.
● *At its best when young and tender. Often served as separate course.*

Courgettes

Season: May–September
Wash, do not peel, cut in slices and cook in boiling salted water for 4–5 min.
● *Courgettes are young marrows. They may also be fried or cooked in the oven with a little finely-chopped garlic and butter or oil.*

Mustard and Cress

Season: all year
Wash well and remove seeds. Served as salad.

Water Cress

Season: all year
Wash well. Served as salad, and can be cooked in soups.

Cucumber

Season: all year
Served raw as salad. Alternatively, peel and dice, and cook in boiling salted water for 10–15 min. Serve in white sauce.
● *Cucumber makes delicious soup.*

Curly Kale

Season: February
Prepare as for cabbage. Cook in boiling salted water for 15–20 min.

Endive

Season: May–November
Served as salad. Alternatively, shred fairly finely, and cook in boiling salted water for 5–10 min.
● *Known as chicory in France.*

Fennel

Season: July–November
A little, finely chopped, can be added to salad. Or cook it in boiling salted water for 10–15 min., and serve in white sauce, or with melted butter and little lemon juice.
● *Finely-chopped feathery leaves of fennel can be used to flavour soups and sauces—particularly with fish.*

Garlic

Season: all year
Garlic, finely chopped or crushed, is used very sparingly as seasoning.
● *Garlic grows in bulbs, made up of several sections. Each section is called a clove.*

Horseradish

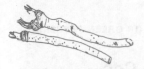

Season: October–March
Wash well, scrape, soak in cold water and then grate. Use for horseradish sauce.
● *Has pungent smell that makes the eyes water.*

Leeks

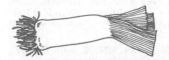

Season: August—May
Cut off roots, most of green ends and outer skin. Either leave whole and split down the middle, or cut into rings. Wash thoroughly. Cook in boiling salted water for 20–30 min. Serve with white sauce.

Lettuce

Season: all year
Cut off roots and wash thoroughly. Usually served as salad, but can be cooked by the same method as cabbage.

Marrows

Season: June–October

Peel thinly, remove seeds in older marrows, cut into even-sized pieces and cook in boiling salted water for 4–5 min. Serve with butter, or coated in white sauce.

● *Marrow is also good peeled and cut in thick slices (or left whole with seed core removed) and stuffed, then baked covered with a piece of greased paper.*

Mushrooms

Season: all year

Field mushrooms should be peeled; cultivated mushrooms wiped with damp cloth. Button ones may be shaken in colander under running water.

Slice large mushrooms—small ones may be cooked whole. Then either fry or grill with butter, or place them in piece of kitchen foil with knob of butter, salt and pepper, wrap into a parcel and cook in fairly hot oven for 15 min.

● *To prevent mushrooms shrinking and drying during grilling, blanch in boiling water first.*

Okra

Season: Imported all the year round

Cook in boiling salted water for about 30 min.

● *Okra is good added to sauces, casseroles or soups.*

Onions

Season: all year

Peel, and either boil whole for 30–40 min. and serve with white sauce, or slice and fry in butter. Also used to give flavour to soups and stews.

Parsnips

Season: August–April

Peel, cut into sticks and cook in boiling salted water for 20–30 min. Serve tossed in butter, or mashed with butter, salt and pepper.

● *Also good roasted, in the same way as potatoes, round the joint.*

Peas

Season: May–September

Shell and cook for 8–10 min. in boiling salted water to which a little sugar and a sprig of mint has been added. Serve tossed in butter.

Green or Sweet Red Peppers (Capsicums)

Season: July–February

Wash, cut in half lengthways, cut out seed core, stalk and any white pith. Blanch first if using as 'boats' for stuffing, or shred and add to casseroles, sauces or salads.

Red or Green Peppers (Chillis)

Season: March–February
Very hot. Used for seasoning, particularly in pickles and curries.

Potatoes

Season: all year
Scrape when new, or peel thinly when old. Cut into evenly-sized pieces and cook in boiling salted water for 20–30 min. (10–15 min. for new potatoes).

To prepare creamy mashed potatoes, mash hot boiled potatoes until smooth with good knob of butter and shake of pepper. Beat in little cream or milk. For fried potatoes, prepare hot fat ½ in. to ¾ in. deep, and add peeled potatoes cut into fingers for chips, or slices for French fried. Turn in hot fat until golden brown.

● *To bake jacket potatoes, prick with fork and cook in moderately hot oven for 1–1½ hours. Roast potatoes by placing in fat round joint in oven.*

Salsify (Vegetable Oyster)

Season: October–March
Wash and scrape, cook in boiling salted water for 30–35 min. Serve with melted butter.
● *Usually served as separate course.*

Seakale

Season: December–April
Trim root, and prepare as celery.
● *Often served as separate course with melted butter.*

Shallots

Season: October–January
Prepare as onions.
● *Used in sauces, stuffings and general cooking to give mild onion flavour.*

Spinach

Season: April–November
Wash thoroughly. Cut away any thick stalk, and place leaves in saucepan with no additional water. Cook for 5–10 min. Drain well. Chop finely with knob of butter.

Sweet Potatoes (Yams)

Season: September–April
Peel, cut into evenly-sized pieces and boil in salted water for 20–30 min. May also be roasted round joint of meat.
● *Delicious chestnut flavour.*

Swedes

Season: September–May
Peel fairly thickly, cut into small pieces and boil in salted water for 20–25 min. Mash with a good knob of butter, salt, pepper and little sugar.

Tomatoes

Season: all year. (English ones April–mid-November)
Raw tomatoes are used as salad. Or they can be grilled, baked or fried whole.
● *To peel tomatoes, dip them in boiling water for 10 seconds.*

Turnips

Season: all year
Peel thickly, and cut into slices. Cook in boiling salted water for about 30 min. Mash with knob of butter, salt and pepper.

HERBS AND SEASONING

Basil. Mild clove flavour. Good in tomato soups, salads and other tomato dishes.
Bay. Distinctive flavour. Add 1 or 2 leaves to meat or poultry casseroles. Keep a bay leaf in a small jar of sugar, and use the sugar for sweetening custards and milk puddings. Good added to mulled wine drinks.
Borage. Slight cucumber taste. Flowers and leaves good added to alcoholic drinks.
Chervil. Looks like fine parsley. Good in egg and fish dishes. A popular herb in Mediterranean countries.
Chives. Delicate onion flavour. Delicious in omelettes and salads, or chopped and sprinkled over soups.
Dill. Use the chopped herb for fish dishes. The seed is excellent for pickling.
Fennel. Has an aniseed flavour that goes particularly well with fish.
Marjoram. Good with pork, beef and soups, stuffings and sauces.
Oregano. A great favourite in Italian cooking. Use it in sauces to go with pasta dishes.
Rosemary. Most popular with lamb. Try a sprig under a lamb chop while it is grilling.

Tarragon. A little of the fresh herb is delicious chopped and mixed with mayonnaise to serve with a cold fish, chicken or hard-boiled egg salad. Put a sprig in a small bottle of vinegar, leave 3–4 weeks, then use vinegar for dressings and sauces.
Thyme. A versatile herb that can be added to almost any soup, stew or casserole.
Pepper. Black pepper is ground peppercorns with their skins on, which makes it milder than white pepper. To obtain the best value from pepper, grind your own. A mixture of white and black peppercorns is good.
Salt. For the best flavour, grind salt at home. Try sea salt (Maldon salt), which is made naturally by the evaporation of sea water.
Paprika Powder. A bright red powder made from dried sweet peppers. It has a delicate flavour, and can be used quite generously. Good for goulash and garnishing.
Cayenne Pepper. Made from dried hot peppers and used to season sauces and cheese dishes.
Chilli Powder. Made from **very** hot chillis. Use sparingly in meat dishes and curries.

SAUCES

BASIC WHITE SAUCE

Coating consistency

1 oz. English or Welsh butter
1 oz. flour
½ pint milk

● *Method as for pouring consistency.*

Pouring consistency

½ oz. English or Welsh butter
½ oz. flour
½ pint milk

1. Melt butter, remove pan from heat and stir in flour. 2. Gradually blend in all the milk to form smooth cream. 3. Stir continuously over medium heat until sauce comes to boil. If savoury, season to taste.

Blending consistency

1 oz. English or Welsh butter
1 oz. flour
¼ pint milk

Same method as for other consistencies, except that it is heated until very thick and leaves side of saucepan cleanly.

● *A wire whisk is ideal for making smooth sauces, but if the sauce does go lumpy it can be rubbed through a sieve. A blending sauce is used as the basis of croquettes and soufflés.*

APPLE SAUCE

½ lb. cooking apples
1 tablespoon water
½ oz. English or Welsh butter
1 level tablespoon sugar

1. Peel and core the apples. Cut them up roughly and cook to a pulp with water and butter. 2. Beat cooked apple until smooth (or pass it through sieve) and sweeten with sugar.
● *For roast pork, duck and goose.*

BARBECUE SAUCE

1 recipe French dressing
½ small onion finely chopped
1 teaspoon Worcester sauce
1 tablespoon tomato ketchup

1. Mix all ingredients well together. 2. Brush sauce on steaks, chicken portions, chops, sausages or hamburgers to be barbecued or grilled. 3. While cooking baste frequently.

BEARNAISE SAUCE

2–3 tablespoons vinegar (wine or tarragon vinegar is best)
1 shallot
1 bayleaf
Blade of mace
4 peppercorns
2 egg yolks
3–4 oz. softened English or Welsh butter
Salt and pepper

1. Heat the vinegar with the spices until it is reduced to one tablespoonful. 2. Place egg yolks in basin over simmering water, taking care to see water does not touch bottom of basin or sauce will overcook. 3. Stir egg yolks and strain in reduced vinegar. Continue stirring, and gradually add knobs of butter until the sauce is as thick as whipped cream. Season.
● *For steaks or shellfish. Thin down with cream if too thick.*

BECHAMEL SAUCE

½ bay leaf
½ chopped onion
Blade of mace
2 cloves
½ sliced carrot
½ pint of milk

1. Slowly cook all the ingredients in the milk. 2. Strain, and make as basic white sauce.

BASIC BROWN SAUCE

1 onion
½ carrot
½ oz. dripping
½ oz. flour
½ pint stock
½ teaspoon tomato purée
Salt and pepper

1. Cut vegetables into small pieces, and fry in dripping over very low heat. 2. Stir in flour, and continue cooking slowly until flour is well browned, **not burned**. 3. Remove pan from heat, and carefully stir in stock, keeping sauce smooth. 4. Cover and simmer sauce for 30–40 min. 5. Strain and season with tomato purée, salt and pepper.

SAUCE BIGARRADE

½ pint basic brown sauce
Rind and juice of ½ orange
2 tablespoons red wine
1 teaspoon redcurrant jelly

Stir finely-grated rind and juice of half an orange, red wine and redcurrant jelly into strained brown sauce.
● *Good with game and rich poultry.*

BREAD SAUCE

½ pint milk
1 small coarsely-chopped onion
2–3 cloves
1 oz. English or Welsh butter
2 oz. fresh breadcrumbs
Salt and pepper

1. Heat milk, onion and cloves together very slowly. 2. When milk boils, remove pan from heat, and leave contents to infuse for at least ½ hour. 3. Strain milk on to breadcrumbs and butter. Re-heat just before serving. Season to taste.
● *For roast turkey and chicken. If you like stronger flavour, leave onions in sauce.*

SAUCE CHASSEUR

½ pint brown sauce
1 shallot (or ½ small onion)
½ oz. English or Welsh butter
2 oz. sliced mushrooms
1 glass white wine
1 teaspoon tomato purée

CAPER SAUCE

1 oz. English or Welsh butter
1 oz. flour
¼ pint milk
¼ pint meat stock
1 tablespoon capers
Little vinegar

Make as for basic white sauce, but use half milk and half stock. Stir in the capers and vinegar to taste.
● *Served with boiled mutton.*

CHEESE SAUCE (MORNAY)

½ pint basic coating white sauce
2–4 oz. grated English cheese
½ teaspoon mixed mustard
Salt and pepper

Beat grated cheese and mustard into the hot white sauce. Season to taste.
● *Makes good supper dish poured over cooked vegetables, hard boiled eggs or ham wrapped round cooked leeks.*

CRANBERRY SAUCE

½ lb. cranberries
¼ pint water
2–3 oz. sugar
Port wine (optional)

1. Stew cranberries in water until skins burst. 2. Rub all through sieve. 3. Sweeten to taste with sugar. Add little port wine if liked.
● *For roast turkey.*

EGG SAUCE

½ pint basic coating white sauce
1 hard-boiled egg
Salt and pepper

Chop the hard-boiled egg, and add to white sauce. Season to taste.
● *Good with veal dishes.*

1. Finely chop shallot and fry until soft. 2. Add sliced mushrooms, and cook them lightly. 3. Add wine, and boil rapidly for a few minutes. Stir in brown sauce and tomato purée.
● *For grilled or roast meat.*

FRENCH DRESSING

1 tablespoon wine vinegar
3 tablespoons olive oil
Pinch sugar
Salt and pepper
½ coffee spoon mixed mustard
Little crushed garlic (optional)

Place all ingredients in stoppered bottle and shake well.
● *For tossing salads.*

HOLLANDAISE SAUCE

2 egg yolks
2 tablespoons stock
Salt and pepper
Cayenne pepper
3–4 oz. softened English or Welsh butter
1 tablespoon lemon juice

1. Beat egg yolks in basin, stir in stock, salt, pepper and cayenne. 2. Stand basin over simmering water (do not let water touch bottom of basin) and whisk until sauce is thick. 3. Remove from heat, and whisk in knobs of butter by degrees, stir in lemon juice and adjust seasoning to taste.
● *For salmon, asparagus and other vegetables served as separate course.*

HORSERADISH CREAM SAUCE

½ pint basic coating white sauce
2 rounded tablespoons finely-grated horseradish
1 dessertspoon vinegar
Pinch of sugar
2 tablespoons fresh double cream

Beat all other ingredients into basic white sauce
● *Good with roast beef or baked trout.*

MADEIRA SAUCE

½ pint brown sauce
1 Sherry glass Madeira wine

Stir wine into brown sauce.
● *For roast beef and grills.*

MAITRE D'HOTEL SAUCE

½ pint basic coating white sauce
1 tablespoon finely chopped parsley
1 tablespoon lemon juice
2 tablespoons fresh double cream
Salt and pepper

Stir all other ingredients into basic white sauce. Season to taste.
● *Good with fish, in which case substitute fish stock for half the milk.*

MAYONNAISE

2 egg yolks
1 tablespoon vinegar
Salt and pepper
¼–½ pint oil

1. Stir egg yolks and vinegar together, season well with salt and plenty of pepper, **stirring continuously** with wire whisk. 2. Add oil a drop at a time. After about 2 tablespoons of oil added, let rest run in in steady trickle. 3. If mayonnaise becomes too thick, thin down with little lemon juice or warm water.
● *For salads and shellfish cocktails.*

MINT SAUCE

2 tablespoons finely-chopped mint
Pinch of salt
2 level teaspoons sugar
1 tablespoon boiling water
3 tablespoons vinegar

1. Stir chopped mint, salt, sugar and boiling water together. 2. When cold, mix in vinegar.
● *Serve with roast lamb. The boiling water helps to hold the green colour of the mint, and dissolves sugar.*

MUSHROOM SAUCE

½ pint basic coating white sauce
2–4 oz. cooked, chopped mushrooms
1 teaspoon lemon juice
Salt and pepper

Stir mushrooms and lemon juice into basic white sauce. Season to taste.

MUSTARD SAUCE

1 oz. English or Welsh butter
1 oz. flour
1 level tablespoon mustard powder
$\frac{1}{2}$ pint milk

Combine mustard powder with flour, then follow method for making basic white sauce.
● *Good with grilled herrings, mackerel and boiled fish.*

ONION SAUCE (SOUBISE)

$\frac{1}{2}$ pint basic coating white sauce
1–2 large onions
1–2 tablespoons fresh double cream
Salt and pepper

Peel and coarsely chop the onions. Cook them in boiling water until tender. Either very finely chop or sieve them into white sauce. Stir in the cream. Season to taste.
● *For lamb and veal dishes, or tripe.*

PARSLEY SAUCE

$\frac{1}{2}$ pint basic coating white sauce
$\frac{1}{4}$ level tablespoon finely chopped parsley

Add parsley to boiling sauce, and cook for one minute.
● *For boiled bacon, ham, chicken or fish.*

SAUCE PIQUANTE

$\frac{1}{2}$ pint brown sauce
1 oz. lightly-fried mushrooms
2 teaspoons Worcester sauce
1 tablespoon vinegar
1 tablespoon finely-chopped capers
2 finely-chopped gherkins

1. Chop the mushrooms and add them with all the other ingredients to the brown sauce. **2.** Simmer for 5 min.
● *For pork, ham and bacon dishes, and hamburgers.*

TARTARE SAUCE

$\frac{1}{4}$ pint mayonnaise
1 teaspoon chopped parsley
1 teaspoon chopped chives
1 tablespoon finely-chopped gherkins or fresh cucumber
1 teaspoon chopped capers

Stir all other ingredients into mayonnaise.
● *Good with fish.*

VINAIGRETTE DRESSING

1 recipe French dressing
1 tablespoon finely-chopped mixed fresh herbs

Combine herbs with French dressing.
● *Cold vegetables can be marinated in this dressing and served as a starter.*

MEAT, POULTRY & GAME

COOKING MEAT

1. Wipe meat clean with damp cloth or paper towel.
2. Salt meats (ham, bacon, salt beef) should be soaked in cold water for 6 to 12 hours before cooking.
3. When boiling meat, always start with cold water—just sufficient to cover the joint. Calculate cooking times from the time the water comes to the boil as follows:
   Salt Beef: 25 min. to the pound plus 25 min.
   Bacon and Ham: 30 min. to the pound plus 30 min.
   Mutton: 20 min. to the pound plus 20 min.

4. When grilling meat, only the most tender cuts should be used. Meat can be made more tender, and given more flavour, by marinating (see Cooking Terms) first. The grill should be pre-heated until it is glowing red, so the meat is quickly cooked under a fierce heat.
5. To stew or casserole meat, cut into bite-sized pieces, toss in seasoned flour and fry in a little very hot fat to seal in the juices. Add stock or water to barely cover the meat and prepared root vegetables. Cover closely, and cook **slowly** on top of the oven (stew) or in the oven (casserole) until the meat is tender.

CUTS OF BEEF AND HOW TO COOK THEM

CUT	COOKING METHODS	POINTS TO NOTE
Chuck Steak	Stew or braise	Needs long, slow cooking
Brisket and Flank	Stew, braise or pot-roast	Can be pickled or boiled
Fillet Steak	Grill, fry or roast	
Oxtail	Stew, braise or use for soups	Good, rich flavour
Ribs	Roast on the bone or rolled	
Rump Steak	Grill or fry	More flavour than fillet, but not so tender
Shin	Stew, or use for soups	Needs long, slow cooking
Silverside	Pickle, boil or pot-roast	
Sirloin	Roast (on the bone or rolled), grill or fry as steak	Good flavour
Topside	Roast or braise	

Leg   **Rolled brisket**   **Thick flank**

Topside   **Shin**   **Rolled loin**

CUTS OF BEEF
1. Thick flank
2. Topside
3. Rump
4. Rump steak
5. Sirloin
6. Best rib
7. Rolled rib
8. Brisket
9. Silverside
10. Shoulder
11. Chuck
12. Neck
13. Shin
14. Oxtail

Thick rib   **Middle rib**   **Fore rib**

Oxtail   **Silverside**   **Sirloin**   **Neck**   **Chuck**   **Rump steak**

CUTS OF LAMB AND MUTTON AND HOW TO COOK THEM

CUT	COOKING METHODS	POINTS TO NOTE
Best End of Neck (Joint and Cutlets)	Roast as a joint, fry, grill or casserole as cutlets	Can be made into a crown roast, which is two Best Ends of Neck, with chine bones removed, tied together to form circle (bone-side out). Centre can be stuffed.
Breast	Stew, braise or roast	For roasting, this joint is best boned, stuffed and rolled
Leg (Whole, or cut into shank and fillet)	Roast or boil	
Loin	Roast on bone, or stuff and roll	
Loin and Chump Chops	Fry or grill	
Middle Neck	Stew or casserole	Good for broths and hot-pots
Saddle	Roast	Saddle is both loins together, from ribs to tail. Saddle of mutton weighs 8–11 lb. Saddle of lamb weighs 5–7 lb.
Scrag End of Neck	Stew	Good for soups
Shoulder (Whole or Half)	Roast	Particularly 'sweet' meat

Leg   **Shank end**   **Fillet of leg**

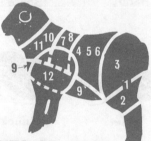

CUTS OF LAMB
1. Leg
2. Shank end
3. Fillet
4. Chump chop
5. Loin
6. Loin chop
7. Best end of neck
8. Chop
9. Breast
10. Middle neck
11. Scrag end of neck
12. Shoulder

Middle neck   **Scrag end of neck**   **Best end of neck**

Rolled shoulder   **Shoulder**   **Loin**   **Loin chop**   **Above: Cutlet Right: Breast**

CUTS OF PORK AND HOW TO COOK THEM

CUT	COOKING METHODS	POINTS TO NOTE
Belly	Boil, braise or roast (stuffed and rolled)	
Leg (whole or divided into Fillet or Knuckle)	Roast or boil	To make crackling on roast pork, score uncooked rind with sharp knife, brush with oil and sprinkle with salt
Loin	Roast or, when cut into chops, grill or fry	
Shoulder (or blade bone)	Roast or braise	
Spare Rib	Roast or, when cut into chops, grill or fry	
Trotters	Stew	Use for brawn

Hand

Spare rib

Fillet

Knuckle

CUTS OF PORK
1. Head
2. Knuckle
3. Fillet
4. Chump chop
5. Hind loin
6. Loin chop
7. Fore loin
8. Chop
9. Belly
10. Spare rib
11. Blade bone
12. Hand

Belly

Chump chop

Hind loin

Chop

Loin chop

Fore loin

CUTS OF BACON AND HOW TO COOK THEM

CUT	COOKING METHODS	POINTS TO NOTE
Corner Gammon	Boil, or grill or fry as rashers	
End Collar	Boil	Very economical. Skin after cooking.
Flank	Boil	
Fore hock	Boil (boned or rolled)	
Fore knuckle	Boil	
Gammon knuckle (or Hock)	Boil	
Long back	Boil, or fry or grill as rashers	
Middle gammon	Bake or boil, or grill in thick rashers	Good sized lean joint
Oyster	Boil	
Prime back	Roast or boil, or cut into rashers and grill or fry	
Prime collar	Boil, or grill or fry as rashers	
Slipper gammon	Boil	Small lean joint
Thin streaky	Fry or grill as rashers	
Top back	Roast or bake, or fry or grill as rashers	An economical cut
Wide streaky (or prime streaky)	Boil, or fry or grill as rashers	

Prime collar   **Top back**   **Long back**

Corner gammon   **Middle gammon**   **Gammon knuckle**

Slipper gammon   **Fore knuckle**

Wide streaky   **Thin streaky**

CUTS OF BACON
1. Slipper gammon
2. Gammon knuckle
3. Middle gammon
4. Corner gammon
5. Long back
6. Oyster
7. Prime back
8. Top back
9. Prime collar
10. End collar
11. Fore hock
12. Fore knuckle
13. Wide streaky
14. Thin streaky
15. Flank

Prime back   **Oyster**   **Flank**   **Fore hock**   **End collar**

CUTS OF VEAL AND HOW TO COOK THEM

CUT	COOKING METHODS	POINTS TO NOTE
Best End of Neck	Roast, fry or grill as cutlets	Because veal is very lean, it is more economical to use than its price sometimes suggests. The delicate flavour of the meat is best combined with highly-flavoured sauces and accompaniments
Breast	Roast or stew	
Fillet Leg	Roast or, when cut into thin slices, fry	
Loin	Roll and roast or, when cut into chops, grill or fry	
Scrag/Middle Neck	Stew or braise	
Shoulder (Whole or Divided)	Roast or stew	
Leg	Roast	
Knuckle	Stew or bake	

Shoulder or oyster

Breast

Loin and chump

Loin cutlets

Leg

Knuckle

Neck

CUTS OF VEAL
1. Fillet leg
2. Loin and chump
3. Best end of neck
4. Shoulder or oyster
5. Breast
6. Middle neck
7. Scrag
8. Leg
9. Head
10. Knuckle

**Best end of
Neck cutlets**

Fillet

STORING MEAT

1. Always thaw out frozen meat and poultry slowly at room temperature. Then cook it straight away.
2. Do not leave meat in its paper wrapping. Remove this, and turn meat on to a plate, and cover or wrap loosely in kitchen foil or a polythene bag.
3. Meat is best purchased, cooked and eaten the same day, but if it must be kept for a short time, keep it in a cold place. The coolest part of a refrigerator is below the freezing box.
4. Once meat has been cooked, it dries out very quickly, so always keep it in a covered container or wrapped in kitchen foil or polythene.

MEAT-ROASTING CHART

MEAT	COOKING TIME	OVEN TEMPERATURE	ACCOMPANIMENTS AND GARNISH
Beef	20–25 min. to the lb., and a further 20–25 min.	375 °F or Gas Mark 5	Thin gravy, Yorkshire pudding, horseradish sauce, mustard
Lamb or Mutton	25 min. to the lb. and a further 25 min.	375 °F or Gas Mark 5	Thin gravy, mint sauce or redcurrant jelly or onion sauce
Pork	25 min. to the lb., and a further 25 min.	425 °F or Gas Mark 7	Sage and onion stuffing, apple sauce, thick gravy
Veal	25 min. to the lb., and a further 25 min.	375 °F or Gas Mark 5	Thick gravy and bacon rolls. Garnish with slices of lemon

● *Allow about 6–8 oz. meat (uncooked) per person. Time chosen depends on quality and thickness of joint. The smallest joint should be cooked for not less than 45 min.*
● *To roast, pre-set oven to required temperature. Heat little fat, put meat in the hot fat and baste well.*
● *To pot roast meat, calculate the time in the same way as for oven roasting. Melt sufficient dripping to cover bottom of large, heavy saucepan, and brown the joint in 'smoking' fat. Reduce heat, cover pan and cook slowly for required time.*

GAME-ROASTING CHART

MEAT	COOKING TIME	OVEN TEMPERATURE	ACCOMPANIMENTS AND GARNISH
Grouse (Season, 12th August– 10th December)	35–45 min. to the Grouse	400 °F or Gas Mark 6	Cranberry sauce or redcurrant jelly, bread sauce, game chips, fried crumbs, watercress
Pheasant (Season, 1st October– 1st February)	15 min. to the lb. plus 15 min.	400 °F or Gas Mark 6	Bread sauce, thin gravy, fried crumbs, watercress, game chips. Tail feathers to decorate

● *A medium grouse will serve 2 people. Game chips are deep-fried thin potato slices— potato crisps are a good substitute.*
● *A medium pheasant will serve 4 people. Although the cock bird is larger, the hen is considered to have more succulent flesh.*

POULTRY-ROASTING CHART

MEAT	COOKING TIME	OVEN TEMPERATURE	ACCOMPANIMENTS AND GARNISH
Chicken	20 min. to the lb., plus 20 min.	375 °F or Gas Mark 5	Veal or sausage meat stuffing, thin gravy, bread sauce, sausages, bacon rolls
Duck	15 min. to the lb., plus 15 min.	400 °F or Gas Mark 6	Sage and onion stuffing, gravy, gooseberry or apple sauce
Goose	Birds under 14 lb., 25 min. to the lb. plus 30 min. Over 14 lb., 20 min. to the lb. plus 15 min.	350 °F or Gas Mark 4	Sage and onion stuffing apple sauce, gravy
Turkey	Birds under 14 lb., 20 min. to the lb. plus 30 min. Over 14 lb., 20 min. to the lb. plus 15 min.	325 °F or Gas Mark 3	Sausage meat and chestnut stuffing, bread sauce, Cranberry sauce, gravy, chipolata sausages wrapped in bacon rashers

● *A 3 lb. chicken will serve 4 or 5 people. A 3½ lb. duck will serve 4 people. Duck and goose are rather rich, so prick the skin with a fork during cooking to allow the fat to run out.*
● *A 10 lb. goose will serve 8 people. As most poultry dries out during cooking, put a little stock in the bottom of the roasting pan and lightly cover the bird with foil. Remove foil ½ hour before the end of cooking.*

FISH

1. Fish should be eaten as fresh as possible.

2. Fish is delicate, and cooks quickly. It should never be over-cooked, as it easily loses its flavour.

3. Properly-cooked fish has tender, opaque flesh which flakes easily away from the bone.

4. **To poach fish,** bring stock or salted water, with a little lemon juice, vinegar or wine, to the boil, carefully lower in the fish, cover and **gently** simmer in a saucepan, or cover in the oven until cooked. White fish is particularly good poached in milk.

5. **To grill fish,** brush with melted butter, rest on a piece of buttered kitchen foil and cook slowly under a pre-heated grill.

6. **Steamed fish** is very easy to digest. To cook, butter two plates, and place the fish on one. Add a little salt, pepper and milk or lemon juice. Cover with the second plate. Place over a pan of boiling water until cooked.

7. **To bake fish,** place in a well-buttered dish or in buttered kitchen foil, season with salt, pepper and a good squeeze of lemon juice. Add a few herbs if liked, cover and cook in the oven until tender.

8. **Fried fish** can be cooked in either deep or shallow fat. To shallow fry, melt enough English or Welsh butter to give ¼ in. depth in the frying pan. When hot, add fish coated in egg and breadcrumbs or seasoned flour. Fry until fish is tender.

To deep fry, heat sufficient fat to well cover the fish. Dip the fish in batter, and when the fat is 'smoking' hot, carefully lower in the fish (a metal basket is best for this). When the fish is cooked, lift it out and drain it on absorbent paper before serving.

9. **Fish cutlets** are thick slices cut across the middle of a fish. There is a hole in the centre of a cutlet where the internal organs of the fish have been removed.

10. **Fish steaks** are thick slices cut across the fattest end of the fish tail. There is no hole in the centre.

11. **A fillet** is cut from one side of the fish backbone from head to tail.

Out-of-the-ordinary
Vegetables

1. Jerusalem (Root) artichoke
2. Globe artichoke
3. French white asparagus
4. Celeriac
5. Avocado pear
6. Courgette
7. Aubergine (egg plant)
8. Sweet potato (yam)
9. Mange Tout
10. Fennel
11. Red cabbage
12. Shallots
13. Salsify
14. Okra
15. Chilli
16. Chicory
17. Green pepper
18. Red pepper
18. American green asparagus
20. French beans
21. Horseradish

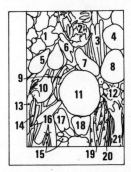

37

BUYING, COOKING AND SERVING FISH

FISH	COOKING METHODS	POINTS TO NOTE
Bass (available, May–July)	Grill, fry or poach	Freshwater or saltwater fish
Bream (all year)	Grill or bake	Freshwater or saltwater fish improved by a stuffing or well-flavoured sauce.
Brill (September–March)	All methods	Saltwater fish usually sold in fillets
Carp (September–February)	Poach	Freshwater fish at its best with a well-flavoured sauce
Cod (all year, best October–February)	All methods	Saltwater fish which can be bought fresh, smoked or salted
Coley (all year)	Fry	
Eel (all year, best in winter)	Stew	Freshwater or saltwater fish which can be bought fresh, jellied or smoked
Flounder (January–March)	All methods	
Haddock (all year, best September–February)	All methods	Well-flavoured fish which can be bought fresh or smoked
Hake (best June–January)	All methods	Saltwater fish with good flavour
Halibut (all year, best July–April)	Poach or bake	Large saltwater flat fish usually sold as steaks or cutlets. Good served with a sauce
Herring (all year, best May–October)	Grill, fry or souse	Saltwater fish. Fresh herrings are firm, bright-eyed and covered in silvery scales. Economical and nourishing. Can be bought as kippers (herrings split and smoked over oak chips) or bloaters (herrings cured whole).
Mackerel (all year, best April–June)	Grill or bake	Saltwater fish. Mackerel should only be eaten very fresh. Full of flavour and particularly good with sieved gooseberry sauce
Mullet—Red and Grey (May–February)	Bake or grill	Saltwater fish. Red mullet is a distinctive-looking fish with a rosy pink skin.

BUYING, COOKING AND SERVING FISH (contd.)

FISH	COOKING METHODS	POINTS TO NOTE
Plaice (May–January)	All methods	
Rock Salmon (all year)	Fry or stew	Particularly good for fish stew or fish salad. Saltwater fish also known as rock eel and huss
Salmon (all year imported. British, February–September)	Poach whole or in cutlets or steaks, or grill. Good hot or cold	With most fish 6 oz. (uncooked) should be allowed per portion, but salmon is very satisfying, and only 4 oz. is necessary
Salmon Grilse (best, late June–July)	Poach or bake whole	Grilse is a young salmon weighing around 3–8 lb.
Salmon Trout (April–August, best May)	Poach or bake whole	Has less pronounced flavour than salmon, and flesh is not so firm
Skate (all year)	Fry, bake or poach. Best if steamed few minutes before frying	Distinctive-looking pinky-white flesh. Usually sold in triangular pieces
Sole (all year, best July–March)	Grill, poach or bake	Saltwater flat fish with fine, firm flesh and good flavour. Dover sole is considered best
Sprats (November–March)	Fry or bake	These small saltwater fish have a particularly good flavour. Remove heads and dust in seasoned flour before frying
Trout (February–August)	Grill, fry bake or poach	Freshwater fish. Has delicate flavour
Turbot (best July–April)	Poach or steam	Saltwater flat fish. Cooked turbot has firm, well-flavoured white flesh and gelatinous skin
Whitebait (all year)	Fry	Baby fish of herrings, sprats or pilchards. Delicious left whole, dusted with seasoned flour and fried until skins are crisp
Whiting (May–December)	Usually cooked whole. Grill, fry or bake	Saltwater fish very easy to digest. Does not travel well, so best eaten near where it is caught

KNOW YOUR FISH

Freshwater Bream

Sea Bream

Brill

Carp

Cod

Conger

Eel

Haddock

Hake

Halibut

Herring

Mackerel

Plaice

Salmon

Skate

Sole

Trout

Turbot

SHELLFISH

Cockles (available all year). Usually sold cooked. Serve with vinegar and pepper.

Crabs (best May–October). Usually sold boiled. Choose a crab which looks clean and wholesome, is heavy for its size and does not sound watery when shaken. The hen crab has a broader tail-flap than the cock crab, which gives more meat and is therefore more economical. Delicious in salads.

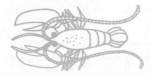

Crayfish (June–March). Look like small lobsters. Taste similar, too.

Scallops (November–March). Try them baked, fried, poached or grilled.

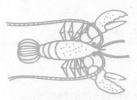

Lobsters (best in summer). Usually sold boiled. By law, lobsters must be at least 9 in. long when offered for sale. Medium-size lobsters are best. Can be cooked in many different ways. Most often eaten cold with salad.

Mussels (September–March). Known as 'the poor man's oyster', a description which speaks for itself. Buy live, and check that shells are tightly shut. Good in soups, sauces and pies, or boiled in their shells and served cold with vinegar and pepper.

Oysters (September–April). Regarded as a great luxury. Easy to digest, and therefore suitable for invalids. Eat them raw, baked, stewed or in sauces and pies.

Prawns (all year). Usually sold cooked —often peeled and frozen. Versatile and delicious. Most often served with salad and in prawn cocktails.

Shrimps (all year). Like small prawns.

PUDDINGS AND DESSERTS

BAKED RICE PUDDING

1½–2 oz. rice (short grain)
1 pint milk
1 oz. sugar
½ oz. English or Welsh butter

1. Wash rice, place it with milk and sugar into well-buttered 1½-pint pie dish. **2.** Place in moderate oven (Gas Mark 4 or 350 °F) for 10–20 min. Then reduce heat to Gas Mark 1 or 275 °F for further 2 hours. **3.** Stir from time to time during first hour of cooking. **Serves 4.**

BOILED RICE PUDDING

1. Use same ingredients as for baked rice pudding, placing them with a knob of butter in a heavy saucepan. **2.** Cook very slowly for about 2 hours until the pudding is thick and creamy.
● *These proportions of rice to milk can be used for most grain or pasta (macaroni) puddings. Rice pudding is delicious served cold with ¼ pint whipped cream folded in.*

CREME CARAMEL

3 oz. granulated sugar
4 tablespoons cold water
2 large eggs
½ oz. caster sugar
½ pint milk
½ teaspoon vanilla essence

1. Using heavy saucepan, dissolve granulated sugar in the water slowly, bring to boil without stirring and continue to boil until rich brown colour. Immediately pour the caramel into warmed mould, and coat the sides. Leave until cold. **2.** Beat eggs and caster sugar together, stir in milk and vanilla essence. Strain into prepared mould. **3.** Stand mould in pan containing sufficient water to come halfway up mould. **4.** Cook at Gas Mark 3 or 325 °F for ¾–1 hour. **5.** When cold, turn out of mould. **Serves 2 or 3.**
● *Crème Caramel is usually expensive in restaurants, but it is quite cheap and simple to prepare at home.*

EGG CUSTARD

1–2 eggs
½ pint milk
1 level tablespoon sugar

1. Beat the egg with 2 tablespoons of the milk. **2.** Heat remaining milk until warm, then slowly stir on to egg and strain into saucepan. **3.** Stir custard over low heat until it thickens and will coat back of spoon. **4.** Sweeten with sugar. **Serves 2 or 3.**
● *Using only one egg, custard does take time to thicken. To speed up process, blend 1 level tablespoon custard powder or cornflour with little milk from ½ pint. Bring rest to boil, then stir on to blended custard. Cool, then add one beaten egg. Stir over medium heat until thick. Sweeten to taste.*

BAKED EGG CUSTARD

2 large eggs
1 oz. caster sugar
1 pint milk
English or Welsh butter

1. Beat eggs with sugar, stir in milk and strain into well-buttered 1-pint pie dish. **2.** Stand pie-dish in pan containing ½ in. warm water, and place in the oven (Gas Mark 3, or 325 °F) for ¾–1 hour, or until set. **Serves 4.**
● *Can be served hot or cold. Very nourishing. Ideal for young children and invalids.*

STEWED FRUIT

¼ pint water
2–4 oz. sugar
1 lb. prepared fruit

1. Bring water to boil in covered saucepan, stir in sugar and cook slowly until it dissolves. **2.** Add fruit, and cook over very low heat for 10–20 min. until tender. **Serves 3 or 4.**
● *Quantities of sugar and water differ according to fruit. Rhubarb and apples need less water because they give off water in cooking.*

APPLE FRITTERS

1 egg
4 oz. plain flour
¼ level teaspoon salt
1 oz. sugar
¼ pint milk
English or Welsh butter
2–3 cooking apples
Deep fat for frying

1. Prepare batter as for pancakes, but use all ¼ pint milk to blend ingredients. Then add sugar. 2. Peel apples and, keeping them whole, remove cores. Slice into ¼-in. rings. 3. Dip apple rings in batter to coat. 4. Heat fat until cube of bread will turn golden brown in 1 min. (if using oil, 30 seconds). Carefully lower in the fritters, and cook for 2–3 min. until golden. 5. Drain on absorbent paper. Serve dusted with icing or caster sugar. **Serves 4–6.**

BAKED APPLES

Cooking apples
Sugar
Cloves
English or Welsh butter

1. Wipe apples, remove cores and slit skin round equator of apples. 2. Fill each core-hole with sugar and a clove. Top with a knob of butter and bake at Gas Mark 4 or 350 °F until tender.
● *Core apples by pushing potato peeler or teaspoon-handle down at side of core and turning it round. Core-holes can be filled with syrup, honey, mincemeat or mixed dried fruit and sugar.*

APPLE SNOW

2 cooking apples
2 tablespoons caster sugar
½ lemon (rind and juice)
1 white of egg
Red colouring (optional)

1. Bake apples whole (without coring) at Gas Mark 4 or 350 °F until tender. Remove skins and cores, and sieve or beat flesh to a purée. Mix apple purée with sugar, lemon juice and finely grated rind. Cool. 2. Whisk egg white until very stiff, and fold into cold purée. 3. If liked, blush the apple snow pink with a little colouring. **Serves 2 to 3.**
● *Good served with egg custard.*

APPLE AMBER

1. Cook apples in same way as for Apple Snow, making them into a purée and stirring in egg yolk. Spoon into individual soufflé dishes. 2. Whisk egg white very stiffly, fold in caster sugar, then pile over apple. Bake at Gas Mark 4 or 350 °F for 15–20 min. **Serves 2 to 3.**
● *Other fruits may be used for Snow or Amber.*

APPLE CHARLOTTE

2 oz. English or Welsh butter
3–4 oz. fresh breadcrumbs
2 oz. brown sugar
1 lb. apples (stewed)

1. Melt butter, and stir in breadcrumbs and sugar. 2. Sprinkle half crumbs over bottom of pie-dish, and cover with stewed apple. 3. Top with remaining crumbs. 4. Bake at Gas Mark 4 or 350 °F for 30–40 min. **Serves 4.**
● *Instead of breadcrumbs, thin fingers of bread can be overlapped to line mould and cover fruit. The dessert can then be turned out to serve. Other fruit may be used.*

QUEEN OF PUDDINGS

½ pint milk
½ oz. English or Welsh butter
2 oz. breadcrumbs or cake crumbs
2 eggs
2 tablespoons jam
4 oz. caster sugar

1. Bring milk and butter to boil, remove from heat and add crumbs. Cover and leave for ½ hour. 2. Separate egg yolks from whites and stir yolks into bread and milk. Turn into buttered 1 pint pie-dish. 3. Place in a moderate oven (Gas Mark 4 or 350 °F) for 20–30 min. or until set. Spread top with jam. 4. Whisk egg whites until they are very stiff, then fold in caster sugar and pile this meringue over pudding. 5. Cook at Gas Mark 3 or 325 °F for 20–30 min. until meringue is golden-tipped. **Serves 4.**
● *For separating egg whites from yolks see Meringues in the cake section.*

BREAD AND BUTTER PUDDING

3 oz. thinly-sliced bread (crusts removed)
English or Welsh butter
1 oz. dried fruit
1 oz. sugar
2 beaten eggs
1 pint milk

1. Butter bread, and cut it into 1 in. squares. Arrange with dried fruit in well-buttered 1½-pint pie dish. **2.** Mix sugar and beaten eggs with milk, and pour over bread. Leave for 1 hour. **3.** Bake at Gas Mark 4 or 350 °F for ¾–1 hour until custard sets and pudding is golden brown on top. **Serves 4–6.**
●*For a change, spread bread squares with jam or marmalade, or use stale cake instead of bread.*

FRUIT CRUMBLE

1 lb. fruit
2–3 oz. sugar
2 tablespoons water
4 oz. flour
¼ level teaspoon salt
2 oz. caster sugar
2 oz. English or Welsh butter

1. Prepare fruit, place half in pie dish, sprinkle sugar and water over, and top with remaining fruit. **2.** Place flour, salt and caster sugar in mixing bowl, and rub in butter to fine crumb. **3.** Sprinkle crumble over fruit, pat down and smooth over. **4.** Bake at Gas Mark 5 or 375 °F for 45–60 min. **Serves 4.**
● *Apples, apricots, blackberry and apple, gooseberries, plums and rhubarb make good crumbles.*

FRUIT FOOL

¼ pint egg custard
½ pint fruit purée
Sugar

1. Prepare thick egg custard (1 egg to ¼ pint milk) and leave until cold. **2.** Combine fruit purée with custard, and mix until smooth. **3.** Sweeten to taste. **Serves 3 or 4.**
● *1 lb. fresh fruit, when cooked gives ½ pint fruit purée.*

YOGURT FRUIT FOOL OR CREAM FRUIT FOOL

½ pint fruit purée
¼ pint natural yogurt or ¼–½ pint whipped cream
Sugar

1. Combine purée with yogurt or whipped cream. **2.** Sweeten to taste. **Serves 3 or 4.**
● *The fruit purée must be thick (use as little water as possible to cook the fruit) or the Fruit Fool will be too sloppy.*

PANCAKES

1 egg
4 oz. plain flour
¼ level teaspoon salt
½ pint milk
English or Welsh butter

1. Beat egg, and gradually blend in flour and salt with about half the milk to form smooth cream. Beat well. Leave for ½ hour. **2.** Stir in 1 tablespoon melted butter and remaining milk. **3.** Melt sufficient butter to moisten bottom of small frying pan. When it is hot, spoon on 2–3 tablespoons batter, tilting pan to coat the bottom. When pancake has browned on underside, toss or turn and brown other side. **4.** Repeat until all batter is used. **Makes 8–12 pancakes.**
● *Pancakes can be served spread with butter, a good squeeze of lemon juice and dredged with sugar, or spread with jam or honey. They are good, too, filled with fruit, folded over and topped with whipped cream.*
● *To re-heat, or keep pancakes hot, wrap in kitchen foil (or put them between two plates) and place in cool oven.*

JUNKET

1 pint fresh milk
1 level tablespoon sugar
1 teaspoon essence of rennet

1. Slowly heat the milk and sugar together until they are only just lukewarm (100 °F) and **not hot. 2.** Remove pan from heat, and quickly stir in the rennet. **3.** Pour at once into serving dishes, and leave in warm place until the junket has set. **Serves 4–6.**

Jellies & blancmanges

1. Vanilla blancmange
2. Chocolate and caramel layer blancmange with whipped cream
3. Quick lemon soufflé
4. Orange jelly with cream

QUICK LEMON SOUFFLE

1 packet lemon jelly
2 tablespoons water
1 lemon (rind and juice)
¼ pint double cream
1 tablespoon milk
2 separated eggs
2 oz. chopped walnuts
Whipped cream to decorate
Lemon slices

1. Dissolve jelly in the water over a low heat. Make up to ¾ pint with cold water. Add the lemon rind and juice and leave aside until almost setting. 2. Whip the cream and milk together until thick. 3. Whisk egg whites until very stiff. 4. When jelly is just setting, add egg yolks and whisk until fluffy. Fold in cream and whisked egg whites, mixing until well blended. 5. Turn souffle into prepared 1 pint souffle dish, and leave to set. 6. Press finely-chopped nuts round side of souffle, and decorate top with swirls of whipped cream and sliced lemon. **Serves 6.** lemon. **Serves 6.**
● *To prepare a soufflé dish, wrap a piece of buttered kitchen foil round dish so top edge protrudes 2 in. above dish. Secure in place with elastic band, string or sticky tape.*

BLANCMANGE

1½ oz. cornflour
1 pint milk
2 oz. sugar
½ oz. English or Welsh butter
1 teaspoon vanilla essence
Fruit (optional)

1. Blend the cornflour to smooth thin paste with little milk. 2. Bring remaining milk to boil and stir into blended cornflour. Pour back into saucepan, and stir over medium heat until mixture comes to boil. 3. Add sugar, butter and vanilla essence, pour into a wetted mould and leave until set. 4. When blancmange has set, turn out of mould, and decorate with fruit if liked. **Serves 4.**
● *Blancmange can be flavoured with grated orange or grated lemon. One level tablespoon instant coffee powder can be added to milk, or 2 oz. chocolate melted in 2 tablespoons milk. Fudge and toffee flavours can be prepared in the same way.*

TRIFLE

¼ pint cold egg custard
¼ pint whipped cream
1 Swiss Roll
1 can raspberries
Lemon or orange juice
2–3 tablespoons sherry
1 oz. almonds, blanched and split

1. Mix egg custard with whipped cream. 2. Arrange Swiss Roll, cut in slices, in dessert dish, add raspberries and sufficient of their juice to moisten Swiss Roll. Spoon over little orange or lemon juice, and the sherry. 3. Lightly spread custard cream on top of trifle, then scatter with split almonds. **Serves 4.**
● *Instead of half custard and half cream, trifle can be topped with half-pint custard and decorated with whipped cream.*

FRESH LEMON JELLY

3 small lemons (rind and juice)
½ oz. powdered gelatine
¾ pint water
4 oz. sugar
Colouring (optional)

1. Peel fruit thinly (a potato peeler does it well), then cut in half and squeeze juice. 2. Place gelatine, water, sugar and peel in saucepan, and slowly heat (without boiling) until the gelatine and sugar have dissolved. Leave to stand for 10 min., then add fruit juice. 3. Strain jelly into wetted 1-pint mould, stirring in little yellow colouring if required. Leave to set. **Serves 4.**

FRESH ORANGE JELLY

½ pint water
½ pint orange juice
Rind of one orange
Juice 1 lemon
¾ oz. powdered gelatine
3 oz. sugar
Orange colouring (optional)

Use same method as for Fresh Lemon Jelly. **Serves 4.**
● *Turn jelly out of mould by using your fingers carefully to loosen jelly from sides of mould. Dip mould in and out of sufficient very hot water to come right up sides of mould. Invert jelly on to plate.*
● *Jellies may also be prepared in variety of flavours, using packet jellies.*

FRUIT JELLY

1 pint prepared jelly
Prepared fresh, canned or frozen
fruit

1. Make jelly, and leave until cool. 2. Pour little jelly in a $1\frac{1}{2}$-pint mould or dish, and leave in a cold place until set. 3. Arrange fruit on top of set jelly, then cover with liquid jelly. Place aside until set. 4. Repeat stage 3 until all the jelly and fruit is used up.
● *The amount of fruit used in fruit jelly can vary to taste. Fruit salad set in jelly is very good.*
● *Fresh pineapple cannot be used to make jelly as it reacts with gelatine and will not set.*

MILK JELLY

$\frac{1}{2}$-$\frac{3}{4}$ oz. gelatine
$\frac{1}{8}$ pint hot water
1 pint milk
2 oz. sugar
$\frac{1}{2}$ teaspoon vanilla essence

1. Dissolve gelatine in hot water, and leave to cool. 2. Heat (not boil) milk with sugar. 3. Stir gelatine into milk, and flavour with vanilla essence. Pour into individual moulds, and turn out when set. **Serves 4.**
● *Flavoured Milk Jelly can be made by dissolving packet jelly in $\frac{1}{4}$ pint boiling water, leaving it to cool, then making it up to 1 pint with cold milk.*

JELLY WHIP

1 pint jelly

1. Prepare jelly, and place aside until it is just beginning to set. 2. Whisk jelly with rotary whisk until it is very frothy. Pour into serving dish. 3. When set, decorate with fruit and whipped cream.

PASTRY

SHORT CRUST PASTRY

8 oz. plain flour
$\frac{1}{4}$ level teaspoon salt
4 oz. English or Welsh butter (or $\frac{1}{2}$
butter and $\frac{1}{2}$ lard)
8 teaspoons cold water

1. Sieve flour and salt into bowl, and cut in butter. 2. Pinch and rub butter into flour, lifting mixture over fingertips until it looks like fine breadcrumbs. 3. Sprinkle water over, one teaspoon at a time, and work it into flour with flat side of round-bladed knife. When 8 teaspoons of water have been added, mixture should hold together, but if flour was dry a little more water may be necessary. 4. Finish by drawing it together with fingertips to form dough. 5. Roll out on board, lightly dusted with flour, to required thickness and shape. 6. Bake at Gas Mark 5 (375 °F).

● *General proportions for Short Crust are: half as much fat as flour, and about 1 teaspoon water to every ounce of flour. Can be stored wrapped in foil or polythene.*
● *Short crust is used mainly for sweet dishes such as fruit pies, tarts and tartlets. Also used for some meat pies, pastries, sweet and savoury flans. Not usually glazed, but served dusted with caster or icing sugar.*
● *If recipe calls for certain weight of pastry, this refers to quantity of flour used to prepare pastry, and not its total weight.*

Bread-making

1 Add the yeast mixture to the warmed flour to give a sticky dough. Beat with an *open* hand

2 Turn the dough on to a lightly floured board and knead by pulling the outside of the dough into the centre

4 Knead the risen dough and shape to fit the loaf tin. Leave to prove until loaf is well risen. Below: The finished loaf

3 Turn the dough into a buttered saucepan, cover, and leave in a warm place until it rises to double the size

RICH SHORT CRUST PASTRY (FLAN OR FLEUR PASTRY)

Made as Short Crust, but butter is increased to 6 oz., 1 oz. caster sugar is added, and egg yolk is used to bind the pastry together instead of water. Because of sugar, this pastry browns quicker, and should be baked at Gas Mark 5 or 375 °F.
● *Used for sweet flans or tarts. 4 oz. pastry (that is, pastry made from 4 oz. flour) will roll out to line 6–7 in. flan tin. 6 oz. pastry will line 8–9 in. tin.*

HOT-WATER CRUST PASTRY

12 oz. plain flour
1 level teaspoon salt
4 oz. lard
¼ pint milk or water

1. Sieve flour and salt into warmed mixing bowl. 2. Place lard and milk or water in saucepan, and bring barely to boil. 3. Pour immediately on to flour, and mix thoroughly with wooden spoon. Knead dough by hand until smooth. 4. Leave third of dough in bowl. 5. Using raised pie tin or small cake tin, press dough with knuckle to line it. 6. Fill the pie case. 7. Press remaining piece of dough to fit top, and seal over with milk or beaten egg. 8. Make hole in pie-top to let steam escape, and later to fill with jelly stock. Decorate the top with pastry leaves. 9. Brush with milk or beaten egg. 10. Bake at Gas Mark 7 or 425 °F for ½ hour, and then at Gas Mark 4 or 350 °F for further 1½–2 hours, depending on filling.
● *Hot-Water Crust is sometimes known as Raised Pie Pastry because it is raised to the shape by hand. It should always be worked warm because, as it cools, it hardens and sets. Used for raised game, poultry, pork, veal etc. pies.*

ROUGH PUFF PASTRY

6 oz. English or Welsh butter
8 oz. plain flour
¼ level teaspoon salt
2 teaspoons lemon juice
¼ pint cold water

1. Cut butter into walnut-size pieces. 2. Sieve flour and salt into mixing bowl, add cut-up butter and quickly mix to dough with lemon juice and water, keeping fat in lumps. 3. Roll pastry into oblong about 6 in. by 12 in., and fold into three. Seal all edges by pressing them with rolling pin, and quarter-turn pastry to left so folded edge is on right. 4. Roll pastry into oblong, and repeat instruction in Stage 3. Repeat once more so pastry has been rolled and folded three times. Cover and leave aside in cold place for 30 min. 5. Roll pastry out fairly thickly, and use as required. 6. Bake at Gas Mark 7 or 425 °F.
● *Rough Puff pastry is used for savoury pies, sausage rolls and turnovers.*
● *General proportion of fat to flour is ¾ as much fat as flour for Rough Puff and Flaky pastry.*
● *Coolness is important in making Rough Puff and Flaky pastry, so if time permits, wrap it in polythene or foil and store in a cool place for 15 min. between each rolling.*

FLAKY PASTRY

8 oz. plain flour
¼ level teaspoon salt
6 oz. English or Welsh butter (or ½ lard and ½ butter)
6–8 tablespoons cold water
2 teaspoons lemon juice

1. Sieve flour and salt into mixing bowl. 2. Divide fat into thirds. Rub one third into flour, and mix to fairly firm dough with water and lemon juice. 3. Roll dough to oblong about 6 in. by 12 in. Dot top two-thirds with small pats of half remaining fat. Fold pastry as illustrated. 4. Repeat Stage 3, and roll again into oblong, fold in three, wrap and put aside in a cool place for 15 minutes. Roll and fold once more before using. 5. Bake at Gas Mark 7 or 425 °F.
● *Flaky pastry is used for puffs, pies, turnovers, vol-au-vents and some flans.*

SUET PASTRY

8 oz. self-raising flour
½ level teaspoon salt
4 oz. grated suet
¼ pint cold water

1. Sieve flour and salt into mixing bowl. 2. Add suet to flour, and mix well with round-bladed knife. 3. Pour in sufficient water to mix soft dough that will leave bowl cleanly. 4. Press and lightly roll pastry to size and shape required.
● *Suet pastry can be used for dumplings, steamed, sweet or savoury puddings. Puddings made from suet pastry should be steamed for at least 2 hours. Pastry can be put on top of filling, in basin, used to line basin and then filled, or made into roly-poly.*

CHOUX PASTRY

¼ pint water
1 oz. English or Welsh butter
3 oz. flour
⅛ level teaspoon salt
2 eggs

1. Heat water and butter until butter melts. Bring to boil. 2. Stir in flour and salt, return pan to low heat and stir with wooden spoon until mixture leaves sides of pan clean. Remove pan from heat and cool slightly. 3. Beat in egg until smooth. Cool. 4. Spoon or pipe the pastry on to well-greased tray and bake at Gas Mark 5 or 375 °F for 25–30 min.
● *If centres are a little moist, lift out moist pastry with a teaspoon, and return choux pastries to cool oven to dry out. Choux pastry is used for eclairs, sweet or savoury puffs and cream buns.*

SCONES

PLAIN SCONES

8 oz. self-raising flour
½ level teaspoon salt
1–2 oz. English or Welsh butter
¼ pint milk
Milk or egg to glaze

1. Sieve flour and salt into mixing bowl. Rub in butter finely. 2. Quickly mix in milk with knife to form soft, spongy dough. 3. Pat or roll out on floured board to ½–¾ in. thickness, and using round cutter dipped in flour to stamp out 8–12 scones. Brush tops with milk or beaten egg if liked. 4. Bake near the top of the oven at Gas Mark 8 or 450 °F for 7–10 minutes.
● *For richer scones, use a beaten egg made up to ¼ pint with milk to mix.*

SPICE SCONES

Ingredients as for Plain Scones, plus:
½ level teaspoon mixed spice
½ level teaspoon cinnamon
2 oz. brown sugar

Follow method for making Plain Scones, but sieve mixed spice and cinnamon with flour and salt, and add sugar before stirring in liquid.

CHEESE SCONES

Ingredients as for Plain Scones, plus:
2 oz. finely-grated English cheese

Follow directions for making Plain Scones, but add grated cheese before stirring in liquid.

DROP SCONES (Scotch Pancakes)

8 oz. self-raising flour
1 level teaspoon baking powder
2 oz. caster sugar
1 beaten egg
½ pint milk
English or Welsh butter

1. Sieve flour with baking powder. Stir in the sugar. 2. Gradually blend in beaten egg and milk to form smooth batter. 3. Lightly brush large heavy frying pan with melted butter, and when hot drop in dessertspoonfuls of batter to form neat rounds. 4. When bubbles come to surface of pancakes and burst, carefully turn over with knife and cook for further 2 min. until golden brown.

BREAD

LOAF AND ROLLS

½ oz. fresh yeast
½ pint tepid milk and water (⅓ boiling
  water, ⅔ cold milk)
1 lb. plain flour
2 level teaspoons salt
1 oz. English or Welsh butter

1. Blend fresh yeast to smooth cream with
2 teaspoons tepid milk and water. Stir
in remainder. 2. Sieve flour and salt into
warmed bowl, and rub in butter. Make
hole in centre, and pour in tepid yeast
mixture. Mix by hand to make soft,
sticky dough. Continue beating with open
hand until dough will leave bowl cleanly.
It may be necessary to sprinkle in more
flour. 3. Turn dough on to lightly-floured
board, and knead by pulling outside of
dough into centre of dough, turning it
round as you do so. 4. When dough is
smooth, place it in large buttered saucepan,
cover with damp tea towel and then
the saucepan lid (alternatively, place in a
buttered large polythene bag) and leave
to rise until dough has swollen to double
its size. Ideally, rising period should take
2–3 hours at average room temperature, but
this process can be speeded up by putting
dough in warm place, such as an airing
cupboard, for 45–60 min. 5. Grease a 1-lb.
(about 7½ in.×3½ in.×2 in.) loaf tin, and
put in warm place. 6. Lightly knead dough,
so as not to lose trapped air, on floured
board, shape into oblong to fit loaf tin, or
cut into 12 and shape into rolls (round,
fingers, plaits, miniature cottage loaves,
knots, twists, etc. See illustrations) and
place on greased baking tray. 7. Slip loaf
or rolls into buttered polythene bag, and
leave to prove until loaf comes to top of
tin, rolls double their size. This will take
1–1½ hours for loaf, and about 30 min. for
rolls at room temperature, or half these
times in warm place. 8. Place proved bread
in pre-heated oven Gas Mark 7 or 425 °F
for 30–40 min. for bread, or Gas Mark 8
or 450 °F for 10–20 min. for rolls. 9. When
cooked, loaf will shrink slightly from
edges of tin, and both loaf and rolls will
sound hollow when removed from tin and
tapped on bottom.

● Two teaspoons of dried yeast can be
substituted for the ½ oz. fresh yeast—
follow directions on pack. Fresh yeast is
obtainable from bakers, and dried yeast
from chemists or health-food shops.
● Brown flour—stoneground whole
wheat is best for flavour—can be used
instead of white flour. It is then necessary
to add a little more tepid milk and water,
making a wetter dough. Brown bread
takes a little longer to cook than white.
● Because your hand is warm, it is the
best and easiest means of mixing bread.
● The dough can also be put in cold room
or larder to rise overnight, or for 24 hours
in main part of domestic refrigerator, but
in these cases dough should be left at
room temperature 20–30 min. before it is
shaped.

QUICK WHOLEWHEAT LOAF
(Without Yeast)

8 oz. plain white flour
1 level teaspoon cream of tartar
1 level teaspoon salt
1 level teaspoon bicarbonate of soda
8 oz. wholewheat flour
1 rounded teaspoon golden syrup
¼–½ pint warm water
¼ pint milk

1. Sieve white flour, cream of tartar, salt
and bicarbonate of soda into mixing bowl.
Stir in wholewheat flour, and mix well.
2. Stir golden syrup into warm water until it
dissolves. 3. Quickly stir milk into flour with
sufficient of the warm water to mix to
stiff dropping consistency. Immediately turn
mixture into greased 1-lb. loaf tin. 4. Cook
at Gas Mark 6 or 400 °F for 15 min. and
reduce heat to Gas Mark 4 or 350 °F for
further 20–30 min.
● Once liquid has been added, get loaf
into oven as quickly as possible.
● A particularly well-flavoured loaf. It is
rather crumbly, so do not cut until next
day.

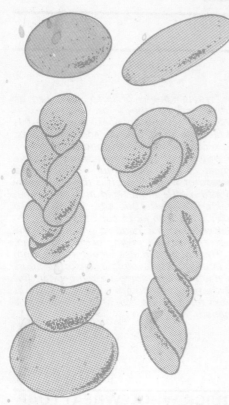

TO LINE A LOAF TIN

1. Mark around base of loaf tin with pencil on to piece of greaseproof paper.

2. Cut rectangle 3 in. larger (all round) than the pencilled rectangle.

3. Cut diagonally from outside corners to pencilled corners.

4. Brush loaf tin with melted fat or oil, and press in greaseproof paper, overlapping the edges and sealing with more fat.

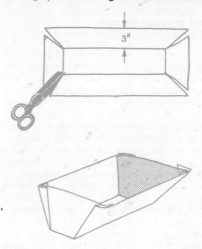

CAKES

Rubbing-in Method

FAMILY FRUIT CAKE

8 oz. self-raising flour
¼ level teaspoon salt
3 oz. sugar
4 oz. English or Welsh butter
6–8 oz. prepared dried fruit
1 teaspoon grated orange or lemon
  rind
1 beaten egg
¼ pint milk

1. Sieve flour and salt into mixing bowl. Stir in sugar. **2.** Rub in butter until mixture resembles fine breadcrumbs. Stir in fruit and grated rind. **3.** Beat egg with 4 tablespoons milk, make hole in centre of dry ingredients and pour in beaten egg and milk. **4.** Mix to form smooth dropping consistency, using the additional milk if necessary. **5.** Spoon into lined round cake tin (6–7 in. diameter). **6.** Bake at Gas Mark 4 or 350°F for about 1½ hours. **7.** Cake is cooked when it feels firm when lightly pressed in middle.

● *Dropping Consistency is when a little mixture will fall from tipped spoon if gently shaken.*

● *Soft Dropping Consistency is when little mixture will drop in dollop by itself when tipped from spoon.*

● *Stiff Dropping Consistency is when spoon has to be shaken well before some mixture will fall off.*

Rubbing in a cake

1 Rub the butter into the flour until the mixture resembles fine bread crumbs

2 Add the fruit to a dropping consistency with beaten eggs and milk

3 Smooth the mixture into a lined cake tin

4 This method makes a good family fruit cake. It should be eaten within a few days

ROCK BUNS

Same ingredients as Family Fruit Cake

1. Follow method for Family Fruit Cake, but use less milk and mix to **stiff** dropping consistency. 2. Using teaspoon and fork, spoon mixture into about 12 rocky heaps on greased baking tray. 3. Cook at Gas Mark 7 or 425 °F for 10–15 min.

DATE AND WALNUT LOAF

12 oz. self-raising flour
½ level teaspoon salt
4 oz. brown sugar
6 oz. English or Welsh butter
2 oz. walnuts
6 oz. chopped dates
2 beaten eggs
¼ pint milk

1. Sieve flour and salt into mixing bowl. Add brown sugar, and rub in butter. 2. Reserving a few nuts, whole, for decoration, chop up remainder fairly coarsely, and add with chopped dates to dry ingredients. 3. Mix to dropping consistency, and spoon into lined loaf tin about 8 in. by 5 in. 4. Stud top of cake with whole walnuts. 5. Bake at Gas Mark 4 or 350 °F for about 1½ hours.

Creaming Method

VICTORIA SANDWICH

4 oz. caster sugar
4 oz. soft English or Welsh butter
2 beaten eggs
4 oz. self-raising flour ⎫
¼ level teaspoon salt ⎬ sieved
2 tablespoons milk ⎭

1. Place sugar and butter in mixing bowl, and cream together by beating vigorously with wooden spoon. They are sufficiently creamed when mixture is much paler (almost white) and has light fluffy texture. 2. Add one beaten egg at a time, beating well after each addition until mixture is smooth again and has become stiffer. 3. Fold in sieved flour with metal spoon. 4. When flour is well folded in, lightly stir in milk (if necessary) to mix to soft dropping consistency. 5. Divide mixture between two lined (bases only) 7-in. sandwich tins. 6. Bake at Gas Mark 4–5 or

350 °F–375 °F for 20–30 min. 7. Leave in tin to cool slightly, then turn out on to cake rack, golden side uppermost. 8. When cold, sandwich the two cakes together with jam, and dust top with caster or icing sugar.

FRESH LEMON OR ORANGE CAKE

Ingredients as for Victoria Sandwich plus:
Finely-grated rind and juice of an orange or lemon

1. Follow method for making Victoria Sandwich, but add half grated rind after creaming butter and sugar. 2. Use the fruit juice instead of the milk to mix to soft dropping consistency. 3. Cook cake in 9-in. sandwich tin for 30–40 min. at Gas Mark 4–5 or 350 °F–375 °F. 4. When cold, top cake with glacé icing mixed with remaining grated rind and fruit juice.

CHOCOLATE CAKE

Ingredients as for Victoria Sandwich, but use 3 oz. self-raising flour, 1 oz. cocoa, and whipped cream

Follow method for making Victoria Sandwich, but sieve cocoa with flour. Sandwich cakes together with whipped cream, and dust top with icing sugar.

COFFEE AND WALNUT SANDWICH CAKE

Ingredients as for Victoria Sandwich, plus (for Coffee Butter Icing):
4 oz. English or Welsh butter
8 oz. icing sugar
2 rounded teaspoons instant coffee powder
2 oz. chopped walnuts

Follow method for making Victoria Sandwich, then prepare coffee butter icing: 1. Cream butter and icing sugar. 2. Dissolve coffee in two teaspoons of hot water, and gradually beat into creamed butter and sugar. 3. Spread little of coffee butter icing over top of cake, and sprinkle with nuts. 4. Sandwich two cake-halves together with remaining icing.

BUTTER CREAM ICING

4 oz. English or Welsh butter
8 oz. icing sugar
Flavouring

1. Cream softened butter with icing sugar.
2. Flavour with vanilla essence, grated orange or lemon rind and juice, cocoa powder or strong coffee to taste. **Tops and fills 7 in.–8 in. Victoria Sandwich.**

RICH DUNDEE CAKE

6 oz. soft English or Welsh butter
6 oz. soft brown sugar
3 beaten eggs
4 oz. plain flour
4 oz. self-raising flour
$\frac{1}{4}$ level teaspoon salt
$\frac{1}{2}$ level teaspoon mixed spice
$\frac{1}{4}$ level teaspoon cinnamon
1 lb. prepared mixed dried fruit
  (sultanas, currants, raisins)
2 oz. quartered glacé cherries
2 oz. chopped mixed peel
Rind and juice of 1 lemon
2 oz. blanched almonds (optional)

1. Cream butter and sugar until soft, fluffy and paler in colour. Beat in eggs one at a time, beating well after each addition. 2. Sieve flours with salt, spice and cinnamon. 3. Lightly fold half flour into creamed fat and sugar, using metal spoon. 4. Fold in prepared fruit, quartered cherries, chopped peel, finely-grated rind, juice of lemon and remaining flour. 5. Spoon mixture into a lined 8-in. round tin, level the top and stud with blanched almonds if liked. 6. Bake just below centre of oven at Gas Mark 3 or 325°F for 2½–3 hours. **Cuts into about 15 portions.**

● *This Rich Dundee Cake recipe makes good birthday cake.*

● *For rich cakes, plain flour or half plain and half self-raising gives better results than all self-raising.*

To test when rich cake is cooked: Insert fine skewer or needle into centre of the cake. If needle comes out cleanly, and top of the cake feels firm all over, it is cooked. If needle comes out with some of mixture still adhering, it is not yet cooked through.

CHRISTMAS CAKE

Ingredients as for Rich Dundee Cake, plus:
2 oz. quartered glacé cherries
4 oz. chopped crystallised pineapple
2 oz. chopped angelica
1 teaspoon liquid gravy browning (optional)
4 oz. chopped almonds or walnuts
2 tablespoons brandy or rum

1. Follow method for making Rich Dundee Cake, and add additional ingredients (except brandy) to dried fruit. 2. Spoon mixture into lined 8-in. round cake tin. 3. Cook at Gas Mark 2 or 300°F for 3½–4 hours. 4. Leave cake in tin to cool. When quite cold, wrap in greaseproof paper and store in airtight tin in cool place.
5. Before covering cake with almond paste, invert it and prick bottom all over with fine knitting needle. Spoon over brandy or rum so it seeps into cake through holes. 6. Cover top and sides of cake with almond paste. Leave to dry in a tin with lid slightly off for a few days, then coat with stiff Royal Icing (see page 58) smoothed round sides and pulled into frosty peaks on top. Tie bright red ribbon round cake.

● *A rich cake improves with keeping. Ideally Christmas Cake should be made six weeks before Christmas, and covered with almond paste one week before.*

EASTER SIMNEL CAKE

Ingredients as for Rich Dundee Cake
Almond paste (see page 58)
Apricot jam (sieved)
Easter chicks to decorate

1. Make almond paste (see below) using 8 oz. ground almonds. Roll just under half mixture into a round 7½ in. in diameter. 2. Prepare cake as instructed for Rich Dundee. Spoon half mixture into an 8-in. lined cake tin, cover with the round of almond paste and top with remaining mixture. Smooth level. 3. Bake just below centre of oven at Gas Mark 4 or 350°F for 1½ hours, then reduce heat to Gas Mark 1 or 275°F for further 2–2½ hours. 4. When cake is cold, turn out of tin and brush top with little jam. Roll remaining almond paste to cover top of cake. 3. Brown almond paste under low grill, and decorate with Easter chicks. **Cuts into about 15 portions.**

Creaming a cake

1 Add one beaten egg at a time to creamed fat and sugar

2 When all eggs have been beaten in the mixture should be paler and smooth

3 Fold in the sieved flour and smooth the mixture into two tins

4 The finished cake should be well risen and with a light, firm texture

To whisk a sponge. .

1 Whisk the caster sugar and eggs together until the whisk will leave a trail in the mixture

2 Lightly fold in the flour with a metal spoon

3 Sandwich the sponge together with jam and plenty of whipped fresh cream

4 The sponge should be *very* light and airy in texture

ALMOND PASTE

8 oz. ground almonds
4 oz. caster sugar
6 oz. icing sugar
¼ teaspoon almond essence
1 beaten egg

1. Combine ground almonds with sugars, add almond essence and mix to a stiff paste with beaten egg. **2.** Knead until smooth. **3.** Makes sufficient to cover top and sides of 8-in. cake.

ROYAL ICING

2 egg whites
1 lb. sieved icing sugar
1 teaspoon lemon juice
2–3 drops glycerine

1. Whisk egg whites until frothy, and gradually blend in icing sugar, beating thoroughly after each addition. **2.** Stir in lemon juice and glycerine. **3.** Icing should be firm enough to stand in upright points when wooden spoon is lifted out of the bowl. Add more icing sugar if necessary.

Whisking Method

WHISKED SPONGE

2 oz. caster sugar
2 eggs
2 oz. sieved flour

1. Whisk caster sugar and eggs together with rotary beater or wire whisk until they are pale frothy and sufficiently thick for whisk to leave trail when dragged across mixture. This takes 5–10 min. **2.** Lightly fold in flour with metal spoon. **3.** Pour mixture into two 6 in.–7 in. sandwich tins, the bottoms greased and lined. **4.** Bake at Gas Mark 5 or 375 °F for 10–12 min. **5.** Carefully turn cakes on to cooling tray. When cold, sandwich together with jam and plenty of whipped cream. Dust top with icing sugar.
● *This method is used for making Swiss Rolls and gateaux.*
● *To test a whisked sponge is cooked, lightly press top with fingertips. This leaves no impression if cake is cooked.*

MERINGUES

2 large egg whites
2 oz. sieved icing sugar
2 oz. caster sugar
¼ pint fresh double cream

1. Place egg whites in clean, dry mixing bowl. Whisk steadily until whites are stiff and dry-looking, with cotton wool appearance. **2.** Mix sugars together, and whisk in half quantity. Then carefully fold in the remainder. **3.** Spoon or pipe about 16 rounds of meringue mixture on to baking tray lined with greaseproof paper and brushed with oil. **4.** Place meringues in the coolest part of the oven at lowest setting, and leave oven door very slightly ajar. Dry out meringues for at least 2–3 hours. **5.** When cold, sandwich together with whipped cream. **Makes about 8 cream meringues.**

● *To separate white of egg from yolk, carefully break shell in half (marking right round egg with knife helps) and tip yolk from one half of shell to other, pouring egg-white into bowl as you do this.*
● *Better results are achieved if egg-whites are chilled before use, and care taken not to get specks of egg yolk included.*
● *A better paper to line baking tray for meringues is non-stick household parchment.*
● *Some ovens have plate-warming compartment that can be kept at low temperature. This is often very suitable for making meringues.*

TO LINE A ROUND CAKE TIN

1. Cut 2 rounds of greaseproof paper the size of the cake tin's base.
2. Cut strip of greaseproof paper the depth of tin, plus 1 in., and long enough to go round tin with overlap.
3. Fold in the 1-in. to make strip of paper the same depth as tin and snip folded-in paper diagonally at 1-in. intervals.
4. Brush tin with melted fat or oil, and put one of rounds in base. Place strip of paper (snipped edge down) round sides of tin. Smooth base and sides with tea towel.
5. Brush bottom of tin with melted fat again, and put in the second round of paper.

Dairy Products

MILK

Grades of Milk

All milk produced in Britain today is tuberculin-tested.

UNTREATED
This is raw milk which has not undergone any form of heat treatment.

UNTREATED FARM BOTTLED
This is raw milk which must be bottled at the farm where it is produced. It may be from any breed of cow, provided the stock conditions on the farm comply with Government regulations and the producer holds a licence to use the special designation 'Untreated'.

PASTEURISED
This is milk which has been subjected to heat treatment which destroys harmful bacteria and prolongs its keeping qualities.

HOMOGENISED
This is pasteurised milk, processed to break up the globules of butterfat evenly throughout the milk.

STERILISED
This is homogenised milk which has been heat treated in the bottle and vacuum-sealed. This extends the keeping quality of the milk. Unopened, it will keep fresh for at least a week.

ULTRA HEAT TREATED (UHT)
This long-keeping milk is homogenised milk which is raised to an ultra-high temperature. This milk will keep for several months.

CHANNEL ISLANDS AND SOUTH DEVON
Milk from Jersey, Guernsey and South Devon breeds of cow—with a minimum butterfat content of 4%.

Legal Standards

Ordinary milk must have a minimum of 3% butterfat and 8.5% solids not fat. Milk sold as Channel Islands, Jersey, Guernsey or South Devon must contain not less than 4% butterfat.

Care of Milk

Ask the milkman to leave it in a shady place away from direct sunlight and avoid leaving it on the doorstep for too long.

If you find the birds are helping themselves, invest in some discs which fit over the bottle tops. When you bring milk indoors, either put it straight into the refrigerator or stand it in a basin or bowl of water, covering it with a clean cloth with its corners dipping into the water. Evaporation of the water keeps the milk cool and fresh.

Never mix new milk with old. And never pour milk into anything but a spotlessly-clean container.

Boiling Milk

If milk must be boiled, then do it quickly, stirring all the time, and cool it immediately. Prolonged heating of milk will not only affect it nutritionally, but will also cause the lactose (milk sugar) to caramelise, giving the milk a cooked flavour. As milk boils over with surprising rapidity, never leave a saucepan of heating milk unwatched.

CREAM

Cream is delicious food which can be used in a wide variety of sweet and savoury dishes. It is easily digested and contains not only butterfat but also protein, milk sugar, minerals and vitamins. Cream is exceptionally rich in energy-giving calories.

Types of Cream

DOUBLE
This must, by law, have a butterfat content of not less than 48%. If desired,

double cream can be whipped. When whipping, add one tablespoon milk. This lowers the butterfat content and minimises any risk of overwhipping.

SINGLE
This must by law, have a minimum butterfat content of not less than 18%. It is generally used as pouring or coffee cream and will not whip.

CLOTTED
This usually contains 50% to 60% butterfat, although the legal minimum requirement is 48%.

LONG-KEEPING
This type of cream is heat treated and has a keeping quality longer than that of fresh cream but shorter than that of sterilised cream. Single cream, double cream and clotted cream may all be treated in this way.

ULTRA HEAT TREATED (UHT)
This cream is ultra heat treated and has a long shelf-life.

STERILISED CREAM
This cream must, by law, have a minimum butterfat content of 23%. It is sterilised with its container to kill all the bacteria and will keep indefinitely. It has a different flavour from fresh cream and will not whip.

Care of Cream

Cream should always be kept cool, clean and covered and away from bright light and strong sunshine. Fresh pasteurised cream will keep three to four days in summer and up to one week in winter if refrigerated. Sterilised, long-keeping and UHT cream will keep for long periods without refrigeration, provided the containers remain unopened. All types of cream must be treated as fresh once the container is opened.

Whipping Cream

Everything must be really cold before cream is whipped—bowl, whisk and the cream itself.
Cream should be whipped quickly until

a matt surface appears—then slowly to avoid over-whipping and making it buttery.

SOURED (OR CULTURED) CREAM

Soured cream has a piquant and refreshing taste, combined with a smooth texture. This enhances the flavour and creaminess of many made-up dishes. It is delicious with raw or cooked fruit, meat, fish and vegetable dishes, soups, stews and sauces. Salad dressings made up with soured cream are ideal for use in the cold buffet.

YOGURT

Yogurt is a delightful way of taking milk. Slightly acidic in taste, it is refreshingly stimulating and very versatile. It is available natural, in a wide variety of flavours and with pieces of fruit added. Yogurt teams well with sweet and savoury dishes, it is particularly delicious with breakfast cereals, stewed and canned fruit, in summer drinks and with freshly-made buttered scones and jam. When added to soups, sauces, stews and casseroles, or poured over white fish before baking, Yogurt not only enhances the flavour of the dish but also adds to the nutritional value.

When cooking with Yogurt, care should be taken not to heat it too vigorously as it might acquire a curdled appearance, although this does not affect the taste.

HOME-MADE SOFT YOGURT
1 pint Pasteurised, Sterilised, Channel Island or South Devon Milk
1 carton (5 oz.) natural yogurt
1. Warm milk to blood heat (about 98°F).
2. Remove from heat. 3. Gently whisk in Yogurt with wire whisk or fork. 4. Transfer to bowl or basin and cover with plate.
5. Leave in warm place for 8 to 12 hours or until set. 6. If cold Yogurt is preferred, refrigerate after it has set.
Approximately 1¼ pints.
● As an alternative to the carton of natural yogurt, yogurt culture (which can be bought from some dairy companies, chemists and health food shops) may be used.

Traditional English cheeses

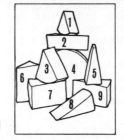

61

1. Wensleydale
2. Leicester
3. Caerphilly
4. Stilton
5. Cheddar
6. Derby
7. Cheshire
8. Lancashire
9. Double Gloucester

FOR FIRMER YOGURT
Use Ultra Heat Treated (UHT) Milk.

FOR FRUIT YOGURT
Stir small pieces of fresh, canned or frozen and thawed fruit into Yogurt after it has set.

BUTTER

Butter has a unique and luxurious flavour and a tremendous versatility of usage. It has always been the foundation of French *haute cuisine.* In ordinary, everyday cooking and baking and as a spread on bread, toast, crumpets, muffins, buns, biscuits and scones, it has no rival.

The Value of Butter

Butter is an energy and protective food usually containing rather more than 80% butterfat. It also contains vitamins A and D (the amount varying with the season) and small amounts of protein, milk sugar and minerals.

Care of Butter

Butter should be kept cool, covered and away from foods with strong flavours or smells. It is, like milk, affected by light and should be stored in a dark place.

CHEESE

There are many varieties of cheese produced in England and Wales and although they are all made from cows' milk, they are, nevertheless, all different in flavour and texture. This is due to slight variations in the manufacturing processes, developed regionally over hundreds of years, and to soil differences which affect the food which the cows eat.

Varieties of Cheese

ENGLISH CHEDDAR
Cheddar, the most popular English cheese, is famed for its unique 'nutty' flavour which becomes deeper as the cheese matures. With its close creamy texture it is used in a wide variety of ways.

CHESHIRE
Cheshire is a mellow, open-textured and crumbly cheese. Its keen tangy flavour is said to be due to the salty soil in Cheshire. Red and white Cheshire both have the same flavour and are delicious for 'elevenses' with fruit, cake or biscuits. Blue Cheshire has a rich flavour and is very rare.

DERBY
This is a pale honey-coloured cheese with a close smooth texture and soft mild flavour. Derby is well suited for interesting flavour combinations such as cheese and pineapple, or for use in a salad garnished with sprigs of mint or parsley.

SAGE DERBY
This is Derby cheese flavoured with sage leaves.

DOUBLE GLOUCESTER
Double Gloucester is a rich straw colour. It has a smooth velvet texture and a full but mellow flavour. Delicious with bread, butter and a pint of ale, or with fresh fruit salad and cream.

LEICESTER
This is a mild orange-coloured cheese with a soft flaky texture. It is especially recommended as a dessert cheese.

CAERPHILLY
Caerphilly is creamy-white with a mild flavour and semi-smooth texture. It is a great favourite with children and excels with celery and thin slices of bread and butter.

LANCASHIRE
Although Lancashire cheese has a mild flavour when young, it develops a full and rather pungent flavour as it matures. Its texture makes it ideal for crumbling over soups and hot-pots and it is renowned for its toasting qualities. A sage Lancashire is also available.

WENSLEYDALE

Wensleydale is pale parchment in colour with a subtle and unique honeyed aftertaste ideal with apple pie. Blue Wensleydale is occasionally made.

BLUE STILTON

Blue Stilton—the 'king of cheeses'—has a close texture intermingled with blue veins which give it its special rich flavour and appearance.

WHITE STILTON

This is a younger version of the Blue Stilton and is milder in flavour, chalky white in colour and crumbly in texture.

COTTAGE CHEESE

This is a creamy, acid curd cheese with a distinctive, delicate flavour. It is made from pasteurised, fat-free milk inoculated with a special curd to develop texture and flavour. It also contains added cream and salt. Cottage cheese is a particularly valuable source of protein and riboflavin (vitamin B2). It is easily digested and is especially useful in the feeding of babies, invalids and old people. It should always be stored in a cool place.

Cheese as a Food

As all well-known English cheeses are made from whole milk, they are rich in protein, fat, calcium, riboflavin and vitamins A and D and contain approximately 120 calories per ounce.

Care of Cheese

English cheese will stay fresh and moist if wrapped in a polythene bag or aluminium foil and then stored in a cool larder or refrigerator. In the latter case it should be brought to room temperature before serving. This takes about half an hour.

Preserves

JAM MAKING

1.   Select ripe or slightly under-ripe fresh, dry fruit. Never use fruit that is soft and over-ripe, or you will get poor setting results, and the jam will tend to go mouldy quickly.

2.   Use a preserving pan or a heavy aluminium saucepan large enough to be only half full once the sugar has been added to the fruit. This allows you to boil the mixture quickly. Use a *long*-handled wooden spoon, as the jam reaches a very high temperature and if it splutters could cause nasty burns.

3.   Fruits contain varying amounts of a natural gum-like setting agent called pectin. Those with little pectin need the addition of juice from a fruit containing a lot of pectin, such as lemons. Fruits with a good amount of pectin are red and blackcurrants, green gooseberries, plums, apricots, early blackberries and raspberries. Fruits low in pectin are strawberries, cherries and late-gathered blackberries.

4.   Fruit should always be cooked until it is soft before the sugar is added, because sugar tends to harden fruit, and it will never soften once sugar has been added.

5.   When sugar is added, stir until it is dissolved before bringing the jam to the boil. Jam boiled before the sugar is dissolved will crystallise.

6.   Once the jam has boiled, stop stirring and boil rapidly—the quicker the setting point is reached, the better the jam. Over-boiling spoils the flavour and colour, and the setting point can be passed, which will mean a thin, runny jam.

7.   With jams made from whole fruit (strawberries, cherries etc.) it is important to leave the jam to cool slightly and then stir it before pouring into jam jars. This ensures that the fruit is evenly distributed through the jam, and will not rise to the top.

8.   If you should burn your hand with hot jam, hold it under a cold-water tap, and then keep it in cold water for as long as possible. For a bad burn, seek your doctor's attention immediately.

Setting-point Tests

1.   Before commencing jam making fill a 1 lb. jam jar with cold water, and tip it into the empty preserving pan. Do this once for every expected pound of jam. Hold a wooden spoon upright in the centre of the pan and mark the spoon clearly where the level of the water reaches.

When the jam has boiled and you think setting point has been reached, remove jam from heat and when it has stopped bubbling, dip in the marked spoon. If the level of the jam matches the mark on the spoon, setting point has been reached.

2.   Place a teaspoonful of the jam on a cold plate, and leave until cool. If the jam wrinkles when pushed with your finger, it has reached setting point.

APRICOT JAM (Dried Fruit)

1 lb. dried apricots
3 pints water
Juice of one lemon
3 lb. sugar
3 oz. blanched almond halves
  (optional)

1.   Soak the apricots in the cold water for at least 24 hours. 2. Slowly simmer fruit in water for about 1¼ hours, then add lemon juice. 3. Add sugar (and almonds) and continue to cook slowly, stirring until sugar has dissolved. 4. Bring jam to boil and boil rapidly for 15–20 minutes until setting point is reached (see this page). 5. Put jam aside to cool slightly. Stir, and ladle into heated jam jars, filling them right to the brim. Cover immediately with waxed-paper discs. Leave until cold. 6. Wipe the jars over with damp cloth, cover with cellophane jam covers after dipping top surface of covers in cold water. Label jars with kind of jam, and date. Store in cool, dark and airy place. **Yield, 5 lb.**

BLACKBERRY AND APPLE JAM

2 lb. blackberries
½ pint water
¾ lb. peeled, cored and sliced cooking apples
3 lb. sugar

1. Wash blackberries thoroughly, then gently simmer them in ¼ pint of the water until soft. Rub them through sieve to remove seeds. 2. Place apples, remaining water and sieved blackberries in saucepan and cook until soft. Add sugar, and continue to cook slowly, stirring until the sugar has dissolved. 3. Boil fruit rapidly for about 10 minutes until setting point is reached. 4. Ladle jam into heated jam jars, filling them right to the brim, and cover with waxed-paper discs. Leave to cool. 5. Bottle and store as for Apricot Jam. **Yield, 5 lb.**

BLACKCURRANT JAM

2 lb. blackcurrants (stalks removed)
1½ pints water
3 lb. sugar

1. Gently wash blackcurrants, and place in large saucepan with the water. Slowly simmer fruit until it is *very* soft. Stir from time to time. 2. Add sugar to fruit, and continue to cook slowly, stirring until sugar has dissolved. 3. Boil fruit rapidly for 10–15 minutes until setting point is reached. 4. Leave jam aside to cool slightly, stir and ladle into heated jam jars, filling them right to the brim. Cover jam with waxed-paper discs and place aside until cold. 5. Bottle and store as for Apricot Jam. **Yield, 5 lb.**

GOOSEBERRY JAM

2¼ lb. gooseberries (topped and tailed)
¾ pint water
3 lb. sugar

1. Wash gooseberries, and simmer in the water until very tender. 2. Add sugar, and continue cooking slowly, stirring until all sugar has dissolved. 3. Bring jam to boil, and boil rapidly for about 10 minutes until setting point is reached. Cool slightly, then stir and ladle into heated jam jars, filling to the brim. Cover with waxed-paper discs, and leave to cool. 4. Bottle and store as for Apricot Jam. **Yield, 5 lb.**

STRAWBERRY JAM

3½ lb. hulled strawberries
Juice of two lemons
3 lb. sugar

1. Gently wash fruit by placing it in colander, and dipping it in and out of bowl of cold water. 2. Place strawberries and lemon juice in large saucepan, and cook very gently until fruit is soft. 3. Add sugar, and slowly dissolve it. From time to time, scrape bottom of pan with wooden spoon to prevent sugar sticking, and to tell when it has all dissolved. 4. Bring jam to boil, and boil rapidly for 5–10 minutes until setting point is reached. Spoon off scum. 5. Remove jam from heat, and leave to cool until thin skin forms on surface. Stir, and ladle the jam into heated jam jars, filling them to the brim and immediately cover with waxed-paper discs. Leave until cold. 6. Bottle and store as for Apricot Jam. **Yield, 5lb.**

RASPBERRY JAM

3 lb. raspberries
3 lb. sugar

1. Gently wash fruit by placing it in colander and dipping it in and out of bowl of cold water. 2. Place raspberries in large saucepan, and cook slowly until fruit is soft, and some juice has come out. 3. Add sugar, and continue to cook slowly, stirring until sugar has dissolved. 4. Bring jam to boil without stirring, and boil for about 10 minutes until setting point has been reached (see page 64). 5. Pour jam into heated jam jars, filling them to brim, and cover with waxed-paper discs. Leave until cold. 6. Bottle and store as for Apricot Jam. **Yield, 5 lb.**

SEVILLE ORANGE MARMALADE

1½ lb. Seville oranges
2 pints water
Juice 1 lemon
3 lb. sugar

1. Scrub oranges, then simmer in the water in a large, covered saucepan for 2 hours until very tender. 2. Lift fruit out of water, and using a sharp knife and fork shred whole fruit thinly, removing the pips. Return pips to water, and boil for 5 minutes to extract pectin. Remove them, and add shredded fruit, lemon juice and sugar. 3. Simmer fruit, stirring until sugar has dissolved, then bring to boil and boil rapidly for 30–40 minutes until setting point is reached. Remove scum. 4. Leave marmalade to cool slightly, stir, then ladle into heated jam jars, filling them to the brim. Cover immediately with waxed-paper discs. 5. Bottle and store as for Apricot Jam. **Yield, 5 lb.**
● *This is one of the easiest methods of preparing marmalade.*

ORANGE AND LEMON MARMALADE

½ lb. Seville oranges
½ lb. sweet oranges
¼ lb. lemons
2½ pints water
3 lb. sugar

Follow the method for Seville Orange Marmalade. **Yield, 5 lb.**

CRAB APPLE JELLY

6 lb. crab apples
3½ pints water
2 cloves (optional)
Lemon peel
Sugar (1 lb. to 1 pint juice)

1. Wash fruit and cut into chunks (without coring or peeling), place in a large saucepan with the water, cloves and lemon peel, and simmer until the fruit is broken up and really soft. 2. Pour boiling water through a jelly bag (or through double thickness of muslin tied to four legs of an inverted stool or chair) to scald it; then pour in the contents of the saucepan and leave it to drip through (without squeezing) into a bowl. This will take a good 2 hours (or overnight). 3. Measure resulting fruit juice, and to every pint of juice allow one pound of sugar. Slowly heat juice and sugar together, and stir until sugar has dissolved. 4. Bring to boil, and boil rapidly for about 10 minutes until setting point is reached. 5. Remove scum and pour jelly into heated jam jars, filling them to the brim. Cover immediately with waxed-paper discs, and leave to cool. 6. Bottle and store as for Apricot Jam. **Yield, 1 lb. to every pound of sugar.**
● *For apple jelly, follow method for crab apple jelly, but use cooking apples.*

REDCURRANT JELLY

6 lb. redcurrants
2½ pints water
Sugar (1 lb. to 1 pint juice)

Follow the method for crab apple jelly, making sure fruit is simmered until *very* soft in first stage. The little stalks need not be removed before cooking.

Yield, 1 lb. to every pound of sugar.

CHUTNEYS AND PICKLES

1. Do not use copper, brass or iron pans when cooking with vinegar, as the metal reacts with the acid.
2. As chutneys and pickles taint wood, use a wooden spoon just for this job, or for savoury dishes later.
3. Vinegar has a pungent smell when it is cooking, so do not be tempted to 'sniff'.
4. Cooking salt is better than table salt for pickles and chutneys.
5. Use a good-quality vinegar—one that contains plenty of acetic acid to prevent the growth of bacteria during storing.
6. As most pickles and chutneys mature with keeping, make sure they are tightly covered to prevent drying out while they are stored. Plastic covers are all right if

they fit *tightly*, or metal lids can be used if they are coated underneath with plastic, or the chutney is covered with a waxed-paper disc.

RED TOMATO CHUTNEY

1 lb. ripe red tomatoes
1 lb. cooking apples
1 lb. onions
1 lb. brown sugar
1 pint good malt vinegar
1 level tablespoon mustard powder
1 level teaspoon Cayenne pepper
1 level teaspoon mixed spice

1. Dip tomatoes in boiling water for a few minutes, then lift out and peel. Cut tomatoes into quarters, and coarsely chop apples. Peel and finely chop onions. 2. Place prepared tomatoes, apples and onions in large heavy saucepan with all other ingredients. Simmer slowly, and stir from time to time to see when sugar has dissolved. 3. Bring chutney to boil, cover pan with lid, and cook for two hours, by which time chutney should be thick, with no unabsorbed liquid. 4. Ladle chutney into heated pickle, bottling or jam jars, filling to brim. Cover with vinegar-resistant lids. Store in a cool, dark place. This chutney improves with keeping.

APPLE CHUTNEY

2 lb. cooking apples
$\frac{3}{4}$ lb. onions
4 large cloves garlic
2 oz. crystallised ginger
1 lb. brown sugar
$\frac{1}{4}$ level teaspoon Cayenne pepper
2 level teaspoons cooking salt
$\frac{1}{2}$ lb. sultanas
$1\frac{1}{4}$ pints good malt vinegar

1. Peel and core apples, and cut into small pieces. Slice onions thinly. Chop garlic very finely. Chop ginger. 2. Place prepared apple, onion, garlic and ginger in large, heavy saucepan with remaining ingredients. Dissolve sugar over low heat. 3. Bring chutney to boil, then cook slowly for $1\frac{1}{2}$–2 hours, stirring from time to time. 4. Ladle chutney into heated jars, and cover with vinegar-resistant lids.

PICKLED ONIONS

Brine
Vinegar
Mixed pickling spice
Baby onions or shallots (peeled with stainless steel knife)
Shredded red cabbage

1. Cover prepared vegetables in strong brine solution (4 oz. cooking salt to 2 pints water) and leave for 24 hours. 2. Prepare spiced vinegar by putting 1 oz. mixed pickling spice in basin to every 2 pints vinegar. Cover basin with plate, and stand it in saucepan of water. Bring water to boil, then remove pan from heat, and let it stand for 2 hours until cold. 3. Rinse vegetables and drain, pack them into jars, leaving at least $\frac{1}{2}$ in. at the top. Cover to top with cold, spiced vinegar, and seal.
●*For pickled cauliflower, follow method for pickled onions, but use cauliflower broken into flowerlets.*

PICKLED RED CABBAGE

Use finely-shredded red cabbage in method for Pickled Onions, but instead of soaking in brine solution, layer shredded cabbage with cooking salt (allowing 4 oz. to every 2 lb. cabbage). Mix thoroughly together in basin, and leave for 24 hours.

PICKLED EGGS

1 pint vinegar
1 oz. pickling spices
3 cloves garlic (optional)
Piece of mace (optional)
Small piece of orange peel
6 eggs

1. Boil vinegar, with spices, garlic, mace and orange peel, for 30 minutes. Leave vinegar to cool, then strain into wide-necked jar with screw lid or tight cork.
2. Hard-boil the eggs, and place under cold running water as soon as they are cooked to stop dark ring forming round yolk.
3. When eggs are cold, shell and place whole in jar, making sure they are well covered by vinegar. Cover with lid.
● *Pickled eggs should not be eaten for at least 4 weeks to ensure the flavour has fully developed.*

PICCALILLI

3 lb. mixed vegetables (cauliflower, shallots, green tomatoes, marrow)
6 oz. kitchen salt
2 level tablespoons plain flour
$\frac{1}{2}$ level tablespoon ground ginger
2 level tablespoons mustard powder
1 level tablespoon turmeric powder
1$\frac{1}{2}$ pints white vinegar
4 oz. white sugar

1. Break cauliflower into small flowerlets, peel shallots, slice tomatoes and dice peeled marrow. Sprinkle prepared vegetables with salt, cover with plate and leave to stand overnight. 2. Rinse vegetables and drain well. 3. Blend flour and spices to smooth paste with $\frac{1}{4}$ -pint of vinegar. 4. Dissolve sugar in remaining vinegar, then add vegetables, bring them to boil and simmer for 20–30 minutes. 5. Drain vegetables (reserving the vinegar), and pack them into hot pickle jars—keep them hot. 6. Stir hot vinegar on to blended flour and spices. Boil this sauce for 2–3 minutes, stirring all time, then pour over hot vegetables in jars.

BOTTLING FRUIT

1. Prepare jars, and use either screw-top bottling jars, or jam jars with clip-on tops. Check there are no chips in glass, and that rubber rings fit well. Wash jars thoroughly, then rinse in cold water. Leave them wet for easier packing.
2. Wash and prepare fruit. (See fruit-bottling chart.)
3. Make sugar syrup—either a heavy or light syrup, according to the fruit. (See chart.)

Light Syrup	Method
8 oz. sugar	Dissolve sugar in water
1 pint water	over low heat. Bring to
Heavy Syrup	boil, and boil for 2–3
12 oz. sugar	minutes
1 pint water	

4. Soak rubber rings and glass lids in water.

Sterilising in water

1. Pack firm fruit tightly in jars with handle of wooden spoon, taking care not to damage. When the jar is full stand it in basin, and pour in cold sugar syrup until it overflows. Lightly tap jar to remove air bubbles, and top up with more syrup if necessary.

For soft fruit, fill the jars half way, cover with syrup, then top up with fruit and fill to overflowing with syrup. This makes it easier for air bubbles to be removed.
2. Dip rubber rings and lids in boiling water for few minutes, then cover the jars. If using screw-top band, screw tightly, then loosen by one half-turn to allow for expansion.
3. Use large pan, deep enough to allow the jars to be completely covered with water. Well-scrubbed zinc bath or bucket would do. Stand chopping board or wads of newspaper on base to prevent jars coming in contact with metal and place jars in so they do not touch one another. Cover entirely with water.
4. Slowly heat water (about 1$\frac{1}{2}$ hours) to the correct temperature (to simmering point if you are not using thermometer), then maintain this heat for the time given in chart.
5. Ladle off some water. Then, using thick, dry cloth, lift out jars one at a time on to dry wooden board, tightening up screw-lid before lifting out the next jar. Leave until quite cold.

● *This is generally considered to be one of the best methods of sterilising, but you can also sterilise in oven.*

Sterilising in the oven

Best results with dark fruits and gooseberries. Not recommended for apples, pears or peaches.
1. Pack fruit tightly in jars so they are as full as possible. Stand the jars about 2 inches apart on baking tray lined with newspaper. Do not add any liquid. Cover the jars with the lids and rubber rings (dipped in boiling water), but do not put on the metal screw-bands or clips.
2. Stand tray of jars in pre-heated oven Gas Mark 2 or 300 °F (if you have an oven thermometer, check the heat in the middle of the oven is 300 °F, and adjust if necessary) for approximately one hour until fruit is cooked (check time with chart).
3. Prepare sugar syrup according to fruit (see chart), and have it ready on boil.

4. Remove the jars from the oven *one at a time.* If the fruit has sunk very much in the jar, top it up quickly from one of the other jars of cooked fruit. Fill the jar to the brim with *boiling* sugar syrup. Put on lid, and clip or screw down tightly before removing next jar from oven.

5. Leave to cool.

● *Fruit preserved in sugar syrup has good colour and flavour, but it sometimes rises in the jars. This can be prevented by preserving in water. Sugar may then be added when fruit is used.*

Bottling test

The day after the bottling, remove screw-bands or clips, and lift each jar by its lid. If there is a vacuum beneath, the lid will not come off, and the fruit should keep well, provided all the other instructions have been followed. If the lids do come off, air has managed to get in, and the fruit should be either re-bottled, or eaten within a few days.

● *Store bottled fruit in a cool, dark place.*

FRUIT-BOTTLING CHART

FRUIT	PREPARATION	SYRUP	LENGTH OF TIME TO MAINTAIN TEMPERATURE		
			Water-bath Method		Oven Method
			With thermometer	Without thermometer	
*Cooking apples	Peel, core and cut into slices or rings	Light	165 °F or 73.9 °C for 10 min.	5 min.	1 hour
Apricots	Remove stalks, use whole or cut in half with stones removed	Heavy	180 °F or 82.2 °C for 15 min.	10 min.	1 hour
Blackberries,	Remove stalks, place in a colander, dip in	Heavy	165 °F or 73.9 °C for 10 min.	5 min.	1 hour
black and red currants	and out of cold water to wash	Heavy	180 °F or 82.2 °C for 15 min.	15 min.	1 hour
*Morello cherries	Remove stalks and wash	Light	180 °F or 82.2 °C for 15 min.	15 min.	1 hour
*Green gooseberries	Top and tail; and snip ends with scissors. Wash	Heavy	165 °F or 73.9 °C for 10 min.	5 min.	1 hour
*Peaches	Dip in boiling water for 1 min., then in cold. Peel, cut in half and remove stones	Heavy	180 °F or 82.2 °C for 15 min.	10 min.	1 hour
*Dessert pears	Peel, core and slice	Heavy	190 °F or 87.8 °C for 30 min.	20 min.	1½ hours
Plums	Remove stalks, wash, use whole, or cut in half and remove stones	Light	180 °F or 82.2 °C for 15 min.	10 min.	1 hour
Raspberries	Remove stalks. Wash as blackberries	Heavy	165 °F or 73.9 °C for 10 min.	5 min.	¾ hour
Rhubarb	Wash, cut into 1 in. lengths	Light	165 °F or 73.9 °C for 10 min.	5 min.	¾ hour

*As fruit is prepared, keep in bowl of cold water to which lemon juice or salt (1 tablespoon to 2 pints) has been added, to prevent discolouration.

Buying A House

Owning your own house is a good investment. If you remain in the same house for 20–25 years the property will be yours entirely and its market value will have approximately doubled during that time.

If you are buying a house on mortgage and decide to move after a period of, say, five years you will find that its market value has increased from the original purchase price by between £100–£500.

Buying a house on mortgage calls for a substantial deposit, usually a minimum of 10% of the **value** of the property, which may be considerably less than the **asking price** of the property. The purchaser is expected to meet this difference in cash.

Young couples unable to raise adequate capital to meet their deposit can enter into a **Guaranteed Deferred House Purchase Scheme.** This means taking out an endowment assurance, paying monthly premiums and, when the policy has been in force for approximately three years, negotiating a loan equal to the valuation of the house.

Whether you obtain the money by this method or a 90% mortgage from a building society there are certain other expenses which must be allowed for:

1. **Building society's survey fee**
2. **Your own surveyor's fee**
3. **Your solicitor's fee for conveyance**
4. **Government stamp duty**
5. **Land registry fee**
6. **Government stamp duty on deeds**
7. **Insuring the property against fire etc.**
8. **Mortgage protection insurance**

Buying a new house should never be done in a hurry. Plan your viewing in three stages:

Situation

1. If the property is on a new estate, are the roads made up or will there be an additional charge for this?
2. Is there reliable public transport? Is it near a railway? Is there a motorway in the vicinity?
3. Is it near shops?
4. Is it near the schools?
5. Are there recreational facilities near at hand?
6. Is there space for the children to play?
7. Are there any nearby hazards for the children, e.g. canals, gravel pits, dangerous main roads, etc?
8. What are the future development plans for the area?
9. Are there any potential disadvantages nearby; e.g. boarding kennels, light industry, clubs, etc?

Construction of the House

1. Is the main structure of brick, stone or timber and what will its maintenance cost? Is there a damp course?
2. What type of roof has it?
3. Are the gutters and downspouts in good condition?
4. Are the doors protected by a porch from prevailing winds?
5. Is the garden laid out with lawns and flower beds?
6. Are all fences in a state of good repair?
7. Is there a garden shed or outside store for bicycles, etc?
8. Is there a garage or carport? Is the garage large enough to take your car?
9. Are all the paths in good repair?
10. Are your boundaries clearly defined?

Accommodation offered

1. Is there a large living room?
2. Is there a separate dining-room?
3. Is the kitchen large enough to accommodate cooker, washing machine, spin dryer, refrigerator, etc?
4. Does the sink unit have a double drainer?
5. Are there adequate worktops and storage space?
6. Is there a pantry?

7. Is there storage space for vacuum cleaner, ironing board, etc?

8. Will the kitchen accommodate a table and chairs/stools?

9. Is there a cupboard under the stairs?

10. Is there a cloakroom in the hall?

11. Where are the gas and electric meters situated? Can they be read from outside the house?

12. Where is the linen cupboard?

13. How many toilets are there? If only one, is it separate from the bathroom?

14. Is the house centrally heated? If so, what type of heating and what are the running costs?

15. Is there adequate storage for fuel?

16. What form of additional heating is available in winter?

17. Is there an immersion heater?

18. Is the loft insulated?

19. Are all walls and woodwork sound and free from any structural defect, dry rot or woodworm?

20. Are window frames in good condition and glazing sound?

21. Are there any signs of damp?

22. Is the electric wiring sound? Are there adequate points in all rooms?

23. What is the rateable value of the property?

24. Are there any additional charges; e.g. ground rent?

ones, or two small bedrooms converted into one large room. You will also be able to select colours of paintwork, tiles, wallpapers, bathroom and kitchen fittings and other accessories.

Having a house built as a single unit will cost more than the equivalent sized house on an estate. Consult a qualified architect. The **Royal Institute of British Architects** will put you in touch with one in your area or you can select from their Directory.

He will draw up all the necessary plans, consult with the builders and instruct a quantity surveyor to estimate the cost.

When briefing your architect it is important to tell him exactly how much money you can afford to spend as well as listing all the things you hope to include.

Once the building starts you may visit the site and watch progress. It is usual, however, to retain your architect and any queries or objections to the materials being used, or the way in which they are being fixed, should be made through him.

Select a builder who is a member of the **Registered House Builders' Association** and you will be covered against any faults which may arise for a period of 10 years.

Before building begins, the financial arrangements should be agreed with your building society or bank. The money is usually paid to the builder in pre-arranged stages as the work progresses.

HAVING YOUR HOUSE BUILT

If you are unable to find a house which meets your requirements you can have one built to your own specification.

The first step is to buy a plot of land which carries outline planning permission for a dwelling house. Or, select a house on a new estate before even the foundations are laid, and enter into an agreement with the builder to modify his plans to your specifications.

If you choose the latter method, the modifications will have to be of a minor nature and probably confined to the interior layout.

It will be possible, however, to have a large bedroom made into two smaller

MOVING HOUSE

Planning is the secret behind a smooth move. Immediately you know the date when you can take possession of your new house:

1. Contact one or two local firms of removal contractors and ask for an estimate. If you are moving to another part of the country, contact a firm there: they may be able to fit you in on a 'return service' basis at a cheaper rate.

2. Read carefully the conditions of contract under which the work is to be carried out.

3. Note the amount of liability given for your goods during transit. If necessary, take out additional cover with your own insurance company. Cost will be about 3/6 per £100.

4. When the representative calls to estimate the amount of furniture to be moved, make clear any special instructions.

5. If you wish to pack your own china/ glassware/books, arrange to have packing cases several days in advance.

Before Removal Day

1. Notify the local **rating authority, telephone area office, gas, electricity** and **water boards** of the date you will be vacating your house so that the various meters can be read and services suspended.

2. Notify **hire purchase firms, insurance companies,** etc., of your intending change of address.

3. Notify your **bank** and any **savings banks** your family use.

4. If you have a **pension** or **family allowance** book, inform the post office of your change of address.

5. Fill in the necessary form at the post office for your letters to be re-directed.

6. Transfer your **radio** and **TV licence.**

7. If you have children, make the necessary arrangements for them to be transferred to **schools** in the new district. If you can plan your move to coincide with the start of a new term this will help the child to settle much easier.

8. Cancel standing orders for deliveries of **milk, bread, newspapers** and **fuel.**

9. Cancel your **window cleaner.**

10. If there are solid fuel fires at your new house, arrange for the **chimneys** to be swept before you move in.

11. Arrange for **carpets** and **lino** to be laid in advance of your moving date.

12. Arrange for **curtains** to be made and hung.

On Removal Day

1. Make an early start. Have breakfast dishes washed and all beds stripped of blankets and linen before the removal men arrive.

2. Leave the removal men to dismantle beds, wardrobes and similar items. Don't try to help or offer advice. Don't distract the men with cups of tea or offers of cigarettes. They are allowed these only during their official break.

3. Any last minute instructions should be given to the foreman, not to individual workmen.

4. Remember to point out any items which are not being taken.

5. Provide a list showing where the different pieces are to go on arrival at your new house. Simple method is to mark items with coloured stick-on tabs; different colours to indicate different rooms.

6. Mark items you are going to need immediately on arrival so that these can be put into the van last.

7. Before the van leaves, take a final look round the house, starting at the top and working down room by room, to see nothing has been forgotten.

8. If you are taking carpets and linos and these have not been sent on ahead, check that they have been lifted.

9. Give the foreman full details on how to find your new house. A sketch map is of great help if it is in an out of the way place, or on a new estate and not numbered.

10. Most removal firms require payment when the goods are unloaded, so have the necessary cash or cheque to hand.

11. Tips should be handed to the foreman, who will share them out.

12. On arrival, concentrate on putting up and making up beds and putting basic cooking utensils and food where you can find them. Don't try to get the whole place straight at once or you will overtire yourself. Allow at least a week to get the house in order. Plan so that a definite proportion is carried out each day.

Insurance

Insurance is a means of buying financial protection against unforeseen happenings —such as fire to the house, or loss of life—which could otherwise have expensive repercussions.

Either an **insurance company** takes on the risk, in return for a premium, or it is placed with underwriters at **Lloyd's**.

Here are some of the ways of fixing up insurance:

1. Direct with an insurance company.
2. Through a full-time agent of an insurance company.
3. Through a part-time agent of a company—such as a garage owner, solicitor or accountant.
4. Through a firm of insurance brokers. If unsure about insurance, this is generally the best course. A broker should be able to make the best arrangements, and will not charge a fee.

HOUSEHOLDER'S INSURANCE

One of the main insurances is a householder's policy, called a different name by some companies. There are basically three types:

1. A BUILDING policy—for the house and outbuildings only.
2. A CONTENTS policy—for all the contents of the house, but not the structure.
3. A joint BUILDING and CONTENTS policy.

Anyone owning a house needs both kinds of policy, but *usually* anyone living in rented accommodation is not responsible for insuring the house, and will need only to insure the contents.

A building society lending money for house purchase has the right to specify the company with which the house should be insured.

In determining the value of a house for insurance, account should be taken of the cost of:

1. **Rebuilding the house.**
2. **Removing the debris of the existing structure.**
3. **The fees of architects and surveyors.**

Among the perils covered are:

1. **Fire and lightning.**
2. **Burglary.**
3. **Riots, but not malicious damage.**
4. **Storm and flood—although flood is not automatically included in all policies, and special arrangements may have to be made.**
5. **Bursting or overflowing of water tanks, apparatus or pipes.**
6. **Impact (for example, a vehicle other than your own crashing into the house).**

Many insurers exclude the first £15 of any claim made under Items 4 and 5. For full cover, it is necessary to make special arrangements in advance, and pay an additional premium over and above the 2s. 6d. per £100, which is the most usual basic rate.

Contents

The policy for contents covers household goods, personal effects, valuables and items such as electricity meters or telephone installations you do not own, but for which you are responsible. It costs about 5s. per £100 insured.

The main cover, very similar to that for the building of the house, applies while anything insured is in the house. The cover is generally more restricted when anything is temporarily removed from the house.

Deciding on the value for which to insure is not easy, and it is best to go round the house, assessing the value for each room separately. To insure for too little would give many insurers the right to void the policy altogether. Others would be able to scale down the amount payable in the event of a claim.

It is generally pointless to insure articles which depreciate in value for the full cost of replacement as new, since insurers do not settle claims on this basis. Allowance will be made for depreciation, and the use gained from an article before its loss or destruction.

Since the insurance gives cover only against specified perils, it is well worth extending a **householder's** policy to give **all risks** cover on jewellery, furs and items of value, such as cameras or binoculars. In this way both accidental loss or breakage are covered. Points to watch are:

1. Specify items of value separately with a fairly full description.

2. Give each item its own value.

3. If possible, be able to support any individual figure with an up-to-date professional valuation. This will help the settlement of any claim.

4. Include a lump sum for items too small in value to be specified separately, and to cover anything of minor value acquired during the year.

Liability

There is cover for claims people may make against you for accidental damage to property or personal injury in your capacity as owner or occupier of a house. Generally the limit is £100,000 for any one accident.

But there is no cover under the building and contents policies for accidents happening away from the house for which you or another member of the household may be responsible. Subject to certain exclusions, this can be arranged as an extension. For about 10s. a year, claims made against members of the family living in the house will be met up to £100,000.

As in the case of most liability insurances, insurers will handle claims made against you, and will pay the legal costs involved. Points to remember are:

1. Never admit liability to anyone else.

2. Pass on to the insurers, unanswered, any communication claiming damages following an accident.

MOTOR INSURANCE

Certain insurance protection is required by law before a car may be driven on the public highway. Compulsory insurance is restricted, and wider cover is generally arranged. The main types of motor insurance are:

Act Only

This is the legal minimum required by the Road Traffic Act 1960. It only covers claims for damages for death or personal injury caused to other individuals on the highway.

It does **not** cover non-fare paying passengers, nor does it give any protection for claims for damage to the property of other people, such as damage to somebody else's car.

Third Party

This gives the basic cover under **Act Only**, and includes accidents off the highway. Generally there **is** cover for liability to non-fare paying passengers (although this may be specifically excluded by the insurers). Also there is cover for damage to other people's property, such as the cost of repairs to another car.

This insurance should be considered the absolute minimum. Only with this is there full cover for claims which may be made against one. Even so, there is **no** cover under this policy for damage to one's own car.

Third Party, Fire and Theft

This is simply a third party policy, plus cover for your own car against fire and theft.

Comprehensive

Comprehensive is the widest cover available, giving everything under **Third Party, Fire and Theft**, plus loss of or damage to the car by any means—apart from exclusions relating to wear and tear, depreciation and other 'running expenses', such as electrical breakdowns, punctures.

Many insurers now require policy-holders to bear the first £15 or so of claims for accidental damage to the car. Often the amount is higher for a young or inexperienced driver.

There are many extras to most comprehensive policies, such as:

1. Cover for accidents to yourself or your wife involving death or serious injury in direct connection with the car.
2. Medical expenses, up to a fixed amount, following an accident with the car.
3. Loss of or damage to rugs, clothing and personal effects, up to a stated value while they are in the car.

Premiums for motor insurance depend on a number of factors, such as:

1. The type of car.
2. The area of the country in which it is garaged.
3. The age of the policy-holder.
4. How the car will be used—whether for business as well as social and domestic purposes.
5. Who else is likely to drive the car.

Many insurers grant a progressive discount if no claim has been made on the previous year's insurance. After four claim-free years the discount may amount to 60 per cent, or more, of the full premium.

One claim during a year generally does not invalidate the discount, but results in a dropping back of two years in the discount scale.

Under the third party section of most policies, there is provision for you to drive another car. Only **third party** risks will be covered; there will be no insurance for damage to the car which is being driven. This, however, may well be covered under the car owner's policy.

Generally, lifts can be given to other people, provided they do not pay—but even sharing expenses may be taken as paying.

The policy will have to be extended for motoring abroad. A **green card** (which is a local insurance certificate) must be obtained from the insurers. They should be told the dates of the journey and the countries involved. An additional charge is made for this service.

HOLIDAY INSURANCE

A great deal of worry and possibly expense can be saved by taking out a special insurance policy solely to cover the period of a holiday, especially a holiday abroad. Generally divided into sections, such a policy is likely to provide cover for the following:

Medical expenses

Although semi-reciprocal arrangements exist with some continental countries, medical treatment generally has to be paid for abroad. Adequate insurance will cover such expenses, and the cost of a companion to stay on with the sick person, should this be necessary.

Personal Accident

This provides a cash payment in the event of death or permanent disablement (or a weekly benefit during temporary disablement) resulting from an injury on holiday.

This section is particularly popular with people travelling by air. Alternatively, cover can be taken out simply for the days of flight. This may cost no more than 2s. per £1,000 for each day.

Cancellation Insurance

If a holiday is cancelled because of sickness or injury to oneself or a member of one's party, the policy will pay the cost of the non-recoverable expenses.

Generally, the cover also applies in the case of the death, illness, quarantine or accidental injury to any relative or friend or a close business colleague of the insured person.

Tickets and Money

Cover for loss of tickets or money generally is included, and the limit may be £100. As a rule, there is no cover for the first £2 10s. of any claim, or for shortages due to error or currency depreciation. And the police must be notified of any loss within a specified period.

Luggage

This can be insured on 'all risks' terms, and it includes such things as cameras, sports equipment, provided they are listed in the policy. Many insurers say that individual items worth more than £50 constitute a special risk, and so must be specified separately.

It is important to insure for an adequate sum for **everything**. This should be the cost of replacement, less a reasonable amount for depreciation.

Bad Weather

Apart from the main type of holiday policy, it is possible to insure against a holiday in the United Kingdom being spoilt by rain. The insurers will pay £5 towards holiday costs for each day during which the rainfall between 10 a.m. and 6 p.m. exceeds a specified amount—often a 10th of an inch, which represents about two hours of steady rain.

There is no cover for the first qualifying day in each week, on the grounds that one wet day during a week's holiday is only to be expected. The premium depends on the area, and the time of the year.

PERSONAL ACCIDENT AND SICKNESS INSURANCE

Many people arrange insurance to cover personal accident or sickness on an annual basis, so that the cover is always in force, irrespective of how an accident may occur. Under a personal accident policy, there is generally cover for the following:

1. Death resulting from an accident.
2. Loss of one or two limbs, and/or the loss of the sight of one or two eyes.
3. Permanent total disablement.

Under each of the headings, the sum insured can be for the same figure.

In addition there may well be:

1. Cover for temporary total disablement (for example, no work, on doctor's orders). A weekly benefit equivalent to one per cent of the capital sum may be paid up to a limit of two years.
2. Cover for temporary partial disablement—in which case a lower weekly benefit will be paid.

A personal accident policy may be extended to cover sickness—say at the rate of £10 a week for a maximum of one year.

Premiums for these policies are usually calculated according to your occupation. These policies are renewable annually, which means that insurers have the right to refuse renewal. Or they can impose terms, such as increasing the premium or excluding claims arising from certain causes.

One way to make sure that cover will be available, and that the claim will continue to be paid in the event of a long illness, which could result in your never returning to work, is to have a non-cancellable or continuous disability policy.

In this case, the premium depends on your age when the policy is taken out. It continues to be payable until the end of the policy period—perhaps until the age of 60 or 65. In the event of accident or sickness, the claim continues to be paid during the period of disability, if necessary until the end of the policy period.

INSURANCE CLAIMS

When an accident occurs, it may be difficult at the time to tell whether there will be a claim under the policy. Nevertheless, the insurers should be advised at the earliest opportunity. Here are some of the steps which should be taken in the event of a fire or loss or damage:

1. Call the fire brigade in the event of a fire.
2. Notify the police in the event of loss if it is possible that an item may be found—or following theft or malicious damage.
3. Obtain the names and addresses of witnesses in the event of a motor accident, as well as the names and addresses of any

other motorists who may have been involved in the accident.

4. Do not admit liability to anybody for injury or damage to their property, even though it may seem as though you were in the wrong.

5. Do everything possible to minimise the loss, and do not put repairs in hand until the insurers have given their consent.

6. Notify the insurers, and keep them advised of all future developments.

LIFE ASSURANCE

A life policy can be used solely to provide financial protection against death, or as a means of saving as well, in which case a lump sum will be payable on a certain date or at earlier death. There are two main categories of life policy.

One is temporary or term, where the policy is in force for only a specified period, and pays a claim only in the event of death during that period.

This insurance is quite cheap, because the policy generally terminates when the children of the family are self-supporting, and thus it is only in cases of premature death that a claim is made.

Under this heading, a policy can provide a lump sum at death, or a tax-free income from the date of death until the policy would have expired, with no further premiums to pay. The second is permanent cover. This is more expensive, since it is known at the outset that a claim will have to be met at some stage.

The two main types of policy are **whole life**, when the benefit is payable only at death, although there may be provision for premiums to cease to be payable at a certain age.

And **endowment**, when the benefits are paid on a certain date agreed at the outset, or at earlier death.

When a policy is arranged on a permanent basis, either the benefit can be a set figure, or, by paying a rather higher premium, the policy can share in the profits of the insurance office. In this case, there is a minimum guaranteed sum assured at the outset.

Periodically, this sum is increased by the allocation of bonuses from the profits of the insurance office. Once allocated, a bonus cannot subsequently be withdrawn.

Also, endowment contracts can be arranged which are linked to the units of a unit trust. Some of these policies have guaranteed minimum values in case there should be a sharp drop in prices on the Stock Exchange.

Income tax relief can be claimed on the premiums for many types of life assurance policy. After a number of premiums have been paid towards a permanent policy, it can often be used as security for a loan from the insurance office, should this prove necessary

Household Budgets and Accounts

A budget is a forecast of income and expenditure over a given period. Accounts are a record of how the income has been spent.

Just as the Chancellor of the Exchequer plans the nation's 'housekeeping' at Budget time, so must you prepare your own personal budget.

YOUR BUDGET

It is important to make a budget, even a very simple one, because it will give you an idea of how much money you have to spend on various items such as food, clothing, insurance and the like.

Both budget and accounts should correspond to the period by which you get paid. Most people in Britain are still paid weekly, and most expenditure on household accounts is incurred weekly.

Remember, however, that there are certain bills which come in at longer intervals for which you have to make weekly provision. Such things as repairs to one of your appliances, or expenditure on an annual holiday, fall into this category. Unless you make provision for them, you will have no money in hand when the time comes.

All this is very simple, but a lot of people do forget it.

YOUR ACCOUNTS

Most people know how much their weekly or monthly wage or salary is going to be throughout the year. If you are one of these you can, within the year's income, allow a certain amount for each of the main categories of expenditure that we all have to meet.

Food, rent, clothes, travel, entertainment, repairs, hire purchase payments and a **reserve amount** should all figure in the budget. It is hard to be dogmatic about categories of expenditure, because these will vary according to the personal habits and taste of each family.

On the income side, one should remember to include such things as contribution towards the household expenses of children who may be at work, or the child allowance.

You can also add into the income amount any interest that you may be earning on any savings, the wife's earnings, or any pension you receive regularly. This then gives you the total income which cannot be exceeded. If it is, you will be forced into the situation where you will have to borrow money.

If you borrow money, it has to be repaid. If you borrow it from a bank or any other financial institution, you will have to pay interest on it. If you are making regular repayments against borrowed money, you will have to make allowances for this in your budget.

However hard the going is, it is absolutely essential to keep your expenditure within your income and, if at all possible, leave something over for a rainy day.

Once you have prepared your statement of weekly or monthly earnings—which must be after tax, national insurance stamps and all other deductions—you can then begin to allocate money for different things.

An elementary, but quite satisfactory, form of financial control is to take the weekly pay packet, and put the amount allowed for various purposes into separate labelled envelopes. You can then spend from each as and when necessary without overspending on any particular item.

With more discipline you can use a more sophisticated—though still simple—system of accounts. All accounting means is that you keep an accurate record of everything you have spent during the budget period.

A simple method is to make a shopping list, and to enter the amount that you have spent on the list itself. At the end of the week, you will be able to see how your accounts have matched up with your budget.

This is really all that needs to be done to keep on an even keel financially. Always remember the expenses which occur at less frequent intervals than your budget period. For these, a reserve must be made.

BUDGETS AND BANKS

Many people these days have a bank account. Although you pay the bank for this privilege, the cost is reasonable. A bank account does away with the need for keeping a lot of cash in the house.

Most people put into their bank account their weekly or monthly salary, and then pay their bills by drawing cheques. A cheque is simply an order to your bank to pay money out of your account. This does not do away with the need for budgeting, but it does simplify the business of keeping accounts because the bank sends you regular statements showing how much money you have put in, and how much you have taken out.

Bills you pay by **cheque** are identifiable on your bank statement—you know exactly how much the grocer or the butcher have cost you—but you must still keep your own records of where the **cash** you spend has gone.

If you get into a muddle, or want advice, there is no better person to whom to turn than the bank manager.

Banks will not allow you to overdraw your account (that is, borrow money from them) unless you make arrangements for paying it back, so do not think that you can start using their money automatically without their permission.

Banks often lend to people who can conduct an account properly, but they expect to be paid back over a fairly short period on the agreed terms. Interest has to be paid on money borrowed for as long as it remains outstanding.

Budgeting Examples

**A simple guide on proportions
of total income to allocate to
different categories of expenditure**

Housing, including travelling to and from work	20%
Fuel—all fuel used (wood, coal, coke, electricity, gas, etc.) ..	10%
Food—including school or canteen meals	30%
Clothing—shoes, repairs, cleaning included	10%
Household expenses, detergents, cleaning, replacements ..	10%
Spending or pocket money ..	5%
Savings, holiday, TV and radio	10%
Reserve for contingencies ..	5%
	100%

Budgeting on two Incomes

One way to divide financial responsibilities

HUSBAND					WIFE				
Housing ..	..	..	..	20%	Food ..	..	..	..	30%
Fuel ..	..	..	..	10%	Clothing ..	..	..	..	10%
Holiday ..	..	..	..	5%	Household expenses	..	..		6%
Savings ..	..	..	..	*5%	Personal money ..	..	..		4%
Personal money	..	..		10%					
				50%					50%

* This is a minimum. It is advisable for the husband to increase this sum as much as he can in relation to his earnings and the money he earns which exceeds the amount earned by his wife.

BUDGET ACCOUNTS AT BANKS

Banks will offer their good customers a Budget Account. This enables you to deposit a regular sum monthly, against which the bank will pay your bills as and when they become due. This evens out your liability to a fixed sum each month.

Even if your bills exceed the sum deposited in one month, the banks will still pay out. Over a period, of course, the bank will have to be satisfied that your average payments do not exceed your regular deposits. Banks make a small charge for this service.

OTHER LIABILITIES

When budgeting, remember your liability for **tax** and **national insurance stamps**. Most people have tax deducted at source, and because they are employed persons, their stamp is also bought by their employer, and the amount deducted from their salaries.

There are, though, a large number of self-employed people who pay tax directly. They must also buy their own national insurance stamps.

If you are self-employed, you must put tax money to one side out of earnings. Do not leave it lying around—put it in some form of deposit account where it will earn some interest until the Inland Revenue demands it.

The only people exempt from income tax are those who have not been required to fill in a tax return and who have no income. Everyone else must do so.

The penalties for not filling in your tax returns are severe—£50 for each failure and £10 a day for each day the failure continues. In cases of incorrect or fraudulent returns, the penalties are even more severe.

If you pay tax directly, then make sure you know how much you will be liable for. There are allowances to be claimed, and a number of perfectly legal ways of avoiding paying too much. The advice of a qualified accountant is almost always worth his fee.

While income tax inspectors are generally very helpful in explaining matters, remember they are essentially tax collectors—**not** tax advisers. If you want good independent advice, you will have to pay for it.

Home Security

Protecting your home and property against theft is very important. The crime rate is soaring, and the police force in many places is undermanned.

Figures show that there is, on average, a burglary or break-in every three minutes. Crime goes on 24 hours a day, seven days a week.

Figures for the Greater London Area alone show that:

1. **Well over 75,000 houses and flats are burgled every year.**
2. **Goods to the value of £5 million are reported stolen from private homes every year. This figure is what the police actually know about. The true figure is probably much higher.**
3. **One in every 30 homes will be broken into during the next 12 months.**
4. **Fewer than one in 100 homes are adequately safeguarded against theft.**

We have an excellent police force, and they are doing their best to combat the soaring crime figures. They are fighting the criminal with the very latest techniques, but they cannot be everywhere at the same time. The first responsibility for protecting the home and its contents lies with the householder.

WHAT CAN BE DONE?

The average householder can help himself and the police in a variety of ways. A few minutes' thought is often all that is needed. Here are a few tips from the top—Scotland Yard itself.

Do not make it easy for the casual housebreaker.

A very high proportion of all break-ins are committed by the 'casual' burglar. He goes for ordinary houses, and is after small items like cash, jewellery and ornaments. He will only enter a house if it is made easy for him. He is easily deterred by closed windows, bolted doors or a bright light burning in the house.

Do not provide bait for the professional crook.

The really professional criminal only goes for homes where he thinks valuables are kept. Wherever possible, place your valuables in the safety of a safe deposit box at your bank. If you must keep valuables or large sums of money in the house, treat yourself to a good strong safe.

The professional is not easily deterred. If faced with locked doors and windows, he will break in to get what he wants. Only an efficient burglar alarm system will foil him.

Do not advertise to the burglar.

Thousands of homes have been burgled because the owners gave open invitations to the criminal. If you are going on holiday, or leaving the house empty for a few days, be sure to prevent anything which will advertise your absence.

1. Cancel milk and newspapers.
2. Lock and bolt all windows, on all floors.
3. Tell your neighbours that you are going away.
4. Place your valuables in a bank or a safe deposit box.
5. Make sure that any ladders are safely locked away.

Ask for free and expert advice on home security.

The police are only too willing to give every property owner advice on all matters of home security. Special Crime Prevention Officers are freely available upon request to the nearest police station. An officer will visit your house, and advise you as to your individual needs regarding locks, alarm systems and all thief-proof devices.

HOW MUCH DOES IT COST?

It need not cost you a fortune to protect your home against theft. For as little as £10 to £15, you can fit anti-thief devices.

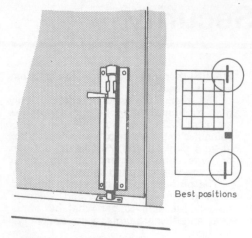

Best positions

Fit two strong bolts to the insides of doors. Place them, wherever possible, away from glass panels.

Doors

Check the locks on all your outside doors, front and back. A mortice lock or a rim lock is best. For added protection, insist on a lock which passes the British Standards specification B.S. 3621/63. Make sure that the lock bears the British Standards Institution mark.

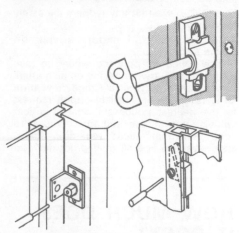

Top: Key-operated casement lock. Bottom left: Key-operated window lock for wooden casement. Bottom right: Key-operated window lock for metal casement.

Fit two strong bolts to the inside of all doors, and make sure you check them every night before going to bed.

Where you have glass panels in doors, make sure that the inside bolt and lock is beyond reach if the thief smashes a pane.

Windows

Ordinary sash and casement fasteners on windows do not give adequate protection. Fit a key-operated window lock wherever possible. On wooden frame windows, the average householder can fit such a lock with little trouble. With metal window frames, it is best to have the locks fitted professionally.

Check all windows before going to bed, including skylights and upper floor windows.

Garages

Fit a stout padlock to your garage doors. Insist upon a closed shackle padlock for maximum protection.

Lock all ladders in your garage at night, as well as any tools which could be used to prise open doors or windows.

Other Safeguards

In addition to the safe and simple precautions listed above, there are dozens of other things you can do to protect your home and belongings. Here are just a few of them:

Anti-climb paint on drainpipes

Anti-climb paint is specially formulated so that it never sets completely hard. You paint the upper part of your drainpipe with it. If a thief attempts to climb the pipe to reach an upper window, he finds that the drainpipe is extremely slippery, and that paint comes off on to his hands and clothing.

Burglar alarms

There are two types of burglar alarm protection open to the average house-holder.

Firstly, he can install any one of a number of audible alarms which will sound if a thief enters his house.

Secondly, he can subscribe to a security company who will fit a burglar alarm system which is connected directly to their own 24-hour crime prevention service.

The advantage of the second system is that the thief is unaware that he has set off an alarm, and is often caught redhanded. Its main disadvantage is that it is expensive.

Check strangers attempting to enter your home.

Always insist on seeing the credentials of any stranger who wants to enter your home. Many thieves pose as gas inspectors, sanitary inspectors and council workers.

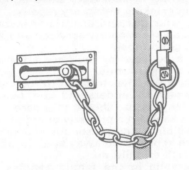

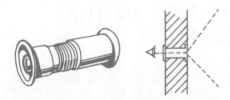

Two useful devices for people living alone. Above: A safety chain which allows the door to be only partially opened. Below: A peephole telescope.

For people who live on their own, it is a good idea to fit a safety chain to the front door, so that callers can be identified before the door is fully opened.

Another useful device which can be fitted to the front door is a peephole telescope, which allows you to see the caller without opening the door.

Safes.

If a safe is to be fitted in your house, make sure it is adequate. A wall-fitting safe offers a little protection, but the experienced criminal can remove it intact and take it away to work on it.

A properly-fitted underfloor safe is one of the best forms of protection you can have.

Keep a sharp lookout.

Keep your eyes open for suspicious characters lurking in your area. If you have any reasonable grounds for suspicion, telephone the police at once. Even if it is a false alarm, the police will thank you for your action. They would rather be safe than sorry.

An automatic deadlock

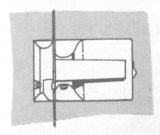

A rim automatic deadlock

A key-operated security bolt

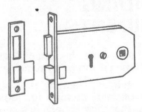

A horizontal mortice lock

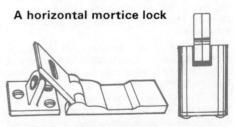

A high-security locking bar and padlock

Safety In The Home

It is a sobering fact that there are more fatal accidents in our homes than on the roads. For every six people who are killed on the roads in England and Wales, eight are killed in our homes. Thousands more are seriously injured.

While accidents in the home happen to people of all ages, two groups are more at risk than others. These are children (particularly those under five years) and old people.

ACCIDENTS

Home accidents fall into these main categories:

1. Falls—the chief danger to old people.
2. Burns and scalds—especially affecting young children and old people.
3. Poisoning—a danger to all, especially from gas and medicines.
4. Suffocation—a major hazard to babies.

AVOIDING ACCIDENTS

There are three important factors to consider when planning to avoid accidents:

1. The human factor. If you have children or old people to look after, remember that their actions will sometimes be governed by curiosity, disobedience, temper, ignorance, absent-mindedness or loneliness.
2. The physical factor—poor eyesight, lack of physical co-ordination or slowness of reaction to danger may be the immediate cause of the accident.
3. The material factor—an article in the wrong place, a hole in a carpet, any one of a hundred possibilities which in 99 cases may not cause an accident, but in the 100th case will.

FORMULA FOR SAFETY

Your home will be safe if:

You consider the home safety carefully, and check up on danger points, putting in necessary extra lighting, undertaking necessary repairs.

All your gas and electricity installations are properly serviced and kept in good repair.

As a housewife, you have a sensible working routine.

You take the trouble to get your family to understand the reasons why they too should take care.

You keep fires properly guarded.

Medicines and poisonous substances are kept locked away and out of the reach of children.

Everyone in the family handles hot liquids with care and they are kept away from children.

You buy only equipment you know is safe and is properly approved.

SAFETY IN THE GARDEN

Having checked your home for security and to prevent accidents, you must also remember to give your garden the 'once over'.

Many berries and leaves look attractive to children, but may be poisonous. Some of the most common poisonous growths are toadstools, the common yew tree, deadly, woody and black nightshade, thorn apple, laburnum, mistletoe and ivy. If you have children, the safest thing is to make sure that you have none of these things in your garden.

AVOIDING FALLS

Clear as you go. Do not leave things lying around on the floor for someone to

POISONOUS PLANTS IN THE GARDEN

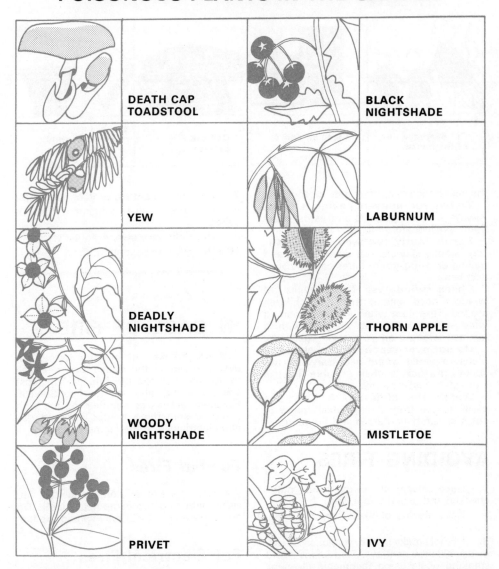

	DEATH CAP TOADSTOOL		**BLACK NIGHTSHADE**
	YEW		**LABURNUM**
	DEADLY NIGHTSHADE		**THORN APPLE**
	WOODY NIGHTSHADE		**MISTLETOE**
	PRIVET		**IVY**

trip over.

Check floor coverings. Worn carpets and rugs, and badly fitting lino, can all cause accidents.

Use non-slip polish. Do not over-polish floors. The shine may look nice, but your vanity may result in a nasty fall for someone you love. And do be sure not to polish under mats.

Avoid trailing flex. This just asks to be tripped over. Remember, too, that it is dangerous to run flex under floor coverings.

Have good lighting. Danger can lurk in the shadows. Ensure that your home is well lit, with no dark corners, especially near the staircase. Wipe up spilt liquids at once. Grease or water spilt on the floor can be a real hazard.

Check the staircase. Watch for loose stair-rods and frail banisters. Keep the staircase clear, and do not have slip mats at the foot of the stairs. Remember

FOUR-POINT FIRE DRILL

| 1 Get everyone out of the house | 2 Close all doors | 3 Call the Fire Service | 4 Smother small fires |

the importance of a safety gate for toddlers.

Watch for uneven paving stones. Always a risk in gardens and yards. Have them levelled, and replace worn ones.

Repair faulty footwear and clothing. Sloppy slippers, run-down shoes and trailing dressing-gown hems can all cause accidents.

Check windows. Some types of window need bars if there are children around. Take care when you are cleaning windows, and do not struggle with a jammed window on your own—get help.

Do not over-reach. Have shelves and meters lowered where necessary. Do not stand on a rickety chair or table. Keep a stout step-ladder handy.

Watch the children. A baby can easily topple from a high-chair, pram or cot. Use safety harnesses and fireguards.

AVOIDING FIRES

1. Have electrical wiring and plugs checked and repaired regularly

2. Have electric blankets serviced regularly.

3. Do not smoke in bed, smoke carelessly or use shallow ashtrays. Particularly avoid smoking while using flammable cleaners.

4. Be sure that tiles fixed with flammable adhesives do not come into contact with flame or strong heat.

5. Do not air clothes or household linen in front of unguarded fires or over gas burners.

6. Keep paraffin heaters in a safe place, and be sure they are properly guarded. Do not carry paraffin heaters while they are alight.

7. Use sparkguards to protect open fires.

8. Use only metal containers for hot ashes.

9. Have chimney swept regularly.

10. Destroy combustible rubbish.

IN CASE OF FIRE

If fire breaks out in your home, get everyone out of the house, and close all the doors. Call the fire brigade—in most cases call 999 and ask for Fire Service. For small outbreaks, smother the fire with a rug or something similar. Turn off gas and electricity—at the mains preferably.

For Fat Fires

Cover the vessel containing the fat, either with a lid or a damp heavy cloth. Do not use water—it will only spread the fire.

For Electrical Fires

Turn off gas or electricity. Switch off the current and unplug if possible. Use water to extinguish fire.

For Paraffin Heater Fires

Throw on buckets of water from at least six feet away. Or use the garden hose. Concentrate on cooling the metal casing.

For a Clothing Fire

A person whose clothing is on fire should be rolled up in a rug. They must not be allowed to run about, particularly outdoors. When the fire is out, wrap the victim up in a blanket and call doctor or ambulance.

If You are Trapped by Fire

Go into a room, and shut the door. Try to keep out smoke by putting carpet or blanket at the bottom of the door. Go to the window and call for help.

AVOIDING SCALDS

1.   Use a pan guard when cooking to avoid saucepans being overturned.
2.   Keep teapots, cups or other vessels containing hot liquids well out of the reach of small children.
3.   Use thick covers on hot-water bottles, and check them regularly for leaks.
4.   Put cold water in before hot when washing and bathing.
5.   Turn kettle spouts and steam vents away from the front of the cooker.

AVOIDING BURNS

1.   Always use fixed fireguards.
2.   See that clothes—especially winter ones—are made of flame-resisting wool, or proofed cotton or nylon.
3.   Keep matches out of the reach of children.
4.   Keep flammable liquids like petrol, paraffin and lighter fuel away from flame or heat.
5.   Use a cloth when handling hot vessels or appliances. Keep these out of the way of children.
6.   When lighting fireworks, follow the instructions exactly.
7.   Control the size and spread of bonfires, and never light them with petrol or paraffin.

AVOIDING POISON

1.   Keep medicines out of the reach of children.
2.   Be careful to take the correct dose of medicine—read the directions carefully. Never keep medicine at your bedside or take it in the dark. Do not allow children to give themselves medicine, and do not pass on your medicine to someone else.
3.   When you are taking a medicine, do not take any other medicine—even a laxative—without your doctor's knowledge.
4.   Be careful where you store medicine. Use a proper cabinet which can be locked. Keep all medicines in their properly-labelled original containers. Do not hoard surplus medicine—when you are no longer taking it, flush it down the lavatory, or ask your chemist to destroy it for you. Never put medicine in the dustbin or on the fire.
5.   Store disinfectants, household bleaches, paraffin, turps and the like away from medicine and out of the children's reach.

AVOIDING SUFFOCATION AND CHOKING

1.   Never share a bed with a baby. While you are asleep, you can easily cause the baby to suffocate.
2.   Make sure that the baby is properly 'winded' after feeding it from a bottle.
3.   Always put a pillow under the mattress in a cot or pram.
4.   Never use soft pillows for babies.
5.   Always remove airtight rubber or plastic bibs after feeding baby.
6.   Never let young children play with plastic bags.

AVOIDING ACCIDENTS WITH GAS

1.   Ensure that your appliances are correctly installed, and Gas Council tested.

2. Check regularly that pilot lights are functioning properly.

3. Watch for loose gas taps and worn connecting tubing.

4. Remember that instantaneous water heaters used for supplying hot water to a bath must be fitted with a flue. And bathrooms need proper ventilation to keep gas burning correctly.

AVOIDING ACCIDENTS WITH ELECTRICITY

1. Treat electricity with respect. Never take chances—make-shift repairs can kill.

2. Be especially careful of using electrical appliances near water. In the bathroom, never use appliances not specifically designed for bathroom use.

BUYING FOR SAFETY

Signs That Mean Something

BSI KITE MARK

This symbol stands for the most valuable assurance possible—the British Standards Institution Kite Mark. It can only be used when the BSI is satisfied that quality and safety of the product are up to the specification of the relevant British Standard and that production facilities are likely to give reliable consistency.

BRITISH ELECTRICAL APPROVALS BOARD

The British Electrical Approvals Board for Domestic Appliances grants this Mark after testing samples to British Standards Institution safety standards and finding that all requirements are met.

Be sure that any electrical appliance you buy has this mark.

COUNCIL OF INDUSTRIAL DESIGN

This black and white triangular label which features the words 'As selected for the Design Centre' was one of the first labelling schemes to put emphasis on the appearance of the product as well as its functional efficiency. The Council of Industrial Design works towards the improvement of design in the products of British Industry. Design Centre labels can be found related to most household goods.

GAS COUNCIL

All gas appliances have to be thoroughly tested to British Standards before they can be put on sale through the Area Gas Boards. This is the symbol which you should look for.

OIL APPLIANCE MANUFACTURERS' ASSOCIATION

This is the sign to look for if you are buying a portable domestic oil heater. All heaters manufactured by member companies of this Association meet the high safety requirements called for by the current British Standard 3300.

TELTAG

Teltag is an informative label, not a mark of quality or approval. Introduced by the Consumer Council, Teltags are designed to give shoppers (and retailers) the basic facts about a product. Teltags give details about a product's performance, how it will wear, what it is capable of doing, in a standardised format, so that comparison of information about different products is easy.

HOW SAFE IS YOUR HOME?

How do your home safety precautions measure up with this list compiled by the British Standards Institution? If you answer 'yes' to every question, you are superhumanly safety-minded. If you have six 'noes' or less you are still doing quite

well. More than six—there is room for improvement.

ENTRANCE
Is it well lit?

HALL AND PASSAGE
Are they well lit?
Is the doormat 'sunk'?
Is the floor surface even?

LIVING ROOM
Are carpets and rugs in good repair?
Are there sufficient electrical power points for all appliances?
Is the fire guarded with a fixed fireguard?
Is the mirror sited away from the fireplace?

KITCHEN
Are all domestic cleaning agents locked away when not in use?
Are kitchen knives and sharp utensils stored safely away from children?
Is the cooker well maintained and functioning correctly?
Is the floor 'non-slip' and free from polish build-up?
Does the first-aid cupboard bear the British Standards Institution seal of approval?
Is the first-aid cupboard out of the children's reach?

STAIRS
Is the stair carpet firmly fixed and in good repair?
Are the banisters firm and strong?
Is the light operated by a return switch for use at top or bottom?
Are the stairs free of obstruction?

BEDROOMS
Is the fire guarded with a fixed fireguard?
Is the fire free from close contact with curtains and furnishings?
Is the electric blanket in good working order?
Does the electric blanket have the BSI seal of approval?

BATHROOM AND LAVATORY
Are there handrails fixed to the bath and toilet?
Is a rubber—or similar—mat available for use in the bath?
Does the light operate on a pull-cord switch?
If warmed by electricity, is the heater sited high on the wall?
Does the heater have a pull-cord switch?

Where To Get Help

Much time and money is spent by consumers on obtaining service on household goods. It is just as well to know from whom one can expect service, how much it is going to cost, how to make a complaint and to whom to make it.

GENERAL PRINCIPLES

There are certain general principles which should be clearly understood. Most goods in this country are bought from shops. Every time you buy something, you enter into a contract with the shopkeeper. The law incorporates into most contracts of sale certain protections for the purchaser, and because of the existence of the contract of sale between yourself and the retailer from whom you purchased the goods, you should complain to him first.

SELLER'S RESPONSIBILITIES

The person who sold you the goods may have sold you a defective article. This may be basically the fault of the manufacturer, but it is the responsibility of the shopkeeper to put it right. He may be able to seek redress from the manufacturer or wholesaler from whom he bought it, but his is the first and primary responsibility. Most retailers in businesses where service is required are anxious to uphold their responsibilities, and a fair complaint will usually produce the desired result.

If you have bought a refrigerator which will not freeze, or a television set which will not get a picture, a good retailer will do his best to put it right.

Such items are normally sold with a guarantee which entitles you to free service for a period. Read the terms of the guarantee carefully to make sure it does not leave you in a less favourable position than if you had relied on your legal rights under the contract of sale.

YOUR RIGHTS

Under a contract of sale you have certain rights.
1. If you are buying by description, the goods supplied must be as described. This sounds obvious, but it is very important. If the goods are not as described, you are entitled to return them and get your money back.
2. Goods sold to you must be of 'merchantable' quality. This is not a very high standard, but it roughly means that they should be fit for the purpose for which they were sold. If they are not you are entitled to redress against the retailer.
3. Contract-of-sale rights are only applicable to the condition of the goods when purchased. After you have had goods for some time they are subject to fair wear and tear, and if defects are caused by this there is no breach of contract.

For example, if a television set will not work at all soon after you have bought it, or the picture is of such poor quality that you cannot watch it, this is a breach of the contract.

But if the set breaks down after three years of continuous use, it is more likely to be due to fair wear and tear, and the consumer must pay.

There are no hard and fast rules for determining whether there has been a breach of contract, but it is sufficient here to say that new goods should work reasonably well for a reasonable length of time. If they go wrong later it is up to you to put them right.

PEOPLE TO TURN TO

If your retailer will not or cannot put things right, the next step is to write to the manufacturer. Most manufacturers of brand name goods are jealous of their reputation, and will treat your complaint seriously.

You could also write to the trade association of which your retailer or the manufacturer is a member. Many of these associations are prepared to investigate complaints made about their members. If all else fails, try the Citizens' Advice Bureau, the Consumer Council or the readers' service of a national newspaper.

COMPLAINTS ABOUT STATE SERVICES

So much for complaining about goods you buy which are not up to standard. But many of the frustrations the consumer suffers concern services. Where these are obtained from a nationalised industry, such as gas or electricity, complain to them—but what about the whole range of services provided by your local authority, and for which you pay your rates?

The first thing to do is to go to your local council offices. If you get no satisfaction you have the right to approach your local councillor or, where national policies are involved, your Member of Parliament.

Remember, though, that these are busy people, and to waste their time with frivolous or unjustified complaints is unfair—and useless.

How the System Works

Everyone in Britain is represented by local councillors and Members of Parliament, and if you do not know their names, inquire at the council offices, giving your address. You will then be told in whose ward or constituency you live.

Most councillors are prepared to see their voters at their homes or places of business at convenient times.

MPs are at Westminster for two-thirds of the year, but normally they visit their constituencies at weekends specifically for the purpose of receiving complaints. You will often see notices in the local newspaper to say when your MP will be at his constituency offices. Write to ask for an appointment, stating your complaint briefly and when you see him, answer his questions as quickly and as fairly as possible.

Role of the Ombudsman

MPs' now have the power to recommend certain matters to the Ombudsman or, to give him his proper title, the Parliamentary Commissioner for Administration. There is no point in writing to this official direct—he can only deal with problems which have been referred to him by MPs.

Broadly speaking, where your complaint concerns the faulty administration of any Government department, the Ombudsman can deal with it. He may want to see you, in which case you can be paid the expenses incurred in visiting his office.

HOW THE LAW HELPS

Recent legislation provides a useful weapon against those who persistently misdescribe the goods and services they sell, or the prices at which they are available. The Trade Descriptions Act 1968 provides that if a firm or an individual describes goods in writing or by word of mouth in a way that is materially false, an offence has been committed which may result in their being prosecuted and fined.

Some firms have made a practice of apparently offering reductions by showing one price with a line through it, and another price, very much lower, suggesting a substantial saving to the purchaser. In some cases the goods were never offered at the higher price, so the benefit to the consumer was fictitious rather than real.

Such pricing claims are now in certain circumstances an offence in the eyes of the law. Note that the Act does not provide for any recompense to be made to you, but simply enables a prosecution to be brought against the retailer concerned.

If you have a complaint about this sort of false price-cutting, go to your local Weights and Measures inspector. You will find his department's address in the telephone book under the local authority.

Here is an easy-to-follow guide to what to do if you need help or want to lodge a complaint:

WRITING LETTERS OF COMPLAINT

The presentation of a letter of complaint is important. It can make all the difference to whether you get quick satisfaction or none at all. Here are some useful tips:

1. Try to address your letter to a person. The time and trouble spent checking on whom to write to is a good investment. Impersonal letters tend to get shunted around, and are not dealt with as promptly as letters addressed to the managing director by name.

2. Make your letter neat and easy to read —and above all keep it short.

3. Letters phrased courteously, stating your case in fair, reasonable terms are more likely to get a friendly and helpful reaction.

4. Give *all* the important facts. Include the nature of the complaint (is it about goods or service?), the reason, the dates involved, the type of products or services, the names and addresses of relevant retailers or manufacturers. If it is a branded product with a serial number, remember to quote this.

5. Do not overstate your case. Be prepared to stand by your words—you may be called upon to prove the truth of your complaint.

COMMERCIAL GOODS AND SERVICES

Complain to:

1. The retailer from whom you purchased the goods or services.

2. The manufacturer. Letters addressed to a person are usually more effective.

3. The trade association to which the retailer or the manufacturer belongs.

IF NECESSARY, WRITE TO:

1. The Consumer Council.

2. Readers' service departments of the national newspapers.

LOCAL AUTHORITY AND GOVERNMENT SERVICES

Complain to:

1. Local council office.

2. Local councillor.

3. Member of Parliament if the matter involves national policies and through him to . . .

4. The Ombudsman.

IF NECESSARY, WRITE TO:

Local newspapers or the national press.

NATIONALISED INDUSTRY SERVICES

Complain to:

1. Local office or showroom.

2. The Consultative Council for the appropriate service. Addresses can be found at showrooms, post offices or railway stations.

IF NECESSARY, WRITE TO:

The national press.

In The Garden

TOOLS

Use good, efficient tools. Making do with broken and rusty tools is false economy, and gives no pleasure.

The basic tools for a beginner are a digging fork and spade, a rake and a hand trowel. Secateurs should also be an early acquisition. A hoe, and equipment for the lawn, will be next on the list.

Do not hesitate to pay a little more for good quality. Stainless steel tools will last a lifetime in good condition, whereas cheap equivalents will soon need replacing. Keep tools under cover after use, preferably in a shed supplied with hanging brackets. Wash away dirt immediately after use, and wipe over with an oily rag before storing for any length of time.

Select digging tools for convenience of weight and height. Many are now made with light alloy shafts and handles.

Small but useful pieces of equipment include a long, stout line with pegs at either end, and a slim dibber for handling seedlings.

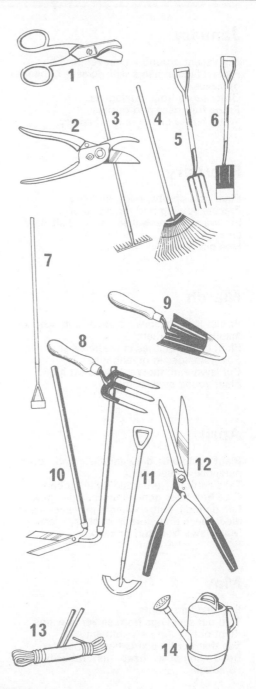

A CHECK LIST OF GARDEN TOOLS

1. **Flower gathering scissors**
2. **Secateurs**
3. **Rake**
4. **Wire lawn rake**
5. **Digging fork**
6. **Digging spade**
7. **Hoe**
8. **Hand fork**
9. **Hand trowel**
10. **Lawn edging shears**
11. **Half-moon lawn edger**
12. **Lawn shears**
13. **Line and pegs**
14. **Watering can with fine rose**

MONTH BY MONTH GUIDE

January

Dig vacant ground whenever possible.
Protect tender plants with screens or heaps of leaves.
Order seeds from catalogues.
Prune fruit trees and bushes.
Water house plants only when dry.

February

Plant new shrubs, trees and roses.
Prepare sowing bed for vegetables.
In warm greenhouse sow half-hardy annuals.
Hoe out weeds.

March

Prune rose bushes; spread compost or manure below them.
Plant early potatoes in sheltered site.
Sow tomatoes in greenhouse.
Cut lawn with mower blades set high.
Plant young strawberries.

April

Plant gladioli, delphiniums, and other perennial flower roots.
Take cuttings from lifted dahlia tubers.
Give fruit trees general insecticide spray.
Lift daffodil bulbs when the leaves have died. Clean and store in cool dry place.
Make lawn from turf or seed.

May

Buy bedding plants.
Thin out seedlings from earlier sowings.
Plant out young chrysanthemums.
See that border plants have supports.
Build compost heap as rubbish accumulates.

June

Plant out dahlias.
Cut back rock garden plants after flowering.
Water with gentle spray during dry spells.
Prune early shrubs like forsythia and mock orange.
Take cuttings of geraniums and fuchsias.
In greenhouse sow cyclamen, primulas and cinerarias.

July

Cut off flower heads as they die.
Lift tulip bulbs as foliage dies, clean and store in cool dry place.
Cut out raspberry canes that have carried fruit.
Apply lawn weedkiller if needed.
Shade and fully ventilate the greenhouse.

August

Tie dahlias to stakes.
Prune out oldest shoots on rambler roses.
Sow cabbage, and more lettuce, for spring.
Remove side shoots from tomato plants.
Spread lawn mowings around shrubs.

September

Plant bulbs in bowls of fibre.
Buy bulbs for outdoor planting.
Plant wallflowers for spring.
Harvest vegetables as needed.
Plant evergreen shrubs and trees. Water them well.

October

Clear away bedding plants and dig beds.
Gather apples when they part easily from spur.
Lift and store begonias, gladioli and dahlias.
Plant tulips.
Apply fertiliser to ground scheduled for new plants.

November

Remove leaves as they fall. Add to compost heap.
Plant hardy border flowers and new rose bushes in prepared ground.
Prune out old wood from currants and gooseberries.
Collect stakes, labels, etc., and store them.

December

Check that wall plants and trees are staked against wind.
Prune fruit trees and spray with tar oil.
Pinch out tops of wallflowers.
Check through fruit and flower bulbs in store for disease.

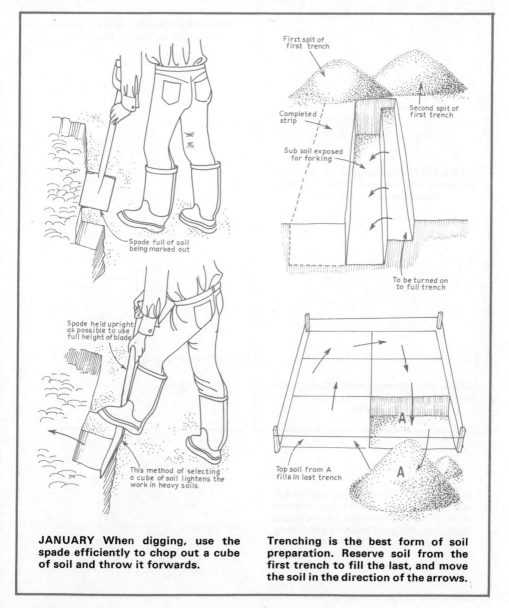

Spade full of soil being marked out

Spade held upright as possible to use full height of blade

This method of selecting a cube of soil lightens the work in heavy soils

First spit of first trench

Completed strip

Second spit of first trench

Sub soil exposed for forking

To be turned on to full trench

Top soil from A fills in last trench

A

JANUARY When digging, use the spade efficiently to chop out a cube of soil and throw it forwards.

Trenching is the best form of soil preparation. Reserve soil from the first trench to fill the last, and move the soil in the direction of the arrows.

JANUARY Above: Apple fruit spur. Do not prune. Below: Growth shoot. Prune as shown.

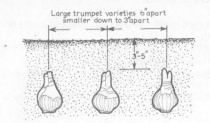

FEBRUARY Plant daffodils in ordinary soil as shown here.

JANUARY Blackcurrant bushes showing before and after pruning. Oldest wood is removed.

This soil corer is used to remove cores of turf before planting bulbs in grass.

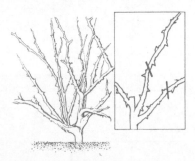

JANUARY Gooseberry: Cut back badly placed main shoots and shorten side shoots.

JANUARY Keep a shine on the glossy leaves of house plants by treating them with the special leaf-shining liquid you can get from the gardening shop. Or use milk—or beer.

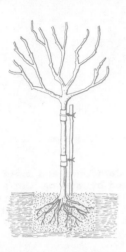

FEBRUARY See that standard roses and other tall subjects are securely supported against gales. Suitable ties are shown below:

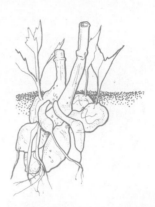

APRIL Dahlia tubers stored over the winter and watered now will throw shoots to take as cuttings. Alternatively, tubers can be divided and grown on for planting out in late May.

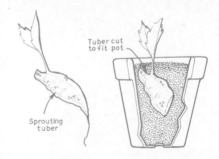

Tuber cut to fit pot

Sprouting tuber

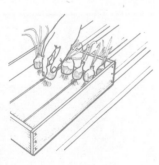

APRIL When spring bulbs finish flowering let the tops die naturally before lifting and storing them.

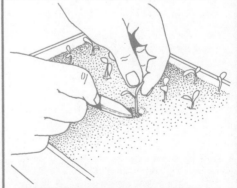

MAY Seedlings need to be spaced out as quickly as possible. Hold gently by the seed leaf and use a dibber to make the hole.

JUNE Geraniums provide suitable shoots for cuttings in this and other months. Let the base of the cutting dry for a few hours before planting.

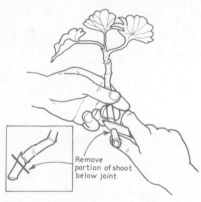

Remove portion of shoot below joint

Cut square below end of leaf joint and plant around edge of a pot of moist compost.

Tongue of cut through joint

JUNE Carnations and pinks can be increased by layering. Cut a tongue (above) **and bury this portion of stem** (below). **Sever from plant when rooted.**

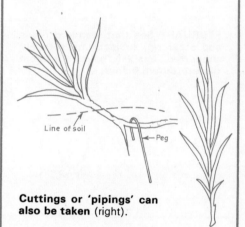

Line of soil

Peg

Cuttings or 'pipings' can also be taken (right).

SEPTEMBER Evergreen shrubs and trees should have their ball of fibrous roots protected until they are settled in the planting hole. Note: soil level will just cover roots.

OCTOBER Lift and label dahlia tubers and allow to drain as shown above. Below: Detach old corms and cormlets from lifted gladioli.

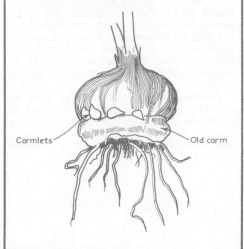

Cormlets   Old corm

NOVEMBER Turn waste material and leaves into compost by making a heap with chemical activator between the layers.

A SELECTION OF ROSES

Hybrid Teas

PINK
Ballet
Eden Rose
Gail Borden (cream reverse)
Percy Thrower
Perfecta
Pink Favourite
Prima Ballerina
Wendy Cussons

CRIMSON
Chrysler Imperial
Ena Harkness
Ernest H. Morse
Milord

RED
Fragrant Cloud

SCARLET
Olé

SALMON-PINK
Mischief

APRICOT-PINK
Shot Silk

VERMILION
Super Star

YELLOW
Dorothy Peach
Grandpa Dickson
King's Ransom
Peace
Spek's Yellow
Sutter's Gold

WHITE
Virgo
Memoriam

ORANGE
Beauté
Bettina
Diorama
Mojave

BICOLOR
Tzigane (red and yellow)
Piccadilly (red and yellow)

99

Floribundas

PINK
Dearest
Paddy McGredy
Pink Parfait
Queen Elizabeth

SCARLET
Arabian Nights
Evelyn Fison
Korona
Sarabande

CRIMSON
Europeana
Red Favourite

SALMON
Elizabeth of Glamis
Jiminy Cricket
Spartan

ORANGE
Alison Wheatcroft
Manx Queen
Orangeade
Woburn Abbey
Zambra

YELLOW
Allgold
Golden Slippers

WHITE
Iceberg
Ivory Fashion

LIGHT MAUVE
Lilac Charm

BICOLOR
Circus (yellow and red)
Masquerade (yellow and red)
Sea Pearl (pink and cream)

Ramblers

Albertine (salmon)
Alberic Barbier (cream)
American Pillar (pink)
Banksian Yellow
Dr W. van Fleet (pale pink)
Crimson Shower
Sander's White

Climbers

Aloha (pink)
Casino (yellow)
Climbing Ena Harkness (crimson)
Climbing Peace (yellow and pink)
Golden Showers (yellow)
Mermaid (primrose)
Zéphirine Drouhin (deep pink)

GROWING ROSES

Planting

Roses are tolerant plants, but they generously repay careful attention from the start. Bushes are supplied from nurseries from the time of leaf fall until late winter, and can also be purchased in leaf as container-grown plants from a garden centre.

Planting should take place as soon as the bushes are received if the soil is workable. If it is very wet or frozen, the roots must be protected with moist soil, peat or sacking until planting is possible.

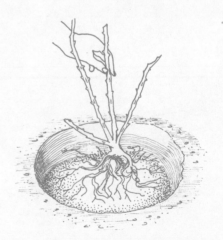

Make the planting hole wide enough for the roots to spread fully. Add best top soil first and firm it around roots.

Roses: a popular selection

1. Gold Crown
2. Bettina
3. Christian Dior
4. Beauté
5. Super Star
6. Silver Lining
7. Sutter's Gold
8. Prima Ballerina
9. Josephine Bruce
10. Piccadilly
11. Mischief
12. Belle Blonde

It is important to fork the soil as deeply as possible prior to planting, adding peat to both very light and very heavy soils to improve the structure. Then the ground needs firming by gentle treading.

A common fault is to plant roses too closely. At less than three feet apart there is a likelihood of overcrowding in a few years.

Dig a hole for the bush a little wider than the span of the roots. Any roots which are broken or damaged should be cut away. When the hole has been cleared, return some fine top soil to the bottom, plus a handful of peat. Mound this slightly, and place the plant with the roots spread naturally.

If you look at the rose stem, you will see a mark where the soil level occurred in the nursery. The plant needs to be buried to this mark or a shade deeper.

Begin to return the best top soil over the roots, and when the hole is half full, tread it down with the toe of the foot. Fill the hole and tread firmly. Test firmness by pulling stem. It should not move.

Examples of good and bad pruning

A good pruning cut is clear of the bud and sloping in the same plane. The bad examples show the cut too high and the slope too steep.

Left: Suitable pruning for a floribunda bush rose. Right: Moderately hard pruning on a hybrid tea bush.

Pruning

March is considered to be the best time to prune bush roses (hybrid teas and floribundas). The act of pruning promotes new growth and improves flower size and quality. Even newly-planted bushes should be pruned. Remove the tops to within about three inches of soil level.

During the next two years or so allow a framework of three or four branches at the base of the plant to develop.

Subsequent pruning consists of removing dead, very thin and crossing shoots, and in keeping the centre of the bush clear of growth. The shape to aim for is that of an open vase. Aim also for even distribution of branches, cutting out competing ones down to the very base of the plant.

Next the remaining branches and shoots need shortening. Prune weak growth hard, and strong growth lightly.

Always use sharp secateurs for pruning, so that the cut is clean and not bruised. Make a gently sloping cut, and whenever possible select a point above a bud which faces outwards. In summer when flowers fade, it pays to cut off the head together with three to six inches of stem. This is a form of pruning, and encourages new flower-bearing shoots from below.

LAWN CARE

Mowing

Mowing the lawn often becomes an unpleasant task because it is not done often enough. Regular light mowing can be done quickly and with little effort; it becomes difficult when the grass is long. Ideally, trim it once a week from spring until late autumn.

At the same time, do not keep the grass too short. This encourages browning in dry weather, and mower-skid when it is wet.

The secret of easy, even mowing is to have an efficient machine. For small lawns, a hand model with roller rather than wheels is adequate. But you can save all effort by using an electric machine. There are two— battery-operated (no cable) and mains-operated.

For the larger lawn, a petrol-engine

mower is a good investment. Always keep your mower clean. Regular servicing pays, and dealers prefer to receive machines for attention in the autumn and winter, rather than at the last minute in spring.

If the grass is maintained at a sensible length—half to one inch tall—it is easy to obtain that professional striped appearance by mowing straight up and down in strips. It is the way the grass lies and reflects light that gives the alternate dark and light effect.

Always attach the grass box, and use the clippings on a compost heap, or as a mulch around shrubs. The only exception is in very dry weather, when you can let the clippings fly.

When you start mowing in the spring, cut rather higher than normal by adjusting the machine. In summer be sure to water the lawn **before** signs of drought appear. In autumn, remove leaves. In winter, it is best not to walk on the lawn.

Spiking

A lawn needs annual spiking in order to break the surface crust and allow air and moisture to percolate, thus improving root growth. Autumn is the best time to do this.

In early spring it will pay thoroughly to scratch the turf with a wire rake. This removes dead grass and moss.

Early summer is when lawn weedkillers are most effective. Applied as instructed

Essential lawn operations include wire raking in spring and forking to aerate in autumn.

on the bottle, these herbicides will get rid of daisies, plantain, dock and other common weeds. Special weedkillers will control clover and other difficult kinds. At the same time, do not neglect the simple remedy of digging up larger weeds.

Should weed control result in bare patches, scratch the surface, apply some good top soil and scatter lawn grass seed.

Repairing

To remove a bump in the lawn, cut the outline of an H-shape across the bump with a spade or half-moon edging tool. Peel back the turf from the centre and remove some soil until the turf, when replaced, lies flat.

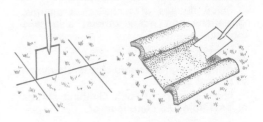

Cut an H-shape across the middle of the bump or hollow. Ease back the turves, add or remove soil until level and replace turves.

Repair crumbled edges by cutting out an oblong turf and reversing it. Sow a little seed to fill the gap where the broken edge lies. Lawn edges should be trimmed cleanly in spring, using a taut line and cutting against the edge of a board.

Remember that grass needs food like any other plant. Fertiliser-makers supply spring and autumn 'tonics'. Use them during showery weather. Scattering peat on the surface is beneficial, as it works downwards.

You can make a new lawn from seed or turf. Seed is very much cheaper, but turf is quicker and less trouble. Use best quality seed and apply at $1\frac{1}{2}$ to 2 oz. per sq. yd. in spring or autumn. The site must be free of weeds and hard lumps, then trodden and raked fine.

If turfing, treat site as for seeding. Buy turves from a specialist firm and lay bonded like wall bricks.

FILLING THE GREENHOUSE

If unheated

SPRING
Make early sowings of hardy flowers and vegetables. Sow tender kinds from mid-March.

Obtain early flowers from bulbs in pots; also from alpine plants in pots.

Give winter-flowering pot plants a rest (e.g. azalea, poinsettia, cyclamen).

SUMMER
Continue with bedding plant sowings; keep back some to flower in pots.

Enjoy flowers of fuchsias, geraniums, carnations and many others; also take cuttings.

AUTUMN
Bring in large-flowered chrysanthemums to protect blooms.

Enjoy flowers of such climbing shrubs as passiflora and clerodendron.

WINTER
Enjoy the orange fruits of winter cherry (solanum) and white flowers of Christmas rose in pots; also azaleas. A camellia in a tub may be brought in to flower.

If heated to keep out frost

The range of all seasons is extended. Sowings can start earlier. Permanent plants such as abutilon, cobaea, plumbago, eucalyptus may be included. During winter protect dahlia and begonia tubers, also gladioli, there.

If heated to about 55 degrees F

Activity proceeds the year-round. Plants to try include clivia, hoya, anthurium, strelitzia, species begonias, saintpaulia, scented jasmine, hibiscus, coleus—and several orchids.

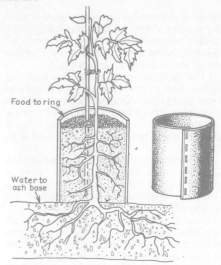

Food to ring

Water to ash base

RING CULTURE enables tomatoes to be grown in the greenhouse without using the border soil, which is often diseased. Cover the ground with a 6 in. layer of gravel or coarse ashes. Set the plant in a bottomless ring of John Innes No 2 compost. Once established, apply only liquid fertiliser to the ring; pure water to the base material.

SIMPLE SOIL TESTING

It is important for a gardener to know the nature of his soil in terms of **acidity** and **alkalinity**. These are chemical terms for which the popular equivalents are 'sour' and 'sweet'.

In an acid soil, the element calcium is in short supply; in an alkaline soil it is plentiful.

Most plants prefer a soil which is slightly acid, which is the condition most commonly found in Britain.

However, in chalky districts and in some clay areas, soil analysis shows an alkaline reaction. In alkaline conditions it is difficult to grow a whole range of shrubs and certain vegetables. Shrubs of the **rhodo-dendron** group and certain **ericas** are notably lime-hating.

At the other extreme—high acidity— there are more serious difficulties, as the nutrient balance of the soil is upset.

Garden weeds

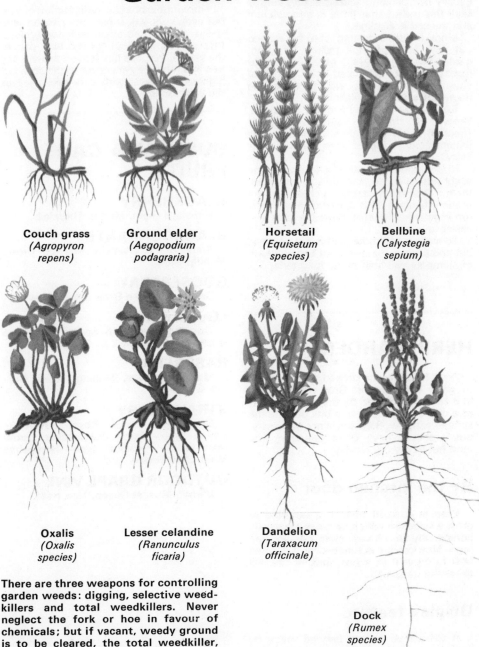

Couch grass
(Agropyron repens)

Ground elder
(Aegopodium podagraria)

Horsetail
(Equisetum species)

Bellbine
(Calystegia sepium)

Oxalis
(Oxalis species)

Lesser celandine
(Ranunculus ficaria)

Dandelion
(Taraxacum officinale)

Dock
(Rumex species)

There are three weapons for controlling garden weeds: digging, selective weed-killers and total weedkillers. Never neglect the fork or hoe in favour of chemicals; but if vacant, weedy ground is to be cleared, the total weedkiller, 'Weedol', will save time. Use selective weedkillers on lawns, where the most persistent weeds are likely to be celandine and dandelion.

Illustrations by courtesy of Plant Protection Ltd.

105

A traditional simple soil test is to shake up a small sample with dilute acid, usually hydrochloric acid. If fizzing can be seen this means that there is free calcium and the soil is alkaline.

More accurate testing can be carried out with a simple soil testing kit (from garden shops) which gives a colour reaction to be compared with a colour chart provided. This will indicate the degree of acidity or alkalinity.

Experts use a scale for these variations, known as the pH values. Mid-point (neutral) is pH 7. Figures lower than this denote acidity; higher ones denote alkalinity.

It is a good general rule to apply lime every other year to acid soils to 'sweeten' them. This really means correcting the nutrient balance, and is particularly useful for vegetables. It also makes a clay soil easier to work.

To make a soil more acid is not so easy, but additions of manure, peat and sulphate of ammonia will help in the long term.

HERB GARDEN

Fresh herbs for the kitchen are a pleasure to grow and prepare. Grow them either in a small, sunny bed by the kitchen door, as a display feature or in a box outside the kitchen window. Rich soil is not necessary, but it should have good drainage, and tend not to dry out rapidly.

By the kitchen door

Even in a small bed, it is possible to grow a selection which includes marjoram, borage, thyme, chives, mint, parsley and sage. Mint produces runners, so it is often best to grow it in a box sunk in the soil to restrict its spread.

Display feature

A decorative feature can be made by forming a pattern of groups of herbs with gravel or paving between them. An old cartwheel makes a pretty herb garden. Plant different kinds between the spokes.

Window box

The window box has the limitation of size, but even so it will supply the kitchen with sprigs of the more essential kinds (chives, thyme, mint, parsley) for the best part of the year. If you like bay leaves, grow a bay tree in a tub. They are rather expensive, but highly decorative, with dark green leaves the year round.

BUSH AND CANE FRUITS

BLACKBERRY
Himalaya Giant, Merton Thornless.

BLACKCURRANTS
Amos Black, Baldwin, Malvern Cross, Mendip Cross.

GOOSEBERRY
Careless, Golden Drop, Lancer, Leveller.

LOGANBERRY
True loganberry has spines, Thornless loganberry has none.

RASPBERRY
Malling Promise, Malling Jewel, Norfolk Giant.

STRAWBERRY
Cambridge Vigour, Royal Sovereign. Alpine type—Baron Solemacher (grow from seed). Perpetual type—Hampshire Maid, Sans Rivale.

OUTDOOR GRAPE VINE
Brandt, Muscat Queen, Noir Hatif.

PLANNING A GARDEN

If you are creating a garden from scratch, re-planning a neglected one, or improving an existing one, it is wise to make a scale plan on paper. Some of the suggestions given below may be helpful.

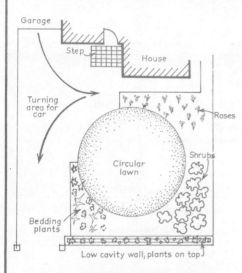

Above: FRONT GARDEN layout should allow for the free movement of a car to and from the garage. Circular lawn and informal groups of plants avoid fussy appearance.

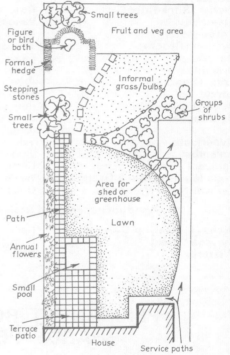

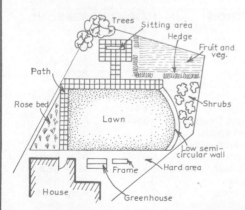

Above: NARROW SITE: Often a problem. Solution is to break the distance by creating two distinct areas of roughly square proportions. Use curves to counter the rigid outline.

Left: AWKWARD ANGLES: Plan the site to follow the lines of the house rather than the boundary fence. Mask the awkward corners with trees and shrubs. This example enables the greenhouse to be brought conveniently near the house.

A SELECTION OF SHOWY SHRUBS

NAME	COLOUR	HEIGHT (feet)
Berberis darwinii	Orange	4
Buddleia	Purple shades	8
Ceanothus 'Gloire de Versailles'	Blue	6
Chaenomeles (Flowering Quince)	Red	5
Cistus (Rock Rose)	Rose, purple	5
Clematis	Various	climbing
Cotoneaster	Red berries	2 to 10 according to type
Cytisus (Broom)	Various	4
Deutzia	Pink	6
Diervilla	Red	5
Erica (Heather)	Purple, red, white	from 6 in.
Forsythia	Yellow	8
Hebe (Veronica)	Purple, Red	1
Hydrangea	Blue or pink according to soil	5
Hypericum	Yellow	3
Lavender	Violet	3
Lonicera (Honeysuckle)	Cream	climbing
Philadelphus (Mock Orange)	White	5
Pyracantha (Firethorn)	Orange or red berries	8 (on a wall)

Rhododendrons and azaleas—only if you have acid soil

NAME	COLOUR	HEIGHT (feet)
Ribes (Flowering Currant)	Red	5
Syringa (Lilac)	Purple, pink, cream	8
Wisteria	Blue	climbing

PERMANENT BORDER PLANTS (HARDY PERENNIALS)

NAME	DESCRIPTION	HEIGHT (feet)	SEASON
Achillea filipendulina	Yellow 'plates'	from 3	June–Sept
Campanula lactiflora	Light blue bells	4	June–July
Dicentra (Bleeding Heart)	Pink	1	April–July
Delphinium	Blue, purple, white	5–6	June
Doronicum (Leopards Bane)	Yellow 'daisies'	3	April–June
Hemerocallis (Day Lily)	Many colours	2	June
Helianthus (Sunflower)	Large yellow heads	from 4	Aug–Oct
Lupin	Multi-hued spikes	3	June
Lysimachia	Yellow spikes; easy	2½	June–July
Michaelmas Daisies	Many shades, a 'must'	from 2	Aug–Nov
Paeonies	Beautiful bowl flowers	2½	May–June
Phlox	Many shades	3	July–Sept
Rudbeckia (Cone Flower)	Various shades	2½	Aug–Sept
Sedum spectabile	Lasting pink heads	1½	Aug–Sept
Solidago (Golden Rod)	Yellow-gold plumes	from 2	July–Aug
Thalictrum	Rose-mauve; dainty	2½	June–July

Herbaceous plants

1. Achillea Coronation Gold
2. Agastache Cana
3. Solidago Golden Gates
4. Thalictrum Dipt. Hewitt's Double
5. Helenium Moerheim Beauty
6. Erigeron Dignity
7. Erigeron Sincerity
8. Solidago Lemore

HARDY ANNUAL FLOWERS TO SOW

NAME	COLOUR	COMMENTS
Alyssum	Pink, purple, white	Ideal for edging
Calendula (Marigold)	Yellow and orange	Will seed itself
Candytuft	Pink, mauve, white	Will seed itself
Clarkia	Pink, mauve, white	Support with twigs
Dimorphotheca	Orange, salmon, white with dark eye	Good for dry ground
Echium	Deep blue; also mixed	Long flowering
Eschscholtzia	Poppy flowers, mixed	Good for poor soil
Godetia	Mainly pink shades	Lovely in mass
Matthiola bicornis (Night Scented Stock)	Mauve	Sweetly scented
Mignonette	Red shades	Sweetly scented
Nasturtium	Yellow, orange, red	Quick ground cover
Nigella (Love-in-a-Mist)	Mainly blue	Feathery foliage
Virginian Stock	Red, lilac, white	Easy, free flowering

● *Best effect is always obtained by fairly close grouping of annuals. Sowings can be made from March onwards.*

SPRING BULBS
Selection and planting guide

NAME	COLOUR	DEPTH TO PLANT (inches)	FLOWERING TIME	HEIGHT (inches)
Crocus	Purple, yellow, white	3	Feb–April	4–6
Crown Imperial	Yellow, red, orange	5	April–May	36
Cyclamen (hardy)	Rose, crimson	3	Feb–April	4
Daffodils	Yellow, white, pink	3–5	March–May	12–18
Dog's Tooth Violet	Rose	2–3	March–April	6
Glory of the Snow	White, pink, blue	2	March	6
Grape Hyacinth	White, blue	3	March–April	6
Hyacinth	White, pink, rose, blue	3–4	April–May	12
Iris (dwarf)	Blue, yellow	2–3	Feb–April	3–6
Narcissus (species)	Yellow, white	2–3	Feb–April	3–18
Anemone	Various	2	March–May	6–12
Siberian Squill	White, blue	2–3	March–April	3–6
Snake's Head Fritillary	White, yellow, purple	3–4	April–May	9–12
Snowdrop	White	3	Feb–March	6–12
Snowflake	White and green	3	March–May	8–10
Star of Bethlehem	White	3–5	April–May	12
Tulip	Various	4–6	March–May	12–24
Tulip (species)	Various	3–5	March–May	3–18
Winter Aconite	Yellow	3	Feb–March	4–6

Notes
● Planting depth is measured from TOP of bulb.
● Space bulbs at not less than twice the depth.
● Plant spring bulbs during September or October.

A DOZEN POPULAR HOUSE PLANTS

POPULAR NAME	BOTANICAL NAME	GUIDE
Wandering Sailor	Tradescantia	Easy
Grape Ivy	Rhoicissus	Easy
Kangaroo Vine	Cissus	Easy
Ivies	Hederas	Easy
Rubber Plant	Ficus elastica	Easy
Spider Plant	Chlorophytum	Easy
Begonia	Begonia	Special care
Saffron Spike	Aphelandra	Special care
Mexican Breadfruit	Monstera	Easy
Mother-in-Law's Tongue	Sansevieria	Easy
African Violet	Saintpaulia	Special care
Sweetheart Plant	Philodendron	Easy

Key

EASY—long lasting given good light, water when drying out and moderate temperatures.
SPECIAL CARE—only short lasting unless given steady warmth and humidity. Best in greenhouse or conservatory.

DON'TS for house plants

DON'T let water stand in the saucer.
DON'T keep them in same room as oil stoves.
DON'T keep them in draughts or in direct fire heat.

VARIETIES OF FRUIT

FRUIT	TYPE	WHEN RIPE
APPLE		
Bramley's Seedling	Cooking	Sept–April
Charles Ross	Dessert	Oct–Nov
Cox's Orange Pippin	Dessert	Nov–Jan
Ellison's Orange	Dessert	Sept–Oct
George Cave	Dessert	Mid July–early Aug
James Grieve	Dessert	Sept–Oct
Worcester Pearmain	Dessert	Sept–Oct
PEARS		
Beurré Hardy	Dessert	Pick Sept, use Oct
Conference	Dessert or cooking	Pick late Sept, use Oct–Nov
Doyenné du Comice	Dessert	Pick Oct, use Nov–Dec
Dr Jules Guyot	Dessert	Pick Aug, use Sept
Pitmaston Duchess	Dessert or cooking	Pick Sept, use Oct–Nov
PLUMS and GAGES		
Early Laxton	Dessert	Late July *
Giant Prune	Cooking	Mid Sept
Victoria	Dessert	End Aug *
Merryweather Damson	Cooking	End Sept

* (Best grown together to pollinate each other)
COOKING CHERRY
Morello — Aug–Sept (suitable for wall training)

(Sweet cherries present too much difficulty for garden growing)
PEACH
Peregrine or Rochester (suitable as a bush)

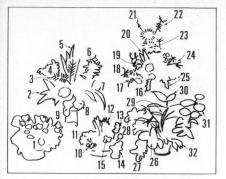

Plants about the house

House plants can be even more decorative if they are arranged in such groupings as these. Here cut flowers, ferns and sprays have been included to add to the effectiveness of the displays.

A VEGETABLE PLAN FOR THE YEAR

NAME	SEED FOR TWO ROWS 20 FT. LONG	SOW	HARVEST
Beans			
Broad	½ pint	February–March	June–July
Runner	½ pint	May	July–September
Dwarf	¼ pint	May–July	July–September
Cabbage	1 pkt.	March–August	All year
Cauliflower			
Summer	1 pkt.	March–April	June–July
Autumn	1 pkt.	April	September–November
Brussels sprouts	1 pkt.	March	Winter
Carrots			
Early	½ oz.	March–July	from June
Maincrop	¼ oz.	April–May	Winter
Parsnips	½ oz.	March	Winter
Turnips	¼ oz.	April–July	June–September
Onions	¼ oz.	March	September
Leeks	⅛ oz.	March	Winter
Potatoes			
Early	5–6 lb.	April	from June
Maincrop	5–6 lb.	April–May	Winter
Peas			
Early	1 pint	March	June
Maincrop	1 pint	April–May	June–August
Beetroot	1 oz.	April–June	June–October
Radish	½ oz.	March–August	from April
Spring onions	½ oz.	March–August	June–October
Marrows	1 pkt.	June	August–September
Tomatoes			
Outdoor	1 pkt.	May	August–September

PEST AND DISEASE CHART

SYMPTOM	CAUSE	CONTROL
Green insects around tips of plants	Greenfly (aphids)	Many insecticide sprays or dusts (see label)
Swollen, flaky areas on apple branches	Apple canker	Cut clean and paint with tar-oil in winter
Holes in apples	Insect grub	Spray with lindane immediately after blossom
Sooty blotches on apples	Apple scab	Spray with captan fungicide before blossom burst
Black spots on rose leaves	Rose black spot	Apply rose fungicide throughout spring
White powder on rose leaves	Rose mildew	Apply karathane fungicide regularly
Grey mould on strawberries	Botrytis	Apply orthocide at flowering and repeat
Nest of caterpillars, particularly in vegetables	Caterpillars	Remove by hand in preference to using DDT
Seedlings topple and rot	Damping-off disease	Use special potting compost which is part-sterilised
White tunnels in leaves (Chrysanthemums)	Leaf miners	Spray with malathion and repeat
Slow moving grubs at root level	Cutworms or leatherjackets	Apply DDT dust to soil
Grubs in raspberry or loganberry	Raspberry beetle	Apply liquid derris after blossom; repeat
Pale stippled leaves on greenhouse plants	Red spider mite (just visible on undersides)	Use greenhouse insecticide or smoke; keep atmosphere moist
Leaves or young plants eaten	Suspect slugs and snails	Lay slug bait nearby
Moss on lawn		Use moss killer or lawn sand as directed; improve drainage by spiking

● *See colour pages overleaf*

Garden pests and diseases

Today there is no excuse for serious failures in the garden due to pest or disease. There are many safe and efficient chemical products for preventing and stamping out troubles. The gardener's emphasis should always be on prevention or quick remedy. This will reduce the amount of pesticide needed and enable plants to give their best.

LEAF MINERS
On chrysanthemums, cinerarias and celery: Use malathion or lindane.

BLACKFLY
Prevent on broad beans by pinching out tops; otherwise as for greenfly.

GREENFLY (APHID)
On roses, chrysanthemums and most flowers. Use a systemic insecticide as directed on label.

RASPBERRY BEETLES
On flowers and fruit use derris.

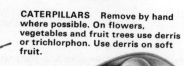

CATERPILLARS Remove by hand where possible. On flowers, vegetables and fruit trees use derris or trichlorphon. Use derris on soft fruit.

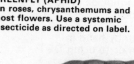

CAPSIDS
On flowers and fruit trees use BHC in spring.

PEA MOTHS
Spray with systemic insecticide as directed.

FLEA BEETLES
Attack brassica, swede and turnip seedlings. Use seed dressing when sowing; derris or BHC later.

LEAF HOPPERS On flowers and fruit use derris or systemic insecticide as directed.

PEA and BEAN WEEVILS Use derris.

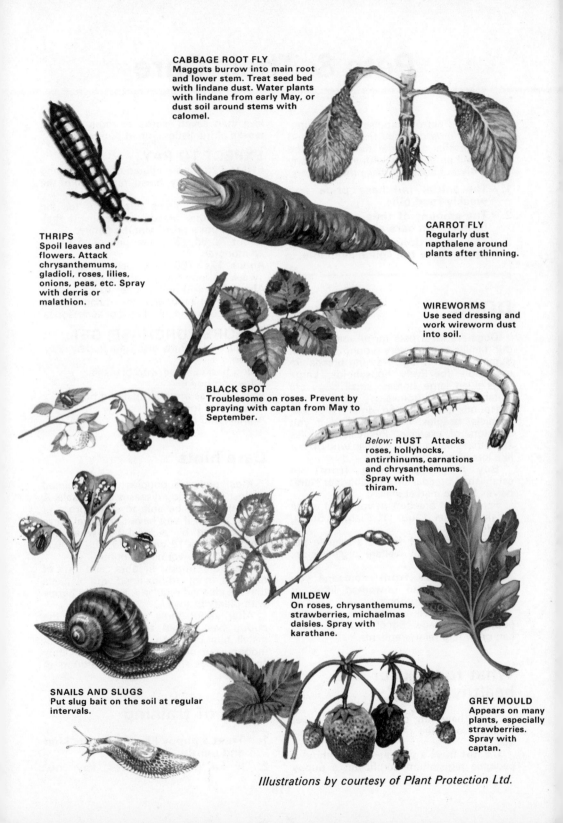

CABBAGE ROOT FLY
Maggots burrow into main root and lower stem. Treat seed bed with lindane dust. Water plants with lindane from early May, or dust soil around stems with calomel.

THRIPS
Spoil leaves and flowers. Attack chrysanthemums, gladioli, roses, lilies, onions, peas, etc. Spray with derris or malathion.

CARROT FLY
Regularly dust napthalene around plants after thinning.

WIREWORMS
Use seed dressing and work wireworm dust into soil.

BLACK SPOT
Troublesome on roses. Prevent by spraying with captan from May to September.

Below: **RUST** Attacks roses, hollyhocks, antirrhinums, carnations and chrysanthemums. Spray with thiram.

MILDEW
On roses, chrysanthemums, strawberries, michaelmas daisies. Spray with karathane.

SNAILS AND SLUGS
Put slug bait on the soil at regular intervals.

GREY MOULD
Appears on many plants, especially strawberries. Spray with captan.

Illustrations by courtesy of Plant Protection Ltd.

Pets & Their Care

Never get a pet on impulse or in a hurry. Take your time over the final choice, and remember that the new member of the family will probably be with you for many years. Always consider these three factors:

1. **The initial purchase price and weekly food bills.**
2. **The amount of time which must be spent on care and exercise.**
3. **The conditions in your home, particularly the space available.**

DOGS

Dogs are ideal pets for all members of the family except very young children. Some exotic and highly-strung breeds are unsuitable for lively households. Large dogs need large homes, small dogs are suitable for small homes.

Hounds and sporting dogs (Afghans, spaniels, beagles, etc.) are good if you like lots of exercise. Pekinese, poodles and other small dogs suit those who do not like lots of running around.

Buy a pedigree dog from: an established breeder or a reliable pet store; **never** from a market stall.

For a list of breeders in your area, write to the Kennel Club, 1 Clarges Street, London W.1.

Buy a mongrel from: a reliable pet store or an animal welfare organisation, such as the R.S.P.C.A.

Get one free from: someone you know who has an unwanted litter, or from a veterinary surgeon.

It helps to have a good idea about the puppy's parentage. Small bundles of fur can grow into mini-elephants.

What to look for in a healthy puppy

If you have any doubts, contact a vet to check over the puppy, or else do not buy it.

Do not buy: a pedigree dog without a pedigree registration certificate; a puppy less than seven weeks or more than 12 weeks old; a listless, timid puppy.

EXPECT TO PAY:

£10 to £25 for a pedigree dog, depending on family history, breed, reputation of the breeder.

Three to four times this figure for the larger, exotic breeds, especially if they come from a prize-winning family.

About 7s. 6d. (37½ new pence) to £1 for a mongrel.

About 12s. (60 new pence) to £2 a week on food for a pedigree dog.

About 12s. (60 new pence) to £1 a week on food for a mongrel, depending on size.

At least £5 on the initial cost of accessories.

BEFORE PURCHASE, GET:

A collar and identity disc (required by law).
A lead.
A dog basket, lined with blankets.
A feeding bowl.
Toys, such as a rubber ball and bones.
A supply of food.
A brush and comb.

Care hints

Most pedigree puppies are inoculated against serious dog diseases before sale. A breeder should be able to show proof of this. If not, or if you have a mongrel, have it inoculated by a local vet when the puppy is 10 to 12 weeks old. The vet will also advise on worming a puppy.

Keep the puppy indoors, and out of draughts, in an old box lined with blankets that are cleaned regularly. Keep him happy with plenty of toys.

After about three months, when the puppy has passed the chewing stage, install him in a dog basket, and keep it indoors, out of the way of people. Only sporting dogs should be kept outdoors in kennels.

Rules of training

1. **Treat a puppy like a baby, be kind and gentle.**
2. **If he makes a mess, say 'no'**

in a stern voice.

3. Take him outside, so that he associates the two. In about a week, he will go of his own accord.

4. Always let a puppy exercise outside immediately after meals, as this is when he is likely to make a mess.

5. People who live in flats can use a tray lined with litter or earth.

Simple obedience training can be started at about six months. Teach him to sit by repeating the command, and at the

same time gently placing one hand under his muzzle and the other pushed down firmly on his flanks. Use tit-bits as a reward, and encouraging words.

Other rules of obedience can be found in special books, or by taking him to a local obedience training class. Write to the Kennel Club for details.

you can decide if he is getting too much or to little to eat. But never hesitate to contact a breeder or veterinary surgeon for further advice.

Follow this table as a general rule. To find out the weight of a dog, weigh yourself and the dog on some scales, then weigh yourself alone. Subtract to get the dog's weight.

Age	No. of meals	Type of food
Up to six months	Four a day	Meat or tinned dog food, mixed with puppy meal. Milky foods like milk mixed with puppy meal, baby cereal foods or even corn flakes. Add lightly-cooked eggs occasionally. Feed two meat and two milky meals.
Six to nine months	Two a day	As above, but milky foods no longer needed
Nine months and over	One a day	Meat or tinned dog food, mixed with meal or biscuits. Feed in the evening, or split the daily ration in two. Keep to a strict habit so that he can expect his food at regular intervals

Feeding guide

Fresh clean water should be available at all times. Dogs like bones to gnaw, but never feed those that can splinter, like rabbit, chicken or fish bones.

Remember that very active dogs, like greyhounds and gun dogs, will need more food to make up for energy they use. By keeping an eye on his general condition

General hints

1. Always keep a dog on a lead in the street.
2. Brush him daily, particularly if he has a long coat. If his coat gets dirty, an occasional bath does no harm.
3. If a bitch has puppies, it should be

Yorkshire Terrier: *Very much the lady's dog. Easy to care for but needs some grooming and exercise.*

Poodle: *Both Toy and Ordinary Poodles are affectionate and intelligent. Easy to train and quick to learn.*

Pembroke Corgi: *Slightly aggressive nature; make good guard dogs. Easy to care for.*

Cocker Spaniel: *Placid and affectionate. Needs plenty of exercise and a fair amount of grooming to keep coat immaculate.*

A gallery of top dogs

Collies and Shetland Sheepdogs: *Collies are one-man dogs, need plenty of grooming. Shetlands, smaller, are better town dogs.*

Labrador: *A placid-natured dog. Easy to groom but needs as much exercise as you can give it.*

Alsatian: *Another one-man dog. Will settle in most unconfined environments. Needs little grooming but a great deal of exercise.*

Boxer: *A good family dog—small enough to be kept in town and easy to look after.*

These are the country's most popular breeds of pedigree dogs as recognised by the Kennel Club. In recent years there has been a swing to larger dogs. Buy your dog from a reputable breeder and make sure you see the certificate of pedigree registration. Buy a breed to suit your needs and environment. The general rule is small dogs for small homes, large dogs for large ones. Regular exercise is essential—so do not choose a sporting dog if you like a lazy life.

Weighing a dog. First, weigh yourself. Then weigh yourself and the dog together and subtract your own weight.

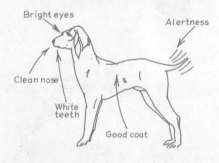

Bright eyes

Alertness

Clean nose

White teeth

Good coat

Above: What to look for in a healthy dog. Below: Food/weight ratio for a rule-of-thumb feeding guide.

HOW MUCH TO FEED YOUR DOG

16 ozs.

30 lbs

½ oz. to 1 oz. food to each 1 lb. of dogs weight

easy to find homes for them. If you do not succeed ask the help of a local animal welfare clinic. Never try to destroy puppies yourself.

4. Dogs need a regular, balanced diet. Meat alone is not enough, and too many table scraps can cause obesity.

5. Do not try to diagnose dog ailments. See a vet at once if your dog is unwell. If you are worried about your dog straying or having puppies, the vet can perform a simple operation for a moderate sum.

6. When the dog is six months old, by law it must be licensed. Get a form from any post office.

CATS

Cats are ideal pets for all members of the family. Some pedigree breeds, such as Siamese, need constant companionship. Long-hairs need companionship, plus daily care. Cats are best neutered or spayed if not used for breeding or kept in a flat.

Buy a pedigree cat from: a cat breeder, the pet section of a large store, a cat show.

For names and addresses of cat breeders in your area, contact the Cat Information Centre, 69 New Oxford Street, London W.C.1.

Buy an ordinary one from: a reliable pet store or an animal welfare clinic, such as the R.S.P.C.A.

Get one free from: someone you know who has an unwanted litter, or from a vet.

Kittens should not be less than seven weeks old when they leave their mothers. Avoid kittens which do not have milk teeth showing, or an early growth of teeth—they are usually too young.

What to look for in a healthy kitten

Soon after getting a kitten, ask a vet to give it a health check. He will also advise on special injections to protect against many cat diseases, including cat flu.

If you do not want kittens later on, or a straying tom, the vet will also advise on spaying or neutering, which should be done no later than five months from birth.

Do not buy: a pedigree kitten without a Cat Fancy registration form, a kitten less than seven weeks old, a very timid or listless kitten.

EXPECT TO PAY:

£7 to £25 for a pedigree kitten, depending on family history, breed.

7s. 6d. (37½ new pence) to £1 for an ordinary kitten.

About 12s. (60 new pence) a week on food for both types.

BEFORE PURCHASE, GET:

A basket lined with blankets.

A feeding bowl.

A tray filled with cat litter or earth.

A few toys, home made ones, like empty cotton reels, balls of paper, will do.

A brush and comb, particularly if it is a long-haired cat.

A supply of food.

Care hints

Keep cats indoors in a warm, quiet place. Cats are very clean, and look after their own personal hygiene, but long-hairs need a daily brush and comb to prevent the coat matting.

The correct way to pick up a cat or kitten is by placing one hand under the chest, and using the other to support the hindquarters. Never pick it up by the scruff of the neck, or by its paws.

How to hold a kitten.

Rules of training

1. Place the tray filled with cat litter or earth near the basket.
2. When the kitten shows signs of making a mess, lift it quickly but gently into the tray.
3. Do this for at least a week, and the kitten will know where to go.
4. Clean the tray as often as possible, using a mild solution of disinfectant and hot water.
5. Fit a special cat door to the door leading to the garden if you live in a house. The cat will soon learn to use it.

Feeding guide

At first, the young kitten will need a mixture of cat food or good quality meat, chopped finely, and baby cereal mixed with plenty of milk. Milk and water should be available at all times. Give two meat meals, two milky meals a day.

At four to six months two of the meals can be cat food or meat, the other the milky type. At nine months, one meal a day, but there is no reason why the daily meal cannot be split in two.

FEEDING YOUR KITTEN			
2 – 4 MONTHS	4 – 6 MONTHS	6 – 9 MONTHS	9 MONTHS & OVER

Above: How many times a day to feed your kitten. Below: The signs of a healthy cat.

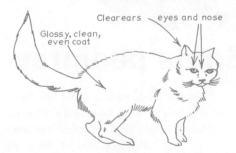

Clear ears   eyes and nose

Glossy, clean, even coat

Some pedigree cats

1. Black Long-hair. 2. English Tabby. 3. Smoke Long-hair. 4 & 5. Seal-point Siamese. 6. Russian Blue. 7. Some pedigree and non-pedigree kittens. 8. Abyssinian. 9. Burmese.

124

An average cat will need between three-quarters and one can of food a day, depending on size. Watch its weight. You will soon see if it is getting too much or too little food.

Fresh-cooked meat, fish, offal, liver, minced meat can all be fed once in a while, but the diet should be varied, if possible, daily.

Do not feed your cat fish all the time. If using a canned cat food, check whether it is a complete diet (fish or meat plus rice and cereals), or a meat or fish food which needs additions to it for a complete diet.

Milk is a **food,** not a drink. Water should be available at all times.

General hints

1. Do not feed bones to a cat. Chicken or rabbit should have all bones removed, and be chopped finely.

2. Cats are fond of exercising their claws. To save furniture, teach the cat to use a log for scratching, or buy a special scratching post from a pet store.

3. Consult a vet if your cat seems unwell —do not try to treat it yourself.

4. Use only a bristle brush on a cat, never the wire type.

BUDGERIGARS

Budgerigars are suitable pets for young and old people, especially those living in flats, single rooms, confined spaces or council property where larger pets are banned. They are unsuitable for people not prepared to give a budgie daily attention, and keep its cage clean.

Buy one from: a pet store or a budgie breeder or fancier.

Material for cat illustrations by courtesy of the Cat Information Centre. Material for the dog and budgerigar illustrations by courtesy of Animal News Service.

Bear in mind that it is easier to teach tricks to a young budgie than to an older bird. Young budgies have bands of dark colour across the feathers at the top of the head. These usually disappear when the bird is about 12 weeks old.

What to look for in a healthy budgie

Brightness, alertness, cleanliness and good feathers.
Clean and well-formed beak, claws and feet.
Clear and unmarked skin around beak, eyes and legs.
Do not buy: a budgie that sits at the bottom of a cage, has small growths on its claws or an overgrown beak or claws.

EXPECT TO PAY:
£1 or 30s. (£1·50) for a budgie.
More if bought from a breeder.
About 3s. (15 new pence) a week on all food items.
About £4 for accessories to start with.

BEFORE PURCHASE, GET:
A cage. Size and shape vary according to cost.
A seed bowl and water hopper.
Sanded sheets for the cage floor.
Plastic bag to catch loose seed.
A few toys, such as a bell and a ladder.
Some commercial grit.
A supply of food.

Care hints

Place the cage in a draught-free spot, and away from sudden changes in tem-

A budgie under 12 weeks old (left) has bands of dark feathers across its forehead. In an adult budgie (right) the bands have disappeared.

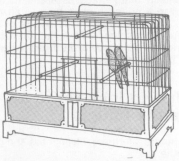

A budgie cage should be as big as possible and kept away from draughts and direct sunlight.

perature and direct sunlight. Clean out the cage once a week. Wash all items in the cage in a solution of hot water and mild disinfectant. Cover the cage at night. Budgies like companionship. Try to get two if possible.

Rules of training

1. Give the budgie a few weeks to settle down in the home.
2. Teach it to be finger tame by talking to it in a soft voice.
3. Teach it to talk after it is finger tame by repeating simple words like 'Joey', 'Hello', 'Pretty Budgie'.
4. If you particularly want to teach a budgie to talk, only keep one.

Feeding guide

Budgies need: a correct mixture of canary and millet seed. This can be bought loose at pet stores, or dust-free and containing added vitamins and minerals in a packet from a pet store or grocer.

A supply of grit in the cage to aid seed digestion, and to provide calcium.

Cuttlefish bone to keep the beak trim, and provide calcium.

Green food or fruit, like lettuce, cabbage leaves, or small pieces of apple.

Millet spray or rings as an occasional treat.

A constant supply of fresh water in the hopper.

Never feed budgies foods like bread, jam, cakes or biscuits.

General hints

1. Give a budgie a small piece of wood to gnaw, and make sure the perches in the cage are all the same diameter.
2. Let the budgie out of his cage once in a while, but guard against open windows, cats and open fires.
3. Blow the husks off the seed-pot each morning so that the budgie can reach its seed more easily.
4. Budgies are very healthy pets, and can live for about nine years. If they ever seem unwell, seek advice from a vet.

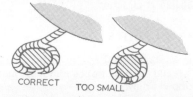

CORRECT   TOO SMALL

Above: There should be at least two perches in a cage, as far apart as possible and at least $\frac{1}{2}$ in. in diameter. Below: How to hold a budgie.

OTHER CAGE BIRDS

There are many different types of cage birds which make good pets. They include canaries, members of the finch family, linnets, siskins, redpolls, and parrots.

If you are considering getting one of these, seek advice from a pet store, as some of them need special diets and cages.

WILD BIRDS

It is not suggested that wild birds should be kept as pets, but many of them are regular garden visitors. During the cold, winter months, when food is scarce, they need help to survive. Wild birds found in the garden can be divided into two basic types:

1. **Hardbills, such as the house sparrow, chaffinch, greenfinch and bullfinch, which feed mainly on seeds.**
2. **Softbills, such as the robin, wren, blackbird and bluetit, which feed mainly on insects.**

When the ground is frosty, the softbills, especially the wren, suffer most. Their beaks cannot penetrate the earth, and without your help they cannot find enough food to stay alive. During a very cold spell, hundreds of thousands of birds die from hunger or exhaustion.

How to Help

Put the food on concrete paths, paving or special bird tables and feeders. Flat-dwellers can put food in window-boxes. Wild birds will soon overcome their initial shyness if food is put out regularly in the same place. Make sure there are no cats around.

Keen bird-spotters can learn more about wild birds by writing to The Royal Society for the Protection of Birds, The Lodge, Sandy, Bedfordshire.

What to Feed

Birds must eat one quarter of their own weight a day to live. Put out table scraps, nuts, grains, cheese or a handful of special wild bird food which can be bought at pet stores or supermarkets.

It is all right to leave white bread in the garden for birds during the winter, but not in spring and summer, when it will be fed to the young and is not very nutritious.

COLD WATER AND TROPICAL AQUARIA

Fish are particularly good pets for people living in confined spaces such as flats and rooms.

Buy them from: a reliable pet store, or a member of a local aquarist society.

The most popular cold water fish are goldfish. There are several types, including shubunkins, comets, fantails and veiltails.

There are about 200 species which can be kept in tropical aquaria. The more popular ones are the guppy, platy, swordtail, mosquito fish, zebra danio, white cloud mountain minnow, beacon or head-and-tail-light fish, dwarf gourami.

Healthy fish are: free from fungus growth, lively and clean-finned. And they swim normally.

Do not buy: tropical and cold water fish together unless you have separate aquaria and heating; fish that can outgrow their aquarium.

EXPECT TO PAY:

Up to £5 for a selection of suitable specimens.
£10 or more for aquarium equipment.
Between 2s. 6d. (12½ new pence) and 7s. 6d. (37½ new pence) a week on food.

BEFORE PURCHASE, GET:

An aquarium, preferably the rectangular type, with metal sides—the largest one possible. And a cover.
Three to four feet of tubing for siphoning water from the aquarium.
A mercury thermometer for checking water temperature.
A net to catch the fish.
For cold water fish, some of these plants: Canadian pondweed, hornwort, Lagaro-siphon major (sometimes called Elodea crispa), Vallisneria spiralis.
For tropical fish some of these plants: Egeria, Cryptocoryne, Vallisneria spiralis, Myriophyllum verticlatum.
Molluscs like the ramshorn snail—the same variety for both tropical and cold water aquaria, but obtained from either a tropical tank or a pond, as appropriate.
Compost or sand for the bottom of the tank and for the plants (about 1½ lb.).
Stones for the tank.
An electric immersion heater and thermo-stat for tropical aquaria (the whole circuit must be earthed, to guard against short circuits).

All these items can be bought at pet stores specialising in aquaria equipment.

Care hints

Place the aquarium near the light, but not in direct sunlight. If necessary, paint

Garden birds

Here are some of the most popular wild birds seen in the garden at most times of the year. Others that may be spotted include Great tit, Coal tit, Missel thrush, Robin, Hedge, House and Tree sparrows, Nuthatch, Bullfinch, Goldfinch, Wren and Spotted fly-catcher.

Starling

Blue tit

Greenfinch

Chaffinch

Hen Blackbird

Songthrush

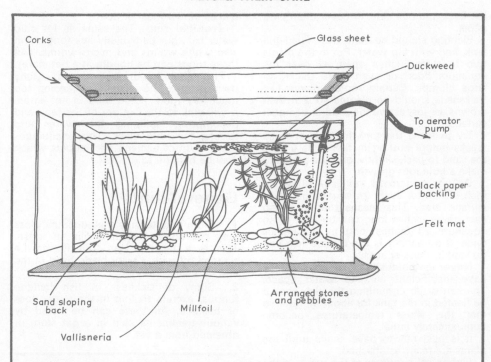

Corks — Glass sheet — Duckweed — To aerator pump — Black paper backing — Felt mat — Arranged stones and pebbles — Millfoil — Vallisneria — Sand sloping back

Above: An aquarium ready to receive the fish. One gallon of water should be allowed for every inch of fish, excluding the tail. Below: Some popular aquarium fish. The guppy and swordtail are tropical fish, the rest are cold-water fish.

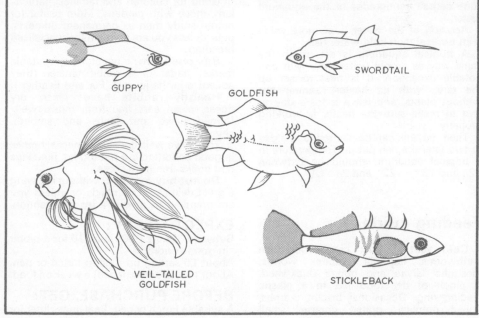

GUPPY

SWORDTAIL

GOLDFISH

VEIL-TAILED GOLDFISH

STICKLEBACK

the back and one side, or cover them with paper.

Planting should be done with a half-full tank, and with tap water. Put in the plants two to three inches apart all over the aquarium floor, or even more thickly in large clumps. Certain rooted plants like Vallisneria should be planted so that their crowns are just above the sand or compost surface.

Try to leave the tank for two or three weeks before putting in fish. This allows the sand to pack slightly, and the plants to make a little root growth.

Do not overcrowd the fish—allow an inch of fish for every 24 square inches of surface area. This means that four fish each three inches long can be kept in an aquarium 24 inches long by 12 inches wide. If an aerator is used, more fish can be kept in these spaces.

Never use goldfish bowls—they usually have insufficient air and water space. The can or jar containing the fish should be floated in the tank for about an hour so that the water temperatures become approximately equal.

It is best not to have snails until the plants are really established.

Siphon off a quarter of the water in the tank weekly and replace it with fresh water. Use the thermometer to check that the temperature of the replacement water is within three to four degrees Fahrenheit (one degree centigrade) of the aquarium water.

Aeration of the water is of more value with tropical than cold water fish.

A tropical aquarium is set up in the same way as a cold water one, with one notable exception. It is best to set up the tank, with its heater running but without plants, and leave it for a day or two to make sure the heater is working properly.

Then the tank can be planted, and a day or two later the fish put in. Temperature in a tropical aquarium should be between 72° and 75° F (22° and 24° C).

Feeding guide

Cold water fish: Live foods, like earthworms, daphnia, Tubifex worms, mosquito larvae and pupae duckweed. A pinch of dry food fed in a plastic feeding ring. Occasional biscuit crumbs, boiled oatmeal, grated cheese, small pieces of raw meat or liver.

Tropical fish: The same as for cold water fish, but particularly live foods, and also white worms and micro-worms. (All these foods can be bought at a pet store).

Fish should not be overfed. Many owners make the mistake of feeding too much dry food. If the food is not eaten, it will sink to the bottom of the tank and decompose, polluting the water and turning the sand black. This encourages the growth of bacteria and moulds which may be harmful to the fish.

General hints

1. From time to time the aquarium glass may get covered with a film of algae. This is a healthy sign, but it can be scraped off with a razor blade fixed in the end of a cane.

2. Signs of sickness in fish include fungus, excreta trailing in the water, loss of balance. All these can be cured by various treatments sold in a pet store or obtained from a vet.

RABBITS

Good for children and families, particularly those with gardens. More useful for nature study than as permanent domestic pets, unless you are going in for specialised breeding.

Buy one from: a pet store, a reputable market trader or a rabbit fancier (they advertise in the journal 'Fur and Feather').

Healthy rabbits have: clean, dry noses, clean ears free from mites, well-formed paws and limbs and smooth, shiny fur.

They have well-developed necks, bodies in good condition but not too fat, hind legs and hocks free from sores.

Do not buy a rabbit: without knowing a great deal about its needs or unless you are prepared to give it a lot of attention.

EXPECT TO PAY:
Between 30s. (£1·50) and £10 for a rabbit in good condition.
About £5 setting up a good hutch or pen.
About 10s. (50 new pence) a week on food.

BEFORE PURCHASE, GET:
A suitable hutch or pen. Peat-moss litter for

bedding, plus straw or wood chips. Suitable water containers.

Care hints

If building a rabbit pen, make sure that the floor slopes down towards the front, and the walls and partitions are at least three feet high. If wire netting is used, it should be half-inch mesh. Have the floor area between three-quarters and one square foot per lb. of rabbit housed.

Hutches are more widely used than pens. They should be at least 1½ feet high inside. A single small or medium rabbit needs a hutch of at least two square feet. A doe with a litter needs twice this space. Ideal hutches are about four feet by two feet, with two doors and a central, removable solid partition. Doors should be covered on the inside of the frame with three-quarter-inch mesh-wire netting.

If the hutch is kept outdoors, the doors should be half solid, with a six-inch overhang on the roof. A good rule is to make the length of the hutch about four times the length of the rabbit, and the height twice its length.

How to lift a rabbit.

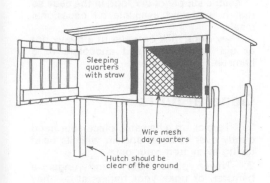

Sleeping quarters with straw

Wire mesh day quarters

Hutch should be clear of the ground

A strongly built rabbit hutch, raised well clear of the ground.

Feeding guide

Give a rabbit grass, meadow and clover hay, all garden greenstuffs, cow parsley, dandelion leaves, the green tops of root crops such as carrots, turnips and swedes. In winter rabbits particularly like clover hay.

Bran can be damped to a crumbly

mass that holds together when squeezed in the hand.

Never feed green raw potatoes, rhubarb, chrysanthemum, foxglove, geranium, hemlock, henbane or any evergreen such as laurel, privet or yew. All stale uneaten food must be removed daily. Food is best given twice a day.

Rabbits have a habit of either scratching the food out of a dish, or lifting it in their teeth and spilling the contents on the floor. The food container must therefore be secured to the floor. Water containers should be secured to the side of the hutch, and fitted with metal drinking tubes at a convenient height to the rabbit.

General hints

1. Never lift a rabbit off the ground by its ears. Gently grasp the scruff of the neck with one hand, and allow the rabbit to rest on the other hand.
2. Food and water containers should be cleaned every day.

HAMSTERS

Ideal for children—and people not terrified by rodents—but they do bite.

Buy one from: a pet store, or a reputable market trader.

THE FOUR VARIETIES ARE:

1. **Normal (colour chestnut brown, fading to cream on the abdomen).**
2. **Cream (deep cream fur over the whole body).**
3. **Piebald (white, with small irregular patches of fawn).**
4. **Fawn (an even, pale fawn. Fairly rare because of reputed low fertility).**

What to look for in a Healthy Hamster

Ears covered in silky hairs. As a hamster gets older, these hairs disappear—size is nothing to go by.

Eyes free from tumours.

Thick, soft fur, without scars or sores.

Do not buy: a hamster that mopes or seems lifeless, a female for children—they can be irritable in season.

EXPECT TO PAY:

About 5s. (25 new pence) to 12s. 6d. (62½ new pence) for a healthy hamster.

About 2s. 6d. (12½ new pence) a week on food.

About 30s. (£1·50) on a cage and bedding.

BEFORE PURCHASE, GET:

A suitable cage.

Some hay for the cage. Straw is too cold.

Sawdust on the floor of the cage.

Some toys like a wheel, cotton reel, nuts and paper.

How to lift a hamster.

Care hints

Hamsters should be housed singly, as they tend to fight. They are happy to live alone as long as they have plenty of toys. Give them an even-temperature room to live in, and never keep them outdoors. Hamsters tend to be more active at night.

Occasionally, especially in cold weather, they will hibernate and appear dead. If this happens, they should be left to waken naturally, but leave some dry food in the cage in case a warm day or night revives them. Cages need to be cleaned only once a week, the damp corner being changed when needed.

Hamsters store more food than they normally eat, and their store should be cleared every week. Do not move the food daily, or the hamster will come to mistrust you.

Feeding guide

Give them special hamster foods sold at pet stores, and a mash of puppy meal with added table scraps, meat, boneless fish, egg, cooked bacon rind, cheese, pudding.

Balance this with green food, or raw root vegetables in winter. Hamsters also like nuts, raisins and cake.

Keep a supply of dry food in the cage so that it is always available for occasional meals.

They drink milk or water in a heavy pot or old jar. **Never** feed chocolate to a hamster.

General hints

1. To pick up a hamster, place your hand gently over its back, and lift with its head facing away from your palm.

2. Never place your hand under a hamster, or poke your fingers at it—they are short-sighted, and could mistake you for food.

3. The more they are handled, the more tame they become.

4. Consult a vet if a hamster seems unwell, but remember they only live for two to four years.

TORTOISES

Pleasing pets but only for people with gardens. They are not indoor pets.

Buy one from: a pet store or a reliable market trader.

What to look for in a healthy tortoise

A crack-free shell.
Limbs free from sores.
A heavy tortoise, proportionate to its size.
When gently shaken, it should hold its limbs stiff.
A head pulled in sharply when alarmed.
Bright, clean eyes; mouth free from fungus.
Do not buy: a tortoise after July—if they are imported after this month, they rarely have time to get used to the British climate, and may die during the winter months.
A tortoise measuring less than four inches across its shell.

EXPECT TO PAY:

Between 10s. (50 new pence) and £1 for a good specimen.
About £1 on building a pen if the garden is easy to escape from.
A few shillings a week on odd tit-bits.

BEFORE PURCHASE, GET:

A box (to prepare for hibernation).

Care hints

Tortoises need very little attention. Make sure all exit holes in the garden are sealed up, or else enclose the tortoise in a large wire pen.

Round about October, when the tortoise appears lethargic, put it in a small box not less than a foot square, fill the box with dry leaves. Cover the tortoise with hay or straw, and a lid pierced with ventilation holes on the box. This will create the right atmosphere for hibernation, and keep out rats.

Do not disturb the tortoise until March. On the first sunny day it may be taken out on the lawn, and left to wake up slowly. It is best to keep the box in an outhouse, and put the tortoise back in it at the slightest sign of night frost.

Never attempt hibernation indoors in a warm room. At the end of hibernation, the change of temperature could kill the creature.

Feeding guide

Tortoises eat: grass, weeds such as dandelion and clover, lettuce, peas, strawberries, rose leaves, virginia creeper.
Sometimes brown bread covered in jam.
Vitamin foods, like liver, halibut oil and orange juice.
Tortoises soon get used to eating food in the same place. They feed early morning and late afternoon, the rest of the day being spent in resting and sunbathing.

General hints

1. Keep a supply of clean, fresh water available at all times.
2. Never give a tortoise milk.
3. Make certain a tortoise can find some shade in hot weather.
4. Tortoises can live for many, many years, but lots die because of inadequate precautions taken during hibernation.

GUINEA PIGS (CAVIES)

Guinea pigs are ideal pets for children. They can be kept indoors, or outside if protected against the cold, rain and draughts. The three varieties are:
1. **Normal—straight hair, about 1½ in. long.**
2. **Abyssinian—short hair which radiates from about six places on the body.**
3. **Peruvian—straight hair several inches long, with white the most common colour.**

Buy one from: a reliable pet store, through advertisements in the journal *Fur & Feather* or from a local cavy society.

EXPECT TO PAY:

About 15s. (75 new pence) for a normal guinea pig.
Up to £5 for a long-haired guinea pig.
Between 5s. (25 new pence) or 10s. (50 new pence) a week on food.
About £2 on the initial cost of accessories and housing.

How to lift a guinea pig

BEFORE PURCHASE GET:
An indoor or outdoor hutch.
Hay for bedding material.
Sawdust for the floor.
A supply of food.

Care Hints

Divide the hutch into two parts, one for sleeping quarters and the other for both feeding and exercise. The second half should be as large as possible. An outdoor hutch should be raised from the ground, and have a sloping, weatherproof roof. It should be cleaned regularly and frequently.

Guinea pigs are very timid, and are easily frightened by sudden movements. They should be held in two hands, with one around the shoulders, with the thumb and forefinger under the chin, the other under the rump to take the weight.

Guinea pigs can breed when they are six months old, and the gestation period is nine to 11 weeks. They can be fed on solid food when only two days old, and are weaned in a fortnight. As soon as a female (sow) becomes pregnant, the male (boar) should be removed from the hutch.

Feeding Guide

Feed bran mash, good hay, mixed corn and rolled oats. You can also give root vegetables and green stuffs, such as lettuce and cabbage. Some pet stores sell special pellets for guinea pigs. Fresh clean water should also be available, and must be changed daily.

General Hints

1. Guinea pigs live happily together, but two sows and two boars together may result in fighting.

2. Make sure all doors are closed, fires guarded and other pets out of the way before letting them have the free run of a room.

3. Given proper care, guinea pigs live on average two and a half to three years—some as long as five years.

4. If they appear unwell, consult a vet or go to an animal welfare clinic.

MICE

Mice are fine pets for children, but not for nervous mothers. They should be kept indoors in cages or special wooden boxes. The most common types are:

1. **White (albino).**

2. **Piebald (large black patches on white).**

3. **Self-black.**

4. **Grey.**

Buy one from: a reliable pet store, or a reputable market trader.

EXPECT TO PAY:
About 5s. (25 new pence) for a pair of mice.
Up to 6d. (2½ new pence) a week on food.
About £1 on a suitable home and bedding material.

BEFORE PURCHASE GET:
A proper home for mice.
Sawdust for the floor, and cotton wool for bedding.
A supply of food.

Care Hints

A wooden box with a glass front and removable zinc tray at the bottom is ideal for a home. An old aquarium with a ventilated lid is also suitable, and some pet stores sell metal cages with mouse-wheels inside. Whichever you choose, make sure you clean it out regularly.

Cover the floor with sawdust, and provide a water supply by attaching a small piece of tubing to an inverted medicine bottle. Provide some paper and wood chippings so that the mouse can build a nest.

Mice can be picked up by closing the hand around them, or holding the base of the tail between the thumb and first finger of one hand, and supporting the body with the other.

A gerbil

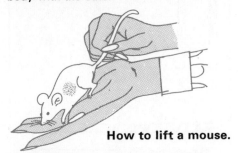

How to lift a mouse.

Feeding Guide

Pet stores sell special mice food, or you can feed mixtures of oats, birdseed and brown breadcrumbs, with addition of lettuce, chickweed and carrot. Occasional bits of meat and scraps can be given, but leftovers should be cleared before they go stale. No more than one fifth of an ounce (about six grams) of dry food should be fed to each mouse daily.

General Hints

1. Mice breed rapidly, so if keeping a pair, remove the male from the nest once the female becomes pregnant.

2. If a pair escape from their home, you may have to place mousetraps round the house to keep down numbers.

GERBILS

A newcomer to the pet world, the gerbil is a little bigger than a mouse with sand-coloured fur, big ears and shiny eyes, long whiskers and tail. It moves along by leaps and bounds, as its hindlegs are longer than the forelegs.

Ideal for children or people who want an 'in' pet, they must be kept indoors in a draught-free room.

Buy one from: a reliable pet store.

EXPECT TO PAY:

About £1 to 30s. (£1·50) for one.
About 2s. (10 new pence) a week on food.
About £1 on a home and other materials.

BEFORE PURCHASE GET:

A cage—a mouse's will do.
A supply of food.

Care Hints

Gerbils are generally free from illness, and they do not smell. If let out of the cage, they will make no attempt to escape.

The cage should be kept in a room of even temperature, and not in damp surroundings. Do not keep them in aquariums or glass-fronted cages—the condensation which forms on the glass makes the bedding damp.

Cover the floor with dry sand or sawdust for burrowing, and small pieces of paper, scraps of wool, dried grass or hay for them to make a nest. Gerbils will mate in warm conditions, and after 23 or 25 days a litter as large as 12 can be born.

Feeding Guide

The best food is sweet, fresh hay, sunflower seeds, wheat, corn, barley, oats, parakeet seed mixtures, a hamster mix, water-melon and pumpkin seeds. Gerbils also need fresh bits of apple, lettuce and other green vegetables. Stale food must be removed. Water can be given in a water hopper, sold at most pet stores, but gerbils drink very rarely.

General Hints

1. Gerbils can live for five to six years, but must always have dry and warm surroundings.

2. Because they drink so little, gerbils make little mess, and do not need their bedding changed every day.

A Catalogue Of Tools

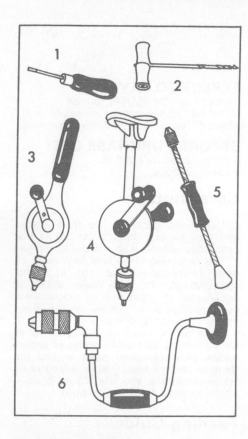

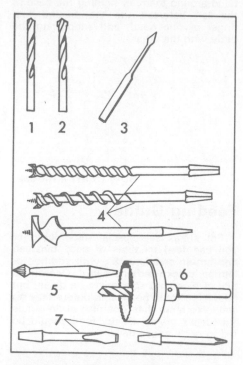

BORING TOOLS

Use a **bradawl** (1) for making starting holes for nails in hardboard, ply or wood or a **gimlet** (2) for deeper starting holes for screws in soft woods.

The ordinary **hand drill** (3) takes various sizes of **twist drills** in the chuck, and can be used for drilling holes in any material. For heavier hand drilling, use a **breast drill** (4). You can press hard on the flattened end with your chest to get more pressure, but be careful not to bend or break the twist drill.

For light drilling jobs, use the **Archimedean drill** (5). This takes special small-diameter drilling bits in its chuck. The **carpenter's brace** (6) is for bigger-diameter drilling jobs in solid wood. Use with auger bits, not twist drills.

BORING-TOOL BITS

Twist drills (1) are used with hand drills or with power drills. Choose the high-speed type (HSS) for longest life and durability. **Special tipped drills** (2) are used for drilling masonry (for inserting Rawlplugs for instance). **Points** (3) are used with the Archimedean drill (maximum diameter usually $\frac{1}{16}$ in.).

Augers (4) are used for all holes in solid wood (twist drills would jam and burn), and are available in larger sizes than twist drills. Use only with a brace, or with a power drill with reduction gear drive. The **countersink** (5) finishes off the top of a hole drilled to take a countersunk head screw, enabling the screw to be pulled down flush.

The **hole saw** (6) cuts larger circles in thin wood, and is usually clamped on to a twist drill to act as a starter and place the hole-centre. You can also use **screwdriver bits** (7) in a hand drill or preferably a brace—for screwing, not boring!

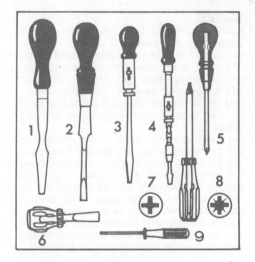

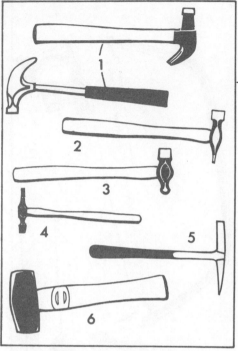

SCREWDRIVERS

The **London** type (1) with flattened handle and **Cabinet** type (2) are for dealing with larger woodscrews. You need several different sizes of one or the other (not both) to match the screw sizes you are likely to come across.

The **ratchet** type (3) is a good general-purpose screwdriver for light work. The **pump-action ratchet** (4) is fine for driving in a lot of screws—but mind it does not slip, or you may trap a finger with the slide.

(5) is a **general-purpose screwdriver** with reversible (plain or Phillips) bit; (6) is a **stub screwdriver**—very useful where access to the screw is limited. (7) **Phillips** and (8) **Pozidriv screwdrivers** for screws with non-slip heads. (9) An **electrician's screwdriver,** for dealing with screwed connections in electrical plugs.

HAMMERS

You cannot go far without a hammer or two. A **claw hammer** (1) is the general-purpose tool for nailing jobs (inserting and withdrawing). The **Warrington hammer** (2) is another general-purpose type, while the **Mechanic's hammer** (3) is intended mainly for metal working. (4) is a **light general-purpose hammer** while (5) is another **light hammer** for tacking or upholstery work. A **short-handled sledge hammer** (6) is also worth including in your tool kit for heavy work.

FOR SINKS

A **plunger** (1) is the tool for clearing a blocked sink. If that fails, try a **'mouse'** (2)—a length of flexible rod to push down the wastepipe and round bends.

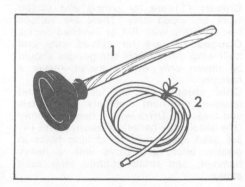

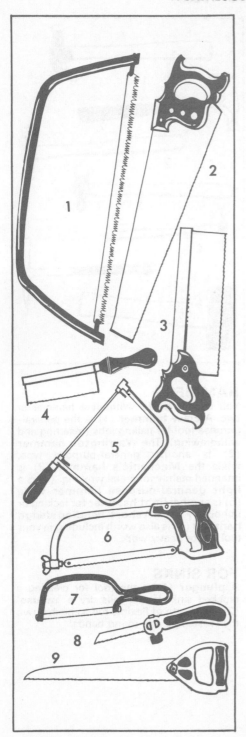

SAWS

Sawing up logs? Then you really need a **woodman's saw** (1). For home carpentry you need two good **hand saws** (2)—one a rip saw and one a crosscut; and a **tenon saw** (3). You might also add a **dovetail saw** (4) for lighter work; and you will probably need a **coping saw** (5) for cutting curves in sheet or solid wood.

For cutting metal there is the **hacksaw** (6) for heavy work, the **junior hacksaw** (7) for light work and the **special type** (8) which takes a hacksaw blade for getting at awkward places impossible to reach with a frame saw. The **multi-purpose saw** (9) is well worth having. This has a specially-hardened blade which can cut most materials, including metal, and the handle attitude can be adjusted.

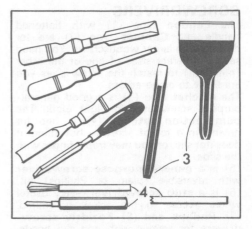

CUTTING AND GOUGING TOOLS

Chisels (1) are for paring and similar work on wood only. There are various blade-widths with flat or bevelled backs. **Gouges** (2) are for curved cuts and hollowing out. Chisels and gouges should be driven only with a mallet—never a hammer.

Cold chisels (3) are for cutting and gouging out hard materials, like metals and masonry. Drive with a heavy hammer (the heavier the better). **Masonry bits** (4) are used specifically for drilling holes in plaster, brick, etc. Drive with a heavy hammer, and rotate slightly after each stroke.

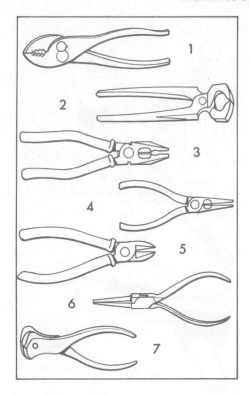

PLIERS

Side-jointed pliers (1) are a general-purpose gripping tool which can often be used in place of a spanner to hold a bolt-head against turning, or even to remove a not-too-tight nut. **Pincers** (2) are specifically a woodworking tool, used for withdrawing nails. **Flat-nose combination pliers** (3) are the chief general-purpose type, and include cutting edges for cutting soft wire. **Radio pliers** (4) are useful for bending the ends of bared flex round terminals, and for light gripping duties. Do not try to use as a spanner, or you will twist and ruin the pointed jaws. **Diagonal cutters** (5) are for cutting wire of all kinds, and you can also use them for stripping insulation. They come in various sizes—small for electrical work and larger for cutting thicker, harder wire. **Half-round pliers** (6) are useful for forming loops in bare wire—to make loops to fit round electrical terminals, for instance. Another type has both jaws fully rounded. **End-cutting nippers** (7) are usually more effective than diagonal nippers for cutting hard wire. A good pair will easily cut $\frac{1}{8}$ in. diameter steel wire.

SPANNERS

Adjustable spanners (1) enable you to tackle all sizes of nuts, and **wrenches** (2) are essential for unscrewing and re-making couplings in plumbing installations.

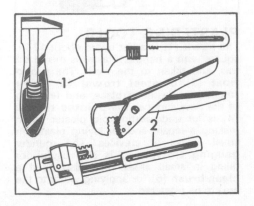

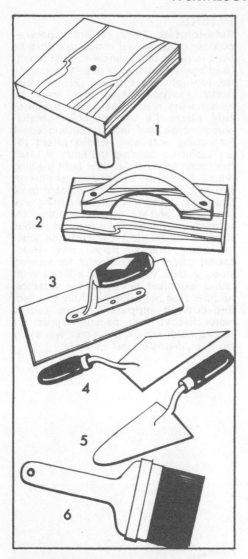

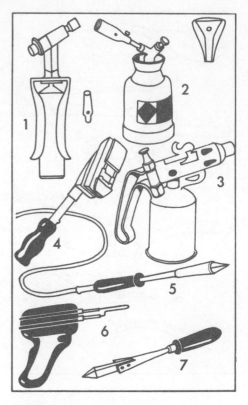

PLASTERING TOOLS

The **hawk** (1) is a flat board about 12 in. square with a handle. Plaster is mixed on this, and taken to the work. The **wood float** (2) or **steel trowel** (3) is for smoothing plaster in place, and levelling of the new surface. The **pointed trowel** (4) is for undercutting old plaster when making a repair, and for laying plaster in small cracks or crevices. The rounder **gauging trowel** (5) is also useful for filling in small areas. You also need a **clean brush** (6) for applying water to the area to be plastered.

STRIPPING TOOLS

Heat speeds paint stripping, and is necessary for soldering and plumbing jobs. The small **blowlamp** (1) which works off a **butane cartridge** is for small jobs only. The larger type working off a **gas cylinder** (2) has similar performance to the **blowlamp** (3) for paint stripping, etc. Both are usually more effective than an **electric paint stripper** (4). For soldering, an **electric iron** (5) is usually the best tool, although a **solder gun** (6) may be preferred for lighter work. The old-fashioned **soldering iron** (7), which you heat in a gas flame still has its uses.

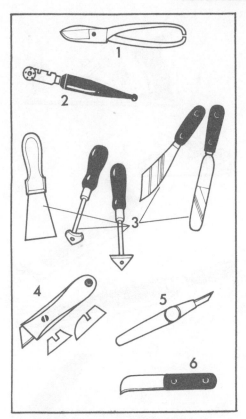

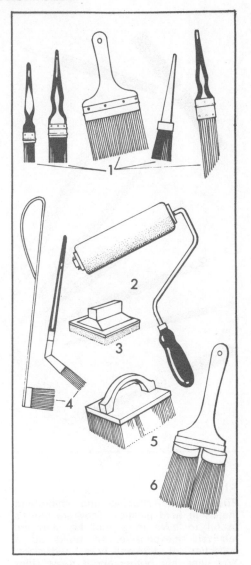

CUTTING AND SCRAPING TOOLS

Snips (1) are used for cutting thin sheet-metal—nothing else. A **glass-cutter** (2) is handy, provided you can use it properly, but it takes a lot of practice to master.

For paint stripping, paper stripping, plastering and similar redecorating jobs, you need the collection of **knives** and **scrapers** shown (3). (4) is a stout **general-purpose knife** with replaceable blades, (5) a **small knife** for light cutting jobs and (6) a **lino knife,** for cutting and trimming lino.

FOR APPLYING PAINT

A variety of **brushes** (1) for household painting. A **roller** (2) covers large areas quickly. A **pad brush** (3) gives a smooth finish, leaving no brush marks or bristles on the paintwork. **Crevice** or **angled brushes** (4) are useful for painting behind radiators, pipes, etc. A **panel stippler** (5) is used for patterning painted or distempered surfaces. A **two-knot distemper brush** (6) is used for distempering and whitewashing.

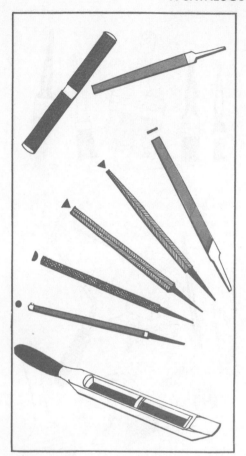

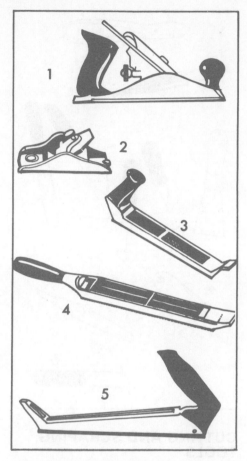

FILES

Files are for shaping and smoothing metals or hard plastics. They are always useful to have in a tool kit, and are relatively inexpensive, so build up a collection of different types and sizes. You need not bother about rasps (files with very coarse teeth for cutting wood) as the **Surform tool** (bottom) will do a better job, and can be used on harder materials as well.

SMOOTHING TOOLS

The general-purpose **metal plane** (1) will be suitable for most smoothing jobs. The smaller version with a full-width blade, known as a **block plane** (2) is used where you need to cut right up to an edge. The most versatile tool in this group is the **Surform,** available either in the form of a plane (3) or flat with a handle like a file (4). The smaller version of the flat Surform (5) is an alternative to a block plane. Surforms can shape, smooth or plane almost any material or surface, including the edges of hard plastic panels, and the blade is replaceable.

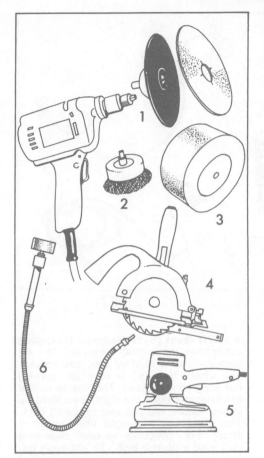

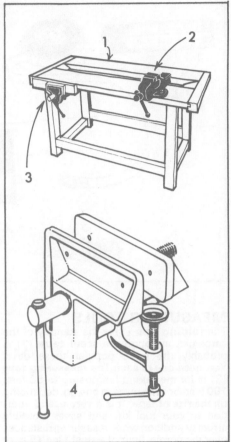

POWER WORKSHOP

The **electric drill** is the heart of a complete power workshop. Only a few of the most widely-used attachments are shown here —the **sanding disc** (1), which is also useful for paint stripping with a special disc; the **wire brush** (2) for cleaning rusty metalwork (there is a variety of different sizes and types of brushes available); and a **polishing mop** (3).

A standard power drill readily converts into a **power saw** (4) with a matching attachment, or into an **orbital sander** for smooth-finish sanding of flat surfaces (5). Also recommended is a flexible **shaft attachment** (6). This can take a variety of small cutting and grinding bits, including drills, to operate in restricted spaces.

ON THE BENCH

A **workbench** (1) is a vital piece of equipment for many jobs. If you do not have room to set one up permanently, there are portable types which fold flat when not in use. A permanent bench can have an **engineer's vice** (2) bolted to it. A **carpenter's vice** (3) is more useful for handling wood. A carpenter's bench has a front apron on to which the carpenter's vice can be fixed.

If you have to use a portable bench—or the kitchen table—a **portable vice** (4) is best. This can be clamped to the edge of the bench or table to hold the work, and stored away when the job is done. You can also take a portable vice *to* the job in many cases.

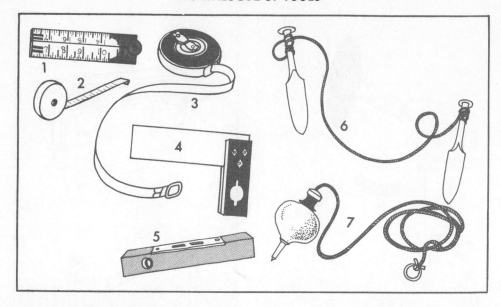

MEASURING TOOLS

The **folding rule** (1) is the standby of the carpenter, although the **steel tape** (2) is probably the more popular these days. You need one of each. The **measuring tape** (3) is for measuring lengths up to 50 feet, 100 feet, or even more in one go, depending on the size of tape. It is a very useful addition to your tool kit, and saves possible errors of addition when measuring distances over the normal limit of a steel tape (5 ft. or 6 ft.). To mark wood-stock for cutting off at right angles, use a **try square** (4).

A **spirit level** (5) is necessary for getting assemblies horizontal—shelves, for instance—and is another tool you require. The **chalk line** (6) is only for marking out long straight lines. The line is coated in chalk, stretched out tight, then lifted up in the middle and allowed to spring back. This gives you a straight line marked in chalk. For checking vertical alignment you need a **plumb bob** (7), although you can improvise this with a weight attached to a length of thin, flexible cord.

BASIC CARPENTRY TOOLS

Tools listed in **black** type can be regarded as essential. Others are designated in order of preference 1 or 2

Tool	Type	Size(s)	Use
HANDSAW 1	Panel	24 in.	General sawing, particularly ply and hardboard
HANDSAW	Crosscut	24 in. or 28 in.	Cutting wood across the grain
HANDSAW 1	Rip	28 in. or 30 in.	Cutting wood with the grain
KEYHOLE SAW 1		18 in.	Cut-outs and curved cuts in wood
TENON SAW		12 in. or 14 in.	Sawing smaller wood stock sizes also ply and hardboard
DOVETAIL SAW 1		10 in.	Lighter work on small wood sizes
COPING SAW		$6\frac{1}{2}$ in.	Cutting curves in sheet ply and hardboard, also thin solid wood
CHISEL	Firmer	$\frac{1}{16}$ in., $\frac{1}{8}$ in., $\frac{3}{16}$ in., $\frac{1}{4}$ in., $\frac{3}{8}$ in., $\frac{1}{2}$ in., $\frac{3}{4}$ in., 1 in.	General paring work, cleaning out grooves, etc.
CHISEL 2	Bevel edge	$\frac{1}{8}$ in., $\frac{1}{4}$ in., $\frac{1}{2}$ in., 1 in.	Finer paring work
GOUGE 1	Firmer	$\frac{1}{4}$ in., $\frac{1}{2}$ in., $\frac{3}{4}$ in., 1 in.	Cleaning out grooves, general paring
HAMMER	Claw	$1\frac{1}{2}$ lb.	General purpose tool
HAMMER 1	Warrington	1 lb.	General purpose tool
PLANE	Metal	8 in.	General smoothing work
PLANE 1	Block		Smoothing and shaping
SURFORM 1	Plane		Shaping, roughing and smoothing wood
SURFORM	File		Shaping, roughing and smoothing wood
SCREWDRIVER	Cabinet or london	6 in., 9 in., 12 in. lengths $\frac{1}{8}$ in., $\frac{3}{16}$ in., $\frac{1}{4}$ in., $\frac{3}{8}$ in. widths	General purpose tool
BRACE 2	Carpenters		For boring holes in wood
AUGERS 2	Wood	$\frac{1}{4}$ in., $\frac{3}{8}$ in., $\frac{1}{2}$ in., $\frac{3}{4}$ in., 1 in.	For use with brace
HAND DRILL 1	$\frac{1}{4}$ in. chuck		Drilling ply, hardboard and thin wood
TWIST DRILLS 1		$\frac{1}{16} - \frac{1}{4}$ in. (set)	For use with hand drill
TRY SQUARE	Metal	9 in., 10 in. or 12 in.	Marking out and squaring off
METAL RULE		12 in. or 18 in.	Measuring and marking out
CARPENTERS RULE		24 in. folding	Measuring and marking out
STEEL TAPE 2		5 ft. or 6 ft.	Measuring and marking out
BRADAWL		$\frac{1}{16}$ in., $\frac{3}{32}$ in.	Starting holes
POINTED AWL			Starting holes
MALLET	Wood		For driving chisels
PINCERS			For withdrawing nails
PLIERS	General purpose		General purpose tool
MITRE BLOCK 1	Wood or metal		Cutting mitres
MITRE SQUARE 2	Metal (adjustable)		Laying off angles for marking out

Do not be put off by the number of tools in this basic list. Quite a number are relatively inexpensive and are particularly useful to have.

Care Of Tools

It is not always true that a poor workman always blames his tools. There **are** poor tools, which can make it difficult, or even impossible, to do a good job. The first golden rule is to buy the best tools you can afford.

It is better to have a small collection of good tools than a large collection of indifferent ones. Budget to build up a collection of **necessary** tools, and if they are **good** tools they can last you a lifetime. Good tools are by far the cheapest in the long run.

Now for the things that damage tools or cause them to deteriorate.

Improper Use

This is probably the most common of all causes, but can be avoided completely by using the right tool for the job. Never, for instance, use screwdrivers or chisels for opening paint tins, never try to cut hard materials with a wood saw, or gouge out plaster with a wood chisel.

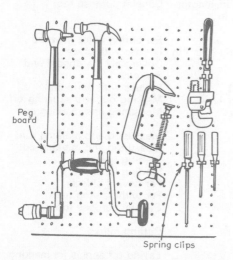

Peg board

Spring clips

Spring clips, wire hooks and a piece of peg board make an ideal storage rack for tools.

Improper Storage

This applies particularly to edge tools, which should always be stored in racks, or on clips—never jumbled together in a box or drawer. Keep steel tools (and electric drills) in a dry place. If they have to be kept in an outside workshop, protect bare metal surfaces with a light smearing of oil to prevent rusting.

Untidiness

Never lay tools down in such a way that they can be damaged. For instance, always lay a plane on its side, not with the cutting edge of the iron resting on the bench or floor. Clean tools after use, and finally wipe with an oily rag. Always wipe a chisel from the handle downwards, **never** the other way round.

Loss of Sharpness

This is inevitable with edge tools after they have been in use for some time, or have suffered damage to the cutting edge. Proper tool care calls for re-sharpening at regular intervals.

Chisels are fairly easy to sharpen on an oilstone. Note that the tip of a chisel has two bevels. It is the extreme end and narrow bevel which requires re-sharpening. Hold the tool at a constant angle of 25 to 30 degrees to the face of the oilstone, and rub it backwards and forwards over the stone.

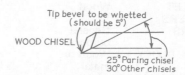

Tip bevel to be whetted
(should be 5°)

WOOD CHISEL

25° Paring chisel
30° Other chisels

Sharpening angles for a wood chisel.

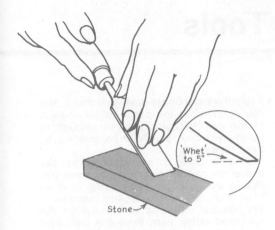

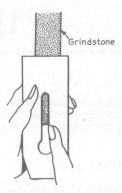

Grindstone

Re-grinding the bevel of a damaged plane iron on a grindstone before finishing the edge on an oilstone.

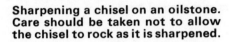

Whet to 5°

Stone

Sharpening a chisel on an oilstone. Care should be taken not to allow the chisel to rock as it is sharpened.

If the chisel is allowed to rock as you rub, the bevel will become rounded. Your check is that the narrow bevel whetted by the stone should be even-looking, straight and parallel.

If the cutting edge has been badly damaged, you must first re-grind the main bevel to the same angle as before, using a grindstone, until the damage is fully removed.

You will now have just one complete bevel on the end of the chisel, which must be perfectly true and even. Form the final narrow bevel to produce a new cutting edge on the oilstone, as when normally re-sharpening.

Plane irons can be re-sharpened in exactly the same way. These will be rather more difficult to get true, since they are wider than chisels, but it is a case of practice makes perfect.

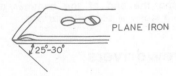

PLANE IRON

25°-30°

Sharpening angles for a plane iron.

Screwdriver blade-tips also work better for re-sharpening from time to time, and particularly if they have been damaged. You can use a grindstone for this job, but avoid producing a sharp edge. The edge should be thick enough to grip in the slot of a matching size of screw, so that the screwdriver will actually support the screw in a horizontal position.

The main thing to watch in re-sharpening a screwdriver is to be sure that the edge is square, and not at an angle.

Edge square

SCREWDRIVER

Maintaining a square edge is all-important when re-sharpening a screwdriver.

Saws can be re-sharpened with a small triangular file, working on each tooth in turn. It will then usually be necessary to re-set the teeth as well with a setting tool. Saw-sharpening is thus really a job for the professional, and most tool shops provide such a service.

You can avoid this problem by using saws with replaceable blades.

Cold chisels can be re-sharpened by grinding. Avoid getting the tool-tip too hot, as this can soften the metal. So grind only for a few seconds at a time, dip in water or oil to cool and repeat this operation as many times as necessary.

Using Tools

Most people are familiar with using the simple, common tools, but not always the best and safest way of handling them.

Hammer

A hammer's chief job about the house is knocking in nails, but the nail has first to be held in position, and it is all too easy to hammer one's fingers instead of the head of the nail, especially if the nail is a short one.

You can avoid this by holding the nail with something else—a pair of pliers, for example, but that is a bit cumbersome.

Instead, if you are positioning a long nail, hold it in place with a looped spill of paper. If it is a short nail, use a strip of corrugated paper or card through which the nail is pushed.

Large nail

Above: Holding a large nail in position with a paper spill. Below: Holding a small nail in place with a strip of card or corrugated paper.

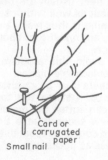

Small nail

Both are real finger-saving methods, and you can remove the paper holder as soon as the nail is located securely enough to stand on its own, and finish hammering the head down flush.

Another thing to remember is that the bigger the nail the bigger the hammer you should use. It is no good trying to drive a six-inch nail with a tacking hammer—the hammer will tend to bounce off the nail-head rather than drive the nail. And the smaller the hammer, the easier it is to miss the nail-head.

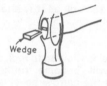

Wedge

Above: Using a wedge to tighten the loose handle of a hammer. Below: Driving the wedge in place by banging the hammer head on a hard surface.

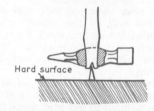

Hard surface

Never use a hammer with a loose head. It may fly off. If the head is loose, get a little metal wedge from an ironmonger and drive it into the end of the handle to tighten the head. You can do this by banging the end of the hammer down on to a stone or concrete surface.

Screwdrivers

Screwdrivers should be used only for driving screws, not for other odd jobs like levering off the lid of a tin of paint.

Screws need a *starting hole* into which

Start hole.

Start a hole for the point of a screw with a bradawl.

Hold the screw in place with the finger and thumb for the first few turns.

Keep the screwdriver square to the head of the screw during the whole of the screwing operation.

the point of the screw can be placed. You can make this hole with a bradawl, or if the screw is large and the wood is hard, you will need a drill. Then hold the screw in place with the fingers for the first few turns of the screwdriver, after which it should not need any more supporting.

The same trick applies when you are inserting a screw into a Rawlplug or similar plug. After tapping in the plug with a hammer, use a bradawl to open up the hole in the plug so that you can place the screw properly.

If the screwdriver slips, then probably you are not keeping it in line with the screw. If you 'angle' the screwdriver, the blade will tend to slip sideways out of the slot in the screw-head. This is a very common fault.

You also have to apply enough pressure on the screw to keep the blade from jumping out of the slot, but the main effort should be applied to turning the screwdriver. Do not try to push the screw home too hard. Let it screw itself home.

On a surface which must not be scarred or damaged, you can avoid a screwdriver slipping by using a Phillips head or Pozidriv screw, and the appropriate screwdriver. This entails buying special screws and screwdriver, which can only be used together. A Phillips or Pozidriv screw cannot be driven with an ordinary screwdriver, nor can a Phillips screwdriver be used to drive ordinary slotted-head screws.

Saw

Using a saw is not as straightforward as it seems. Much depends on whether you are going to saw across, or in the same direction, as the grain in solid wood.

Sawing **across** the grain—which you do when you cut off a length of wood— the saw needs to be held at an angle of 45°. Sawing **with** the grain, the saw needs to be kept at a steeper angle, about 60°. For sawing hardboard and plywood, use the same angle (45°) as for sawing across the grain.

Sawing is accomplished by moving the saw upwards and downwards, while maintaining the right angle. Do not allow the saw to rock so that the cutting angle changes.

At the same time, the saw must be kept upright, not tilted to one side or the other.

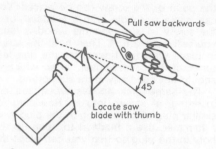

Pull saw backwards

45°

Locate saw blade with thumb

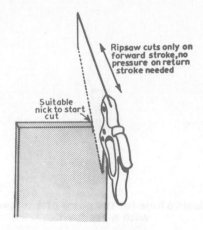

Ripsaw cuts only on forward stroke, no pressure on return stroke needed

Suitable nick to start cut

Above: When sawing across the grain, keep the saw at an angle of 45 degrees. Below: When sawing with the grain, the angle of the saw should be 60 degrees.

Using a ripsaw

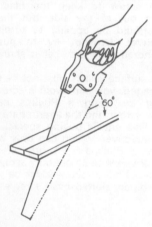

60°

The idea is also to let the saw do the work— do not use excessive force on the saw, and use smooth, full strokes rather than rapid, short strokes.

Most saws cut in both directions, but a **ripsaw** cuts only on the forward stroke, so you need no pressure on the ripsaw at all for the return stroke. With all saws, in fact, you will find it easier to saw on the down stroke, and regard the up stroke merely as a means of getting it into position.

The first thing is to get the saw-cut started. If you begin with a down stroke, the saw will probably skid sideways rather than cut into the edge.

You should first place the saw on the edge of the wood, establish the correct saw-angle and place the thumb along the side of the blade as a guide. Now draw the saw backwards gently. Repeat this until you have made a suitable nick to start the

cut. Then you can remove your thumb and begin sawing properly, the saw being guided by the cut you have started.

Before sawing old wood, check if there are any nails in it which could damage the saw-teeth. To remove them, tap the pointed end of the nail with a hammer to drive the nail-head above the surface. Then turn the wood over, grip under the head of the nail with **pincers**, and lever the nail out with a sideways rocking motion of the pincers. It is no good trying to pull the nail straight out.

If you do not want to mark the surface of the wood, place a scrap piece of hard-board under the pincers.

Hand drill

A hand drill is not so familiar to most people as a hammer or screwdriver, but it has many uses around the home. To insert a twist drill into the chuck of a hand drill, hold the chuck firmly in the left hand, and rotate the handle anti-clockwise to open the chuck's jaws (the three little wedge-shaped pieces inside the opening). Insert the drill in the chuck as far as it will go and, still holding the chuck, turn the handle in a clockwise direction until it stops. Get it as tight as you can by levering down on the handle. If you do not tighten the jaws of the chuck enough, the drill will slip when you start drilling.

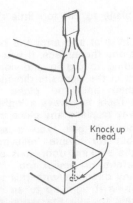

Knock up head

Before sawing old wood, take out any nails remaining in it. Begin by tapping the pointed end of a nail to raise the head above the surface on the other side of the wood.

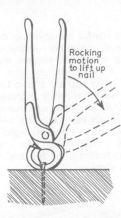

Rocking motion to lift up nail

Finish off the removal of the nails with a pair of pincers. A piece of hardboard placed under the pincers (below) will prevent damage to the surface of the wood.

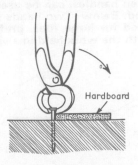

Hardboard

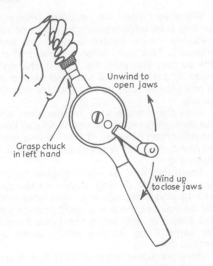

Unwind to open jaws

Grasp chuck in left hand

Wind up to close jaws

How to hold a hand drill for inserting a twist drill in the chuck.

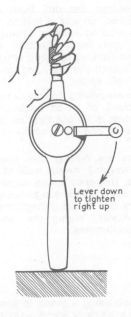

Lever down to tighten right up

Close the jaws of the hand drill chuck, after inserting the bit, as firmly as possible by levering down on the handle. If the bit is not held firmly, it can slip during drilling.

Whatever you are drilling, make a starting hole with an awl (in wood or soft material) or a centre punch (in hard material). This will locate the point of the drill so that you start the hole in the right place, and the drill will not tend to skid off to one side as soon as you start turning the handle.

Turn the handle at a regular rate, and use enough pressure on the handle to keep the drill biting properly. If you have to press very hard, your drill is blunt, and you should replace it.

Keep the drill at right angles to the surface you are drilling. If you let the drill lean to one side, not only will your hole not be true but there is a good chance you will snap the drill off in the hole. Exactly the same thing applies when using an electric drill.

Here are some other drilling tips worth remembering:

1. For a clean 'through' hole, stop when the point of the drill begins to emerge from the opposite surface. Remove the drill, turn the work over, and complete the hole by drilling from the other side.

2. To remove the drill from the hole when finished, do not at first try to pull it out, or to unwind it. Keep turning the drill gently in the same direction as when drilling, but without applying any pressure. This will loosen the drill, and enable it to be withdrawn easily.

3. If you are drilling thin ply or hardboard, place a block of wood under the work. You can then drill right through the ply or hardboard in one go, and have a clean exit hole.

4. If you are drilling thin sheet metal with a power drill, **never hold the metal with the fingers.** It can catch on the drill and spin round dangerously as the point of the drill breaks through the bottom surface. Always clamp the work to a bench in such cases.

Plane

If you are using a plane to smooth the surface of a piece of wood—say the edge of a door which is sticking—there are really only two rules to remember:

1. Adjust the depth of the iron by twisting the knurled knob in the centre of the iron assembly so that the plane takes a smooth, even cut. It is better to

adjust a plane to cut too little than too much.

2. Find by trial and error the best way to plane along the surface. If you find the plane tending to dig in and come to a stop, work in the opposite direction. You should then find the plane running smoothly. There is always a 'right' and a 'wrong' way to plane any piece of wood.

A plane will give you a smoother surface, but for simple 'relieving' jobs such as the sticking door, it is easier to use a Surform or similar tool. You can work in any direction with this tool, but avoid running it right up to an edge, as this is likely to split the wood there. A Surform will not produce such a smooth surface as an ordinary plane, but you can always finish off with glasspaper.

File

A file is useful for shaping or finishing jobs in hard materials—especially metal. Files come in various shapes and lengths, and you should choose the one best suited for what you are trying to do. Small files can be fitted with wooden handles and you can use them one-handed. Large files should always be used two-handed.

It helps to have the work rigidly clamped in a vice. Then you can concentrate entirely on holding the file and working it with push strokes.

Use handles on small files

Above: Small files, fitted with wooden handles, can be used one-handed. Below: Two hands should be used for large files, preferably with the work held in a vice.

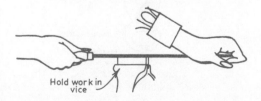

Hold work in vice

Hacksaw

If you have to cut off a piece of metal, a hacksaw is the right tool for the job. Again clamp the work tightly in a vice, and make a starting nick with a small triangular file.

Grasp the hacksaw by the handle and the front end of the frame, place in the starting notch and start sawing with a firm push stroke. Keep up a steady to-and-fro sawing motion, but apply only light pressure on each return stroke. If the blade does not appear to cut on the forward stroke, it is the wrong way round. Take it out of the frame and reassemble it the other way round.

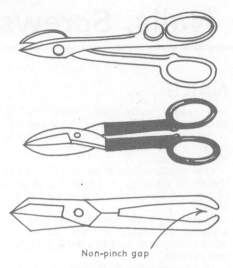

Non-pinch gap

Three kinds of snips.

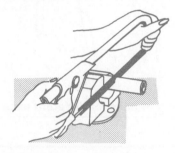

Hacksaw work should be firmly clamped in a vice. Make a nick with a triangular file to start the cut.

Snips

To cut thin sheet metal, you can use snips—not kitchen scissors, which will not be tough enough for the job. (You will only ruin them, too).

Snips are like scissors in appearance, with short blades and curved rather than looped handle-ends. Use them carefully with a scissors action, and take care not to nip the palm of your hand between the ends of the handles.

For clean cutting stop each cut before the jaws are fully closed. If you take full cuts you will produce a series of burrs or jagged edges. Be careful when handling sheet metal, as any edge can give you a nasty cut.

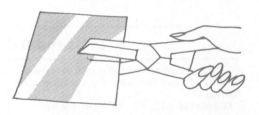

Above: Stop each cut with a pair of snips before the jaws are fully closed. Otherwise the cutting line will be full of burrs and jagged edges (below).

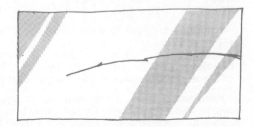

Nails, Screws, Nuts & Bolts

NAILS

Use **round nails** (wire nails) for all general nailing jobs where the wood size is generous, and there is little danger of splitting. The round-head provides good holding power.

Oval nails where there is a chance of the wood splitting, or where it is desired to hide the head below the surface of the wood.

Panel pins or **hardboard pins** for securing hardboard or ply panels to wooden frames or wood backing. Tacks are **not** suitable.

Hardened nails for driving into plaster.

For special jobs, use special nails—lath nails for laths, floorboard nails for floorboards, large-headed galvanised nails for attaching roofing felt.

Use ordinary steel nails for interiors, galvanised nails for all exteriors.

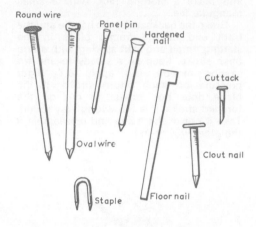

A variety of nails for different uses.

Standard Nail Sizes

Round nails. The most useful sizes will probably be 1 in., 1¼ in., 1½ in., 2 in. and 3 in. A ½ lb. of each provides a good basic stock.

Length	¾ in.	1 in.	1¼ in.	1½ in.	1¾ in.	2 in.
*Diameter	16, 17, 18	14, 15, 16	14, 15	12, 13, 14	12, 13, 14	10, 11, 12
Length	2¼ in.	2½ in.	3 in.	3½ in.	4 in.	10 in.
*Diameter	10, 11	9, 10, 11	8, 9, 10	7, 8	6, 7	⅜ in.

Oval nails. Most useful sizes—½ in. (2 oz.), ¾ in. (2 oz.), and ½ lb. each of 1 in., 1½ in., 2 in., 3 in. and 4 in.

Length	½ in.	¾ in.	1 in.	1¼ in.	1½ in.	1¾ in.
*Shank	16×20	15×19	14×18	13×17	12×16	11×15
Length	2 in.	2¼ in.	2½ in.	3 in.	3½ in.	up to 6 in.
*Shank	10×14	9×13	8×12	6×10	5×9	2×6

Panel pins. Easier to drive down flush than oval nails to hide the heads. Buy a ¼ lb. or ½ lb. at a time.

Length	½ in.	⅝ in.	¾ in.	1 in.	1¼ in.	1½ in.	2 in.
*Diameter	18	18, 19	17, 18	16, 17	16, 17	15, 16	14

*These numbers refer to standard wire gauge sizes.

Hardboard pins. These may be of square section, copper coated and thus rust-resistant. Sold in packets. Or use gimp pins or panel pins ¾ in. or 1 in. long (17 gauge preferred). Recommended spacing is 4 in. to 6 in., and approximately ½ in. in from edge of board.

Softboard pins. For building or insulating boards up to ½ in. thick, use 1¼ in. or 1½ in. round nails. For thicker boards use 2 in. nails or longer. Do not use oval nails or panel pins with softboards, as the heads will not provide sufficient grip.

USING SCREWS EFFICIENTLY

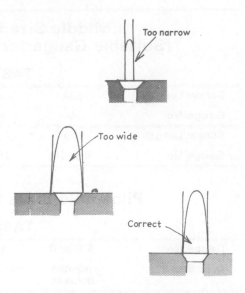

Too narrow

Too wide

Correct

1. Choose a suitable length for the job. For instance, if you are screwing a hardboard panel to a wooden frame, choose a length that allows the screw to penetrate about half-way into the frame, or at least half an inch, whichever is the greater.

2. Choose a suitable diameter for the strength required. If in doubt, use a middle size. (See Table 2 under *Woodscrew Sizes*)

3. If inserting the screw near the edge of a hardboard or ply panel, or in thin wood, or in any size of **hard** wood, first drill a pilot hole to take the screw.

4. Use the right size (blade-width) of screwdriver. See Table 3. This is particularly important with larger screw sizes, or where the screw is being driven into hard wood.

5. When driving **brass** screws into **hard** wood, first dip the tip of the screw in grease. This will make it easier to drive home without the screw becoming tight and possibly shearing in half.

Make sure that the blade-width of the screwdriver is the right one for the screw.

WOODSCREW SIZES

TABLE 1

Gauge No.	4/0	3/0	2/0	0	1
Nominal Diameter	·054 in.	·057 in.	·060 in.	·063 in.	·066 in.
Gauge No.	2	3	4	6	8
Nominal Diameter	·080 in.	·094 in.	·108 in.	·136 in.	·164 in.
Gauge No.	10	12	14	16	18
Nominal Diameter	·192 in.	·220 in.	·248 in.	·276 in.	·304 in.
Gauge No.	20	22	24	26	28
Nominal Diameter	·332 in.	·360 in.	·388 in.	·416 in.	·444 in.

Note: woodscrews are specified by **length** and **gauge** number. The table above gives the actual diameter equivalents of gauge numbers. Thus a 1½ in. × 10 screw would have a nominal diameter of ·192 in. or approx. $\frac{1}{5}$ in.

Middle Size Woodscrews
(Suitable Gauge for Average purposes)

TABLE 2

Screw Length	$\frac{3}{8}$ in.	$\frac{1}{2}$ in.	$\frac{3}{4}$ in.	1 in.	$1\frac{1}{4}$ in.
Gauge No.	0	1 or 2	4	6 or 8	6 or 8
Screw Length	$1\frac{1}{2}$ in.	$1\frac{3}{4}$ in.	2 in.	$2\frac{1}{2}$ in.	3 in.
Gauge No.	8 or 10	10	10 or 12	12	12 or 14

Pilot-hole Sizes for Woodscrews

TABLE 3

Gauge No.	4/0 to 0	1	2	3, 4	5
Drill Size	pointed bradawl	bradawl	$\frac{1}{16}$ in.	$\frac{5}{64}$ in.	$\frac{3}{32}$ in.
Gauge No.	6	8	10	12	14	over 14
Drill Size	$\frac{7}{64}$ in.	$\frac{1}{8}$ in.	$\frac{1}{8}$ in.	$\frac{1}{8}$ in.	$\frac{5}{32}$ in.	$\frac{3}{16}$ in.

SELF-TAPPING SCREWS

Self-tapping screws are useful for gripping in holes drilled in hard materials, like thin sheet metal, especially where one side only of the work can be reached. The trick lies in drilling the right hole-size for the screw, so that it grips strongly and permanently, and at the same time is easy to screw home properly.

Self-tapping screws are identified by a number size. Use the table below to find suitable matching-hole sizes.

Screw No.	2	4	6
Suitable twist drill	$\frac{1}{16}$ in.	$\frac{5}{64}$ or $\frac{3}{32}$ in.	$\frac{7}{64}$ in.

Screw No.	7	8	10	12
Suitable twist drill	$\frac{1}{8}$ in.	$\frac{9}{64}$ in.	$\frac{5}{32}$ in.	$\frac{11}{64}$ in.

TACKLING STUCK SCREWS

A freeing oil or 'Plus Gas' is usually partially effective in loosening the grip of a screw stuck in metal, or a nut 'frozen' on to its bolt. To be more certain, leave the fluid for an hour to work on the rust.

If necessary try these more drastic methods:

Phillips-head Screws

There is a trick here which nearly always works. Use a plastic-handled Phillips screwdriver, locate in the screw-head and tap the end of the screwdriver sharply with a hammer. This will break the grip of the rust. Then the screw can be removed by unscrewing in the usual way.

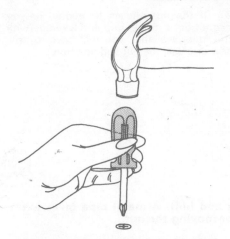

Freeing a rust-gripped Phillips-head screw by tapping the end of a screwdriver sharply with a hammer.

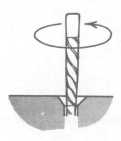

The two stages of taking out a large stuck screw. Above: Drilling a hole into the screw. Below: Using a screw extractor, inserted into the hole, to lift out the drilled screw.

Slotted-head Screws

Apply freeing oil generously so that it can penetrate under the head and on to the screw threads. Select a screwdriver with a large handle (such as the Cabinet type), and a blade-width which exactly matches the screw-head slot.

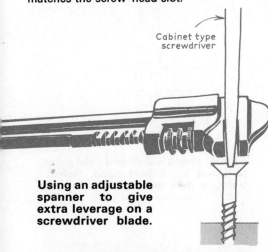

Cabinet type screwdriver

Using an adjustable spanner to give extra leverage on a screwdriver blade.

If you cannot turn the screw, grip the flat part of the screwdriver blade between the jaws of an adjustable spanner. The screw should then free with the extra leverage available.

If it does not—or the screw-head breaks—the screw will have to be drilled out. Alternatively, if it is a large screw you can drill a smaller hole down into the screw, then insert a screw extractor into the hole. Use a tap wrench on the square end of the extractor, and turn anti-clockwise to move the screw.

Screw extractors are like headless screws with an opposite-hand thread, made in specially hardened steel. They are relatively inexpensive, and available in various sizes.

Nuts and Bolts

Most 'frozen' nuts and bolts can be removed with a socket spanner set because this can usually provide sufficient leverage even to shear the bolt, if necessary. But socket spanner sets are expensive, and not usually part of a family tool set.

Again, try to get as much leverage as possible. The leverage of an ordinary spanner can be increased by slipping a length of metal piping over the end. Use freeing oil on the nut first, and note the following points:

1. The spanner used must exactly fit the nut. A sloppy fit is not good enough.

Equally, an adjustable spanner will not be suitable, for the same reason.

2. It will almost certainly be necessary to hold the bolt-head against rotating, using another spanner of the same size.

3. If the nut refuses to budge, or you cannot get a proper grip and leverage with the tools available, you will have to drill, saw or chisel the nut and bolt free.

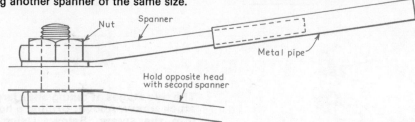

Using two spanners to free a stuck nut and bolt. A metal pipe gives extra leverage to the spanner moving the nut.

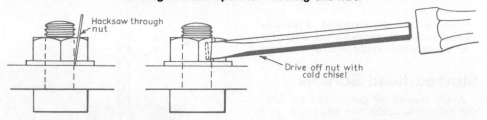

Tackling a seized-up nut and bolt from the nut side with a hacksaw and cold chisel.

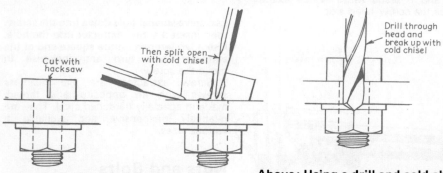

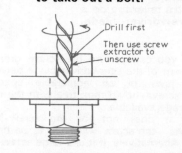

Above: Tackling a seized-up nut and bolt from the bolt head side with a hacksaw and cold chisel. Below: Cutting off a bolt head using a cold chisel and hammer only.

Above: Using a drill and cold chisel to break up a bolt head. Below: Using a drill and screw extractor to take out a bolt.

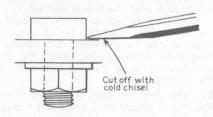

Materials & Their Uses

PAINTS

Primers

Primers can only be applied over clean, grease-free and bare surfaces. They will not work over old paint.

Use as a first coat. Remember that different primers are required for different materials. Primer is not essential for interior woodwork, but use pink primer for first-class work. Metallic wood primer for exterior woodwork.

Hardboard requires a hardboard sealer, otherwise subsequent paint-coats will soak in and leave a blotchy appearance.

Iron and steel need a red oxide primer, a high-zinc (galvanising) paint or aluminium paint.

Galvanised iron requires high-zinc paint or calcium primers.

Aluminium—use a light alloy etching primer, or the paint will not adhere.

Glass-fibre—special glass-fibre primer. Alternatively, sand the surface until all gloss is removed, and then go straight on to an undercoat paint.

Cement and plaster—cement and plaster primer, though you can start with undercoat on old plaster.

Undercoat

Apply an undercoat after the priming coat is completely dry.

Use thin paints of same colour as finish required. Apply two or more coats, sanding lightly between each coat to remove any surface imperfections. The undercoat must be a suitable type for the finish paint.

Jelly Paints

Thick, one-coat paints which do not drip, sag or run. Use over an undercoat or old paint surface rubbed down flat with sandpaper. Do not stir paint in the can, or attempt to brush out like ordinary paints.

Distempers

Low-cost finish for plaster walls and ceilings. Use soft, non-washable distempers for ceilings only—washable for walls (oil-free types best for new plaster). Oil-bound distempers are suitable for exterior work.

Emulsion paints are now generally preferred to distempers for interior work.

Cellulose Paints

Most useful for painting small articles. Do not apply over oil-bound paints, or mix with other paints. For best results, apply by spray. For brush work, use brushing cellulose paints where possible.

Cement Paints

Various types and colours for painting exterior concrete, etc.

Heat-resisting Paints

Use on boiler flues, fire surrounds, car-exhaust manifolds and other hot areas (radiators can take ordinary paints). Chief colours are black, red and aluminium.

Varnish

Slow-drying, clear high-gloss finish for applying to bare woodwork with a good colour and grain. Varnishing appreciably darkens the wood colour.

Emulsion Paints

Better than other types over plaster and plasterboard. Also suitable for interior woodwork, walls and ceilings.

Emulsion paints do not require a primer or undercoat and they are an excellent primer on absorbent surfaces to be finished in other paints. Less suitable for damp, steamy atmospheres, or for exterior work.

Gloss Paints

Modern household paints of this type are usually based on synthetic resins. Suitable for interior and exterior use. Apply only over a suitable undercoat.

Gloss or semi-gloss paints are better than emulsion paints for interior work in damp atmospheres.

Polyurethane Paints

Special type of synthetic resin paint, very durable and waterproof and high gloss. Two-part mixtures are most durable, but must be applied only over polyurethane primer and undercoats. One-shot polyurethane paints can be applied over ordinary undercoat.

Woodwork must be quite dry if painted with polyurethane, or paint will later tend to lift and peel. Apply second coat before the first coat has dried hard.

Synthetic Varnish

Fast drying, clear finish with very high gloss. Main types are polyurethane and polyester. Generally superior to traditional varnishes. Less darkening of the wood.

HOW MUCH PAINT TO USE

Use this table to estimate the amount of paint you require for any given job.

Type of paint	Typical covering power (brushed on)	
	1 gallon sufficient for sq. yd.	1 pint tin sufficient for sq. ft.
Primer:		
on wood	50–60	60
on plaster	50–55	55
on wallboard	40	40
on hardboard	30–40	35
on metal	60–80	70
Undercoat:		
on wood	55	55
on plaster	50–55	55
over primer	55–65	60
Gloss:		
over undercoat	50–70	60
Flat paint:		
over undercoat	60–75	65
Emulsion:		
on hardboard	30–40	35
other surfaces	80–120	90–120
Varnish:		
*first coat	50–70	60
other coats	70–100	75–100

*Thin down with equal part thinners

PLYWOODS

Standard plywood panels are 8 ft. by 4 ft., but ply can be cut to any smaller size required. Plywood thickness is always manufactured to millimetre sizes. Approximate equivalents are:

Specified mm thickness	3	4	5	6	7	8	9
Approx. inch equivalent	$\frac{1}{8}$	$\frac{5}{32}$	$\frac{13}{64}$	$\frac{1}{4}$	$\frac{9}{32}$	$\frac{5}{16}$	$\frac{23}{64}$

Specified mm thickness	9.5	10	13	19	25
Approx. inch equivalent	$\frac{3}{8}$	$\frac{25}{64}$	$\frac{1}{2}$	$\frac{3}{4}$	1

Practically all modern plywood is made with water-resistant glues. Here are three general classifications:

Unspecified or interior ply. For indoor use only.

Generally this is white wood, or sometimes mahogany. Avoid ply which has a thick core, and very thin-facing plies, if durability and strength are required.

Exterior grade. For interior or exterior use.

White to reddish, such as fir.

Marine. For interior or exterior use. Suitable for extreme exposure to damp. Mahogany only.

Plywood is suitable for the same purposes as hardboards, but is less suitable for exposure to damp unless of exterior or marine quality. It is generally stronger and less brittle than hardboard, and available in a wider range of thicknesses.

Use a sharp handsaw or tenon saw to

cut plywood. For curved cuts, a padsaw, coping saw or fretsaw.

Fasten with small wire nails, small oval nails or screws. For greatest strength and durability, use UF Resin glue and fastenings.

Finish with paint of any kind, or natural wood finish sealed, stained and polished, or varnished.

HARDBOARDS

Standard panels are usually 8 ft. by 4 ft., but you can normally buy any smaller size cut to the dimensions you require. Hardboard also comes in various thicknesses from $\frac{3}{32}$ in. up to $\frac{1}{2}$ in., but $\frac{1}{8}$ in. is the usual thickness stocked.

As a rule the finish is smooth one side, with a canvas texture on the other, but you can get hardboards with a smooth finish both sides. There are various types of hardboards suitable for different jobs.

Standard hardboards

Colours: from light brown to dark brown.

Suitable for: interior and exterior work. General panelling, furniture construction (on wood frames), door panels, tiling or covering floors.

Cut with: handsaw or tenon saw for straight and slightly curved cuts. Padsaw for sharp curves. Clean up edge with plane or Surform.

Fasten with: UF resin glue and/or hardboard pins.

Finish with: preliminary coat of hardboard sealer. Then undercoat or emulsion. Finish coat, or second coat of emulsion.

Medium hardboards

Colours: from dark brown to grey.

Suitable for: interiors only. Wall and ceiling panelling, general building construction, underlay for floor covering.

Cut with: handsaw or tenon saw.

Fasten with: as for standard hardboards.

Finish with: as for standard hardboards.

Super hardboards

Colours: dark brown.

Suitable for: bath panels, exteriors and flooring because it has good resistance to moisture and wear.

Cut with: handsaw or tenon saw. Padsaw for sharp curves. Clean up edge with plane or Surform.

Fasten with: as for standard hardboards.

Finish with: as for medium hardboards.

Pegboard

Suitable for: display panels, ventilation panels, vent panels.

Cut with: handsaw or tenon saw.

Fasten with: UF resin glue and/or hardboard pins.

Finish with: as for standard hardboards.

Enamelled hardboards

Suitable for: washable surface for partitions, splashbacks and bath panels.

Cut with: tenon saw.

Fasten with: UF resin glue and/or chrome-plated screws.

Finish with: none required.

Plastic-faced hardboards

Colours: All. Also grained and patterned.

Suitable for: partitions, splashbacks, bath panels, decorative washable panelling.

Cut with: tenon saw.

Fasten with: as for enamelled hardboards.

Finish with: none required.

Embossed hardboards

Colours: striated, fluted, grained and other decorative surfaces.

Suitable for: decorative panelling and partitions.

Cut with: handsaw or tenon saw.

Fasten with: UF resin glue and/or hardboard pins.

Finish with: as for standard hardboards.

SOFTBOARDS

The softboard type of panelling material is divided into two main types—wallboard and insulating board. All can be used for panelling walls, partitions and ceilings, but insulating board provides additional insulation against heat loss and sound. They are for interior use only.

Wallboard (homogeneous)

Use for: panelling walls, ceilings and partitions. As underlay for carpets or linoleum.
Standard sizes: length 6 ft. to 12 ft., width 3 ft. and 4 ft., thickness $\frac{5}{16}$ in. and $\frac{3}{8}$ in.
Cut with: fine-tooth saw or knife.
Fix with: wire nails.
Finish with: plaster or emulsion paint. If plaster, specify suitable sort of board.

Wallboard (laminated fibre)

Use for: panelling walls, ceilings and partitions.
Standard sizes: length 6 ft. to 12 ft., width 3 ft. and 4 ft., thickness $\frac{3}{16}$ in. and $\frac{1}{4}$ in.
Cut with: fine-tooth saw.
Fix with: wire nails.
Finish with: plaster or emulsion paint.

Insulating Board (homogeneous)

Use for: lining walls and ceilings. Thermal or acoustic insulation. Preventing condensation.
Standard sizes: length 6 ft. to 16 ft., width 2 ft., 3 ft., 4 ft. and 6 ft., thickness $\frac{1}{2}$ in. to 2 in.
Cut with: fine-tooth saw or knife.
Fix with: wire nails.
Finish with: plaster or emulsion paint.

Insulating Board (laminated)

Use for: lining walls and ceilings. Thermal and acoustic insulation.

Standard sizes: length 6 ft. to 12 ft., width 3 ft. and 4 ft., thickness $\frac{3}{16}$ in. and $\frac{3}{8}$ in.
Cut with: fine-tooth saw.
Fix with: wire nails.
Finish with: emulsion paint or plaster. If plaster, specify suitable type of board.

Insulating Board (bitumen bonded)

Use for: lining roofs—it has improved resistance to moisture.
Standard sizes: length 6 ft. to 12 ft., width 4 ft., thickness $\frac{1}{2}$ in. to $1\frac{1}{2}$ in.
Cut with: fine-tooth saw.
Fix with: wire nails.
Finish with: nothing.

Insulating Board) (bitumen impregnated)

Use for: jobs where maximum resistance to moisture is required.
Standard sizes: length 6 ft. to 16 ft., width 4 ft., thickness $\frac{1}{2}$ in.
Cut with: fine-tooth saw.
Fix with: wire nails.
Finish with: nothing or emulsion paint.

Acoustic Tiles

Use for: lining ceilings, and on walls where sound-deadening and/or thermal insulation is required.
Standard sizes: 12 in. by 6 in. up to 24 sq. in. Thickness $\frac{1}{2}$ in. to $1\frac{1}{4}$ in.
Cut with: very fine-tooth saw. Hot wire best for plastic tiles.
Fix with: suitable adhesive.
Finish with: nothing.

GLUES AND ADHESIVES

For gluing wood to wood, ply to wood, hardboard to wood. Use UF resin—powdered one-shot glue mixed with water. This is the best all-round glue for woodworking joints, except greasy woods. Waterproof. Follow instructions for mixing, and use carefully.

Or use PVA—white glue. Good general-purpose woodworking glue. Slow drying, non-staining. Not waterproof.

Or casein. Cheaper resin glue, which makes strong joints, but is not fully waterproof.

Laminated plastic panels to wood. Use impact or contact adhesive, which gives strong, permanent joints.

Wood veneer to wood. Use PVA, which is non-staining. Veneer will need clamping down flat while drying. Or try UF resin, which makes the strongest joint but will possibly stain. Clamp down veneer. With impact adhesive there is no chance of 'shuffling' the veneer once it is in place, but no clamping down is required. Smooth veneer with a roller.

Paper to wood or hardboard. Use a wallpaper adhesive for large areas. PVA is very suitable, but more costly. Try Cow Gum for attaching patterns—they can be peeled off when you like—or office gum for small areas.

Paper to plaster or plasterboard. Wallpaper adhesive is best.

Porcelain tiles. Use tile cement. Impact adhesive is useful for refitting loose tiles.

Plastic tiles. Use the adhesive specified by the manufacturer. Impact adhesive is all right for quick repairs, but check that the adhesive does not attack the material.

Repairs

Hard, brittle plastics. Use epoxy resin adhesive for permanent repairs. Impact or general-purpose adhesives make semi-permanent repairs.

Thermoplastics. Use a matching plastic cement, or a suitable solvent. Unglueable thermoplastics can often be welded together by using a hot smoothing iron.

Pottery, china or porcelain. Epoxy resin adhesive or a general-purpose rubber-base adhesive produces strong, permanent joints, though the joint-line usually shows as a discolouration.

Cracks in wash-basins. Use polyester resin to apply a bandage-type pack of glass-fibre over crack on underside of basin.

Metal articles. Epoxy resin adhesive produces strong, permanent joints, or consider mechanical repair with rivets, or by soldering.

Glassware. Use epoxy resin adhesive, but joint-line will show.

Glass roofing. Use polyester resin and glass-fibre bandage strip. Apply to clean, dry glass along line of crack. Permanent but ugly repair.

Be prepared

Suggested stock adhesives to meet most requirements.

1. **Tin of UF resin, for all woodworking joints.**
2. **Squeeze-bottle of PVA white glue.**
3. **Packet of wallpaper adhesive.**
4. **Tube or tin of Impact or Contact adhesive.**
5. **Tube of general-purpose (rubber-base) adhesive—interior type for non-porous surfaces. Another for exterior use.**
6. **Epoxy resin adhesive. Separate tubes of resin and hardener.**

163

Plumbing

Instead of large and unsightly lead pipes emerging from the walls and running to sinks and basins, modern plumbing consists of smaller bore copper tubing joined together and connected to equipment by compression joints.

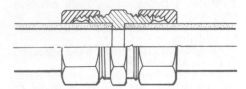

A common type of compression joint.

These pipe-runs stand free from the walls and are thus at 'room temperature', so they do not need protection against frost unless they run in unheated areas, like the loft, or are outside pipes.

IN THE LOFT

The main centre of the plumbing system is in the loft, so it pays to insulate lofts in order to prevent freeze-ups. Insulation will also keep the whole interior of the house warmer by preventing heat loss through the loft and roof. The pipes and the cold water storage tank should receive further treatment.

Pipes in the loft should be properly lagged, either with special insulating wrappings or shaped polystyrene covers, or else tightly bound with strips of sacking wound in place like a spiral bandage and tied in position with string at suitable intervals. Sacking is usually the simplest and cheapest material.

The tank needs insulating on the sides and top only. Leave the underside open, as warm air rising through the roof will help keep the tank warm.

There are two basic methods of insulating a tank. You can either use insulating

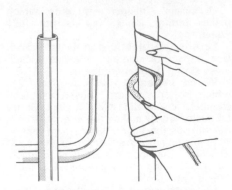

Lagging pipes with (left) shaped polystyrene covers and (right) insulating wrappings.

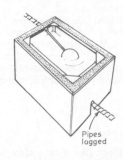

Pipes lagged

Water tank fitted with an insulating box. The top is covered with a tray of insulating material.

blankets or tank covers tied in place, or else build a hardboard or ply box around the tank, leaving a two-to-three-inch space which can be filled with vermiculite or shredded polystyrene.

In the latter case, make a separate shallow tray to rest on top of the box containing the filling to insulate the top of the tank. This tray can then easily be lifted off should you ever need to get to the inside of the tank.

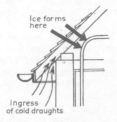

Pipes in the loft can be affected by cold draughts. Sources of draught should be blocked.

While in the loft, block sources of cold draughts from the outside as well. This can make your pipe-lagging doubly effective. In very cold weather, leave the trap door to the loft slightly open to allow heat from the house to enter the loft.

Two methods of insulating the loft. Above: With glass fibre lengths between the joists. Below: With packaged in-filling in the joist spaces.

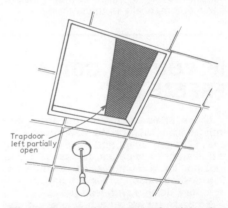

The loft can be warmed with air from the house by leaving the trapdoor slightly open.

All outside taps and the exposed pipes leading to them should be lagged. Strips of sacking or carpet underlay can be used, but will become waterlogged if left exposed. Ideally, such lagging should be fitted with a waterproof cover, such as a binding of polythene sheeting.

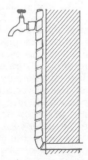

HOT-WATER TANK

The hot-water tank will be situated in an airing cupboard. This also needs covering with an insulating blanket or

Lag all exposed pipes leading to outside taps.

special 'jacket' made to fit the tank. The object this time is to reduce heat loss from the tank.

You can leave a small area of the top of the tank exposed to keep the cupboard warm, but usually sufficient warm air for airing purposes comes from the exposed pipe at the bottom of the tank, which should not be lagged.

If the house has central heating there will be a mixer valve on or near the boiler. Set one way, this valve will direct most of the hot water through the pipes to the radiators. The other way, it will direct most of the hot water to the hot taps.

Before going to bed, turn the heat control down to a low setting, and the mixer valve to direct hot water, to the taps. This will give minimum heat loss through the pipes overnight. You can get even better economy by having a time-switch installed which switches off the hot-water supply at night and switches it on again automatically in the morning.

IF YOU DO GET A FREEZE-UP

If the pipes *do* freeze, the usual first indication is that no water flows from a tap. Leave the tap open, and trace back along the length of pipe as far as you can, looking for a compression joint which has pushed open, or for a bulge or split if you are dealing with lead pipes.

You will not get an actual leak until the pipe unfreezes, so if you can find the affected area first and repair it, so much the better. If not, or you are faced with a burst, isolate that pipe by turning off the appropriate stopcock.

To unfreeze a pipe, wrap with a towel or similar material soaked in hot water. This is particularly useful for frozen waste-pipes. In the case of an outside tap or pipe, you can pour hot water over it from a kettle.

Bursts are rare with copper piping installations, although occasionally there may be seepage at joints.

Freezing can also strain and open a joint. Quite often this can be stopped simply by re-tightening the nuts on the joint. If this is not effective, make a temporary repair by coating the joint with paint, and then wrapping tightly with a cloth bandage, finishing off with a final

Hot water poured over cloth

Unfreezing a pipe with a cloth and hot water.

wrapping of waterproof insulating tape if the water seeps through the cloth.

For a permanent repair, isolate the pipe by turning off the right stopcock so that you can disassemble the joint completely, replace the little ring-shaped 'olives' and then re-assemble the joint tightly.

With lead piping, you will be repairing a split in the pipe-wall. You can try the same treatment as above for a temporary repair, after first using a hammer to close the split as tightly as possible. A permanent repair is a job for a competent plumber.

LOCATING STOPCOCKS

The incoming water supply from the mains is controlled by two stopcocks. One is an outside stop valve, usually located under a small manhole in the pavement outside, and the second is inside the house.

You should know the position of the second stopcock, as this is the one you normally use to shut off the water supply to the house. The outside stop valve is the responsibility of the water authority, and should not be touched by a householder except in the sort of emergency where you need to turn off the water supply in a hurry, and cannot locate the inside stopcock.

Turning off the supply by the inside stopcock means that no more water will flow from the mains to the house, but the cold-water storage tank will still be full of water. To isolate this tank from the

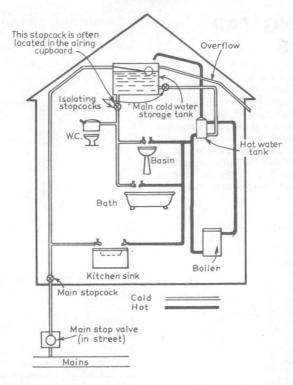

Labels on diagram:
This stopcock is often located in the airing cupboard
Overflow
Isolating stopcocks
Main cold water storage tank
W.C.
Hot water tank
Basin
Bath
Boiler
Kitchen sink
Main stopcock
Cold
Hot
Main stop valve (in street)
Mains

A typical household water system, showing the likely position of stopcocks.

piping system there is usually another stopcock located near the tank, and possibly other stopcocks in other parts of the distribution system.

To work on disassembling any appliance connected directly to the plumbing, such as a tap, you must know which stopcock to close to isolate that appliance from the supply.

Our diagram can help, but remember:

1. The kitchen-sink cold-water tap is the only one fed directly from the mains (except in some older buildings). To isolate the kitchen tap it is thus only necessary to turn off the main stopcock.

2. Turning off the main stopcock will isolate the storage tank from a further supply of water. Drain the tank by turning on any cold-water tap other than the kitchen tap.

3. To work on any cold tap other than the kitchen tap, you need only turn off the stopcock in the feed line from the cold-water tank.

If you cannot find the stopcock which isolates the main cold-water tank from the internal piping—many houses do not have one—you can fit a temporary plug in the tank outlet. A length of broomstick with the end carved to a taper shape to fit the outlet is handy for this.

Otherwise, to work on cold-water taps you will have to turn off the main stopcock and drain the tank.

4. The hot-water system is on a separate circuit. In most systems there is a stopcock between the feed line from the cold-water tank to the hot tank. This is the one to close to work on a hot tap, but **be sure to open it again after the job is finished.**

5. If you cannot find a stopcock on the water supply to the hot tank, you will have to isolate the main tank by closing the main stopcock and draining the whole system (both hot and cold water). Normal supply should then be restored as soon as possible.

167

REPLACING TAP WASHERS

To replace washers in old-style taps, first isolate the tap by turning off the appropriate stopcock. Then:

1. Undo the small inset screw under the tap handle, remove the handle and unscrew the outer cover with a wrench. This will reveal a large nut, which is undone with a spanner. This discloses the 'jumper', which can be pulled out. Some may be held in place with a split pin which must be removed first.

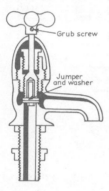

Grub screw

Jumper and washer

Cross-section of an older type of tap.

2. Undo the nut on the 'jumper', and remove the old washer. Replace with a new washer, then re-assemble the tap in the reverse order.

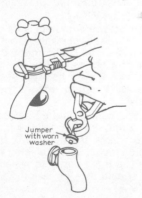

Jumper with worn washer

Most modern taps can be re-washered without having to turn off a stopcock to isolate the tap.

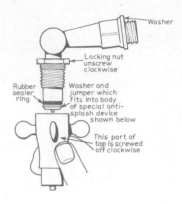

Washer

Locking nut unscrew clockwise

Rubber sealer ring

Washer and jumper which fits into body of special anti-splash device shown below

This part of tap is screwed off clockwise

The parts of a modern tap.

1. Partially open the nozzle, and undo the top nut.

2. Undo the nozzle completely. Water will first escape from the tap, but stop completely as the nozzle is fully unscrewed. You now have the nozzle unit detached to work on.

3. Projecting from the bottom of the nozzle you will see a small anti-splash fitting. Press this upwards to loosen, then turn the tap upside down, so that this unit and the 'jumper' will fall out of the tap. Remove the 'jumper', and replace with a new one.

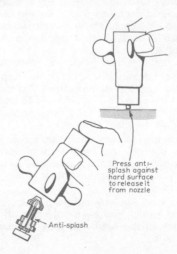

Press anti-splash against hard surface to release it from nozzle

Anti-splash

4. Re-assemble the tap, taking care that the anti-splash unit is properly located, and then screw the nozzle back in place, finally tightening the top nut.

LEAKING OVERFLOW

The main cold-water storage tank has an overflow pipe running out through the roof. Normally this pipe is above tank-water level, and if water does drip or flow from this pipe it is usually an indication of trouble at the tank ball-valve, allowing the water level in the tank to rise too high. Go up into the loft, take the top off the tank and have a look at what is happening inside the tank.

Ball valves

The ball valve works like this:
A hollow ball on a long arm floats on the surface of the water in the tank. As the water level rises in the tank, the lever movement reaches a point where it closes a valve on the tank inlet so that no more water will flow into the tank.
If water is drawn off, the water level will fall and with it the ball, opening the valve and allowing more water to flow from the mains into the tank until the original level is reached and the valve is closed again.
If the valve does not work properly, the water level will continue to rise past its proper point, and eventually run out through the overflow pipe. Check the following possibilities:
1. Punctured ball. The ball will not float properly if it is punctured. Check by unscrewing the ball from the end of the lever and shaking it. If there is water inside the ball, replace it with a plastic one
2. Damaged valve washer. The arm carrying the ball is held at the other end by a split pin. Remove this pin, and withdraw the arm. You can then withdraw the piston from the valve, and examine the washer. If damaged, screw off the head of the piston and fit a new washer.
Sometimes the cause of a leaky valve is dirt or grit between the washer and valve seat, so clean if necessary as well as, or instead of, replacing the washer.

3. Not enough pressure on the valve. In this case pressure can be increased by bending the arm gently downwards, but **avoid putting force on the valve itself.** Use two adjustable spanners to apply leverage to bend the arm slightly, as shown in the diagram.

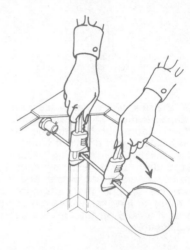

You can do this without turning off the mains stopcock, as even if the valve is completely disassembled excess water supply will merely escape through the overflow pipe. This will save several journeys between the loft and the downstairs stopcock to check whether or not your adjustments are producing the required result.
When working properly, the ball valve should shut off the main water supply completely when the water level in the tank is about an inch below the overflow pipe. If you cannot achieve this with the treatments described above, call in a professional plumber, as you may need a new valve unit.

BLOCKED WASTE PIPES

The kitchen sink and the bathroom basin are the two most likely to become blocked with waste in the drain pipes.
1. Simple blockage due to accumulation of food waste, grease or hair can usually be cleared by flushing with a jug of hot

water in which is dissolved a cup of washing soda. Repeat two or three times if necessary. If this does not work:

2. Fill the sink with water, place a rubber force cup over the drain hole and pump up and down vigorously, holding the handle in both hands. If *that* does not work:
3. Try mechanical cleaning. Place a bucket under the U-bend beneath the sink to collect water and waste, and then unscrew the plug at the bottom of the bend using a file, screwdriver or some similar tool locked on the lugs, as shown in the diagram.

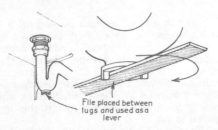

File placed between lugs and used as a lever

If the sink empties at once, the blockage is in the pipe from the U-bend onwards. Clear whichever length of pipe is affected by poking a length of fairly stiff wire through it. Use galvanised iron wire, or a special coiled flexible wire cleaner.

If the blockage is near the opening in the bottom of the U-bend, use thin wire to *pull* the waste out through the hole, rather than try to *push* it farther down the pipe.

LAVATORY BLOCKINGS

Lavatory blockages may need slightly different treatment. Instead of soda water, use caustic soda for a preliminary treatment and a wire-handled cleaning brush. Take care not to splash caustic on your hands or face. Then use stiff wire, if necessary, to pull out paper or tissue waste.

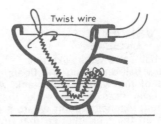

Twist wire

Using a stiff wire to pull out a paper or tissue blockage in the toilet bend.

Sometimes the blockage may be farther down the system, so that even with the U-bend cleared the lavatory pan still fills with water when the cistern is flushed and drains only very slowly. In that case it may be necessary to rod through the drains.

HOW A CISTERN WORKS

Lavatory cisterns vary in design, but filling is controlled by a floating ball-and-valve assembly like that in the main cold-water storage tank. Similar faults can develop, allowing a continual seepage of water through the overflow pipe which passes through the outside wall of the house.

In addition, there is a handle (operated

either with or without a chain) attached to a plunger fitted into a dome-shaped bell inside the cistern.

When the handle is operated, the plunger is lifted, water is sucked under the lip of the bell into the pipe leading to the lavatory pan, and continues to siphon through until the cistern is nearly empty and the siphon is 'broken'. The cistern then refills through the delivery pipe and its valve.

The mechanism should give little trouble provided the cistern is cleared out regularly —say once a year. Isolate the cistern by turning off the stopcock on the outflow of the main cold-water tank, drain the cistern by flushing and take the whole mechanism to pieces for cleaning. It comes apart quite easily.

If necessary, you can adjust the water level by bending the ball arm gently, and sometimes trouble is caused by the arm fouling the bell or the sides of the cistern. That again you can adjust by bending gently, but avoid putting any load on the valve itself.

CLEARING DRAINS

Outside drains need occasional attention. Surface drains are accessible through grid covers and manholes, both of which can be removed and debris flushed away with a hose. Lavatory drains are always covered by manholes which would normally not be lifted unless there is a definite blockage which needs attention.

Blocked drains can only be cleared by rodding, using a series of canes which fit or screw together to form a long, flexible rod. The drain passages are exposed by lifting the manhole cover, the end of the rod inserted and the length of rod pushed through, using a push-pull motion.

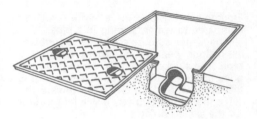

A manhole cover removed to show the drain below.

Some properties have only one manhole, several houses being linked together in the drainage system. In this case the obstruction may have to be cleared backwards or forwards along the piping routes, working from the manholes of neighbouring houses.

If lifting a manhole cover reveals a flooded manhole, then there is a definite blockage, and if the next manhole in line is empty, the blockage is between the two. If both are full, then the blockage is after the second one in the run.

Where the run can be inspected by a series of manholes, therefore, it is possible to locate the position of the blockage, provided the direction of the run is clearly established. The flow is from the house to the main drain.

Clearing drains can be an unpleasant job, as well as requiring rods for the job. Unless there is an emergency, it is usually best to call in professional assistance.

Electricity In The Home

Electricity flowing in a wire can be compared to water flowing in a pipe.

The water current could be thought of as gallons per second going through a pipe. The thicker the pipe the more water goes through with the same pressure. It is the same with electricity—the thicker the **wire** the more electricity it will let through for the same **voltage**.

● Remember—thick wires pass more **amps** than thin wires.

The mains pressure (voltage) is constant. The appliance determines how much electricity is used. The easier it is for the electricity to flow through the appliance the more will flow, and the more power (watts) will be produced. This power can be used to produce light, heat, motion, sound and so on, depending on the purpose of the appliance.

Volts

The volts in electricity are the pushing force behind the electrons flowing along the wire. With water this would be the pressure pushing it along the pipe.

Amperes (amps)

Amps are the amount of electrons getting along the wire per second. Another word for amps is **current**.

Watts

Electric power is measured in **watts**. One thousand of these are called a **kilowatt** (kW.). Every appliance—even a light bulb—should have its power marked on it.

To obtain this power, a **current** of electricity flows through a wire from the supply to the appliance, through the appliance to do its job, and back to the supply again in a second wire. These two wires are combined in one **cable**.

Mains **voltage** (usually 240/250v), **power** (watts) and **current** (amps) are linked by a simple rule:

$$\text{Volts} \times \text{amps} = \text{watts}$$
From which:
$$\text{Amps} = \text{watts} \div \text{volts}$$

For example, a one bar electric fire has a power of one kilowatt (1,000 watts). From a supply of 250 volts it will draw a current of:

$$1,000 \div 250 \text{ volts}$$

Which is 4 amps.

Units

The **unit** of electricity, on which your bill is based, is the amount of electricity needed to produce one kilowatt of power for one hour. It is called a **kilowatt-hour**.

A kilowatt bar fire uses one unit in one hour of continuous operation. A two bar fire uses two units per hour—or one unit in half an hour. A 100 watt bulb uses one-tenth of a unit in an hour—or one unit in ten hours.

The power consumption of various appliances, together with their current, and the cost of running per hour (at 2d. per unit for the sake of argument) is shown in the table.

Electric power points

15-amp round-pin sockets.

The fuse for each individual point should be found in one of the fuse-boxes near the meter (usually under the stairs). Each point will take up to 3,000 watts (3 kW.).

5-amp round-pin sockets.

These may be wired together and fed through one 5-amp fuse in the fuse-box, or be provided with individual 5-amp fuses in the box. Each point will take up to 1,000 watts (1 kW.).

2-amp round-pin sockets.

These are usually wired together and fed through one 5-amp fuse in the fuse-box, or connected directly to the lighting wiring. Each point can take up to 500 watts ($\frac{1}{2}$ kW.).

APPLIANCES AND RUNNING COSTS

Appliance	Power (Watts)	Current (Amps)	Cost per hour
Clock, doorbell	$\frac{1}{2}$	$\frac{1}{480}$	$\frac{1}{1000}$d.
Lamp—very dim	20	$\frac{1}{12}$	$\frac{1}{24}$d.
Lamp—dim	40	$\frac{1}{6}$	$\frac{1}{12}$d.
Lamp—medium	60	$\frac{1}{4}$	$\frac{1}{8}$d.
Lamp—bright	100	$\frac{2}{5}$	$\frac{1}{5}$d.
Lamp—very bright	150	$\frac{5}{8}$	$\frac{3}{8}$d.
Radio Record player Radiogram	60	$\frac{1}{4}$	$\frac{1}{8}$d.
Television Tape recorder Guitar amplifier	90	$\frac{3}{8}$	$\frac{3}{16}$d.
Electric blanket	110	$\frac{1}{2}$ approx.	$\frac{1}{4}$ d.
Food mixer	250	1	$\frac{1}{2}$ d.
Drill	300	$1\frac{1}{4}$	$\frac{5}{8}$d.
Vacuum cleaner Bowl fire Small one-bar fire One glass-type infra-red bar Non-steam iron One-element toaster (non-pop-up)	750	3	$1\frac{1}{2}$d.
Small wash boiler Large one-bar fire Slow kettle Small immersion heater Steam iron Washing machine (no heater)	1,000 (1 kW.)	4	2d.
Two small fire bars Two infra-red fire bars	1,500 ($1\frac{1}{2}$ kW.)	6	3d.
Large two-bar fire Medium immersion heater Medium speed kettle	2,000 (2 kW.)	8	4d.
Three-element toaster (pop-up) Small three-bar fire Infra-red three-bar fire	2,250 ($2\frac{1}{4}$ kW.)	9	$4\frac{1}{2}$d.
Fast boiling kettle	2,750 ($2\frac{3}{4}$ kW.)	11	$5\frac{1}{2}$d.
Large three-bar fire Large (bath) immersion heater Ten-gallon wash boiler Washing machine with water heater Large convector fire Small plug-in cooker	3,000 (3 kW.)	12	6d.
Fixed cooker	Up to 7,000 (7 kW.)	Up to 28	Up to 1s. 2d.

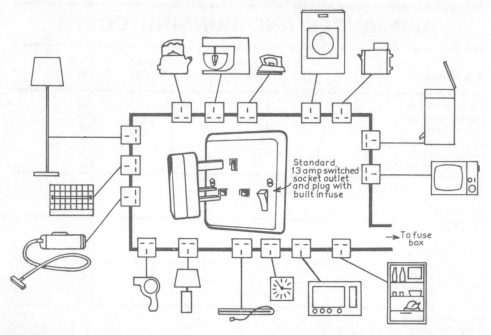

Standard 13 amp switched socket outlet and plug with built in fuse

To fuse box

Appliances which can be run from 13-amp flat-pin sockets on a ring circuit. Fuses which match the appliances' current rating (see table) are fitted in the plug.

Lighting points.

Wall lights, ceiling lights and wall switches are usually wired together and fed in sections—often floor by floor in the building—with a 5-amp fuse for each section in a fuse-box near the meter.

13-amp flat-pin sockets.

These sockets are wired in a ring circuit, and do not have individual fuses at the fuse-box. Each point is joined to the next, and the two ends of the circuit are brought to one pair of terminals in the fuse-box, and fed by a 30-amp fuse. Most houses would have one ring circuit per floor.

It is the most up-to-date system and it is easier to add new points to a ring circuit.

The important difference between this system and others is that each appliance has its own fuse inside its plug. The fuses are available in values up to 13 amps, and each appliance requires a fuse just a little higher in current value than the current that the appliance normally uses (see table).

Although the ring circuit is an excellent system, there are two points where it tends to fall down in operation.

1. Every plug is sold fitted with a 13-amp fuse, which makes people tend to fit 13-amp fuses to every appliance. **This can be dangerous**. If a flex for a low-powered appliance is designed to carry only 5 amps safely, it can overheat and catch fire should a fault occur in the appliance which causes the full 13 amps to flow in the thin flex.

To combat this it is necessary to know the current that the appliance uses (see table) and to ask the electrical shop to provide you with a fuse just above this value in exchange for the fuse in the new plug when you buy it. To be on the safe side, keep a stock of fuses of lower value than 13 amps for the appliances that need them.

2. Many of 13-amp adaptors for flat-pin plugs do not contain a fuse, but only a warning, in small letters, not to put a load of more than 13 amps on the adaptor. To the unknowing this means little, but these adaptors enable a total current of up to 26 amps to be taken from one socket. Should this happen the socket will become dangerously overheated, and soon need replacing.

These two situations can be avoided if you:
● *Fit fuses of the right current value to the plugs.*
● *Avoid using adaptors unless they have the word 'fused' written on them.*

TO REPLACE A FUSE IN A 13-AMP PLUG

Tool needed : Screwdriver.
1. Take off plug-lid by removing retaining screws.
2. Pull out blown cartridge fuse from contact clips.
3. Replace with correct fuse according to the current required by the appliance. (See section on 13-amp flat-pin sockets.)

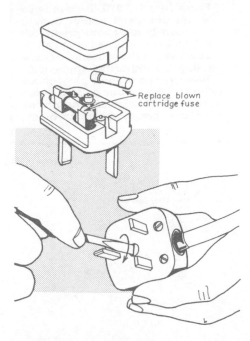

Replace blown cartridge fuse

4. Replace plug-lid and tighten screws.
5. Check that the appliance is no longer at fault before plugging it in again
6. Some plugs are fitted with a small plastic trapdoor in the base which is opened by the thumb-nail so that the fuse can be instantly changed.

TO FIX A PLUG ON TO A FLEX

Tools needed : Small screwdriver, sharp knife or scissors, wire-cutters or patent wire-strippers.
1. Take off plug-lid by removing retaining screws.
2. Inside the plug are brass screws where the wires of the flex are connected. There will be two or three, depending on whether the plug is two-pin or three-pin.
3. If your plugs are two-pin, and the appliance has a three-core flex, it may not be safe to use it with a two-pin plug. If the appliance has a casing wholly or partly made of metal, it must be earthed by the means of the third wire connected to the earth pin of a three-pin plug. This is the pin that is missing from two-pin systems so two-pin plugs should only be used on appliances with non-metal cases, or those which are double insulated.
4. Using the knife or scissors, carefully trim back the outer protective covering of the flex to reveal about $2\frac{1}{2}$ in. of the coloured cores. Take care not to damage them.
5. Using the wire-cutters or patent wire-strippers, trim about $\frac{3}{4}$ in. of the rubber or plastic covering from the ends of the coloured wires. If you damage the wire strands when doing this, start again, because the wire can overheat if some of the strands are not used.

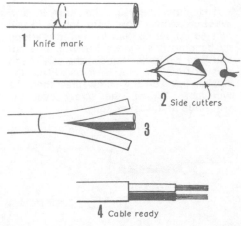

1 Knife mark

2 Side cutters

3

4 Cable ready

6. Connect the wires according to this table. (The pins are marked on the plug L for live, N for neutral and E for earth):

	2 wires: both the same colour	2 wires: red and black
Pin L	Either	Red
Pin N	Either	Black
Pin E	Leave blank	Leave blank

	3 wires: red black and green	3 wires: brown, blue and green— with-yellow
Pin L	Red	Brown
Pin N	Black	Blue
Pin E	Green	Green–with– yellow

There are two types of terminal screws in plugs. One is the **clamp screw**, where the bare end of the wire is twisted up and bent double before being pushed into a small hole below the screw. The screw is then tightened on to the doubled-up bare end to make a solid connection, thus:

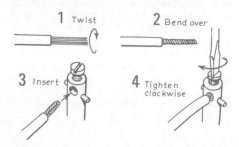

The other type is the **screw and washer**, where the wire-end is again twisted up, but is then formed into a loop by bending it around a screwdriver shaft and back on itself. Remove the screw and washer from the plug terminal. Place the washer back on the screw first, then the wire-loop. Tighten the screw over the wire-loop and washer, thus:

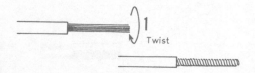

EUROPEAN COLOUR CODING

British colour coding

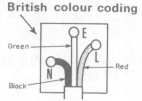

European colour coding

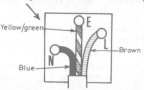

From July 1, 1970, Britain is to use the European colour coding of brown-blue-yellow/green for electrical wiring. The coding eliminates the potential hazard of connecting up imported appliances. Before connecting a plug, check whether the colour coding being used is the European one or the old British one of red-green-black.

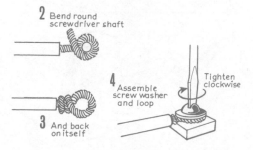

The screw and washer connection is electrically more sound, but the clamp screw is adequate.

7. If the plug is fitted with a cord grip, which is a strap of fibre or plastic designed to prevent the flex being pulled out of the plug accidentally, this is tightened over the beginning of the flex covering, **not** the coloured wires, thus:

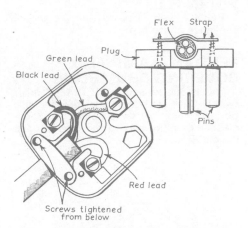

Wiring a three-point plug. (Wires are in the old British colours).

8. If the plug is equipped with a fuse, this must be snapped into its contacts. To check its value see under **13-amp flat-pin sockets**.

9. Replace lid on plug. Tighten screws securely.

TO MEND A FUSE

Tools needed: Screwdriver, fusewire, torch (for lights fuses).

1. Switch off the mains at the fuse-box. Modern fuse-boxes are clearly marked **on** and **off**, and the normal rule is **up** for **off**, **down** for **on**. Some older, cast-iron boxes have a lever at one side. These usually work the opposite way—**up** for **on**, **down** for **off**. If you have a large number of different fuses and boxes they should be labelled.

2. Open the fuse-box. The lid is usually released by the removal of one or more screws.

3. Inside are plastic or china fuse-holders plugged into the box. These have to be withdrawn, and examined one at a time. Withdraw a fuse-holder and look at it. If there is a complete fuse-wire connected between two terminal screws, that fuse has not blown, and must be replaced in the box. If there are signs that the fuse-wire

has melted, indicated by a sooty and coppery mark on the holder, the fuse has blown.

4. Loosen the terminal screws, remove the remaining parts of the old fuse-wire and clean up the fuse-holder.

5. Fit new fuse-wire of the **correct** thickness. Whether the thickness is for 5, 15, 20 or 30 amps is marked on the fuse-holder. Make sure you keep a stock of fuse-wire of all the grades for the fuses you have. Use only one strand of fuse-wire, and connect the terminal screws in the same way as on a plug, thus:

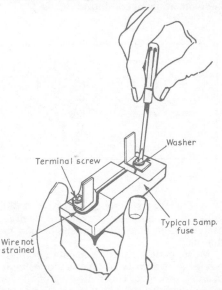

Look at an adjacent similar fuse to check your work.

7. If possible, remove the cause of the blow. Fuse-blowing is mainly caused by:

● *Faulty flex or wiring, causing the live and neutral wires to touch.*

● *Too much load on the fuse. See that the point served by the fuse is not being used by an appliance of too high a power, or by too many appliances adding up to too high a power.*

● *'Blown' bulbs or elements.*

8. Replace the fuse-box lid and switch on the supply again.

9. Some fuse-boxes are now equipped with spare fuses which can be used to replace blown ones immediately. The blown fuses can be mended at your leisure. Or you can lay in a spare supply of fuses for such emergencies.

The Electric Meter

All electric current entering a building has to be measured, in order to be charged for, by the Electricity Board. That is the purpose of the meter, which is situated close to the fuse-boxes—usually under the stairs.

On the front of the meter there are a number of small pointers and dials which show how many units have been used. The unit of electric power is the kilowatt-hour, and each dial shows ten-thousands, thousands, hundreds, tens and ones of kilowatt-hours according to its label:

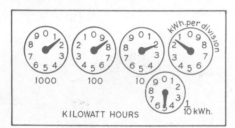

In the diagram the reading is 1,822 units. Unless a needle is exactly on a digit, the next digit below the needle is read for that dial.

Most meters have adjacent pointers going in opposite rotations for simple gearing, so this must be watched for when reading individual dials. Disregard the dial for one tenth of a unit.

When your meter is read by the electricity man, he puts down the reading and takes away the previous bill's reading from it. This gives the number of units used since the last bill. For instance:

Reading in December: 2,849 units
Reading in March: 4,061 units
Amount to be paid for: 1,212 units

This method is used because meters cannot be wound back to zero at each reading.

You are normally charged for the number of units at a certain rate per unit. Added to this is the flat rate, or standing charge, for the quarter. For instance:

Flat rate December to March:	£2	
1,212 units at 2d. per unit	£10	2s.
TOTAL	£12	2s.

Common Electrical Faults

WORN FLEX

Replace with flex to suit power of appliance concerned.

PENDANT LAMP-FLEX COVERING CRUMBLING

This is due to lamp heat. Turn off main switch. Check that the lights are in fact off. Connect flex to lamp-holder in same manner as plug, and to the rose as was the old flex.

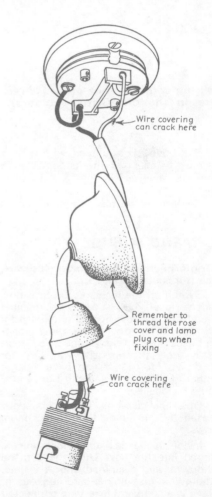

Wire covering can crack here

Remember to thread the rose cover and lamp plug cap when fixing

Wire covering can crack here

Remember to thread the rose-lid on to the new flex before making connections to the rose.

HOT PLUG

Usually occurs with high-power appliances. Caused by poor plug-to-wire or plug-to-socket contact. Re-connect flex if plug-to-wire contact is at fault. Fit a new socket if plug-to-socket contact is poor.

Open plug and examine for looseness at the terminals. Check socket by using a sound high-power appliance in it. If its plug overheats, the socket is at fault. Any fitting damaged by charring must be replaced.

FUSE BLOWN THROUGH OVERLOAD

This is caused by the incorrect use of adaptors or by a high current appliance plugged into a low current socket, resulting in too much current being demanded by the appliances plugged in. See table of current values for various appliances, and make sure they do not add up to more than the point is designed for. Have extra points fitted or re-distribute appliances if they are all required at the same time.

BLOWN FIRE BAR

Remove guard. Undo screws at each end of the element. Take old element to an electrical shop as a pattern, as there are many types. Fit new element in the reverse order. Keep reflectors clean and dust free.

Rules to Remember

1. **Use as few adaptors as possible.**
2. **Do not plug heavy current appliances into the lights or low current points.**
3. **Keep flexes as short as is convenient.**
4. **Keep flexes in one length from plug to appliance and avoid taped up joints.**
5. **Have installation checked for safety if over 10 years old.**

● *Sometimes new switches and plugs are fitted to old wires, so when you move in do not assume that their presence means the place has recently been re-wired. A better check is to see that you do not have an untidy set of varied fuse-boxes of antique design. The sign of a full re-wire is a neat, single fuse-box with one switch for all the dwelling's points and lights.*

Even with newer installations, the fittings with the greatest demand could need replacement, so a thorough check every so often by a competent electrician is advised.

(Also see **Electrical 'Shorts': a Warning** in **Emergency Repairs** Section.)

Central Heating

The term 'central heating' has become so loosely used that without qualification it no longer bears a specific meaning.

There are many types of house heating. Some are complete, others are partial heating systems. *True* central heating is an installation which maintains high temperatures (60–75°F or 16–24°C) throughout the house.

All heating systems fall into four main groups, based upon the choice of fuel. The four main fuels are:
- *Solid fuel (coke, anthracite, etc.).*
- *Gas.*
- *Oil (kerosene, gas oil).*
- *Electricity.*

Installation and running costs vary with the type of system. And different houses require different systems.

To find out which system is most suitable, each householder must take several factors into account.

1. How much of the house is to be heated? This will tell you whether you need full or only partial heating.

2. How large is the house? Certain types of heating systems are only suitable for the smaller, two- to three-bedroom family house.

3. How old is the house? Many of the available central heating systems are difficult to instal in very old houses. Some are out of the question.

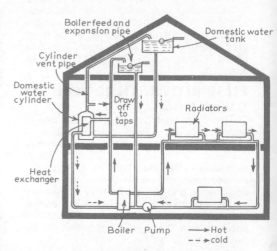

Small-bore hot water heating system layout combined with hot water supply.

4. How much space is available for installation? Some systems take up more space than others. In a multi-story block of flats, for instance, most solid fuel systems are out of the question, since there is no room for the storage of large quantities of fuel.

Keeping these considerations in mind, the householder can begin to make a choice from the many alternatives available. Here are a few of the more popular systems:

OIL-FILLED ELECTRIC RADIATORS

The simplest and most convenient type of house heating. Each radiator is thermostatically controlled and capable of fingertip adjustment. Radiators can be purchased separately, and simply plugged into the mains. They are not permanent fixtures, and can be moved from room to room

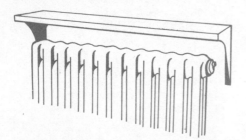

A shelf above the radiator, made of metal or wood, helps to prevent dust-stains on the wall above. The shelf should be screwed in 4 inches above the radiator, and should project at least 2 inches at the front and at each end.

as required. They can also be taken with you if you move house.

The main disadvantage is that although there are no installation costs, the running cost is comparatively high. Each radiator consumes electricity at the standard rate, and uses a lot of current.

OVERNIGHT ELECTRIC STORAGE HEATERS

The next step upwards in electric house heating. Installation costs are reasonable, and the system consumes only off-peak electricity at half the normal rates. The storage unit may be used to power either a warm-air heating system, or can be connected into a hot-water heating installation.

Advantages: Ease of installation and low running costs.

Disadvantages: Little or no control over the amount of heat put out. Heating cannot be provided in less than 12 hours, and it takes the same time to be turned down or off. It gives off the greatest heat in the early morning, and starts to cool off in the evening, often the time when most heat is required.

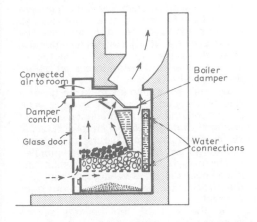

High output back boiler in solid fuel room heater.

ELECTRIC UNDERFLOOR HEATING

Can be installed in new houses, when they are being built. It consists of coils of electric wiring laid in a concrete foundation under the floor. Trouble free, and cheap to run, usually working in conjunction with a night-storage unit. It suffers from the same lack of control as overnight electric storage heaters.

SOLID FUEL BOILER SYSTEMS

Solid fuel is less costly than other types of fuel, particularly if purchased at cheap rates during the summer.

The simpler systems require hand firing, and can be used to provide central heating by means of warm air grilles or water-filled radiators and small-bore pipes. Installation can be easily made in most houses, but there must be space provision for the storage of large quantities of fuel. The boiler will fit easily into a normal-sized kitchen.

In larger systems, a self-feeding automatic boiler may be used, but this piece of equipment is bulky, and needs to be installed in a cellar, or outside the house. It is unsuitable for installation in the kitchen. An automatic solid fuel boiler can cost up to twice that of a hand-fired unit.

OIL-FIRED BOILER SYSTEMS

Most domestic oil-fired systems burn kerosene (a slightly modified form of paraffin). There are two main types of boilers—vapourising or wallflame. Oil boilers are compact, noiseless and clean. They are also trouble free, and run automatically from bulk storage tanks.

The larger your storage tank, the cheaper your running costs, since most major oil suppliers offer price reductions for bulk orders. The storage tank (which holds between 300 and 1,000 gallons) needs to be installed outside the house, under cover if possible. The boiler itself fits neatly into the average-sized kitchen.

As with solid fuel boilers, the heat produced may be used for different types of central heating systems. Small-bore water pipes and radiators are the most popular, but oil boilers will also power a warm air ventilation system.

Both uses of oil-fired central heating offer fairly low running costs, and excellent control over heat. Installation costs are fairly high, and the system needs to be planned in advance, as it is not easy to modify at a later date. It becomes an integral part of the house, and cannot be removed if you move.

GAS-FIRED HEATING

As the price of gas varies slightly from town to town, the running costs of a gas-operated central heating system are not consistent. The initial installation costs are much lower than for other systems and little servicing is required. There is no smoke, smell or fuss and it operates quietly and gives instant heat control. Gas can be used with a hot water or warm air system.

Attic and Roof Insulation

With **all** central heating systems, the roof of the house must be insulated against heat loss. Without insulation, up to 30 per cent of the heat produced can be lost, with a corresponding increase in fuel costs.

It is not an expensive operation, in many cases a do-it-yourself job. Using rolls of insulating material laid between the joists of the loft, the average-sized house can be effectively insulated for between £20 and £30.

The space between cavity walls can also be treated for insulation by filling with plastic foam. This treatment needs to be carried out by a specialist, but can save up to 60 per cent of total heat loss, and reduce fuel bills by as much as a quarter. Average cost for a three-bedroom house is between £60 and £75.

Double glazing also reduces heat-loss in the house.

Servicing

The air-venting valves of radiators should be opened at the beginning of every heating season, after the first firing has been in operation for several hours. Hold a small tin under the valve, and turn the loose key anti-clockwise. If a jet of water emerges, close the valve, but allow a splutter of air and water to develop into a jet before re-closing the valve.

Oil and gas systems should be given a service inspection at least once a year, preferably under a maintenance contract arranged through the fuel supplier. Electric systems need no do-it-yourself servicing. If they go wrong, send for the supplier.

The only regular attention a solid fuel boiler needs is the sweeping of soot and dust from the inside flueways about once a month.

At the end of the heating season remove the ash of the last fire, and give all accessible heating surfaces a stiff brushing down. Leave the air inlet open to ensure good ventilation. Do not use the boiler as an incinerator during the off-season.

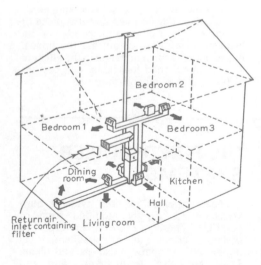

Warm air heating layout, gas fired and fan operated.

Home Decorating

PART ONE: PAINTING

BEFORE YOU BEGIN

The key to success in decorating, as in all forms of home improvement is preparation and patience.

A smooth matt or gloss surface without marks or runs—despite the quality of modern paint brushes or of paint—is virtually impossible without careful pre-treatment of the surface.

This rule applies whatever the working surface and particularly in the case of plaster, wood or metal.

The more careful the filling of abrasions, the more fine the sandpapering and the more care taken on the gradual build up of the surface, the better the result.

Before paint is applied, surfaces should be bone dry and free of grease. Do not paint on those occasional days when surfaces 'bloom' with fine moisture.

Rarely, indoors, does any major damp-ness affect paintwork. Woodwork which is already painted needs only a thorough wash down and sanding to provide a suitable base.

● *Remember to remove all dust before the job starts.*

PAINTING ON WOOD

Painting raw wood—which is largely a question of protection—includes treatment of knots in the wood with shellac to stop 'bleed-through'.

Then a **primer** is applied to deaden suction of the wood. This is followed by an **undercoat**—in the case of oil paints—

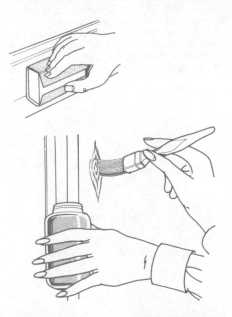

Before painting, dig out loose plaster from cracks and fill in. Allow filling to dry thoroughly before sanding down. See *Filling up Holes And Cracks* **in Section** Walls And Windows.

Sand down raw wood and treat the knots with shellac before painting. See Section Woodwork Care.

183

followed by the **final coat** which is a standard gloss or matt finish paint.

If the modern one-coat paints—i.e. polyurethanes which dry exceptionally hard or those which are jellied to become non-drip—are used, then the finishing paint can also be used for undercoating.

Choice of paint is a matter of personal preference, but because labour normally represents the highest proportion of cost of any home job, it does not pay to buy cheap materials.

Normally, a quality gloss paint, a pint of which will cover about 10 square yards, dries in some four hours and hardens in 12–14 hours. Gloss paint should not be thinned.

Undercoats—which can be thinned—take slightly longer.

● See also section **Woodwork Care.**

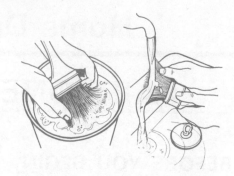

Brush care after using emulsion paint: wash most of the paint off with warm water, then wash thoroughly in soapy water. Give a final rinse under the cold tap.

redecorate a room in a morning.

The emulsion can be thinned with water, but it is best not to.

The usual method is to work with a criss-cross action over the surface, easing the pressure as the paint is 'stroked' towards the light.

Wipe up paint splashes as the job progresses. Do not allow them to harden.

Walls or ceilings covered with old emulsion should be lightly washed before adding a new coat. On bad surfaces, loose material should be removed and it may be necessary to use a primer sealer as an initial base.

After using emulsion, remove most of the paint from brush or roller with plenty of warm water. Then wash thoroughly in soapy water and rinse under cold tap.

With other paints, brushes can be cleaned with turpentine substitute or a proprietary cleaner. Most manufacturers advise on the most suitable solvent for their product.

● See also *Paints* in Section **Materials & How to Use them.**

EMULSION PAINT

The application of emulsion paint with a roller is one of the quickest and most effective ways of redecorating a room.

Emulsions have remarkable coverage power, are supplied in a variety of colours and finishes, and dry out very quickly.

With care, it should be possible to

Use a criss-cross action for best results with a roller.

BRUSHES

The best paint, however, will not make the best job without the best brush and its proper use.

Brushes of professional decorator quality are certainly worth the investment. With proper care brushes give first-class work for years.

The brush should have long bristles and

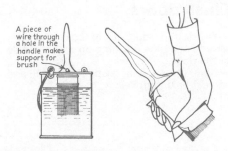

A piece of wire through a hole in the handle makes support for brush

During a temporary pause in the painting, immerse the bristles of the brush in a can of turpentine. Rough-dry the bristles before starting again.

a lively feel. The wedge holding the bristle to the handle should not be too large. The longer the bristle, the easier the brush is to clean, and the better to handle.

Buy several sizes of brushes, including 'angled' brushes for painting behind fixtures.

'Brush control' is important. This means that the brush is held gently yet with sufficient pressure to guide its direction.

With a wide brush, the handle should rest between thumb and forefinger with the fingers supporting the back of the brush.

A small brush should be held loosely like a pen, the forefinger guiding the direction, the second finger acting as a rest.

Brushes should be flexed before starting to paint to ensure that all loose hairs are removed. New brushes should be broken in on undercoats to improve the taper of the bristles.

Brushes should be thoroughly cleaned if a job is to be temporarily abandoned or postponed during meal breaks, etc. Once paint settles in the stock of the brush it can become difficult to remove.

The brush can be suspended over a tin of turpentine substitute with the bristles just immersed. Rough-dry the bristles with a cloth before starting to paint again to discourage runs.

Linseed oil keeps bristles flexible.

PAINTING A ROOM

1. Clear away furniture and furnishings.
2. Wash down ceiling.

3. Strip walls.
4. Wash down and sand woodwork.
5. Apply ceiling cover (paper or paint or both).
6. Paint woodwork.
7. Paint walls.

Equipment

Brushes from ½ in. upwards, including sash brush and dusting brush
Cans to hold turpentine for brush storage during use
Bottle of turpentine substitute
Cloths
Newspaper to protect flooring
Piece of hardboard or tin to aid 'cutting in' of paint to difficult areas (i.e. window frames)
Razor blade trimmer to remove dried paint blobs from glass

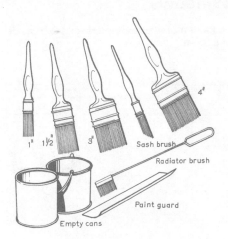

1" 1½" 3" 4"
Sash brush
Radiator brush
Paint guard
Empty cans

Some basic painting equipment.

Techniques

GLOSS PAINTS
Stir briskly before use. Apply as evenly as possible.

JELLY PAINTS
Load the brush well. This paint does not need brushing out.

EMULSIONS

Better spread is obtained by not brushing out. The roller (if used) should be well and evenly loaded, held to the work and smoothly rolled over the surface.

Some emulsions are non-drip. Too much stirring will spoil this. If clear liquid has formed over the 'solid' paint, the liquid should be gently turned in to the paint.

Quantities

A **quart** of gloss paint should be more than enough for woodwork in a room 13 ft. by 12 ft.

A gallon of emulsion is enough for two coats on the walls of a similar room.

PAINTING PROBLEMS

Windows

Paint all the woodwork seen from inside the room.

Painting the top frame of a sash window.
1. Push the bottom frame up to the top.
2. Lower the top frame and paint a third of it.
3. Drop the bottom frame, push the top frame back up (without closing it completely) and finish the painting.

Flush doors

Divide the door into quarters. Tackle a section at a time finishing up at the middle of the door.

Join the sections with horizontal and vertical brush strokes.

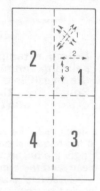

Painting order for a flush door.

Panel doors

Paint in this order (see illustration):
1. **The moulds.**
2. **The panels.**
3. **The verticals between the panels.**
4. **The horizontals.**
5. **The outer verticals.**
● *Check runs throughout with dry brush.*

Painting order for a panel door.

Outside procedure

1. Secure ladders.

2. Clean and repair guttering.

3. Paint inside gutter.

4. Work downwards on guttering from then on.

5. Use a semi-gloss anti-corrosive paint on down pipes.

6. Wash down outside paintwork.

7. Thoroughly sand.

8. Break paint blemishes. Sand well and prime.

9. Apply undercoat and/or top coats.

Paint kettle
hooked to ladder

Safety first

● *Never over-reach when standing on a ladder.*

● *Use a paint kettle hooked on to a rung.*

● *Hold tight with one hand: paint with the other.*

Painting the outside of the house is quite safe so long as the basic safety rules are observed.

PART TWO: PAPERING

EQUIPMENT

Steps (two pairs)
1 plank
1 wide stripping knife
Sponges
Buckets
Wallpaper brush (sized to suit hand)
Long bladed scissors
Plumb-line
Chalk
Mechanical hand trimmer (or metal straight edged ruler and knife) if trimming at home
Wooden ruler (3 ft.)
Sandpaper (medium and rough)
Cork block
Small hand seam roller
Thin, flexibly bladed knife (to use with plaster filler)
Paste board
Paste brush
½-in. paint brush (to remove surplus paste from surface of paper,
Concentrated glue size (if using flour pastes)
Ample cellulose adhesive (out of which also size can be made), or flour paste if preferred, or special-strength adhesive for heavy papers or leatherwork
Wallpaper remover (if needed)
Dry cloths
Sweeping brush
Plastic sheets, dust covers or news-papers
Sack to store debris

Equipment care

Thoroughly clean all equipment before and after use.

Wash down and dry paste board and plank, taking care to extract paste from crevices.

Wash out brushes, dry, and store in mothproof bag.

Clothing

Older the better. Wear an apron with a deep front pocket to hold brushes, etc.

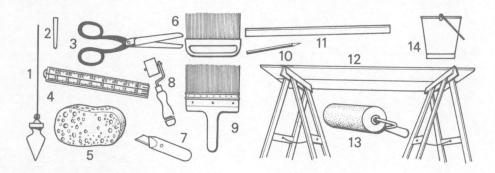

PAPERHANGING TOOLS & EQUIPMENT

1. Plumb-line
2. Chalk
3. Long-bladed scissors
4. 3 ft. wooden ruler
5. Sponge
6. Wallpaper brush
7. Trimming knife
8. Seam roller
9. Paste brush
10. Pencil
11. Straight edge
12. Paste boards mounted on trestles
13. Paint roller for smoothing out air bubbles
14. Bucket

BUYING WALLPAPER

Blend of colours, quality, quantity, and whether home or foreign produced, are matters of personal choice and proper measurement.

U.K. machine printed papers are 21 in. wide after trimming. Length of roll is 11½ yards.

Have your paper trimmed in the shop. Don't attempt to do it yourself.

Papers made abroad often vary in size. An average sized living room in Britain needs about eight rolls of machine printed paper.

To check number of rolls:

1. Measure length of walls in feet. Include all door spaces, recesses, and window space.

2. Measure height of the room in feet from skirting board to ceiling (or to cornice or picture moulding).

3. Match these measurements on a wallpaper chart (given here) and read off the exact number of rolls needed.

Borders are normally sold by the yard.

Ceiling papers can also be calculated from the chart, using the initial room measurement.

Paper Points

Rolls of paper are produced in batches. Each roll has a serial number: make a note of it in case of re-ordering.

Check that your initial order is all from the same batch. If batches are mixed then papers with the same pattern may have different shading.

If buying a job-lot of wallpaper in a sale, always buy more than you need. After the sale it may be difficult to get an extra roll.

PASTE

Increase or reduce the paste strength by varying the amount of cold water used in the mixing.

One pound of paste to eight pints of water is adequate for lightweight papers: six pints of water produces a mix suitable for the heavy duplex and embossed papers.

Read the instructions on the packet very carefully.

ROLL CHART

Height in feet from skirting to cornice or picture-moulding	The top line is the measurement round the walls in feet, including doors, windows, etc.									
	20	24	28	32	36	40	44	48	52	56	60
6 to 6½	2	3	3	4	4	5	5	5	6	6	7
6½ to 7	3	3	4	4	4	5	5	6	6	7	7
7 to 7½	3	3	4	4	5	5	6	6	7	7	8
7½ to 8	3	3	4	4	5	5	6	6	7	8	8
8 to 8½	3	3	4	5	5	6	6	7	7	8	8
8½ to 9	3	4	4	5	5	6	7	7	8	8	9
9 to 9½	3	4	4	5	6	6	7	7	8	9	9
9½ to 10	3	4	5	6	6	7	7	8	9	9	10
10 to 10½	4	4	5	6	6	7	8	8	9	10	10
10½ to 11	4	4	5	6	7	7	8	9	9	10	11
TABLE FOR BORDERS No. of yards	7	8	10	11	12	14	15	16	18	19	20

TABLE FOR CEILING PAPERS (rooms not passages)				
Measurement in feet round room	20–28	30–40	42–50	52–60
Number of Rolls	1	2	3	4

To make Paste

1. Pour the water into the bucket.
2. Start stirring vigorously.
3. Feed in the flour paste powder or cellulose, stirring the whole time, and avoiding lumps.

ROOM PREPARATION

Remove floor coverings or cover the floor with plastic sheets, newspaper or dust sheets. Remove pelmets, curtains and furniture. Or pack the furniture in the centre of the room and cover.

If the ceiling is to be papered or painted, remove light fitments. Switch off electricity supply at mains. Remove fitment, separate the terminals and wrap each in insulating tape. Switch on current again, if needed.

Stripping old Paper

Remove old wallpaper. Give the paper two soakings with warm water, to which has been added a chemical remover. Work upwards from the skirting boards, tackling a section at a time.

If paintwork is splashed with the chemical, wipe off immediately.

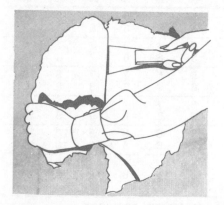

Stripping the old wallpaper. Properly soaked, it should come away easily.

Once the paper becomes pulpy, insert the blade of the broad stripping knife under the edge and ease from wall. Properly soaked paper will come away cleanly.

Gather up stripped paper as job progresses and place in sack. Pasty paper on the floor can be dangerous and is difficult to remove once dry.

Treatment of Walls

New plaster should be neutralised with vinegar and water mixture before papering —one pint of vinegar to one quart of water.

Allow walls to dry after stripping. Lightly sandpaper, with medium paper wrapped round the cork block, to remove surface blemishes, small pieces of paper, old paint runs, etc.

Fill any hair cracks with filler material. Smooth over when wet: sandpaper when dry.

Make up a mix of glue size (follow instructions on packet) and thoroughly size the surface. This reduces porosity and helps movement of paper on the walls during hanging.

If the walls previously were distempered, any loose distemper should be removed. Wash down thoroughly and remove thickened distemper with knife. Try to avoid damaging the plaster. Wipe up debris as the job progresses.

Shiny walls (e.g. painted walls) need dulling with rough sandpaper. Clean off any dirt or grease before starting to wallpaper.

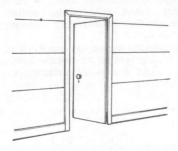

Lining paper is hung horizontally round the walls and joined edge to edge with no overlap.

LINING THE WALLS

Best surface is obtainable by lining the walls. It is necessary on old plaster if hanging heavy textured papers or if working on shiny surfaces.

Lining paper is normally hung horizontally around the walls and butt-jointed (i.e. edge to edge) with no overlap.

The paper is allowed to dry. It is then sized and the wallpaper is hung vertically over the top of it.

Buy best quality lining paper. It is cheap, the price difference between grades is small, and there is little wastage. Any left over is useful for lining drawers, cupboards and shelves.

CUTTING THE PAPER

Set up paste board or the kitchen table. Unroll a length of the pattern paper and measure six inches over the height from skirting board to ceiling or picture rail.

Mark on the non-pattern side and cut the first length. (First to cut; first to hang.) Leave the length on the board pattern side up.

Unroll a second length and match the pattern exactly: right hand edge of the second length to left hand edge of the first. Cut.

Repeat until roll is finished. (Should be about four lengths to the roll).

Ceilings are sometimes not at the same height throughout the room. So check height of room at different points and adjust length of paper to be cut, if necessary.

There is now a bundle of wallpaper lengths on the table, pattern side upwards. Turn the bundle over so that the non-pattern sides face upwards. The pieces are now in the right order for pasting and hanging.

PASTING

Use either flour paste, cellulose adhesive or special strength adhesive, depending on type and weight of paper or personal choice.

1. Place the paper with one edge and one end slightly overlapping the table. If the paper is longer than the table, allow the other end to hang down.

2. Paste down the centre of the length on the table.

3. Brush from the centre to the edge overlapping the table.

Begin pasting by brushing down the centre of the length and then brushing to the edge overlapping the table.

4. Slide the paper to the other edge of the table, overlapping slightly, and brush from the centre to this edge.

5. Fold over the pasted end to halfway along the length. Avoid heavy creasing.

6. Slide the paper along the table so that the unpasted end overlaps slightly.

7. Repeat the pasting process on the remainder of the length.

8. Fold the newly-pasted end to halfway along the length. Avoid heavy creasing.

9. Fold again from each end, until the sheet is in a 'concertina' which can be carried easily.

10. Allow time for the paste to soak in

(paste the next piece meanwhile, if you wish). It takes a minute or two for light papers to become supple enought to hang, longer for heavy papers.

Above: Pasting the second half of the length, with the pasted half folded over. Below: Folding in the newly-pasted end of the length for easy carrying.

Pasting Tips

Paste should be of firm consistency.

Do not use too much or the paper may be marked.

Whether marks can be cleaned depends on whether the colours on the paper are fast or not. To test for fastness, paste the surface of a spare piece of paper and gently rub to see the effect. Never rub to remove a mark whether the colour is fast or not.

Wet paste on the face of the paper should be lifted off with either a small paint brush or a dry cloth.

If colours are not 'runners' a slightly damp sponge or cloth can be used—but very lightly.

Cellulose adhesives tend to be non-staining. Once cold water pastes are wiped off the surface they normally dry out unseen.

Lightweight papers dry out more quickly than double-weight or heavily embossed papers. And the latter sometimes need two pastings.

Rest your paste brush across string

PUTTING ON THE PAPER

Take the plumb-line, chalk the string and hold against the wall, about 19 inches away from the window frame.

Allow the weighted end of the plumb-line to become stationary. Then pluck the string away from the wall and let it snap back to mark out the vertical line. As the paper is 21 inches wide, there are two inches spare for any trimming needed around the window frame.

Using plumbline

● *This system can apply whether the window frame is flush to the wall or fitted in a recess. It is simpler to use offcuts of wallpaper to fit a recess than to try and cover the main wall and recess in one operation, especially as the corners may be out of true. (See* **Obstructions: Corners and Fireplaces.***)*

Always start from the window and work round, from both sides, towards the door. Work around obstructions in the same direction.

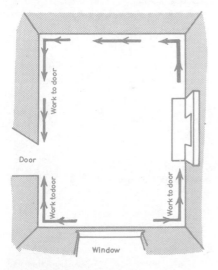

Door

Work to door

Work to door

Work to door

Window

Working round a room, on both sides, from the window to the door.

matched to the vertical chalk line.

4. With the wallpaper brush, brush the paper to the wall downwards and across.

5. Unfold the bottom half of the paper and repeat the brushing. The edge of the pasted length should not overlap the chalk line. If the paper has been buckled or is not properly sited, it should be removed immediately and rehung.

6. Edge the paper into the window fitment. Lightly mark it by running the blunt edge of the scissors down the paper next to the framework. Then ease it back, trim, and brush it into position.

7. Make adjustments at ceiling, picture rail and skirting board level.

8. Remove any surplus paste on paintwork or at the edges of the paper.

A dry sheepskin or plastic paint roller, run over the surface of the paper, helps to remove air bubbles and aids adhesion. This is **not** advisable, however, on heavily embossed papers in case of damage to the finish.

Once the paper is in position, properly trimmed, truly vertical, with air bubbles brushed out and surplus paste removed, a seam roller can be run down the edge on the chalk line to ensure a firm fixture. It is best to wait until the paste is properly set before doing this.

The next length of paper is then hung. This time the edge of the new length is butt-jointed (see illustration) to the edge of the first length. The pattern must be properly matched.

Thus, lengths of paper which were cut and pasted in sequence are now hung in sequence.

After hanging a few lengths of paper, check the edge of the last length with the plumb-line. If the edge is out of vertical, adjust when hanging the next piece.

● *Remember: errors are magnified, if not checked as the work progresses*

Hanging the Paper

1. Stand with both feet on steps at a comfortable height.

2. Unfold half of one pasted length, holding it by the corners between fingers and thumbs. Leave the bottom half folded.

3. Hold the paper to the wall, allowing three inches more than necessary at the top. The side edge of the paper (left or right depending on which side of the window you are working) should be

OBSTRUCTIONS

It is best to remove fitments before papering and to refix them when papering is complete.

Measure the exact positions of screw and plug holes in the wall, and prick out on the paper.

PAPERING STEP BY STEP

1. Carry the pasted and folded length like this.

2. Unfold half of the length and position it on the wall.

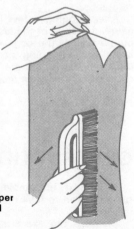

3. Brush the paper downwards and across.

4. Check that the paper hangs in line with the vertical chalk mark.

5. Unfold the bottom half of the length.

6. Mark the top trim line of the paper with the blunt edge of the scissors.

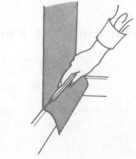

7. Repeat the marking on the bottom edge.

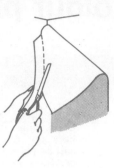

8. Peel back the paper, trim, and brush back in position.

11. Edge the paper into a window fitment with the wallpaper brush before marking it for trim.

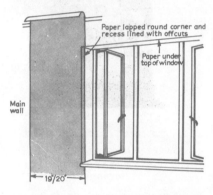

12. Work into a recess by turning about two inches of paper from the main length. Then paper inside the recess with offcuts.

9. Hang the next length of paper, butt-jointing it with the first, and making sure that the pattern matches properly.

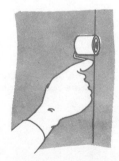

10. When the paste has set, run a seam roller over the joints.

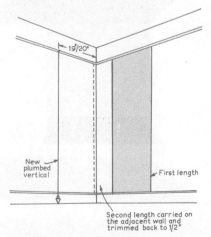

13. Papering into a corner.

Colour schemes are too much a matte
of personal choice to discuss in detail, bu
here are some basic optical tricks whicl
can be played.
● *White enlarges a small room. Use .
white wall to bounce light to othe
coloured walls and dark corners.*
● *Heighten ceilings with light colours
Lower them with dark.*
● *'Square off' lozenge shaped rooms wit.
strong colour patterns on end walls.*
● *Use brilliant colours in ill lit passages.*

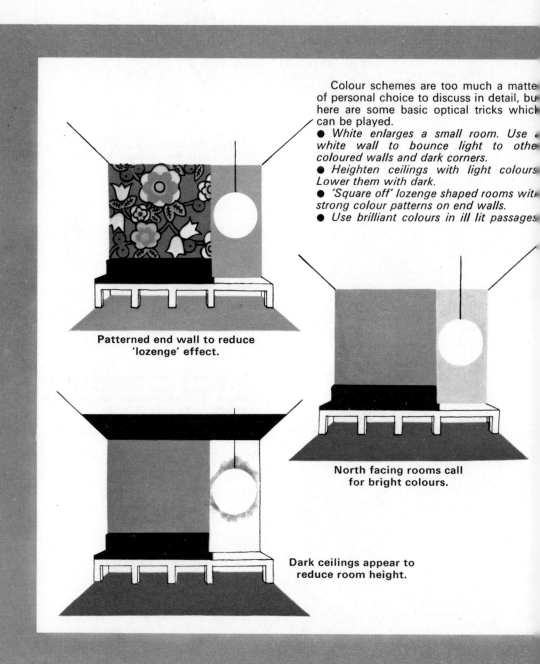

**Patterned end wall to reduce
'lozenge' effect.**

**North facing rooms call
for bright colours.**

**Dark ceilings appear to
reduce room height.**

home decoration

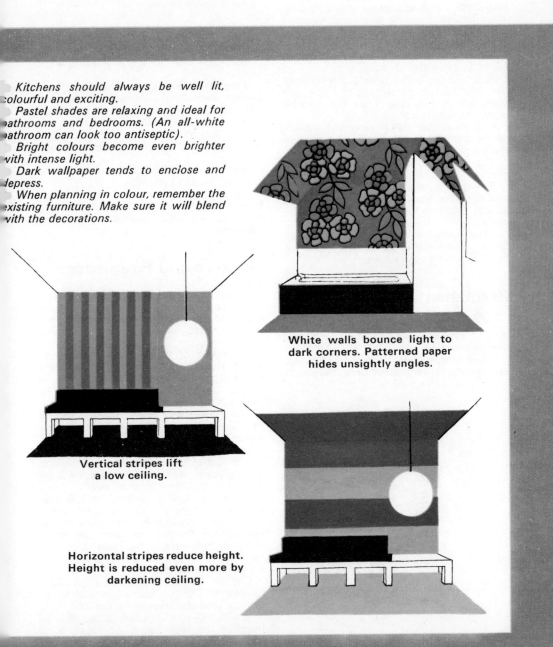

Kitchens should always be well lit, colourful and exciting.

Pastel shades are relaxing and ideal for bathrooms and bedrooms. (An all-white bathroom can look too antiseptic).

Bright colours become even brighter with intense light.

Dark wallpaper tends to enclose and depress.

When planning in colour, remember the existing furniture. Make sure it will blend with the decorations.

White walls bounce light to dark corners. Patterned paper hides unsightly angles.

Vertical stripes lift a low ceiling.

Horizontal stripes reduce height. Height is reduced even more by darkening ceiling.

Papering Around Switches

Electric switch fronts vary. Flush, or near flush, fitments present little difficulty. They can be papered over and trimmed afterwards. It makes a tidier job, however, to remove the switch front.

Turn off the electricity at the mains (see **Electricity in the Home**).

Take out the two retaining screws from the switch front and remove it. The paper then has a full drop over the fitment without obstruction.

Cut away the paper over the switch space, paste the rest down, and replace the switch front.

Circular switches can be dealt with similarly.

To paper round a circular switch without removing the front, allow the toggle (the switch itself) to burst through the wallpaper.

Make a series of cross cuts with scissors to allow the paper to be pressed round the fitment, and trim the edges.

Permanent Fixtures

Some special fitments like bookcases, built-in shelves, china cabinets, etc., are permanent.

Paper around them, taking care to pick up the pattern. If this is not done, the visual

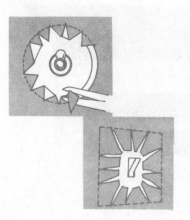

Papering around switch fitments without removing the fronts.

balance of the wall will be upset.

If these fitments are at eye level, it is important to neaten off the edge of the paper adjoining them.

Water Pipes

It is not easy to paper around water pipes.

Care must be taken to maintain the correct vertical line. If necessary, make an extra chalked vertical and work to that on the other side of the pipe.

Normally, cuts are made in the edge of the paper to enable it to be fitted behind the pipes.

Turn off all the heating and allow the paste to dry out naturally.

Pipe clips should **not** be removed. And it is best not to upset central heating radiators or other permanent heating equipment.

Corners and Fireplaces

There are four main corners in every room and often many angles. Despite these, it is essential to maintain the pattern match, and to keep the vertical line.

Thickness of plaster in corners often varies. The top of the corner may need less paper than the bottom. If the paper is simply carried round a corner like this, the working edge will be out of vertical.

The correct way is to paper up to and into the corner, firming the paper into the angle by using the hand in a 'chopping' action.

The rest of the width is carried over on the adjacent wall and trimmed back to allow only half an inch carry over.

A fresh vertical is chalked on the new wall. A new length is pasted to this edge. The paper is brushed back into the corner, overlapping the half an inch previously allowed. Pulpy paper tears easily, so any tailoring to fit around a fireplace should be done with the paper dry.

Cut the piece slightly oversize to allow for correct fitting. Then paste and hang, making final adjustments on the job.

In dealing with recesses, particularly in hanging the first length of paper, it is simpler *not* to try and paper both the recess and the main wall at the same time. It *can* be done, but often leads to inaccuracies.

Paper the main wall, working to the first vertical at the 19 inches width. Then smooth the remaining two inches around the recess corner. Paper the recess with a separate length from suitable offcuts at the end of the main papering.

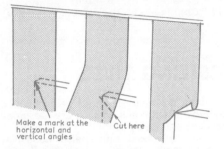

Make a mark at the horizontal and vertical angles | Cut here

Cutting paper to fit around the angles of a fireplace should be done with the paper dry to avoid tearing.

DRYING OUT

A newly decorated wall will carry damp patches. This is quite normal: paste takes time to dry out.

Open a window for ventilation, leave the room and close the door.

Sometimes patterns appear to have dulled, and glossy stripes to have blurred. This, again, is quite normal and corrects in the drying process.

Tears and how to treat them

When the paper is drying out, try to prevent damage by careless handling of steps or other equipment.

Sharp pressure on pulpy wallpaper will produce a triangular tear. The torn piece tends to concertina.

Gently ease the torn piece of paper to produce as flat a surface as possible, see that it is adequately pasted, and then smooth back into position.

If the piece has been torn out and lost, hunt through the scrap for a matching piece. The edges of the new piece should be torn, not cut.

The new piece should be slightly oversize. Once pasted in position, the edges will not be seen.

SPECIAL PAPERS

Papers needing special treatment are always accompanied by instructions from the manufacturers. In case of doubt, check with the wallpaper supplier or send a sample of the paper to a paste manufacturer.

Flock papers and some washables need extra care. Occasionally one might have difficulty with synthetic covered papers, as their edges tend to 'roll' if not properly treated.

LINING A CEILING

Ceiling papers are wide in variety and supplied in differing weights and textures.

The ceiling can, of course be treated as an extra wall and covered with ordinary wallpaper.

As defects tend to show up more on a ceiling, however, this is not advisable.

Ceilings generally are painted white or cream. The painting can be done direct on to the plaster or on to a lining paper or special ceiling paper.

The technique of lining a ceiling is similar to papering the wall, the main differences being that the decorator has to work awkwardly, the lengths of paper are longer, and the folding is different.

To line a ceiling:

1.   Set up the two sets of steps with the plank between them. Check that they are secure.

2.   Work away from the light.

3.   Mark a chalk line, with string and blue chalk, to lay the first length against. Mark out an inch less than the width of the paper on the ceiling. With someone to help, hold each end of the chalked string to these marks and snap it against the ceiling.

4.   Cut the paper about six inches over the length or width (depending which way you are working) of the ceiling.

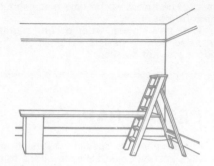

Before starting to paper a ceiling, make sure that the plank is secure.

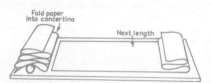

Above: Folding ceiling paper into a concertina before hanging. Below: Putting on the ceiling paper, supporting the concertina with a length of broom handle.

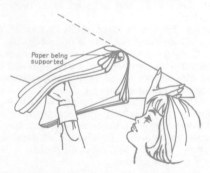

5. After pasting, fold the paper into a series of concertinas, pasted side to pasted side, about 18 inches across.

6. Lay the folded paper across a piece of smooth wood, or broom handle, about 20 inches long. Hold this in your left hand (if you are right-handed) and work from the right hand side of the room.

7. Unfold the first concertina. Fit the paper to the line, overlapping about three inches at the end wall.

8. With the wallpaper brush, smooth down the centre of the piece, then out towards the line, and then in towards the facing wall.

9. Repeat the process, fold by fold, until the whole length is in position.

10. Mark the trim lines with the blunt edge of the scissors. Ease back the paper, trim, and brush back into position.

11. Continue with the remaining lengths.

CEILING TILES

There are many types of ceiling cover, including decorative tiles in a wide range of sizes and designs.

These are fixed with special adhesives using a 'blob' method. A blob of adhesive is put on each corner, another in the centre, and the tile is pressed gently on to the plaster.

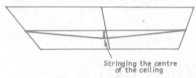

Above: Marking the centre of the ceiling before fixing tiles. Below: Tiles should be fixed from the centre of the ceiling, working outwards.

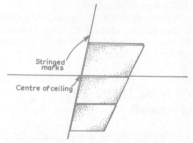

Work is from the centre point of the ceiling outwards.

To remove these tiles, a broad stripping knife is held against the dry adhesive and lightly tapped. Normally the adhesive will come away in one piece.

Normally, when decorating a room completely, you should tackle the ceiling first. But with decorative tiles, a better visual finish is had by papering first and tiling afterwards.

Household Troubles:
Causes & Cures

EVIDENCE	WHEREABOUTS	PROBABLE CAUSE	WHAT TO DO
Powdery rust-red dust	On floors and furniture	Spores of dry rot fungus	
Flat, pancake-like substance, mustard yellow or rust-red, corrugated in centre. White round edges with yellow staining.	Round doors, near skirtings, on wood plaster or brickwork	Fruit body of dry rot fungus	
Deep cracks in wood making cubical pieces.	Any wood in damp situation	Wood attacked by dry rot fungus	Act *immediately*. Ask for a free timber survey, as this fungus can soon cause widespread damage
Thin sheets of silvery or grey growth, sometimes tinged with yellow or lilac. Snowy cotton-wool growth sometimes tinged with bright yellow	On wood or plaster associated with above	Mycelium of dry rot fungus	
Warping and darkening of timber, often with lengthwise cracking	Skirtings, window frames, floorboards etc. in very damp situations	Wood attacked by wet rot fungus	Ask for a free timber survey and advice without obligation
$\frac{1}{16}$ in. diameter round holes in wood	Structural timber and floorboards	Exit holes of woodworm (common furniture beetle)	Ask for a free timber survey without obligation from a timber treatment company
Small heaps of gritty wood dust	On or below structural timbers and floorboards	Boredust of woodworm	
$\frac{1}{16}$ in. diameter round holes in wood	Furniture	Exit holes of woodworm	Use woodworm fluid and wax or cream polish. Fumigation services are also available
Small heaps of gritty wood dust	Under furniture	Boredust of woodworm	
$\frac{1}{8}$ in. diameter round holes, probably in oak or other hardwoods	Structural timber of old houses	Exit holes of death watch beetle	Ask for a free timber survey without obligation from a timber treatment company
Small heaps of wood dust, with bun-shaped pellets	On or below structural timbers	Boredust of death watch beetle	

HOUSEHOLD TROUBLES: CAUSES AND CURES

EVIDENCE	WHEREABOUTS	PROBABLE CAUSE	WHAT TO DO
$\frac{1}{10}$ in. diameter round holes in or near bark left on softwoods	Roof timbers or floor joists with unbarked edges	Exit holes of bark borer	Remove bark. This woodborer does not cause significant damage, but ask a timber treatment company for a free survey to check identification
Large oval holes, occasionally with blistered appearance, on surface of softwoods	Roofing and flooring timbers in houses mainly in N.W. Surrey area	Exit holes of house longhorn beetle	Act *immediately* and ask for a free timber survey without obligation from a timber treatment company
Ragged holes in woollen garments, carpets, furs. Small woolly-bear grubs, shed skins or adult moths	Airing cupboard, upper rooms, wardrobes and drawers	Carpet beetles, clothes moths or house moths	Check loft for old birds' nests, dead birds or debris. Spray cupboards and affected carpets or garments with mothproofer
Small dark animal droppings, gnawed wires, woodwork, food containers, stored bulbs etc.	Usually ground floor, near skirting or in cupboards	Mice	Lay poison bait in numerous small piles near signs of damage
Flying insects	Any room	Flies, wasps, gnats etc.	Spray with insecticide, or ask pest controller to trace source of trouble
Crawling insects		Cockroaches, silverfish, bread beetles etc.	
Dull patches, stains or fading of unpolished hardwood	Teak and afrormosia furniture	Sunlight and heat drying out natural oils	Apply teak oil two or three times a year
Greying of cedarwood exterior covering, warping or swelling of outdoor timbers	On outside walls, or in garden sheds, fencing, exterior rooms, greenhouses etc.	Effects of weathering, especially exposure to moisture	Treat with cedarwood water repellent or clear water repellent finish

● *Even if the wood in your home shows no sign of trouble, consider taking out a woodworm and wood rot insurance policy.*

Woodwork Care

FINISHING

Plain woodwork nearly always needs finishing, otherwise it will readily become stained or discoloured, or gradually turn grey. Select the most suitable method of treatment from the following:

Sealing

USE FOR:
1.   Interior wood panelling, furniture and fitments made in veneer-faced boards or mahogany ply.
2.   Garden sheds, house extensions, etc. in cedar.
3.   Outside timberwork.

MATERIALS AND METHOD
1.   Modern polyurethane sealers provide a quick and efficient method of sealing and finishing wood in one go. Apply by brush, mop or sponge, and rub well in. When dry, the surface may be rough, so sand down flat with very fine sandpaper.
   Further coats of sealer can then be applied, each coat heightening the gloss obtained. A 'sealed' finish can thus range from semi-mat (or almost mat if lightly sanded) through semi-gloss to high gloss. Gloss can be further enhanced by wax polishing.
2.   Paint with cedar preservative, which provides a seal for the wood and gives a rich colour.
   Untreated exposed cedar (or any wood) turns grey when exposed to an outside atmosphere. Cedar preservative will **not** restore the colour in such cases. The wood must first be scraped and sanded down until all the grey has been removed.
3.   Plain outside woodwork, such as fence-posts, should be treated with a good preservative to seal the wood and protect it from rot. Creosote preserves, but is unattractive in colour. Most proprietary fluids are green, but some are colourless.

French polishing

USE FOR:
   Mahogany or walnut furniture—or furniture veneered in these woods.

MATERIALS AND METHOD
   French polishing is really a job for the professional or the really experienced amateur. If you want to try it, buy a French polishing kit; and follow the instructions carefully.

Using a French polishing kit. Follow the instructions on the kit carefully.

   For the unskilled, sealing with a polyurethane sealer, followed by wax polishing, will give a better result, and be much quicker.

Varnishing

USE FOR:
1.   Mahogany or similar decorative woods where a high-gloss finish is required.
2.   High-gloss, water-resistant finish for decorative woods exposed to damp conditions, or exterior panelling.

MATERIALS AND METHOD
1.   Use a modern polyurethane varnish for easiest application. All varnishing must be carried out in a dry and dust-free atmosphere.
2.   Polyurethane varnish is more durable and waterproof than oil-bound varnish. Use two-part polyurethane for exposed conditions.

Damage to woodwork
by woodworm .

Adult common furniture beetle
(Anobium punctatum)

Damage to wicker work by common
furniture beetles

Adult Death Watch beetle
(xestobium rufovillosum)

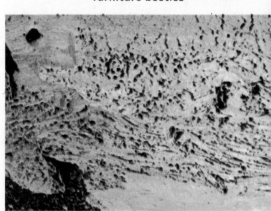

Wood damaged by Death Watch beetle

Adult wood boring weevil

Wood damaged by weevil

. . and fungus

Dry rot can flourish in damp conditions, particularly in places where no air circulates. It is a living fungus which feeds on the moisture in the wood and literally sucks it dry, leaving it soft and weak. The only treatment is to cut out damaged areas of woodwork and replace it. So make sure that the insides of cupboards and similar enclosures do not remain full of damp, stagnant air. Drill holes or vents to allow air to circulate in the enclosure. Wet rot is less harmful. It results from wood becoming thoroughly waterlogged. It can be cured by drying out the wood completely, but it can start again if the source of waterlogging is not also cured. *See also* Woodwork Care *under* Dry Rot *and* Wet Rot.

Dry rot fruiting body of Merulius lacrymans

Dry rot damage to skirting and floor

Mycelium, or strands of dry rot fungus

Wet rot fungus (Coniophora Cerebella)

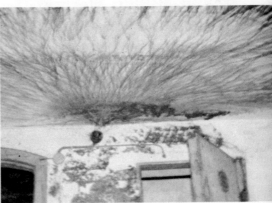

The cellar fungus growing on a ceiling

Illustrations by courtesy of Rentokil Laboratories

Staining

USE FOR:
1. Wood which needs its appearance improving before polishing or varnishing.
2. Matching the colour of wood assemblies, or masking rub marks. Simple finish for wood flooring.

MATERIALS AND METHOD
1. Staining cheap white woods to make them look expensive is usually highly unsatisfactory because of the poor grain pattern brought out, and uneven absorption of the stain. Try the effect on a piece of scrap wood first.
2. Tackle carefully, otherwise the stained area will be too dark. A much lighter stain is needed to colour end grain, due to the higher penetration.

Only a professional, or an experienced amateur, can be relied upon to produce really satisfactory results with stains.

Painting

USE FOR:
1. Whitewood furniture and fittings, where a finished appearance is required.
2. Colouring wood-surrounds, skirting boards, etc. to conform to an overall colour scheme.
3. Water-proofing and weather-proofing exterior wood assemblies.

Materials and Method
1. Painting is the best method of finishing. Sealing is an alternative, but varnishing is generally less satisfactory. Do not try staining the wood, as the result will almost certainly be blotchy and unattractive.
2. Standard practice.
3. Standard practice, but use exterior paints.

REMOVING STAINS
See Stain Removal Section.

RENOVATING OLD WOODWORK

If the wood originally had a decorative appearance and was finished by sealing, polishing or varnishing, the only satisfactory ways to restore it to its original appearance are:

1. If finished by sealing or polishing, sand or scrape down until all the surface exposed is new wood, with its original colour. Then re-finish completely, as for new wood.
2. If the original finish is varnish, use paint or varnish stripper to remove all old varnish. Then sand down until a new wood surface is restored. Re-varnish as for new wood, or seal if a quicker treatment is required.

Defects such as deep scores can be filled in, using a suitable filler to match the original colour of the wood. But such areas will always show up through sealing or varnishing.

3. If the original finish is paint, you may be able to take a few short cuts.

For old paint in reasonable condition, sand over thoroughly, using fine grade wet-or-dry abrasive paper. Fill any uneven patches carefully with a suitable filler. When dry, sand down flat. Then repaint

Filling in uneven patches on woodwork and (top) sanding down when dry.

Cleaning off old paint with a blow-lamp and stripping knife.

with one or two coats of undercoat, followed by a finishing coat.

If the old paint is badly peeled, it should all be stripped off. Use a paint stripper or a blowlamp and stripping knife. Make good any surface defects, and then sand all over. Re-paint as for new wood.

DRY ROT

Areas of dry rot must be cut right out well past the boundaries of attack, and the rotten wood burnt. Thoroughly wire-brush and clean surrounding areas, and paint with a dry rot fluid.

Make good the damage by cutting new wood to fit, and soak this in dry-rot fluid before fixing in place. If this is impossible, paint back of wood with dry-rot fluid before fitting, and the remainder after fitting. When dry, paint to finish in the usual way.

The main cause of dry rot is a damp, stagnant atmosphere. It can be avoided by providing ventilation.

WET ROT

Wet rot is caused by wood becoming waterlogged and never drying out again properly. It is most likely to occur in wooden floors in bathrooms near a leaking pipe, or in windowsills.

Wet rot can be stopped if the wood is dried out properly, and then painted with a dry-rot fluid. It will start again if the wood can still get saturated, so seal the surface by painting, or similar treatment, to prevent this happening.

If the wood is badly affected, and has become very soft and useless, it will have to be replaced. The new wood can develop wet rot under the same conditions as before, so if the source of damp cannot be stopped, seal the wood surface.

Walls & Windows

GLAZING

Tools and Equipment

Glass cutter
Putty (linseed oil for wood frames; metal glazing for metal frames)
Wedge shaped nails
Pin hammer
Mallet
Wooden ruler
Paint
1 in. brush
Hacking knife
Putty knife
Chisel
Pliers

CUTTING GLASS

1. Work on flat surface.
2. Hold ruler firmly against surface of glass.
3. Holding cutter like a pen, run cutting wheel firmly over the surface against the ruler edge. The wheel must run freely and should be lubricated if necessary with turpentine. Cutting mark should be made in one movement.

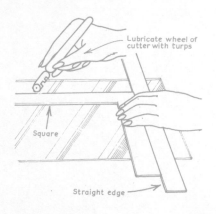

Lubricate wheel of cutter with turps

Square

Straight edge

4. Tap the opposite side of the cut with cutter handle.

5. Holding glass firmly on flat surface, move the cut to edge of the table and snap off waste piece of glass.

● *Experts snap off glass with fingers. Do not expect to be an expert first time. Wear protective gloves or hold edge of glass with folded cloth. Beware of splinters and slivers of glass. Keep children and pets well away.*

Replacing a Window Pane

1. Break away as much as possible of damaged glass.
2. Working from **outside**, remove the old putty. Use hacking knife or chisel and mallet (never a hammer).
3. With pliers, withdraw any wedge shaped nails holding glass in rebate.

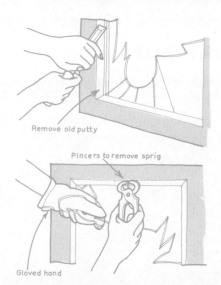

Remove old putty

Pincers to remove sprig

Gloved hand

4. Working from **inside**, insert chisel in putty between glass and wooden framework. Break up old putty, levering out pieces of glass. Take utmost care not to damage woodwork.
5. Clean up the rebate and then add coat of priming paint.

6. Measure space. Cut replacement pane (or have it cut at the glaziers) slightly undersize.

7. Work linseed oil putty well in hands until pliable.

8. Skim the rebate with putty to make bed for one side of pane.

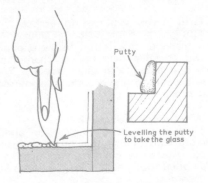

Putty

Levelling the putty to take the glass

9. Fit the new pane, pressing firmly on to putty.

10. Tap in a few wedge shaped headless nails to hold glass in position.

11. With putty knife, trim off surplus putty inside room.

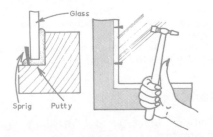

Glass

Sprig   Putty

12. Work additional putty into long 'sausage' and place against outside face of glass and against woodwork.

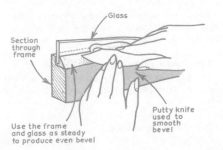

Glass

Section through frame

Use the frame and glass as steady to produce even bevel

Putty knife used to smooth bevel

13. Angle the putty knife against glass, putty and woodwork and run blade downwards or across in a smooth firm action.

14. Neaten off corners.

15. Take care in trimming the bottom horizontal: this edge acts as a watershed.

16. When putty surface is firm, coat with priming or undercoating. When this is dry, add top coat of paint.

17. Clean windows and remove debris.

PLUGGING WALLS

Plugging a wall to take Rawlplugs or similar plugs for fixing screws is simple in theory, but there are snags in practice. You have a choice of two basic tools:

1. Rawlplug tool (or hole plug for larger diameters), for driving with a hammer. The

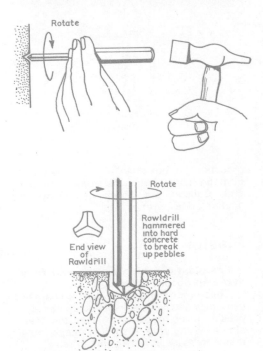

Rotate

Rotate

End view of Rawldrill

Rawldrill hammered into hard concrete to break up pebbles

technique is to strike the end of the tool smartly and repeatedly, rotating the tool slightly after each stroke. The heavier the hammer the better.

2. Masonry drill or tipped drill, normally used in a power drill. In other than soft surfaces (plaster, for instance), the drill should run at a **low speed** (the lowest speed with a two-speed drill, or using a

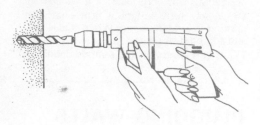

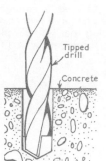

Tipped drill

Concrete

reduction gearbox attachment on the drill). Firm pressure should be applied to the drill. Consult the check list below if anything goes wrong.

Plaster

For plaster which cracks and falls away on outer surface.
Check that the tool or drill is sharp—use a new one if possible. If you do damage plaster, make good with asbestos filler after inserting plug. Also, drill deeper hole than necessary and use a longer plug.

When hole enlarges towards bottom end.
Probably you are not holding the tool or drill at right angles to the surface. Make good with asbestos filler before fitting plug.

When hole breaks through back of plaster.
Not a suitable position for a plug. Try to find a better position—you can always fill in trial holes.

Concrete

Drill or tool will not penetrate.
You are probably using a blunt tool, or a hammer that is not heavy enough.
Old concrete may be very hard, and almost impossible to plug properly. You may be able to find a softer spot by trial and error.

When concrete cracks.
There is not much you can do about this other than finish hole, and then make good. Always avoid plugging near the edge of concrete, as this very likely results in cracking.

Brick

Drill or tool will not penetrate.
As for concrete, but note that the mortar between bricks may be harder than the brick itself.

Brick flakes, or shows signs of cracking.
Stop and try another spot. Avoid plugging near the edge of a brick.

General

When material is difficult to penetrate.
A hand tool and a heavy hammer, better than a power drill and a masonry drill.

Plug pulls out of hole when screw is in position.
Plug too small for hole. Always use a plug size to match tool or drill size, or next size up if this will fit.

Plug will not drive into hole.
Plug is too large. Try chamfering off the edge of the plug with a razor blade to make it fit.

Final fixing weak.
If the hole is well formed, and the

FILLING UP HOLES AND CRACKS

Roll moistened filler into plug

Ram Asbestos filler into hole

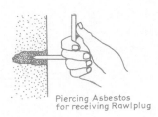

Piercing Asbestos for receiving Rawlplug

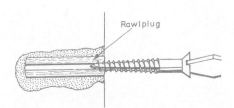

Rawlplug

Filling up or making-good holes and cracks in walls or ceilings requires just two tools, a hawk and a small pointed trowel, plus a packet of modern filler powder, which is better than ordinary plaster. Then tackle the job step by step.

1. Use the trowel to dig out all loose plaster in the crack or hole.

2. Work round the edges of the area so treated to cut-back or 'undercut' the edge to act as a key for the new filler.

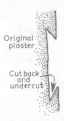

Original plaster

Cut back and undercut

3. Brush over the damaged area to remove loose plaster and dust.

4. Pour a quantity of filler powder into a heap on the hawk. Then use your finger to form a hole in the middle.

5. Add a little water in the hole, and mix with the plaster, working from the centre outwards with the trowel. Add more water as necessary, and carry on until the filler is completely mixed with water to the consistency of a fairly thick paste.

6. Brush the edges of the area to be treated with clean water.

plug the proper size, the trouble probably is that the hole is not deep enough. Always drill as deep as possible, and use long screws to match.

Screw will not screw down flush.
Hole is not deep enough, or the screw is longer than the plug.

An unsatisfactory or weak fixing can generally be improved by re-drilling the hole much deeper, or by fitting the plug to the full depth of the new hole, and packing any clearance at the front of the hole with asbestos filler.

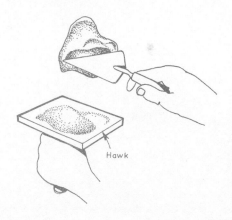

Hawk

7. Lift filler off the hawk on the blade of the trowel, and push into place. Continue until the damaged area is filled in, then level off with sweeping strokes, working

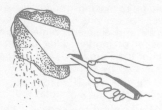

Criss cross cuts

excess plaster over the edges. Scrape off excess plaster with the trowel.

8. If the plaster repair is not perfectly level or flush, leave until thoroughly dry, and then flatten off with sandpaper.

Note: if there is a large damaged area to be filled in, do not attempt to fill it in one go.

Fill in below the surface of the wall or ceiling, and leave to dry. Before it is quite dry, score in criss-cross cuts with the point of the trowel. When completely dry and hard, paint over with water, then use more filler to complete filling in flush.

Emergency Repairs

When an appliance breaks down, or some other domestic mishap occurs, it is useful to know what emergency action can be taken to get things working again for the time being.

ELECTRICAL FAULTS

Electrical appliances are probably the most likely to develop faults after long use. The cause quite often is a simple one which you can put right in a matter of minutes, provided you know what to look for.

Suppose an electric iron or an electric kettle does not work when it is plugged in and switched on. The cause of the fault is a disconnection somewhere. You can check where this is likely to be, and perhaps save the cost of calling in an electrician.

Try the Fuse

First unplug the appliance. *Never leave it plugged in while you are working on it.* If the plug is a fused type, check the fuse. Unscrew the big screw in the back of the plug which holds it together, and remove the top. You can then remove the fuse from its clips, but you will not be able to tell if it is blown just by looking at it. Check it with a simple test circuit, using

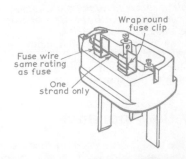

Fig. B. Using a fuse wire as a temporary replacement for a plug fuse.

two short lengths of wire and an ordinary dry battery taken from a torch as shown in Fig. A.

Bare the ends of the two lengths of wire. Wrap one end of one piece round the metal body of a torch bulb, and one end of the other piece round one end of the fuse. Hold the two free ends of the wires on each end of the battery and touch the other end of the fuse on the bottom of the bulb. If the bulb lights, the fuse is all right.

If the fuse is obviously blown, use the same test to check that the fuse you are fitting is all right. You could have picked up another blown fuse by mistake. If you have not got a new fuse, use fuse wire of the same rating as the fuse, as shown in Fig. B.

● *For directions on how to mend a fuse in a fuse-box, see the Electricity section.*

Try the Plug

If the test shows the fuse to be all right, examine the wires attached to the terminals of the plug. One of these could have worked loose to cause the disconnection. The remedy is to remake the connection properly.

Try the Flex

More likely, the fault will be in the flex at a point where it has been repeatedly bent

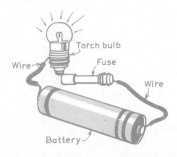

Fig. A. Checking a plug fuse with a simple test circuit.

or chafed, and has eventually broken. Search for damage by running the length of flex through your fingers. You can repair breaks by twisting the ends of broken wire together, and binding any bare wire with insulating tape.

This is only an emergency repair, and the complete length of flex should be replaced as soon as possible.

If the position of the damage leaves enough flex running to the appliance, cut the flex at the point of damage and refit the plug to this shorter length.

Try the Appliance

If the fuse is sound and the flex is sound the disconnection is in the appliance. Dismantle the appliance as far as necessary to expose the internal connections of the flex. These may be loose or broken. If not, the element of the appliance probably needs replacing, and that is a job for an electrician.

To prove the connections right through to the inside of the appliance, you can use the bulb-and-battery test again. Connect to the two opposite pair of pins of the plug, as shown in Fig. C, and use a loop of bare wire (a paper clip will do) to connect the red and black wire terminals in the appliance itself.

If the bulb lights, this proves the circuit right through to the internal connections of the appliance. The fault is then in the appliance, from that point on.

Quite often a disconnection fault is intermittent. This will almost certainly be due to:
1.   Loose or broken connections in the plug or at the appliance end of the flex, or
2.   Damage at one particular point along the length of flex.

Repairing Elements

The one element failure you can readily tackle is that of an electric fire. Examine the length of the faulty element thoroughly. The break may be at one end, or more likely somewhere in the length of coil.

You can repair such a break by twisting the two ends together with pliers. This is not easy, for the wire will be brittle and tend to break. Also, if you do manage a success-full repair, it will be strictly temporary, and the element should be replaced as soon as possible.

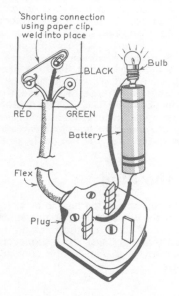

Fig. C. A simple test circuit to check the wiring to an appliance.

ELECTRICAL 'SHORTS': A WARNING

A burning or fishy smell coming from any electrical appliance which is switched on warns of a 'short'—and a possible danger. **Do not touch the appliance.** Switch off and disconnect completely by removing its plug from the mains supply socket. You can *then* examine the appliance. The trouble may be a broken or frayed wire inside the appliance or in the plug—you can usually trace it by smell. If the damage is in the wiring in the run of the flex the point of damage will usually be evident by a charred or burnt area on the flex covering.

If the damage is at either end of the flex, you can make it good by cutting the damaged length of wiring back by about 6 inches and re-making the flex connections to the plug, or appliance. If the trouble is in the length of flex, *the whole length of flex should be replaced with a new flex.*

Provided you *can* find *and* remedy the source of the 'short', the appliance is then fit for re-use—but check the fuse in the plug first to see that it is the right rating. The fact that it has not 'blown' and allowed the 'short' to overheat the wires may mean that the fuse originally fitted was too high a rating. If you *cannot* find the source of the trouble get the appliance serviced by an expert.

There is very little risk of fire developing from an electrical 'short', provided you disconnect the appliance concerned **as soon as you trace a burning smell coming from it.** It will only be insulation burning, and once the heating effect of the mains supply is removed (by disconnection), it will tend to go out on its own. If you cannot conveniently disconnect the appliance, switch off the electricity at the main fuse-box.

Electrical fires can lead to extensive damage if they are undetected; the localised burning can set fire to other inflammable materials nearby. So it is important that mains wiring should be in good condition, for it is hidden behind walls, or in the loft. **Mains circuits should never be overloaded by plugging too many appliances into them**— they must be rated to carry the total load involved (see **Electricity in the Home** Section). You can *protect* mains circuits by making sure that the correct size fuse is always fitted to plugs which fit into wall sockets.

If you do find it necessary to deal with a smouldering flex, simply smother it with a *dry* cloth. Do not pour or throw water on to an electric fire and **never touch it, nor use any type of fire extinguisher on it if the appliance or circuit is still 'live'** (i.e. connected to the mains).

If you are very worried about fires from electric appliances there are various small 'household type' fire extinguishers which can be used to deal with any such fire— **provided the appliance is first disconnected from the mains.** But electrical fires are usually 'smoke without fire'— unless they are allowed to go on long enough for something else to be set alight. Then a fire extinguisher can provide the quickest way of dealing with them. And if you buy a type of household fire extinguisher which *is* suitable for coping with electrical fires, then it will not do any additional damage to the appliance. Spraying the inside of a television set with an *unsuitable* type of extinguisher could do extensive damage to the electrical components.

TV AND RADIO

Television and radio repairs are not for the amateur—even though the time-honoured method of banging a dead set will often bring it to life. This is a very temporary 'repair', and does the set no good at all in the long run. One obvious point to check if a set is dead, however— the fuse in the plug, and the fuse in the back of the set in the case of television receivers.

Loss of picture on a TV set can also be due to the aerial plug having fallen out, or worked loose. Also if you have a loft aerial, poor picture quality can often be traced to the aerial having been knocked out of position when you put something in the loft.

GAS APPLIANCES

Anything other than a simple fault with gas appliances is a job for the expert gas fitter—you cannot afford to take chances with possible gas leaks. However, a smell of gas may simply be due to a tap being left partially on, or the pilot light on the cooker having blown out. Check *regularly* that the pilot light is working properly. If not, it is probably dirty, so try cleaning the dirt off with an old toothbrush.

Tracing a Leak

Gas leaks are best located by smell. The nearer you get to the source of the leak, the stronger the smell. If you suspect a pipe or a pipe-joint of leaking, dribble soapy water on it and smear in place with the fingers. If there is a leak, it will show up by blowing bubbles at that point.
● *Never, never, never look for a gas leak with a naked flame.*

As a temporary measure you can coat a

leak with paint, wrap with cloth torn into a bandage and then apply a final wrapping of insulating tape. Check that you have cleared the leak by smelling close to the area.

In all cases, *report a gas leak caused by a definite fault to your local gas office at once.* They will treat it as an emergency measure. Provided you can definitely trace the source of the leak, a temporary repair should enable you to continue to use gas if absolutely necessary. Otherwise, turn off the gas supply at the meter.

Broken Elements

Broken gas-fire elements are easily replaced, provided you get exactly the right type of replacement element. Take an old one along as a sample, just to be sure of getting an exact match, especially in the case of older fires with ceramic elements. These elements are refitted merely by standing in place.

Metal radiants are held in place with screws. If they have to be removed, it will often be found the fixing screws are stuck fast. A drop of Plus Gas or paraffin will make them easier to remove.

Jet Troubles

Jets on gas fires normally do not need much cleaning, as the force of the flame keeps them clean. However, if a jet *is* dirty, clean carefully with a soft toothbrush.

If a ceramic jet gets broken, it should be replaced by an exact match (the number is usually stamped on it). Be sure that the small slot in the face of the new jet lines up exactly with the slots in the other jets, so that all the gas flames will match.

Most modern geysers and storage heaters have ceramic jets. Check occasionally to see that they are clean, and replace a jet if it is cracked. If you are cleaning the interior of the appliance—which should be done fairly regularly—cover the jet with a piece of cloth so that dirt cannot fall on to it.

Other Faults

Two annoying faults you may experience with the gas supply are:

1. Varying pressure. If there is a lack of pressure at peak times (especially in cold weather), the supply system is probably at fault, and there is nothing you can do about it. If it occurs at other times,though, the gas-pipe sizes in your house may be inadequate—you may be trying to use too many gas appliances off pipes that are too small. Get them checked.

2. Surging pressure, usually accompanied by a sort of musical noise. This is usually due to excess water collecting in the gas pipes. Call the gas company, and they will send someone to 'de-water' the pipes.

MOTOR FAULTS

With motor-driven appliances, the fault is often the simple one of a drive belt breaking or slipping off a pulley. Such a fault is obvious once you have removed enough of the casing to look inside. If the belt has slipped, simply put it back on, but you cannot do much about a broken belt except replace it with a new one of the correct type and size.

Never disregard an unusual noise made by a motor-driven appliance. This is usually an indication that something is wrong. Try to discover what is wrong before an expensive breakdown results. If you cannot, leave the appliance out of action until an expert can examine it. It is always worth having a look yourself first, for the trouble may be caused by something fairly obvious—such as part of the machine needing cleaning out, or requiring lubrication. Consult the maker's instructions for simple maintenance requirements.

BROKEN WINDOWS

There is not much you can do about a badly broken window except block it up with a sheet of hardboard cut to size and tacked in place to keep the weather out, until the pane is replaced.

A crack is a different matter. You can seal this temporarily with a strip of clear cellulose tape applied on the inside (it will not stay on long if applied to the outside). Or you can make a semi-permanent, if unsightly, repair with a strip of glass tissue cut to bandage width and stuck in place with glass-fibre resin. The same resin can be used to stick an ordinary bandage over a crack.

CRACKED WASHBASINS

Exactly the same sort of treatment as for broken windows—stick a strip of glass tissue or bandage over the length of the crack with glass-fibre resin, preferably on the underside where it will not show.

The main thing is to make sure that the crack area is dry before you attempt this repair, so warm the basin with an electric fire first. Leave the fire in place to speed hardening of the repair. Leave for as long as possible before you fill the basin with water again.

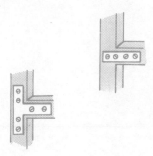

Above: Repair plates used to reinforce T-joints. Below: Repair plates used to reinforce corner joints.

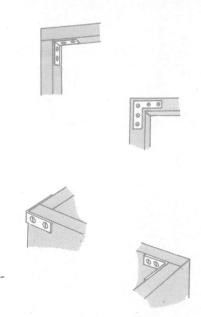

FURNITURE REPAIRS

A common fault with older, well-used furniture—especially chairs—is loosened joints. It is almost impossible to repair such joints by glueing, especially as part of the original joint will probably be broken.

The most effective treatment is to use repair plates, which are screwed in place. These come in various shapes (Fig. D) and should be fitted on the 'hidden' side if possible. Even if exposed they need not look ugly as you can get them in brass as well as steel. Use brass screws with brass plates and steel screws with steel plates.

Fig. D. Four basic shapes of repair plates.

Repair plates can be used to stiffen loose joints in furniture, picture frames, drawers, cabinets, garden gates—in fact, practically any wooden assembly which has worked loose.

They can even be used to repair a broken leg, or chair-seat frame, although if the member is broken right through rather than just cracked, you will need a repair plate on both sides. For the neatest appearance, inset repair plates which show flush with the surface of the wood.

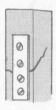

Above: Repair plates used on a fracture. Below: Repair plates used on each side of a complete break.

STICKING DOORS

It may be that the door has warped, or that the door frame has settled slightly, causing the door to bind or jam. The cure is to mark the position of the tight spot or spots, then plane down the edge of the door until it is an easy fit again.

You may have to take the door right off to do this, but before you go to all that trouble, though, check that the cause of jamming is not due to a loose hinge. Screws holding door-hinges can work loose, especially on the door-frame. In such a case it is no good just re-tightening the screws. They will probably work loose again. Replace the original screws, one at a time, with new screws of the same diameter size, but $\frac{1}{4}$ in. or $\frac{3}{8}$ in. longer.

You can also often adjust a badly-hung door by loosening the screws holding the hinges to the frame, and inserting packing under either the top or bottom hinge to cant the door slightly in the required direction once the screws are tightened right up again.

● *For repairs around the house not included in Emergency Repairs, see under the appropriate sections.*

Home Dyeing

Commercial dyeing is a very complex operation, but some manufacturers have now produced dyes suitable for successful home dyeing. Nowadays it is possible to obtain good results at low cost, and with little effort—provided that the instructions are followed carefully.

TYPES OF HOME DYES

MULTI-PURPOSE DYE*
Sold in small tins in powder form.

Suitable for use on all natural and most synthetic fabrics including acetate, viscose and every type of nylon.

WASH 'N DYE*
Contains the same dye constituents as Multi-Purpose Dye, but the powder is pre-blended with detergent to provide a unique washing-machine product.

Particularly suitable for large articles such as curtains and candlewick bedspreads.

LIQUID DYE*
Suitable for all natural fibres and most synthetics including rayon and the entire nylon family.

COLD DYE*
A fast dye for use on all household articles made of natural fibres which need frequent laundering.

This dye can be used on wool, when vinegar should be substituted for salt and soda as the fixative.

ALL PURPOSE DYE†
Recommended for use on all natural and most synthetic fabrics.

Marketed in paper sachets in small boxes.

CARPET DYE*
Although carpet dyeing is a much bigger job than dyeing household articles, it can be done very successfully at home and with the carpet in place on the floor.

This dye is suitable for use on wool, nylon and some carpet mixtures.

For the best effect, choose a new colour similar to that of the original.

Remember that the original colour will always slightly change the final result in over-dyeing (a red carpet dyed blue will become purple, for example).

Patterned carpets can be over-dyed just as successfully as plain ones if the colour used for over-dying matches the strongest colour of the pattern.

The thickness of the pile will determine the amount of dye needed: thick carpets absorb more than thin ones.

Colour Removal

In some cases, it may be necessary to remove the original strong or dark colours from the fabric before dyeing.

Colour-removing products are Dygon* or Colour Remover†.

Test a small piece of the fabric first. If the original dye is fast, then it may still be possible to over-dye with a darker colour.
- *By Dylon.
- †By Drummer.

For Successful Home Dyeing

THE DYE
There are different types of dye available for almost every type of fabric, and the correct type of dye must be used.

It is not as yet possible to dye acrylic fibres such as Orlon, Acrilan and Courtelle. The nature of the fibre causes it to distort when raised to temperatures necessary for home dyeing.

Nor is it wise to attempt to dye material that has a special finish—resin-treated to produce drip-dry, crease-resistant material, or weatherproofed. The dye cannot penetrate evenly, and this results in a patchy effect.

THE AMOUNT
Each article first must be weighed dry

so that the correct quantity of dye for the dry weight can be bought.

If an article weighs very little—stockings or tights, for instance—it will only be necessary to use a small proportion of one tin of dye. The easiest method is to dissolve the entire tin in one pint of boiling water as directed, then to use only the required quantity. If the whole tin is used, an over-strong colour will result.

Correct **quantity** of dye for the **weight** of material is most important, especially where exact colours are desired.

THE VESSEL

The dye vessel or bath should be large enough not only for the water to cover the material completely, but to allow room for the thorough movement of the fabric during the dyeing operation.

Small articles can be dyed easily in an enamel or galvanised vessel (or in plastic where no heat is required) but it will, of course, be necessary to stir by hand. A washing machine makes an ideal dye bath. Twin tub machines, in particular, are excellent.

The machine should be loaded only to half the advised maximum wash-load to ensure thorough agitation and even dyeing.

There will be little or no staining of the machine if it is emptied immediately after use, washed thoroughly with hot soapy water to which a cupful of bleach has been added, rinsed and dried.

Dye manufacturers' special instructions should be followed for fully automatic machines with individual wash pro-grammes.

POINTS TO WATCH

1. Every article to be dyed must be clean and unstained. Dyes cannot cover stains and may, in some cases, even make them more noticeable. Even when an article is merely faded unevenly—when curtains have been faded by sunshine for example—it will still be necessary to pre-treat the material with a colour-removing agent.

2. Where a dye **powder** is being used, it should be thoroughly dissolved in the boiling water before it is added to the dye vessel.

3. Make certain, when a fabric needs to be wetted before dyeing, that this is done very thoroughly. If the article is new, wash and rinse it thoroughly first.

4. Open out the wet article before putting it into the dye bath to allow even penetration of the dye.

5. During dyeing, keep the article fully submerged and constantly moving to avoid a streaky or patchy result.

6. Do **not** use the same dye solution twice. Correctly mixed, it should have lost all dyeing properties after being used once.

7. Do not omit the additives (salt, soda, vinegar, etc.) advised in the instructions. They are essential if the dye is to be successfully fixed.

8. Maintain the correct temperature during the dyeing process. Otherwise, the required depth of colour cannot be obtained.

9. Rinse all dyed articles until the water runs absolutely clear.

10. Dry the articles away from strong sunlight or direct heat.

Over-Dyeing Chart

When existing colour cannot be removed (i.e. in fast dyed fabrics) the following chart may be useful:

Red + yellow = red orange
Blue + yellow = green
Yellow + pink = coral
Green + yellow = lime
Light brown + medium Red = rust
Red + blue = purple
Pale blue + pink = lilac
Dark brown + red = reddish brown

HOME DYEING EQUIPMENT

● *By Dylon.*
● †By Drummer.

Cold Water Dye*

● *For small articles such as hand-towels, use an enamel, galvanised or plastic bucket. For large articles such as bed-linen, use a washing machine. Do not use an aluminium dye-bath, as soda reacts on aluminium.*
● *Rubber gloves. This super-fast dye stains hands very quickly.*
● *Wooden spoon.*
● *Metal spoon.*

220

The art of tie and dye

'Limitless scope for the adventurous'—by the *Tie and Dye* and *Tie and Stitch* methods of dyeing patterns of colours into cloth. Here are examples of both simple and elaborate designs. Remember: Use fine materials which have been well laundered, tie the patterns tightly to get sharp, definite shapes and use super-fast dyes such as Dylon cold dyes. *See page 224.*

A picture produced by using, first, Dylon cold dye Nasturtium; then after retying, Coral red.

The colour order used for this picture is Nasturtium, red and lastly Navy, the strongest colour.

Patterns for neckties produced by using a selection of ties and knots.

An example of stitching and dyeing Tartan green, then Navy. Red sequins have been sewn on the finished pattern.

- *Kitchen knife.*
- *Salt.*
- *Soda.*
- *Detergent.*
- *Pint measuring jug.*
- *Kettle.*
- *Adequate dye powder.*

METHOD

1. Fill dye-bath with sufficient cold water to cover the article.

2. Dissolve dye in pint of warm water.

3. Add the dissolved dye to cold-water dye-bath with the required quantity of salt (four tablespoons to one tin of dye).

4. Dissolve the soda in boiling water, and add to dye-bath (one tablespoon of soda to one tin of dye). Soda can be substituted with a product called Cold-fix, by Dylon. Vinegar is used only on woollen garments.

5. Stir water to blend liquids thoroughly.

6. Carefully lift in the thoroughly wet article to be dyed, and stir continually for 10 minutes. Stir intermittently for a further 20 minutes.

7. Pour away dye liquid, add detergent and boiling water to cover the article and leave for five minutes.

8. Pour off detergent water, and rinse until water clears. Spin and dry.

Multi-Purpose Dye*

- *For small articles, use an enamel or galvanised bucket. For large articles, washing machine.*
- *Wooden spoon.*
- *Metal spoon.*
- *Kitchen knife.*
- *Salt.*
- *Measuring jug.*
- *Kettle.*
- *Adequate dye.*

METHOD

1. Fill dye-bath with sufficient very hot water to cover the article.

2. Dissolve the dye powder in pint of boiling water.

3. Add dissolved dye to boiling water in dye-bath with required quantity of salt (one tablespoon per tin).

4. Stir to blend then add the thoroughly wet article.

5. Stir continually for 15 minutes. Raise to boiling point.

6. Rinse article in running water until water clears.

7. Spin and dry.

Wash'n Dye*

- *Designed for use in washing machines, the combination of dye and detergent eliminating the need to pre-wash the article. All you need is a washing machine of adequate size.*

METHOD

1. Fill machine and heat to approximately 180°F. Add tin of Wash 'n Dye. Agitate to dissolve detergent and dye powder. Stop machine.

2. Place in opened-out article, which does not need to be wet.

3. Agitate machine for 12 minutes.

4. Spin out excess dye water if possible, then rinse thoroughly.

5. Spin and dry.

Liquid Dye*

- *Enamel, galvanised or aluminium bucket or bowl for small articles. Plastic utensil will do where no heat is required. Washing machine for large articles.*
- *Salt.*
- *Adequate amount of dye.*

METHOD

1. Fill dye-bath with very hot water. Heat to boiling point if you want a dark or strong colour.

2. Add salt, and correct quantity of the liquid dye.

3. Add thoroughly wet article, and stir for 20 minutes.

4. Rinse in running water.

All Purpose Dye†

- *Enamel dye-bath or washing machine.*
- *Wooden stick or spoon.*
- *Salt.*
- *Pint measuring jug.*
- *Kettle.*
- *Adequate dye powder.*

METHOD

1. Fill dye-bath or washing machine with very hot water.

2. Dissolve dye powder by boiling one pint of water. Add to dye-bath or washing machine.

3. For each box of dye used, add two tablespoonfuls of salt.

4. Carefully put in the article to be dyed. Simmer for 10 minutes.

5. Lift article out, and rinse under running water until clear.

Note: Nylon and acetate fabrics must not be boiled. Keep the dye just below boiling point.

Colour Remover†

● *One carton of colour remover is sufficient to remove the colour from one pound of material, dyed to a medium shade. More stripping powder must be used for dark colours.*

METHOD

1. Enamel or aluminium bowl, or a washing machine.

2. Prepare solution by pouring a quart of hot water into the bowl or washing machine, add not less than ¼ pint vinegar to each carton of colour remover poured into the hot water. Add colour remover.

3. Fill the bowl or washing machine with sufficient hot water to cover the article, so that it can be moved about freely while immersed.

4. Bring the solution to the boil, simmer until the colour is removed. Always keep the article moving and immersed. Do not boil artificial silk, rayon, nylons. If, after 10 minutes, the colour has not been reduced sufficiently for re-dyeing, add more vinegar and colour remover.

5. Rinse thoroughly in warm water before re-dyeing.

Dygon Colour Remover*

● *Washing machine or enamel bucket.*
● *Pint measuring jug.*
● *Wooden spoon.*

METHOD

1. Fill dye vessel of adequate size with hot water.

2. Dissolve Dygon (one tin to ½ lb. dry weight of material or one capful for 4–5 oz. large size) in 1 pint boiling water, stir well and add to vessel.

3. Lift in wet article, and stir for 5 to 15 minutes until colour has been removed, stirring continually. Raise to boiling point.

4. Rinse in hot, soapy water and under running water to remove all traces of Dygon.

Carpet Dye*

● *Enamel bucket and enamel bowl or saucepan.*
● *Measuring jug.*
● *Wooden spoon.*
● *Scrubbing brush.*
● *Rubber gloves.*
● *Adequate dye.*

METHOD

1. In the case of fitted carpets, protect the skirting board or wainscot with newspaper.

2. To protect floorboards or underfelt, place layers of newspapers under the carpet to absorb the dye.

3. First clean the carpet with a suction cleaner, then shampoo with a reputable cleaner to remove all stains.

4. Dissolve the dye powder in a metal bucket by adding boiling water in the quantities directed by the manufacturers.

5. Stir well until all the dye powder has dissolved. Bring to simmering point, and keep bucket on the heat.

6. Pour a small quantity of the solution into a small enamel bowl or saucepan. While the carpet is damp, apply the dye, nearly boiling.

7. Use a clean brush—a hearth brush with a handle is very suitable. Brush the dye solution in, working fast and working well down into the pile. Wear rubber gloves for this job.

8. Avoid saturating the carpet.

9. The dye solution must be kept near boiling point throughout the dyeing process, because colour fastness depends on very high temperature. So frequently replenish the small container from the bucket, which must remain on the heat.

10. Drying time depends on the thickness of the carpet, and the surrounding temperature. Generally two days should be allowed.

TIE AND DYE

Tie and Dye is a means of dyeing patterns of colour into cloth. The penetration of the dye is controlled by knotting or stitching. The idea is that when the material is placed in the dye-bath, the colour cannot penetrate the tied areas. The combination of dyed and undyed shapes forms interesting and colourful patterns.

Tie and Dye is a creative skill which can be practised with little equipment or experience, and offers limitless scope to the adventurous.

Dylon Cold Dye is widely used for instruction on tie dyeing because it is totally colourfast, and can stand repeated launderings. Experiment on a small piece of cotton material (an old sheet is ideal) which can be framed as a picture or made into interesting ties and scarves. Progress on to unique cushions, curtains or household articles.

Cold Dye should only be used on natural fibres.

METHOD

1. Wash and iron cloth.

2. Mark out the design in pencil.

3. Tie up the sample in preparation for dyeing.

4. Make up one pint of Cold Dye— together with salt and soda or Cold Fix.

5. Wet the tied material—to give deeper penetration on bulky articles leave dry.

6. Dye in the usual way, and stir continu- ally for 10 minutes, then intermittently for a further 20 minutes.

7. When the dyeing process is complete, lift out the sample and rinse until water clears. Cover with boiling water and detergent. Leave for five minutes, stirring occasionally.

8. Rinse well, untie while wet and iron while damp.

9. When a second colour is to be dyed, dry the sample and re-tie. Then follow the same procedure.

Simple Techniques

KNOTTING

Tie a test knot to see how much cloth it takes, then mark position of knots. Fold cloth in half lengthwise, twist it and tie a knot on the first mark. Repeat along the cloth, leaving a gap between knots. Pull the knots tightly, and dye the first colour. Rinse and untie. Tie knots in different places on the cloth and dye in a second colour. Produces an irregular mottled effect.

STRIPES

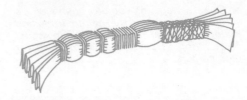

Pleat the fabric, and hold firmly. At intervals make bindings—narrow or wide, even criss-cross to give a variety of patterns. Bind very tightly and fasten off securely. Use strong white cotton or linen thread for binding.

SQUARES

Fold a square of fine material into four, then across to form a triangle. Bind all corners, and dye.

MARBLING

Bunch up the cloth by hand. Secure the thread, and bind in all directions, making a solid ball.

CLUMP TYING

Small objects such as pebbles, corks and buttons can be tied into the cloth. Mark each position with pencil dots, so that you can keep track of the pattern. Hold the object in place, and bind tightly into position with thread.

CIRCLES

Pick up a point of cloth, and secure near

the end for a small circle—farther away for a larger one. Add additional bindings if required for extra pattern.

OVALS AND DIAMONDS

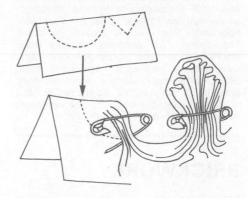

Fold the cloth along the centre of the shape. Weave a safety pin along the marking line. Close the pin and bind, then remove pin.

Stain Removal

The most effective ways of treating stains vary with the object or material involved, so consult the following list for a suitable approach. But do not expect miracles. You cannot, for example, remove deep stains or scars from highly-polished furniture without leaving a permanent mark. Some proprietary surface repairers may produce a satisfactory compromise, but in many cases the only cure is complete re-finishing of the whole surface.

BRICKWORK

Stain

1.   Discolouration.
2.   Smoky discolouration.
3.   White encrustation (most common on new brickwork).
4.   Persistent discolouration.

Treatment

1.   Wash thoroughly with soda soap.
2.   Wash thoroughly with soap solution mixed with household ammonia.
3.   Clean off with wire brush. Paint any remainder with spirits of salt, leave for a while and wash off with clean water.
4.   Best painted over. You can get suitable brick-coloured paints.

CONCRETE

Stain

1.   Rust.
2.   Dirty colour.

Treatment

1.   Paint on strong solution of oxalic acid, and scrub with a stiff brush. Wash off with clean water.
2.   Wash with a strong soap-and-water mixture. If this is not effective, paint with cement paint.

WOOD

Stain

1.   Oil (soaked into bare wood).
2.   Paint.
3.   Tar.
4.   Rubber scuff marks.
5.   Coffee (on bare wood).
6.   Tea (on bare wood).
7.   General discolouration.
8.   Ink.

Treatment

1.   Apply a paste of talc or whiting and trisodium phosphate mixed with a little water. Leave in position for as long as necessary.
2.   Scrape off as much as possible. Treat remainder with trisodium phosphate or paint stripper. Scrape clean, then wash with water.
3.   Try 'lifting' with a rag soaked in petrol or paraffin after scraping off as much as possible with a knife.
4.   Remove by rubbing with fine steel wool.
5.   Wash out as much as possible with soap and water. Rub on carbon tetrachloride or similar solvent cleaner to remove remainder.
6.   Apply strong borax solution and leave. Wipe off.
7.   Paint on strong oxalic acid solution, and leave. This will have a bleaching action on the wood. Wash generously with water.
● In all the above cases, or if the stain is unidentifiable, remove stains which resist these methods by scrubbing with fine steel wool. Re-finish exposed wood with sealer to match surrounds.
8.   Try soap and water. If this is not effective, paint with citric acid and leave

for about fifteen minutes. Wash off with water, and dry.

LINOLEUM

Stain
General.

Treatment

Scrape off carefully without damaging the surface of the lino. For persistent stains, paint with glycerine and leave for about fifteen minutes. If this does not work, try ammonia, carbon tetrachloride or acetone, in that order. Do **not** use strong alkaline cleaners or paint strippers on lino.

FABRICS

If possible, first test that the proposed treatment does not attack or discolour the material.

Stain
1. Beer.
2. Blood.
3. Coffee.
4. Tea.
5. Wine.
6. Fruit juice.
7. Ice cream.
8. Grease.
9. Ink.
10. Grass.
11. Milk.
12. Nail varnish.
13. Lipstick.
14. Oil.
15. Paint.

Treatment

1. Clean with a solution of one part sal ammoniac, one part methylated spirits and four parts warm water.

2. Soak area well in mixture of tepid water and household ammonia. Allow to dry out. If not fully removed, treat with tri-sodium phosphate (one part to eight of water).

3. Sponge with warm, soapy water, then dry. Complete removal of stain with carbon tetrachloride or similar cleaning fluid.

4. Sponge with, or soak in, strong solution of borax.

5. Sponge or soak in acetic acid. One part of hydrogen peroxide to five parts ammonium chloride is also effective, but may bleach the material.

6. Hydrogen peroxide is usually effective, but may bleach the material.

7. Warm, soapy water should remove most of the stain. Get rid of the remainder with carbon tetrachloride or similar solvent cleaner.

8. Lay a piece of blotting paper over the stain, and apply hot iron on top to draw up as much of the grease as possible. Remove remainder with carbon tetrachloride or similar solvent cleaner.

9. Hydrogen peroxide is usually effective.

10. Warm soap and water solution to which has been added a teaspoonful of methylated spirits. Ether is even more effective.

11. Clean off as far as possible with ether. Any remainder can then usually be removed with strong borax solution. Finally wash with clean water.

12. Remove with acetone. The acetone itself will become coloured during this process, and so leave a fainter stain. Remove this with methylated spirits.

13. Remove with carbon tetrachloride or similar solvent cleaner. Area will retain a light stain, which can be removed with hydrogen peroxide.

14. Strong detergent solution, lighter fuel (not ordinary petrol, which will stain), or carbon tetrachloride or similar solvent cleaner. Remove any remaining faint stain with detergent or soap and water.

15. Try paint thinner, methylated spirit, or a mixture of both. Turps substitute can also be used, leaving a fainter stain which can be removed with carbon tetrachloride or similar solvent cleaner. If paint is not softened by above treatment it is probably cellulose. Use acetone to remove this.

Carpets & Floor Coverings

Buying a new carpet is a major investment so it is important that you get value for money and select the right carpet for the job.·

It is important to buy a carpet with a brand name since the name of the manufacturer is a guarantee in itself that the carpet is a good one.

Leading manufacturers, in collaboration with the British Carpet Centre have a standard labelling scheme which states clearly which area of the home the carpet should be used in.

There are five classifications:

1. **Light domestic use, e.g. bedroom use.**
2. **Light to medium domestic use.**
3. **Medium domestic or light contract use.**
4. **Heavy domestic or medium contract use.**
5. **Luxury domestic or heavy contract use.**

TYPES OF CARPET

AXMINSTER
Woven. (The tufts are looped through the back of the carpet and not sealed in as in tufted carpets.)

WILTON
Woven.

TUFTED
Tufts are introduced into a woven jute backing and bound by a coating of latex.

FOAM BACKED
Carpets to which an additional backing of sponge foam has been added and which replaces a separate underlay.

UNDERLAY
Felt, rubber or foam which is laid under the carpet to produce a softer tread and help promote the life of the carpet.

WOOL
Traditional carpet fibre. Its natural springiness ensures the carpet maintains its good looks. Wool is warm, resists dirt and requires the least amount of cleaning attention.

Plain Wilton has a velvety surface; twist pile Wilton in all wool or wool/nylon mixture is extremely hard wearing and crush resistant. Axminster in 80% wool/ 20% nylon is hard wearing for general domestic use.

COTTON
Rarely used except in imported carpets, and for some loop pile rugs. Hard wearing but flattens easily. Rugs can usually be washed and are ideal for bathrooms and nurseries.

BRI-NYLON
The most hard wearing of all carpet fibres, nylon is often mixed with wool to give extra wear resistance. Or it can be used on its own.

Loop pile carpets made from continuous filament nylon are durable enough to use anywhere in the home. New ones, with the loops set close together, are excellent for stairs.

Since nylon has low moisture absorbency it can be shampooed easily and dries quickly. Static is sometimes a nuisance, but it can be overcome by shampooing.

COURTELLE (Acrylic fibre)
Hard wearing and can be used on its own or with other man-made fibres. Good appearance and handling.

ACRILAN (Acrylic fibre)
Man-made fibre nearest to wool in looks. Ideal used on its own, sometimes used in mixtures. Unlike nylon, it does not build up static.

EVLAN (Rayon viscose)
Not as resilient or hard wearing as wool or nylon. Used on its own it is only suitable for light wear. Usually mixed with other fibres to produce a medium quality inexpensive carpet.

EVLAN (Modified Rayon)
More durable and resilient than normal carpet rayon staple, but not as resilient as wool or as hard-wearing as nylon and the acrylics. Suitable for all types of use—

but many 100% Evlan carpets are light-weight and most suitable for lighter wear. Often mixed with other fibres (wool, nylon or acrylic fibres) to produce good performance in inexpensive carpets.

SHAPES OF CARPET

BROADLOOM

Is a term given to carpets over 2 yards wide—usually 9 to 12 ft. or more. Using Broadloom, a fitted carpet can be laid in rooms of up to 15 ft. wide without any joins being necessary.

BODY CARPET

27 in. or 36 in. wide carpet used for stairs and corridors. It can also be laid in strips seamed together and is sometimes the most economical method of close-covering an awkwardly shaped room.

CARPET SQUARE

Is laid loosely so that it can be taken up for cleaning, turned round to equalise wear, or even moved from room to room. It can be any rectangular shape. Broadloom is often sold with the edges bound to be used as a 'square'.

LAYING CARPET

If you have bought a top grade carpet it is false economy to try to lay it yourself. How it is laid can affect its life. If the seams are badly joined or, through bad planning, are made in the wrong places this will hasten wear. Seams which are not sewn securely will loosen and allow the carpet to slide. Laying the pile the wrong way will also cause more wear—an important factor when laying the carpet.

If you do plan to lay your own carpet, then choose from tufted, foam-backed or an Axminster or Wilton that has a non-fray back.

Estimating and Planning

To estimate the amount of carpet you will require to close cover a room make a scale drawing of the room allowing $\frac{1}{4}$ inch to represent 1 foot. In a reasonably rectangular room, calculate by changing

the feet into yards and multiply width by breadth. This will give you the overall square yardage.

Carpet is priced by the square yard so from this you can work out the approximate cost of your carpet, working to the nearest standard width of carpet: i.e. 27 in.; 36 in.; 54 in.; 6 ft.; 7 ft. 6 in.; 9 ft.; 10 ft. 6 in.; 12 ft.; 13 ft. 6 in.; 15 ft.

●*See overleaf.*

Additional extras to allow for when pricing include:
underlay
metal edging strips for doorways
smoothedge or tacks for pinning the carpet into place.

If seams are necessary, try to avoid having these in the doorway or main traffic areas. It is better to have a seam across the room than down the room. Make sure your pile runs the same way on all pieces.

With patterned carpet, allow for pattern matching if it is necessary to have a join. When more than one piece of carpet is needed, ask when ordering that these should be colour matched.

When estimating for stairs, allow additional material for bends and turns plus an additional $\frac{1}{2}$ yard to allow carpet to be moved each year to even up wear.

Methods of Fitting

TACK AND TURN

Edge of the carpet turned under and carpet secured to floor by $1\frac{3}{4}$ in. or $1\frac{1}{2}$ in. tacks.

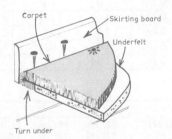

Tack and turn, with the edge of the carpet turned to meet the underfelt.

PINS AND SOCKETS

Large headed brass pins driven through

SQUARE YARDAGE RECKONER

● *If your room is, say, 10 ft. 6 in. wide and 15 ft. long, find 10 ft. 6 in. in the first vertical column and 15 ft. in the top horizontal column. Where the vertical and horizontal lines meet is the figure for the square yardage: in this case $17\frac{1}{2}$.*

WIDTH	LENGTH							
	ft. in. 6 0	ft. in. 6 6	ft. in. 7 0	ft. in. 7 6	ft. in. 8 0	ft. in. 8 6	ft. in. 9 0	ft. in. 9 6
6 ft. 0 in.	4	$4\frac{1}{3}$	$4\frac{2}{3}$	5	$5\frac{1}{3}$	$5\frac{2}{3}$	6	$6\frac{1}{3}$
7 ft. 6 in.	5	$5\frac{5}{12}$	$5\frac{5}{6}$	$6\frac{1}{4}$	$6\frac{2}{3}$	$7\frac{1}{12}$	$7\frac{1}{2}$	$7\frac{11}{12}$
9 ft. 0 in.	6	$6\frac{1}{2}$	7	$7\frac{1}{2}$	8	$8\frac{1}{2}$	9	$9\frac{1}{2}$
10 ft. 6 in.	7	$7\frac{7}{12}$	$8\frac{1}{6}$	$8\frac{3}{4}$	$9\frac{1}{3}$	$9\frac{11}{12}$	$10\frac{1}{2}$	$11\frac{1}{12}$
12 ft. 0 in.	8	$8\frac{2}{3}$	$9\frac{1}{3}$	10	$10\frac{2}{3}$	$11\frac{1}{3}$	12	$12\frac{2}{3}$

WIDTH	LENGTH							
	ft. in. 10 0	ft. in. 10 6	ft. in. 11 0	ft. in. 11 6	ft. in. 12 0	ft. in. 12 6	ft. in. 13 0	ft. in. 13 6
6 ft. 0 in.	$6\frac{2}{3}$	7	$7\frac{1}{3}$	$7\frac{2}{3}$	8	$8\frac{1}{3}$	$8\frac{2}{3}$	9
7 ft. 6 in.	$8\frac{1}{3}$	$8\frac{3}{4}$	$9\frac{1}{6}$	$9\frac{7}{12}$	10	$10\frac{5}{12}$	$10\frac{5}{6}$	$11\frac{1}{4}$
9 ft. 0 in.	10	$10\frac{1}{2}$	11	$11\frac{1}{2}$	12	$12\frac{1}{2}$	13	$13\frac{1}{2}$
10 ft. 6 in.	$11\frac{2}{3}$	$12\frac{1}{4}$	$12\frac{5}{6}$	$13\frac{5}{12}$	14	$14\frac{7}{12}$	$15\frac{1}{6}$	$15\frac{3}{4}$
12 ft. 0 in.	$13\frac{1}{3}$	14	$14\frac{2}{3}$	$15\frac{1}{3}$	16	$16\frac{2}{3}$	$17\frac{1}{3}$	18

WIDTH	LENGTH							
	ft. in. 14 0	ft. in. 14 6	ft. in. 15 0	ft. in. 15 6	ft. in. 16 0	ft. in. 16 6	ft. in. 17 0	ft. in. 17 6
6 ft. 0 in.	$9\frac{1}{3}$	$9\frac{2}{3}$	10	$10\frac{1}{3}$	$10\frac{2}{3}$	11	$11\frac{1}{3}$	$11\frac{2}{3}$
7 ft. 6 in.	$11\frac{2}{3}$	$12\frac{1}{12}$	$12\frac{1}{2}$	$12\frac{11}{12}$	$13\frac{1}{3}$	$13\frac{3}{4}$	$14\frac{1}{6}$	$14\frac{7}{12}$
9 ft. 0 in.	14	$14\frac{1}{2}$	15	$15\frac{1}{2}$	16	$16\frac{1}{2}$	17	$17\frac{1}{2}$
10 ft. 6 in.	$16\frac{1}{3}$	$16\frac{11}{12}$	$17\frac{1}{2}$	$18\frac{1}{12}$	$18\frac{2}{3}$	$19\frac{1}{4}$	$19\frac{5}{6}$	$20\frac{5}{12}$
12 ft. 0 in.	$18\frac{2}{3}$	$19\frac{1}{3}$	20	$20\frac{2}{3}$	$21\frac{1}{3}$	22	$22\frac{2}{3}$	$23\frac{1}{3}$

WIDTH	LENGTH							
	ft. in. 18 0	ft. in. 18 6	ft. in. 19 0	ft. in. 19 6	ft. in. 20 0	ft. in. 20 6	ft. in. 21 0	ft. in. 21 6
6 ft. 0 in.	12	$12\frac{1}{3}$	$12\frac{2}{3}$	13	$13\frac{1}{3}$	$13\frac{2}{3}$	14	$14\frac{1}{3}$
7 ft. 6 in.	15	$15\frac{5}{12}$	$15\frac{5}{6}$	$16\frac{1}{4}$	$16\frac{2}{3}$	$17\frac{1}{12}$	$17\frac{1}{2}$	$17\frac{11}{12}$
9 ft. 0 in.	18	$18\frac{1}{2}$	19	$19\frac{1}{2}$	20	$20\frac{1}{2}$	21	$21\frac{1}{2}$
10 ft. 6 in.	21	$21\frac{7}{12}$	$22\frac{1}{6}$	$22\frac{3}{4}$	$23\frac{1}{3}$	$23\frac{11}{12}$	$24\frac{1}{2}$	$25\frac{1}{12}$
12 ft. 0 in.	24	$24\frac{2}{3}$	$25\frac{1}{3}$	26	$26\frac{2}{3}$	$27\frac{1}{3}$	28	$28\frac{2}{3}$

carpet and into brass socket previously sunk into the floor.

RINGING AND PINNING

Edges of carpet are hemmed or bound all round and metal rings are sewn on to the underside of the hem about 4½ in. apart. Stout pins or nails are driven into the floor at the same distance apart and the rings looped over them.

SMOOTHEDGE

Most popular method as the securing is invisible. Special pre-nailed strips of wood or metal designed with angled nails or teeth to hold the carpet are laid around the edges of the room; carpet is stretched on to these and the teeth/nails hold it in place. Raw edges are tucked down behind the smoothedge out of sight.

A knee-kicker should be used with care. An alternative is to use the back of a broom head to spread the carpet.

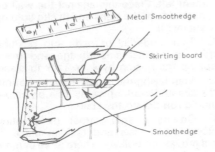

Fitting the smoothedge into the corner of a room.

Fitting

1. Clear the room of all furniture, brush floor and make sure it is free from any roughness, protruding nails, etc.

2. If using smoothedge, stick or nail this into position round the room positioning it about the thickness of the carpet away from the wall to allow raw edges to be tucked down.

Materials for Fitting

Underlay
Carpet
Smoothedge
Tacks
Hammer
Metal edging strip
Carpet needle and carpet thread
Carpet scissors
Stanley knife
Pliers
Stapling machine or gun
Knee-kicker *This needs some skill to use. Uneven stretching can cause buckling. Excessive use of the knee-kicker can damage the back of the carpet.*

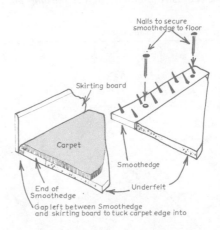

Fitting a carpet to a smoothedge.

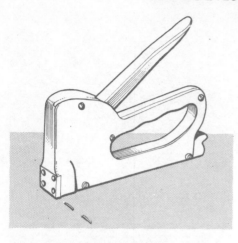

Use a stapling machine (preferably a heavy duty model) or tacks to secure the underlay.

3. Fit underlay; secure to floor with stapling machine or tacks.

4. Start laying the carpet in a corner of the straight side of the room.

5. Lift carpet into position. Do not drag it, or this will move the underfelt.

6. Tack along walls for two or three feet in each direction. Use knee-kicker to stretch for a distance of about six feet sideways and tack in place down the length of the room. Go back to corner and tack across width of room and then down the other side. Finally, stretch and tack across the end of room. *(See diagram.)*

7. Work on each stretch alternately to ensure the carpet is stretched evenly.

8. When the carpet has been fitted right round the room and stretched into position cut any corners, alcoves, etc. to shape.

9. When fitting round pipes it is better to bind the carpet to prevent possible fraying.

Fitting Stairs

1. When fitting stairs, nail smoothedge into place or, if using clips, fit these into position. To do this accurately:
   (a) measure width of stairs.
   (b) subtract width of carpet.
   (c) divide remaining amount by two.
   (d) Subtract the width of the clip.
Cut a block of wood to fit the measurement left. Place this against the wall on each side of the stairs and fit clip tight up against it.

2. Tack underlay or pads into position tight up against smoothedge and overlapping the nosing by 4 in. Tack in place.

3. Start laying the carpet from the bottom of stairs and work upwards. Pile on carpet should run **down** the stairs.

4. On turns, fold carpet by pleating excess under riser and tack in place. If this proves too bulky—where three or more turns come in quick succession, for example—cut and trim away excess. But in this case the carpet cannot be repositioned later for even wear.

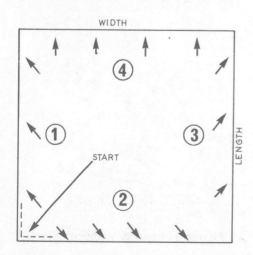

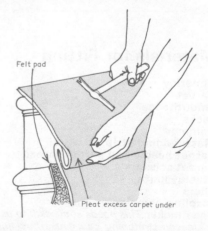

Fold stair carpet on turns by pleating the excess under the riser.

5. Joins should always lie along the joint of the tread and riser. The horizontal threads of the carpet should run parallel with the nosing, even on turns.

6. Leave ½ yard excess at the bottom of the stairs, folded under, to allow carpet to be moved a few inches each year to even wear.

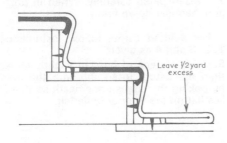

Leave ½ yard excess

CARING FOR YOUR CARPET

It is quite normal for cut pile carpets to shed fluff when they are first laid. After the first vacuuming leave for a week or two to allow some of this excess shedding to bed down into the carpet. Once the carpet has settled, vacuum regularly to remove all particles of dust and grit which otherwise may damage the base of the pile.

Occasionally have your carpet professionally cleaned. In between times use a reliable dry-cleaning solvent to remove odd stains.

There are also several shampooers on the market. If using a wet cleaner make sure the carpet is completely dry before you walk on it or replace furniture in the room. When shampooing do not wet the backing; it can result in shrinkage and even rotting.

Don't use solvents on a rubber-backed carpet: they will damage the backing.

Accidents

If someone spills food or liquid, act quickly. Dab up liquids, scrape up foods with a spoon.

If the pile has been penetrated, put an old absorbent cloth under the carpet to keep the area as dry as possible.

Treat with non-alkaline detergent or a suitable proprietary cleaner.

If the carpet is fitted, beware that the heat from the fire or radiators does not dry out damp patches too quickly and so cause the area to shrink, stretch or buckle.

Quick action can often prevent permanent stain or damage. If the damage is severe, however, it is sometimes better to call in expert assistance immediately.

When attempting to clean stains yourself, remember to always use clean white fabric or tissue and work from the outside towards the centre of the stain.

First Aid Treatments

BALLPOINT INK
Dab with methylated spirits. Sponge with warm water.

BLOOD
Blot first, then sponge with cold water.

BUTTER
Scrape off, then remove final traces by spongeing with warm water and detergent.

BEVERAGES
Mop up surplus, then sponge with lukewarm water and detergent. If black coffee, rub with glycerine first.

FRUIT JUICES
Sponge with warm water and detergent. If necessary, follow by dabbing with methylated spirits.

GREASE
Scrape off, then dab with a proprietary dry cleaning solvent or use carbon tetrachloride.
●—**Important.** Work away from open fire and avoid smoking while carrying out treatment. Well ventilate the room afterwards.

INK
Sponge fresh stains with warm water and detergent. If stain persists, seek professional advice.

MUD
Leave to dry then brush off firmly. Do not attempt to remove it while damp, or

it will penetrate further into the pile.

WAX POLISH

Dab with dry cleaning solvent or carbon tetrachloride.

WINES, BEERS AND SPIRITS

Sponge with warm water and detergent. Old stains can often be removed with methylated spirits.

BURNS AND HOLES

Cigarette burns or holes caused through hot coals or sparks from the fire can be repaired. Cut away the damaged area and let in a patch of matching colour or design.

If the carpet is not fitted, use this method:

1. With the right side uppermost, cut out the damaged part with a razor blade.

2. Cut a patch to fit exactly.

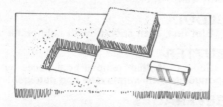

3. Prevent the edges fraying by pasting round the cut edges of both the carpet and patch, half way up the pile, with Copydex or similar adhesive.

4. Allow about 15 minutes to dry.

Glue halfway up the pile

5. Cut a piece of hessian ½ in. larger all round than the patch. Stick this over the hole on the back of the carpet.

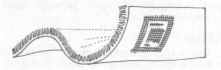

6. With the carpet right side up, paste through the hole on to the hessian.

7. Insert patch carefully. When in position, hammer down firmly.

For a fitted carpet follow instructions **1, 2, 3** and **4** as given.

5. Cut a piece of hessian slightly larger than the patch; insert this into the hole by poking the edges underneath so that it lies flat on the floor or underfelt.

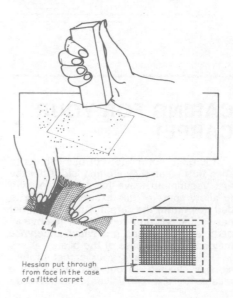

Hessian put through from face in the case of a fitted carpet

6 and **7** as detailed above.

If the carpet is an Axminster, remove 2 or 3 strands from the edge of the hole. Paste the fringed ends now left on to the back of the carpet to prevent fraying, before proceeding as above.

Frayed Edges

Remove strands as above and paste. Additional reinforcement can be given by sticking a length of tape along back.

LINO AND VINYL FLOORING

Equipment

Hammer ⎫
Pincers ⎬ **For preparing floor**
Heavy scissors
Lino knife
Straight edge
Pencil
Paper felt (for underlaying lino)

Linoleum and vinyl should never be laid directly on to the floor. First prepare floor as follows:

1. The floor should be thoroughly cleaned, and dry.

2. All protruding nails should be removed or flattened and rough patches smoothed over.

3. Felt paper underlay should be fastened down; if adhesive is used this should be allowed to dry thoroughly.

Flexible vinyl takes the shape of the floor beneath so, unless the floor is absolutely even, an underlay of resin bonded plywood, felt or rubber is more suitable than felt paper. This applies to flexible vinyl in both sheet and tile form but not to flexible vinyl with felt or foam backing.

Vinyl flooring is more flexible than linoleum. Linoleum has a tendency to stretch and should be laid an inch or so short of the skirting all round the room. It may still be necessary to trim off surplus after a few days.

Vinyl shrinks a little so when laying remember:

1. Overlap all joints by at least ½ in.

2. Allow about 1 in. extra all round the room and abutments.

3. It can be cut with ordinary scissors and is easy to shape around units or fitments.

4. It can be marked with a pencil for cutting and the marks wiped off afterwards.

5. It needs trimming after about four days.

Before laying either vinyl or linoleum leave the rolls overnight in a warm room to make them easier to handle.

LAYING LINO OR VINYL TILES

1. Prepare floor as for sheet linoleum or vinyl.

2. Measure the two end walls, excluding bays and recesses. Mark centre points by driving nails into floor.

3. Tie string tightly from nail to nail. Chalk the string, lift it and let it snap back to give chalk line on floor.

4. Measure the two side walls and make chalk line as **3**.

5. Work from the centre point where chalk lines cross. Place first tile in any of the four right angles.

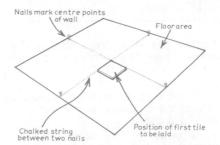

Above: Marking out an unobstructed room. Below: Marking out an irregularly-shaped room.

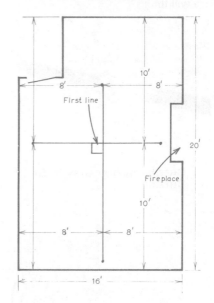

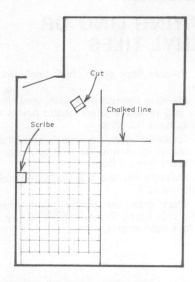

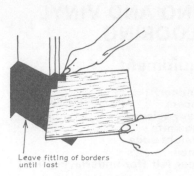

Fitting a tile into an irregular corner.

Fitting the tiles from the centre mark. Leave the border tiles until last.

6. Fit the tiles into position, leaving the fitting of the borders until the rest of the floor is completed.

7. To fit border tiles, place a tile tight against wall and draw a line where it overlaps last tile in the final row of completed tiles. Cut off overlap. Remaining piece will then fit into place.

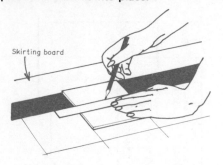

Cutting border tiles to fit.

8. When there are irregularities (e.g. pipes) first cut tile round these. Then push tile tight to wall and cut as in 7.

9. At corners, make sure tile is tight into the angle of the wall. Then cut to two adjacent tiles.

Maintenance

Vinyl flooring has an attractive satiny sheen and needs the minimum maintenance. Normal household spillages can be wiped up with a damp cloth. All-over cleaning is simply a matter of wiping over with mild soap and water. Stains can be rubbed gently with scouring powder and a damp cloth but should not be bleached or cleaned with spirit. Harsh abrasives damage the surface.

Vinyl floors do not require polishing but if a higher gloss is wanted, use a water-based emulsion.

Linoleum needs regular cleaning with a wax polish to help replace the natural oils which cleaning with soap or detergents may remove. Unless linoleum is waxed regularly it will dry out and crack

Home Laundry

There was a time when the only way to get clothes clean was to boil them, and then scrub with hard soap. Today the situation has been made much easier by a variety of products and equipment constantly developing to meet our changing needs. This makes it important for the housewife to understand the subject, and how to relate her needs to what she can afford.

Equipment

The aids now available in home laundry include:
- *Washing machines*
- *Ironing machines and irons of many types*
- *Dryers and airers*
- *Detergents—greatly improved*

The **Home Laundering Consultative Council**, an organisation formed from the major industries concerned with the home washing of garments and textiles, has agreed on washing temperatures for various fabrics, and also on domestic iron settings and terminology.

They have selected eight different washing processes (seven for machine and one for hand-washing), and they use a single process number to describe water temperature, amount of agitation and method of water extraction. These instructions appear on garment labels, on washing product packs and in the instructions given by washing machine manufacturers.

Working from an official definition for what is meant by a maximum, medium or minimum wash, the HLCC agrees on the following washing temperatures and their description:

Maximum wash means the recommended best amount of agitation for any given machine.
Medium wash means between 40 and 60 per cent of the maximum.
Minimum wash means the recommended minimum amount of agitation, normally between 20 and 30 per cent of the maximum.

Examples of the application of the HLCC code and processes are shown in the following table. Use the terms explained above for guidance.

WASHING MACHINES

Your choice is between:

1. **Automatic machine, which you just connect to the water supply (unless the machine is already plumbed in).**
2. **Semi-automatic.**
3. **Twin tub, which divides washing and spin drying.**
4. **Wringer machine–washing machine with hand wringer or electric wringer.**

The trend is to the automatic machine. A major problem for the makers of home laundry equipment in this country is how to get the clothes dry.

Washing machines are now starting to incorporate more sophisticated equipment to this end. One machine even adds heated drying to the spin drying, so that the washing, drying and airing of clothes is done in one machine.

Term	Temperature	Description
Warm Wash	104 °F (40 °C)	Pleasantly warm to the hand
Hand-hot Wash	118 °F (48 °C)	As hot as the hand can bear
Hot Wash	140 °F (60 °C)	Hotter than the hand can bear—the temperature of water coming from many domestic taps
Very Hot	185 °F (85 °C)	Water heated to near-boiling temperature
Boil	212 °F (100 °C)	Self-explanatory

How to choose

1. Get expert advice from local showroom or electrical dealer. If you can, try to buy where you have the advantage of the Safe Shopping Plan—a free advisory and complaints service offered by members of the Electrical Appliance Association.

2. Decide which machine suits your pocket best. Think of the initial cost and the running costs.

3. Study all available literature on new models.

4. Check on seals of approval, safety and performance.

5. Check on financial terms, and do be sure that if you get a reduction in price you are not losing out by paying additional interest on hire purchase terms, or running the risk of not being able to get spares or service.

6. As so many machines are made outside the United Kingdom, it is worth checking where the machine is made, and what assurances are available on spares and service.

Types of machine

FULLY AUTOMATIC

Fully automatic machines will wash, rinse and extract most of the water with the minimum of attention. You select the programme, push the button and the machine does the work.

Refinements include capacities which vary from 6–12 lb. dry weight of clothes, different varieties of 'wash programmes', the incorporation of a tumbler dryer to boost the spin-drying operation.

Some machines need to be plumbed in and even bolted to the floor. Others can be connected to the taps by a length of hose. Permanent plumbing is best. Time for the washing cycle can vary from 75 to 90 minutes or longer, but in the case of automatic machines the operation time is less important. Small loads washed in an automatic machine can be extravagant on current, detergent and water.

SEMI-AUTOMATIC

Semi-automatic machines work rather like the fully automatic ones except that

What, where and how

Fabrics	Machine rating	Hand wash	Method
Washable pleated garments containing acrylics, nylon, polyester or triacetate.	Not for machines	Warm	Warm rinse. Hand-hot final rinse. Drip dry
Wool, including blankets and wool mixtures with cotton and rayon. Silk.	Warm minimum wash	Warm. Do not rub	Spin. Do not hand wring
Acrylics. Acetate and triacetate, including mixtures with wool. Polyester-and-wool blends.	Warm minimum wash	Warm	Cold rinse. Short spin. Do not wring
Cotton, linen or rayon articles where colours are fast at 104 °F (40 °C) but not at 140 °F (60 °C).	Warm medium wash	Warm	Spin or wring
Coloured nylon. Polyester. Cotton and rayon articles with special finishes. Acrylic-and-cotton mixtures.	Hand-hot medium wash	Hand-hot	Cold rinse. Short spin or drip dry
White nylon.	Hot medium wash	Hand-hot	Cold rinse. Short spin or drip dry
Cotton, linen or rayon articles without special finishes where colours are fast at 140 °F (60 °C).	Hot maximum wash	Hand-hot	Spin or wring
White cotton and linen articles without special finishes.	Very hot to boil maximum wash	Hand-hot or boil	Spin or wring

you have to adjust the controls from one cycle to the next. Control of temperature and washing time is automatic.

TWIN-TUB

Twin-tub appliances incorporate a washing machine and a spin drier in one overall cabinet. They have a capacity varying from 5½ to 7 lb. dry weight of clothes, and they are flexible in that they can be moved and stored beneath a draining board or working surface as necessary. Clothes must be removed by hand from the tub to the drier. Most models enable rinsing to be done in the spin drier.

WRINGER MACHINE

Wringer machines consist of a washing machine with hand wringer or electric wringer. There are many different types.

Washing-machine action

There are two main types of automatic washing-machine action:

1. **Tumble action.** A horizontal drum rotates slowly, lifting the clothes through the water. Occasionally the clothes can tumble into a hard ball, so the drum on some machines is designed to revolve in one direction, pause, then turn the opposite way.

2. **Agitator action.** The drum is stationary, and the water is stirred by a fin-shaped spindle in the centre. The spindle moves to and fro. A larger load is possible with an automatic of this type, and also a better spin speed, but it does use a lot more water, and so costs more to run.

Before you buy

Before buying a washing machine, ask yourself:

1. Is the type and dimension right, and will it fit neatly into your kitchen?

2. Will the machine suit your priorities? For example, if time is important, the automatic machine is right for you if you can afford it. If your laundry consists of many loads of different materials, but you want to do all your washing on the same day, then the combined washer and spin drier will suit you best. If you can stay around while the machine is operating, the semi-automatic will suit you and could save your money.

3. Does the washing cycle fit your needs, particularly in relation to the length of time?

4. Is there a noise or vibration problem?

5. Does the nature of the detergent or powder recommended by the machine's maker limit your freedom of choice of washing agent and increase costs?

6. Is the machine large enough to hold the amount of washing you wish to do at any one time?

Looking after the machine

1. Do not overload the machine. The instructions will tell you how much it will take. Follow them, and clothes will get cleaner, and the machine last longer.

2. Use the correct amount of powder. Using more powder **will not** produce a cleaner wash, but it **will** clog the clothes and make rinsing more difficult.

3. Use the correct amount of water. Too much or too little will lead to inefficiency, and you may be overloading the machine.

4. Rinse the machine through with clear water after you have used it to avoid corrosion.

5. Wipe the machine down with a damp cloth to keep it bright and shining. Do not use abrasive powders—they can ruin the finish of enamel and stainless steel parts.

6. If the instructions say 'grease this part', make sure you do, but do not oil anything else.

7. Keep all the filters clean—they are there to stop fluff and the odd button or safety-pin getting caught up, and the water should be able to circulate freely through.

8. Disconnect before you start to clean the machine.

9. Get it serviced from time to time.

IRONS AND IRONING MACHINES

Irons have to cope with man-made fibres needing more heat control than cottons and silks, so manufacturers are including all sorts of refinements.

Most modern irons are automatically controlled. Makers often use the following four recommended settings, and sometimes No. 5:

1. **COOL. For fabrics which will withstand temperatures up to 110 °C —Acrilan, Courtelle, Orlon.**
2. **WARM. Up to 150 °C—Acetate, rayon, Tricel, nylon, wool and terylene.**
3. **MEDIUM HOT. Up to 180 °C— viscose rayon.**
4. **HOT. Up to 200 °C—cotton and linen.**
5. **VERY HOT. Above 200 °C, and should be used with caution, as this setting is not usually suggested on the labels on the garments.**

Types to choose from

1. **Dry Irons.** Cheap and light. The open front handle on many models makes it easy to iron sleeves.
2. **Steam Irons.** The modern 'drip' models work on cold water dripping from a tank in the iron on to a hot spot to make the steam. Only one temperature setting is required for all fabrics when steam ironing, and the iron is simply altered back to dry ironing by a turn of the dial.

The spray iron features a water container spraying water on to the material for turning into steam. Combined steam-spray irons have a push-button container fitted to the side.
3. **Ironing Machines.** Flat-bed ironers look like the domestic version of the tailor's press. Rotary ironers feature a cylinder turned by a small foot-controlled electric motor.

DRIERS AND AIRERS

Most people regard driers and airers as essential in the British climate. The various possibilities are:
1. Airing cupboard converted into a drying cabinet simply by taking the lagging jacket off the hot-water tank. Puts the fuel bill up considerably, because the water loses heat quickly. Not recommended.

2. Cupboard converted into a drier-airer. Small heaters are sold for this purpose, using less than ½d. worth of electricity an hour.
3. Spin drier. There are two types— gravity-outlet and pump. Advantage of the pump is that continuous rinsing can be done in the drum using a second hose attached to a tap. Most separate spin-driers will take about six pounds dry weight of clothes, and maximum extraction will take about four minutes, most of the water being extracted during the first two minutes.
4. Tumble drier. Takes drying one stage further. Clothes that have been spin dried can be damp dried in a tumble drier for ironing, or completely dried for wearing. They are gently tumbled through a current of warm air. Tumble driers are front loading, and some can be mounted on top of automatic washing machines. Some are small enough to fit into a cupboard or under a sink.

LOOKING AFTER THE SPIN DRIER

1. Do not drop things down between the casing and the drum—apart from being bad for the article concerned it will probably either block the outlet, or get caught up in the mechanism.
2. Load the drier correctly. Unnecessary strain on the machine may result in early failure.
3. After you have used the drier, unplug it and wipe it down with a damp cloth to prevent corrosion.

DETERGENTS

There are so many detergents, all claiming to do the job best, that it is difficult to make a choice. A detergent is anything that cleans. Soap is therefore a detergent, and so are soap powders, soapflakes, synthetic powders and liquids. The choice lies between:
1. PURE SOAP. Including soapflakes and pure soap powder. The disadvantage is that in hard-water areas soap combines with calcium and magnesium salts in the water to form the dirty, insoluble scum which gives your wash that grey or yellow look.

2. SOAPFLAKES AND SOAP POWDERS which do contain synthetic washing ingredients to counter-balance the scum problem. Bleaching agents like sodium perborate (to remove stains) and an optical whitener which is really a colourless fluorescent dye, give better results.

3. SYNTHETIC DETERGENTS. Available as powders and as liquid. These can be used in hard or soft water, and in water where vinegar has been added to prevent the dye bleeding. Special low-lather detergents are also available, and these suit some washing machines better.

SORTING HOME LAUNDRY

First divide your washing into two main groups—sturdy fabrics and fine or delicate materials.

They need different methods of washing, different types of soap powder, flakes or detergent and different temperatures of water.

1. Sturdy Fabrics. Including strong white nylon and terylene. Coloured cottons and linens should be sorted into those with fast dyes and those that might run.

2. Fine or Delicate Materials. Silks, rayons and woollens need careful individual washing. So do many of the other man-made fibres.

3. Extra Dirty Articles. Should be soaked in warm detergent suds for 15 minutes before washing. After washing, rinse and wash again.

4. Non Colour-fast Articles. Need special care. Wash separately by hand in warm suds, and dry quickly.

Fashion

Current fashion trends govern the type of clothes you buy, but to dress well and feel confident about what you are wearing there are certain guide rules which should be followed. Before buying ask yourself:

1. Is it a colour I can wear?
2. Will this new item fit into my existing wardrobe and team with the dress and coat I shall be wearing with it?
3. Does it fit properly and hang well?
4. Does the style suit me as an individual; does it flatter my particular figure?
5. Have I accessories to team with it, or must I buy new ones?
6. Is it a good buy, and will I be able to wear it often?

DRESS SENSE

When buying a complete new outfit, know what you are looking for, and know what suits you and flatters you. Points to remember:

If You are Tall

You can wear dramatic clothes, bright colours, exaggerated styles, large prints, widebrimmed hats, large handbags. To lessen your height, choose horizontal stripes, not vertical ones, clothes which cut across the figure, broad belts, contrasting tops, three-quarter jackets.

Flat-heeled shoes do not necessarily reduce the appearance of height. Wear the heel height you feel most comfortable in so that you balance well and walk tall.

If You are Plump

Avoid large patterns, horizontal stripes, very vivid colours, bunchy skirts or very tight ones which over-emphasise the width of your hips. Do not wear very short skirts—an extra inch in length can make hips look two inches slimmer.

Avoid wide belts, gathers and frills, as these add bulk. Avoid tight sweaters, materials that cling, high necklines and big collars.

If You are Thin

Exactly the opposite to If You are Plump. You can wear bright colours, large prints, horizontal stripes or full skirts.

Colour

The colours you wear can affect how you look, so study your complexion, and dress in colours that flatter.

Sallow complexion. Choose warm pinks, flaming reds, warm tans and orange shades, blue-greens.

Avoid yellows and browns; grey and black.

Very pale. Choose glowing reds and pinks, bright oranges and yellows, pastel shades.

Avoid dark green, browns and purples.

Pink complexion. Choose black, shades of blue, lavender, purple, greens and greys.

Avoid bright pink, bright red, orange or yellow—these will make you look florid.

FITTING

Choose materials which hang well and keep their shape. Avoid over-tight clothes which will wrinkle and crease and lose their shape because seams are stretched. Skirts and dresses hang better and last longer if they are lined, half-lining will help avoid seating in a straight skirt.

When buying a dress or coat, look for smooth fitting over the shoulders. Collars should fit evenly, and lie well. Collarless necklines should be free of bulges. Avoid necklines that gape.

PACKING

If you are travelling by air, your cases need to be lightweight since the amount of luggage you can take is strictly limited.

For those last-minute items, or overnight requirements if you are breaking the journey, travel grips are ideal. Check that zip openings are good and wide for easy packing.

Choose clothes that are in crease-resistant fabrics—Crimplene, Terylene, Terylene and cotton mixtures, Acrilan, Courtelle and Trevira fabrics. Wool is good too, since creases will drop out if the garment is left to hang for a few hours after you unpack it.

Many creases can be avoided by careful packing. Use tissues or tissue paper to pad folds, and pack heavy garments as flat as possible.

Plan your basics around two or three colours at the most, and see that everything you take along will mix or match. For instance, your cardigan should team with slacks, skirts and dresses; little tops should team with a suit or slacks.

Keep accessories to a minimum. Shoes and handbags are heavy and cumbersome, so select a basic colour rather than try to match up to each outfit.

Conserve space. Fill the toes of shoes with jewellery wrapped in tissues; slip small items that cannot be crushed down the sides and corners to stabilise your packing. The less the contents move around, the less creased everything will be.

If you have to go through Customs, leave a list of the contents just inside each case. Such a list is also helpful in locating items on an overnight stay, or making a last-minute check as to whether a certain item has been included or not.

PACKING ORDER

1. Pack heavy items such as shoes, brushes, bottles (wrapped in plastic bags for safety) at the bottom of your case.

2. Heavy garments and woollens. Always fold as flat as possible, and cover collars with tissue paper. Pleated skirts are the exception. They travel best rolled length-ways and pulled into a nylon stocking that has the foot cut off, and then placed down the side of a suitcase without further folding.

3. Undies should be packed next.

4. Silk and cotton dresses should be packed last, interleaved with tissue paper and covered over with tissue paper before the lid of the case is closed.

FOOTWEAR

1. Never buy shoes without first trying them on.

2. Have your feet measured regularly; their size can change. If your weight has increased you may find your foot is plumper or broader. Your foot may broaden if you have changed your job and you are doing more walking or standing.

3. When you buy shoes, make sure they are long enough and broad enough.

4. Make sure your shoes grip firmly at the heel.

5. When buying sling-backs, make sure that when the strap is adjusted your heel is resting on the platform of the heel—and not spreading over it at the back or sides.

6. For walking, choose lace-up or bar shoes with a low to medium heel.

7. Wet shoes should be dried out slowly, and the toes kept in shape with trees or rolled up newspaper.

8. Air your shoes before putting shoe trees in them.

9. Rest your shoes by wearing them on alternate days. If you are doing a lot of walking or standing, change your shoes once or twice a day.

10. Clean your shoes regularly. Leather uppers need polish to keep them supple. Clean them before you put them away so that they are always ready to wear.

11. Brush suede shoes with a wire brush or stiff bristle brush. Occasionally use a liquid suede cleaner to revive the pile.

12. Have your shoes repaired regularly. Apart from looking untidy, down-at-heel shoes are bad for your posture.

CARE OF YOUR CLOTHES

1. Coats, suits and dresses should always be hung on hangers, and kept under cover to avoid soiling by dust.

2. Never put more than one garment on each hanger. Make sure the hanger is the right size for the garment.

3. Use padded hangers for flimsy garments.

4. Use specially adapted hangers for skirts.

5. Keep all clothes under cover to avoid soiling. Hang either in a wardrobe or in large plastic bags which completely cover them.

6. Do not overcrowd your wardrobe, or your clothes will be permanently creased.

7. Regular brushing, spongeing and pressing under a cloth will keep clothes looking smart and increase their life.

8. Launder clothes regularly, or have them dry cleaned, especially before putting them away for winter or summer.

9. Keep woollies folded flat in drawers or on shelves. Never bundle them up, or they will be creased and unwearable.

10. Keep lingerie folded flat.

11. Keep belts, stockings, gloves, handkerchiefs and scarves in polythene bags so that they remain clean and readily available.

12. Keep a bottle of spot-remover and a needle and thread handy for on-the-spot first aid.

GROOMING

One of the finest aids to good grooming is a full-length mirror either at the top of the stairs or in the hall, so that you have a full view of yourself several times a day, and always before you leave the house.

Grooming covers all the small details which add up to perfection in dress and appearance. Neglect of any one can spoil the overall effect.

Hair. Should be washed regularly, and kept in healthy condition. Dry, dull hair is usually a sign of neglect or the need for attention to diet. Styles should be in keeping with the occasion.

Hands. Clean, with nails neatly trimmed. If nail varnish is used, it should not be chipped, and should tone with the colours you are wearing.

Feet. Shoes neat, clean and right for the occasion. Feet should be clean, free of corns and callouses. Toe-nails should be clean and neatly trimmed. If varnish is used, it should match finger-nail varnish in colour.

Legs. Free from hair and fuzz, scaly skin and blotches. Stockings should be clean, properly adjusted, and if they have seams these should be properly adjusted. When wearing tights, make sure they are pulled up well, and are not baggy round the knees or ankles.

Figure. Good posture is all important. Stand well and walk with smooth, co-ordinated movements. A well-cut bra and girdle, or all-in-one foundation garment, will help correct figure faults, but exercise is also important.

Clothes. Well cut, well pressed and right for the occasion. It is better to be under-dressed than over-dressed, so keep jewellery to the minimum.

Diets For Healthy Living

You are what you eat—every part of your body, every organ, every bone, your skin and even the condition of your hair results from the foods you eat. Your diet also affects the way you feel, and the amount of energy you have for work and play. Waking or sleeping, your body needs energy for every breath and movement.

To remain healthy and grow normally it is essential that you eat a balanced, mixed diet containing protein, carbohydrates (sugar and starches), fat, minerals and vitamins. These last two play a very important part in maintaining your health. For details of their properties, and the foods they are found in see the chart on Page 249.

Foods vary in the number of calories they contain. Fats contain the highest number of calories; sugar and starch are also rich in calories. Starches include cereals, everything containing flour, potatoes, peas, beans and corn.

Reducing diets are based on the simple principle of restricting your intake of calories, and making your body use up stored fat.

When considering a slimming diet, always ensure that the foods listed are high in protein, since protein is essential to replace worn-out body cells. Foods high in protein include milk, meat, fish, poultry, eggs and cheese. Vitamins and minerals are also essential for health, so check to see that the foods you are eating do have a vitamin and mineral content.

Different diets are required by different age groups. The small child, for example, needs a diet rich in body-building foods, calcium and vitamins. Milk, which contains all these, therefore figures high in diets for this age group.

Many adults eat far too many carbohydrates, usually in the form of bread, pastry, potatoes and sweet foods. Others over-eat compulsively often because of emotional problems which lead them to eat for comfort. Eating is a momentary solace, but the results show and health usually suffers.

There is no perfect food—no one single food which will supply every need essential to the body. The food which comes nearest to doing this, however, is milk. A pint of milk will give you at least one sixth of your daily needs of calories, good protein, calcium, Vitamin A, Vitamin B group especially riboflavine. It will not give you an adequate supply of iron, or nicotinic acid or Vitamin C.

Small children on whole milk will need added vitamins in the form of cod liver oil or similar Vitamin D supplements, and fruit or fruit juice for Vitamin C. The recommended daily allowances of milk are:
Children—1–1½ pints
Adolescents—1½ pints or more
Adults—1 pint

DIET FOR EXPECTANT MOTHERS

From the food you eat will come the strong bones and teeth, firm muscle and healthy tissue of the unborn child. Your diet should include milk, meat, fish, eggs and cheese—all high in protein.

Milk. The most valuable all-round food, since it contains protein, fat, sugar, minerals—especially calcium, which is vital for building bones and teeth—and vitamins.

Meat or fish. Should be eaten at least once a day, preferably grilled, steamed or stewed. Avoid frying.

Eggs. At least one each day.

Cheese. Eaten at main meals or as a between-meal snack.

Yogurt. As a between-meal snack, or eaten with fruit or on its own instead of cakes or puddings.

Vegetables, Salads and Fruits. Include both fresh and cooked fruits and vegetables each day.

Fats. Eat some fresh butter every day.

IMPORTANT

Before beginning any diet, consult your doctor

245

DIET FOR INFANTS UP TO 5 YEARS

Under 1 Year

Breast feeding. The ideal and most well-balanced food available. Optional extras include cod liver oil and liquids containing Vitamin C, such as rose hip syrup.

Artificial foods. According to medical advice.

Weaning. See *Feeding a Baby* in **Child Care** section.

1—5 Years

Milk remains the most important single food throughout this age span. Allow at least one pint each day.

Proteins are essential for strong bones, muscles and healthy tissues. Dairy produce such as cheese, natural yogurt and eggs should be included daily. Peas, beans, nuts, cereals included frequently.

Fats are a rich source of energy. Butter is the most important, but children also absorb the fats in milk, cheese, fish and meat.

Carbohydrates are valuable and energy-producing. They include cereals, bread, cakes, biscuits and potatoes. Also sugars, sweets, honey, syrup and jam, but not in excessive quantities.

Vitamins are important in promoting growth and maintaining health. *See Vitamin Chart for their sources.*

Minerals, in particular iron and calcium, are essential for good health. To ensure the child has these, include plenty of eggs, green leaf vegetables, milk and cheese.

DAILY DIET SUMMARY

1. At least one pint of milk.
2. One helping of meat, poultry or fish.
3. One egg.
4. One helping of vegetables, cooked or raw.
5. Fruit at least twice a day—more if the child refuses vegetables.
6. Starches such as cereals, potatoes and bread (preferably wholemeal).
7. Cod liver oil and orange juice, or rose hip syrup.

8. If sweets, chocolate and ice cream are to be given this should be done after a main meal.
9. Cakes, biscuits, pastries and highly-sweetened foods—in very limited quantities.

DIET FOR CHILDREN OVER 5

For general health, proper functioning of the body, maintenance of a good blood supply and protection against illness, children need a well-balanced diet containing adequate amounts of vitamins and certain minerals. They need a generous supply of good-quality protein and calcium for the growth and development of bones, teeth and body tissues.

Carbohydrates and fats are also important to supply energy. Because children are more active than adults, they require more energy foods for their size than adults do, especially in the form of fats, sugar, milk and eggs.

Milk is vital to their development, especially during their adolescent period, when they require an abundance of first-class protein and minerals, especially calcium. Milk contains them all.

School Dinners

A great deal of controversy exists over the matter of school dinners, and most children grumble about their content. Basically, however, school dinners are nutritionally balanced, and it is far better for a child to eat school dinners than to take sandwiches, and eat large quantities of carbohydrates.

School Milk

Children should be encouraged to take advantage of their school milk as long as they are entitled to it (until the end of their primary school days).

When they get to secondary school they should be encouraged to drink at least one pint of milk a day at home, more if possible.

7-DAY MILK DIET

In this diet you can eat normal portions of the foods listed, except when otherwise indicated. You should drink a pint of milk a day, some of which can be used in tea or coffee. You can also drink as much water as you like.

You do not have to follow the diet day by day in the way it is arranged. For example, you can switch the evening and midday meal or eat Tuesday's meals on Monday.

On this diet you can lose up to seven pounds in one week, but the exact amount will depend on personal factors, such as how active you are. If you do not lose as much as you would like in the first week, continue the diet for another seven days.

Breakfast*

1 egg (scrambled, fried or boiled)
1 starch-reduced crispbread with
  butter
Tea or coffee with milk**

Midday Meal

MONDAY
Clear soup
Cold meat or cottage cheese
Green salad
Slice of melon or half a grapefruit**
1 glass milk

TUESDAY
3 fish fingers
Peas, fresh or frozen (small portion)
1 glass milk

WEDNESDAY
Cauliflower with cheese
1 starch-reduced crispbread with
  butter
1 glass milk

THURSDAY
1 Scotch egg or a plain omelette made
  with 2 eggs
1 starch-reduced crispbread with
  butter
English cheese (1 inch cube)
1 glass milk

FRIDAY
Sardines, salmon or prawns
Green salad
Apple or orange
1 glass milk

SATURDAY
Gammon
Green salad or braised celery
Plain yogurt or an apple
1 glass milk

SUNDAY
Roast beef or lamb
1 small potato
Brussels sprouts or cabbage
Fresh fruit salad**
Real dairy cream

Evening Meal

MONDAY
Minced beef
Brussels sprouts or cabbage
Stewed fruit** and/or plain yogurt

TUESDAY
Chicken casserole (no potatoes)
1 starch-reduced crispbread with
  butter
English cheese (1 inch cube)

WEDNESDAY
Grilled liver or lean ham
Spinach or cabbage
Apple, pear or orange

THURSDAY
Clear soup
Grilled steak
1 small potato
Broccoli or cauliflower

FRIDAY
Baked fish or lamb chop
French or runner beans
1 starch-reduced crispbread with
  butter
English cheese (1 inch cube)

SATURDAY
Poached haddock and egg
1 starch-reduced crispbread with
  butter
English cheese (1 inch cube)

SUNDAY
Cold meat
Peas, fresh or frozen (small portion)
Apple or orange
1 glass milk

Nightcap*
One glass milk, hot or cold

*Every day for seven days.
**You may use a few drops of artificial sweetener, but not sorbitol because it is fattening.

247

DIET FOR THE ELDERLY

As people grow older, they need less bulk foods, and perhaps less carbohydrates. But they need as much, if not more, protein than during their more active days. By ensuring a high intake of protein, elderly people can guard against infection and ill-health.

Protein in the form of meat is expensive, but milk, cheese, eggs and fish are also valuable sources of protein. There is almost twice as much first-class animal protein in English Cheddar cheese as there is in the same weight of prime raw beef. Milk is also a valuable food, and at least one pint a day should be included in the diet.

Since the body cannot store Vitamin C, it is important that a regular supply is maintained. This is provided by fresh fruit and vegetables.

DIET FOR INVALIDS AND CONVALESCENTS

Diets for patients suffering from and recovering from illness have to be outlined by the doctor. The general principle is to give the least bulky, most nutritive, most digestible food available, so the body can have the maximum benefit with the least effort.

Apart from liver and gall-bladder disease, there are few conditions in which large quantities of milk are not beneficial. There are many easily-digestible proprietary protein foods. If in any doubt about invalid diets, seek medical advice.

YOUR FOOD CONTAINS . . .

Per Ounce	Calories	Protein grams	Fats grams	Carbo-hydrate grams	Per Ounce	Calories	Protein grams	Fats grams	Carbo-hydrate grams
Beef	91	4.2	7.9	—	Watercress	4	0.8	—	0.2
Mutton	97	3.7	8.8	—	Apples,				
Pork	119	3.4	11.3	—	eating	13	0.1	—	3.3
Sausage,					Bananas	22	0.3	—	5.5
pork	97	2.5	8.2	2.8	Gooseberries	5	0.3	—	1.0
Haddock	20	4.5	0.2	—	Oranges	10	0.2	—	2.4
Herring	67	4.7	5.1	—	Pears	11	0.1	—	3.0
Kippers	62	5.4	4.5	—	Plums	9	0.2	—	2.2
Sardines	84	5.8	6.4	—	Strawberries	7	0.2	—	1.8
Beans,					Tomatoes	4	0.3	—	0.8
haricot	73	6.1	—	12.9	Butter	226	0.1	24.2	—
Beans,					Cheese,				
runner	4	0.3	—	0.8	Cheddar	120	7.2	9.8	—
Beetroot	13	0.5	—	2.8	Eggs, fresh	46	3.4	3.5	—
Brussels	9	1.0	—	1.3	Margarine	226	—	24.2	—
Cabbage	7	0.8	—	1.1	Milk, whole	19	0.9	1.1	1.4
Carrots	6	0.2	—	1.5	Biscuits,				
Cauliflower	7	1.0	—	0.8	plain	123	2.1	3.8	21.4
Lettuce	3	0.3	—	0.5	Biscuits,				
Onions	7	0.3	—	1.5	sweet	158	1.6	8.7	18.9
Peas,					Bread, white	69	2.2	0.4	14.9
canned,					Bread,				
processed	24	1.7	—	4.7	wholemeal	65	2.3	0.6	13.4
Peas, fresh	18	1.6	—	3.0					
Potatoes	25	0.6	—	5.9	FROM MANUAL OF NUTRITION,				
Spinach	6	0.8	—	0.7	HMSO				

MINERAL CHART

Mineral	What it does	Foods that contain it
Calcium	Builds strong bones and teeth Helps blood to clot Helps muscles and nerves to work Helps regulate the use of other minerals in the body	Milk; eggs; ice-cream; cheese; sardines; herrings; whitebait; spinach; cress; broccoli; kale; cabbage; turnip tops; cauliflower; lentils; beans; dried fruits; summer fruits; bread
Phosphorous	Helps build bones and teeth Important for nerve fibres and body cells Helps use of nourishment for energy	Milk; cheese; liver; eggs; whitebait; sardines; herrings; spinach; cereals; most fresh and dried vegetables
Iodine	Helps to control rate at which body uses energy	Fish and shellfish; vegetables; iodised table salt
Iron	Needed by all cells Needed to form haemoglobin in red blood corpuscles	Liver; eggs; cress; spinach; sardines; ham; whitebait; beef; bread; radishes; cabbage; turnip tops; potatoes
Copper	Needed by red blood corpuscles	Same foods as iron

VITAMIN CHART

Vitamin	What it does	Foods that contain it
Vitamin A	Essential for growth Keeps skin healthy Keeps eyes healthy Guards against infection	Halibut liver oil; sardines; cod liver oil; herrings; milk; butter; cheese; eggs; carrots; bananas; spinach; tomatoes; margarine
Vitamin B.1 (Thiamin)	Keeps heart and nerves healthy Improves appetite and digestion Helps body to use carbohydrates for energy	Yeast; bread; liver; kidney; wholemeal; eggs; potatoes; spinach; sprouts; cress; raw cabbage; peas; beans; lettuce; lentils; nuts; milk
Vitamin B.2 (Riboflavine)	Keeps skin healthy Keeps mucous membranes healthy Prevents sore tongue and sore mouth Helps cells to use oxygen Keeps eyes healthy	Milk; cheese; dairy ice-cream; all foods containing Vitamin B. 1 listed above
Vitamin C	Keeps gums, skin, muscles and bones healthy Increases resistance to infection	Fresh milk; fresh fruits and vegetables; potatoes; black currants; rose hips; citrus fruits
Vitamin D	Helps bone to use calcium and so promotes strong teeth and bones	Milk; eggs; butter; halibut liver oil; cod liver oil; sardines; herring; salmon; margarine

Beauty Care

The secret of a well-planned beauty kit lies in deciding which items are basic to your own beauty requirements.

Buy new products in small quantities to test and experiment with before investing in a large economy size.

Do not hoard—half-used creams go dry, colours in lipstick fashions change.

Learn to use your equipment well. Make sure your makeup mirror is well lit, and do not be afraid to try out new products, so that you keep up to date with changing fashions, and with your own changing skin conditions and beauty requirements.

AIDS TO BEAUTY

Soap and water is excellent for cleansing, provided you use a mild, gentle soap—baby soap or cosmetic soap. Avoid highly-scented soaps for the face, as these are usually very drying.

Cosmetic cleansers are efficient and gentle, and essential if you use a tinted foundation or waterproof mascara. They remove makeup and grime from deep down in the pores.

Cream cleansers do a very thorough job at bedtime. They remove even the heaviest makeup and are suitable for all skin types. But since they leave a residue on the skin, a toning lotion should also be used. The same applies to liquid creams.

Cleansing milks are the most suitable for daytime. They are quick and easy to use, and need not be followed by a toner.

Cleansing pads are easy to carry, and to use at the office or while travelling. They will remove makeup and grime in seconds.

Toners should be used after cream or liquid cleansers. They have a spirit base, and are designed to remove any traces of oil remaining on the skin. They also act as a mild antiseptic, stimulate circulation and help to tighten pores.

Face packs can be used for extra toning, to deep cleanse pores and lighten the skin.

Nourishers help replace natural oils and moisture. They usually contain lanolin, and are for night time use. They can be mild or rich. Use rich ones on the throat, mild ones for the sensitive skin around the eyes.

Moisturisers help combat the drying effects of the weather and central heating, and slow down the dehydration of ageing skin.

Tissues are invaluable for taking off surplus creams, removing stale makeup, blotting lipsticks or creaming away makeup mistakes. Keep them on the dressing table, and in your handbag.

ART OF MAKEUP

Applying makeup is a skilful art. Apart from choosing the correct shade of cream or liquid foundation, and blending it with the right tone of powder, skill is required in applying the powder.

Brushes are ideal for many purposes— applying powder, putting on eye shadow, eye liner, lipstick or rouge. Use them for cleaning away particles of powder from around the hairline.

Pencils can be used for eyebrows, eye liners and for outlining lips.

Sprays can be used for applying deodorants, perfume, hair lacquer.

MAKEUP TIPS

Makeup can do a great deal to improve the shape and contours of the face. First identify the shape of your face.

Remove existing makeup. Scrutinise your face under a good light and pull your hair well back from your face. You will find that the shape of your face falls into one of four basic categories—oval, round, long or square.

To make the best of each shape, watch these points:

Oval should be all softness and gentle curves. Apply cheek-tint, starting high on cheeks and fading upwards along the line of the cheekbones towards temples. Area beneath cheekbones will appear gently hollowed.

Round. Slim this face with dark foundation at the sides. Cheek-tint should be started fairly high on cheeks, blending upwards and outwards. Use a little cream face-shaper on top of the cheekbones close to the eye, and also at the sides of the nose to thin down. Broaden eyebrows, and lengthen upwards.

Long. Subdue the angle of the jaw and the depth of the chin with a darker shade of foundation, or brown-tint face-shaper. Decrease the depth of the forehead by fading the shaper to merge with the hairline. Make eyes wider and rounder to balance the length of the face.

Square. Shade the angle of the jawbone into a long sweeping crescent towards the chin, and hollow the lower part of the cheeks slightly with brown-tint. Eyes and eyebrows should be uptilted at the corners.

The other facial features can also be improved by skilled makeup.

Nose

A too **large** nose can be made to appear smaller by using a dark shade of foundation or a darker powder.

A nose that is too **long** should be given a touch of shadow on the tip.

A **broad** nose can be slimmed down by applying brown tint down the sides.

A **flat** nose needs a cream tint on the bridge, running down the complete length of it.

A **narrow** nose should be given a brown tint at the sides, starting low down.

A **crooked** nose needs shadow and highlights at the crucial places to minimise or emphasise the shape.

Chin

For a too prominent chin use a darker shade of foundation over the chin. Bring a receding chin forward by tipping with a warm tone.

Eyes

Choose eye shadow that tones with your eyes and the colour of your clothes. Apply with the cushion of third finger, or an eye shadow brush. When using a cream eye shadow, powder after application to soften and prevent creasing into lines.

Lips

The texture of your lipstick should be fine, smooth and light, with the colour blending in with your general colouring and with the colours you are wearing. Make sure your lips are dry, and free from cream. If applying with a brush use one with a chisel end.

If your mouth is big, use unobtrusive colours and keep slightly within the natural lines. With a small mouth, use bolder shades and carry to the edge of the natural lines, or just over.

● *See* **Makeup & Hairstyles** *in colour on pages* 260 *and* 261.

PERSPIRATION

The two common problems associated with perspiration are excessive sweating and malodour or 'body odour'.

Body odour arises from substances produced by bacterial action on the ingredients of sweat. **Deodorants** and **anti-perspirants** are available to combat these problems.

Deodorants include an antiseptic ingredient to inhibit the activity of the bacteria which produce the unpleasant odour. This type of product does not normally reduce the rate or amount of perspiration.

Anti-perspirants contain an astringent ingredient which tends to reduce the rate of perspiration significantly, but does not stop it completely.

Although the astringent materials used have some anti-bacterial activity in their own right, it is normal for an antiseptic ingredient to be included to make the products doubly effective against excessive perspiration and unpleasant odours.

In all deodorants and anti-perspirant products, the perfume makes an important contribution to the effectiveness by helping to mask the odours that may eventually develop.

Deodorants and anti-perspirants are available in cream, liquid and powder form, and are packed in jars, bottles, sticks and sprays.

LEGS

Legs must be slim, trim and well shaped, and free from hair and fuzz, dry skin and scorch marks, to be really beautiful. Hair can be removed with a razor or with a depilatory cream. Hand cream will prevent dry skin and chapping, and should be applied immediately after your bath.

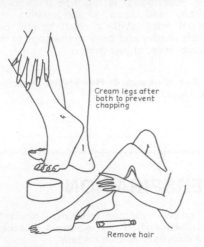

Cream legs after bath to prevent chapping

Remove hair

To trim and firm your legs there is an excellent series of exercises called Legometrics which is based on the principle that a muscle works hardest when it tenses against a solid object.

Scholl wooden exercise sandals with a patented toe grip designed to hold the foot in the correct position should be worn for these exercises.

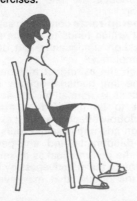

To trim the ankles. Sit on an upright chair, cross right knee over left and brace toes of right foot against the special

sandal gripper bar so that the foot is arched and you feel a pull in the ankle. Hold for the count of two, then relax. Repeat with other foot. Repeat three times with each leg.

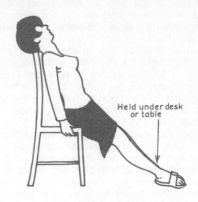

Held under desk or table

To trim thighs and hips. Perch on the edge of upright chair and lean back. Stretch legs out straight, anchoring them under a desk or table with the heels on the floor. Grip toes against bar of sandal until you feel pull in the muscles of thighs and buttocks. Hold for count of two. Repeat six times.

To trim and firm calves. Wearing the exercise sandals, stand on a book or block of wood about 2 in. thick. Rise on to your toes, gripping bar of sandal for count of two. Then rock back to floor on heels. Repeat six times.

EYES

The importance of eye care cannot be over emphasised. Because our eyes are in continual use, rest is of the utmost importance to avoid eye strain. If you spend the whole day doing office work, your eye muscles will contract and relax as often as 100,000 times.

Shield your eyes from dust, grit and bright sunshine with protective glasses. Foreign bodies which will not wash out are one of the most frequent causes of eye irritation. Tears are the finest cleaner of all, and will either wash the particles out of the eye, or to one side of it, where they can be removed with a tissue.

Do not try to remove foreign bodies which have become embedded in the eye surface. For these, seek professional advice.

Eyesight can deteriorate over the years, so it is wise to have regular eye examinations, even if you think your sight is good.

If you are over 40, eye tests should be taken about every two years. If impaired or defective sight is treated as soon as the trouble starts, the chances of preventing it from worsening are better.

Artificial lighting has an important bearing on eyesight. Direct lighting is better than overhead lighting in a main room. Ideally, it should come from behind, and glance down over the left shoulder.

Too much television viewing can cause eyestrain. Avoid viewing in complete darkness, and also avoid lights which reflect off the screen into your eyes. Eyestrain can also be caused through sitting too near the screen—a particularly important point when children are viewing. The ideal distance is 10 ft.

It is important that your eyes are in good condition for driving. Take frequent rests if you are on a long journey. Eye drops will refresh tired eyes, so keep a bottle of them in your car.

Exposure to glare, draughts, dust and oil fumes can also cause eyestrain, so if you are driving with the windows down, make sure you wear protective glasses. Scooter drivers and motor cyclists should always protect their eyes with goggles.

When driving at night, remember your vision is not as acute as it is in daytime. Always proceed with extra caution when travelling from a well lit street into a dark road—eyes need a period of adjustment.

Look beyond and to the left of approaching headlights; reduce speed immediately if you are dazzled by oncoming cars. Recovery from glare may take three or four seconds, or even longer. If you wear tinted glasses to help reduce dazzle, remember that, like sunglasses, they also reduce visibility.

TEETH

The foundations of good teeth are laid early in pregnancy. Most of the new baby's teeth are already formed in the gums at birth, which is why an expectant mother needs a balanced diet rich in the vitamins and minerals that provide building materials for her baby's teeth.

These are found in all dairy products, especially milk, fish and fresh fruit and vegetables.

There is no set rule for when a baby should start teething; it could be any time between three months and nine months. Usually baby cuts his first tooth at six months, has between eight and twelve teeth at one year, his full set of 20 baby teeth at $2\frac{1}{2}$ years.

Decayed baby teeth can lead to gum trouble in adult life, so even before the first tooth appears, baby should be given a selection of hard foods to chew on.

These can include small pieces of raw apple, raw carrot, crispy bacon, rusks and hard crusts of bread. Avoid too many sloppy or sweetened foods.

Although it is impossible to eliminate tooth decay and gum disease entirely, they can be controlled by good dental hygiene habits.

Tooth decay is mainly caused by bacteria (germs) which live on tiny particles of food clinging to the surface of the teeth, and in the crevices between them.

The acids of the bacteria eat their way through the enamel coating of a tooth, and then attack the dentine which forms the main body of the tooth. Once the decay reaches the nerve, it is difficult to save the tooth.

The most common type of severe gum disease is *pyorrhea* caused by germs sticking in the crease where the gum meets the tooth. The gums lose their grip on the teeth as a result.

For healthy white teeth:

1. **Brush your teeth regularly—if possible after every meal.**
2. **Brush your teeth properly.**

3. **Eat as few sweets, pastries and syrups as possible.**

4. **Go to your dentist regularly— every six months for check-ups and early treatment of troubles which can develop without your knowing about them.**

If you cannot clean your teeth after every meal, brush them after breakfast and last thing at night. Concentrate on cleaning each tooth separately. Brush from the gum to the biting edge of the tooth, getting the tufts of the bristle between the teeth to dislodge food particles. Repeat each brush stroke six times.

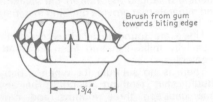

Brush teeth with an up-and-down movement to dislodge food particles between the teeth.

Regular gum massage is also important for healthy teeth. This stimulates blood circulation in the gums, and helps prevent tartar forming in the small hollows where the teeth meet gums—the place where pyorrhea usually starts.

For adults, the toothbrush should have a head between 1¼ in. and 1¾ in. long and a third of an inch wide. For young children the brush head should be about 1¼ in. long.

Do not continue using a toothbrush after its tufts have lost their firmness. To do its job of cleaning your teeth properly, your toothbrush must be in good condition.

Toothpaste's main job is to clean your teeth safely and effectively while whitening your teeth and refreshing your mouth. The toothpaste should not be too harsh—it should polish your teeth, but not damage them. In addition, toothpaste should neutralise mouth acids and be antiseptic.

HANDS

Clean nails and hands are of the utmost importance, not only because they are continually on view, but also for health reasons. Always wash your hands before handling or preparing food.

Divide your hand care into two parts— daily attention and weekly manicure.

Daily

1. Wash hands thoroughly in warm soapy water.

2. Scrub nails briskly with a firm bristle brush.

3. Dry thoroughly.

4. Rub in a little hand cream, paying particular attention to nails and cuticles.

5. Run the tip of a manicure stick round under each cuticle, this keeps the skin soft and fine, and prevents roughness at nail corners. It also promotes healthy nail growth.

6. If necessary, renew nail varnish topcoat.

Before undertaking dirty work, or using harsh soaps, powders or detergents, apply a barrier cream or wear protective gloves.

Weekly

Once a week give your nails a full manicure. For this you will need:
Small bowl of hot, sudsy water
Nailbrush
Soft absorbent towel
Cotton wool
Nail enamel solvent or remover
Cuticle cream or oil
Manicure scissors or cuticle clippers
Long emery board
Manicure stick with fine flat point
Enamel: base coat, topcoat or sealer

DO IT LIKE THIS

1. Remove enamel, using solvent and large wads of cotton wool.
2. Holding emery board at an angle of 45 degrees and using the rough side of it, shape nails with one-direction sweeps. Do not use saw-like movements, as this encourages splitting. Bevel off the edges with the smooth side of the board. Do not file down too low at corners.
3. Soak both hands in the hot suds for several minutes until skin is softened.
4. Dry on soft towel.
5. Coat each cuticle with cream or lotion.
6. Use the pointed end of the manicure stick carefully to loosen cuticle skin and work oil in underneath.
7. Massage in any remaining oil treating each nail separately.
8. Scrub nails in soapy water to remove surplus oil. Dry carefully.
9. Trim away any surplus skin around nail corners. Do not cut round cuticles, since this makes them thick and coarse.
10. Dampen a piece of cotton wool with remover, and wipe over each nail carefully.
11. Apply base, and allow to dry thoroughly.
12. Apply topcoat or sealer.

NAIL VARNISH TIPS

1. Never overload brush. Clean off surplus against side of bottle.
2. Steady the hand you are painting, and the hand you are painting with, on the same flat surface.
3. Paint from the base of the nail to the tip.
4. Use long, slow steady strokes.
5. Leave either a half-moon or a thin line of unpainted nail next to the cuticle to allow oils and creams to soak in.
6. Remove a hairline of varnish from each tip. This helps to prevent varnish chipping.
7. Make sure your nails are scrupulously clean before applying varnish. Traces of grease or soap will make varnish peel. Wipe over each nail with a solvent before applying varnish.

Unpainted nails require a high standard of grooming. They should never be worn too long, and regular buffing with paste or powder will give them a surface shine and a healthy pink colour.

FEET

Too often feet are neglected. They determine grace in walking, posture and even the expression on your face, and so deserve regular attention. Choice of shoes is important (see Footwear, Page 243).

Care of the Feet

1. Wash daily.
2. Dry carefully, especially between the toes.
3. Rub a little hand cream into your feet, paying special attention to the toes and area between them.
4. Cut toe nails straight across, preferably with clippers.
5. Smooth down thick or horny toe nails with emery board.
6. Smooth patches of hard skin with pumice stone.

7. Clean under nail tips with manicure stick.

8. If applying nail varnish, separate the toes first with pads of cotton wool.

Feet need exercise, and walking is one of the best provided that all your toes function and the whole foot is exercised as you walk. Special exercises to keep the toes active are also beneficial.

Try to move each toe by itself

1. Spread out your toes, and try to make each one behave separately as if it were a finger.

2. Draw up your toes in a knuckling movement, first with toes held down to the floor, then with foot raised.

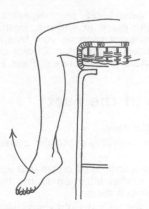

3. Sit on a high chair or stool and let your legs dangle. Turn each foot inwards towards the leg—this helps to strengthen the inner arch of foot.

HAIR

The condition of your hair indicates the state of your general health, and can vary considerably. To keep your hair healthy it is also important to keep it clean, and to keep your scalp clean and free from dandruff.

Your shampoo is important; soapless detergents degrease the hair, and if used too frequently, or if the shampoo is too concentrated, will remove all the natural oils from the hair, making it look dull and lifeless as well as very brittle.

Never use household detergents, washing powders or block soaps. They are all extremely harmful to the hair. Cream type soapless shampoo is the safest, since it contains lanolin and acts as a conditioner.

Shampooing

1. Dampen hair, apply half the quantity of shampoo and work up into a lather.

2. Rinse and reapply shampoo.

3. Work into a rich foamy lather and work well into hair.

4. Rinse in three changes of water, or under running water until the water is clear.

Greasy hair. Use the above method with the water as hot as you can bear it. To reduce over-oiliness, wash frequently. Start with every other day, increasing the length of the intervals between washing as the oiliness decreases.

Dry hair. If your hair is deficient in natural oils, use an oil-enriched cream shampoo. Use sufficient to work up a good lather in one application. Rinse thoroughly, and then apply a little conditioning cream and work well into scalp. Comb through and rinse.

Drying the Hair

DON'T

Dry your hair in front of a coal or electric fire.

Go to bed with it wet.

Put it into rollers all night—the strain on the roots is harmful.

DO

Dry it as naturally as possible—outdoors in fresh air and sunshine is a real tonic.

Dry it with a hand dryer or hood dryer at medium heat.

Under a hood at the hairdresser's, using medium setting.

Brushes and Combs

Brushing helps to keep the scalp clean, and polishes the hair.

Keep brushes and combs scrupulously clean. Wash them daily, and rinse in a mild antiseptic solution if you have dandruff.

Brush hair upwards and sideways as well as downwards to allow air to circulate around the roots.

Choose combs with smoothly rounded teeth which will not damage the hair or scratch the scalp.

Dandruff

Dandruff will cause loss of vitality and gloss, and in severe cases will cause hair to fall or become very thin.

It is infectious, so never lend or borrow combs, brushes or even hair grips.

Keep everything that comes in contact with your hair exceptionally clean.

Wash hair frequently—as soon as any particles appear.

Brush hair daily with a clean brush.

Massage scalp daily with a cream dressing to stimulate and improve circulation to the roots of the hair.

Cutting

Ideally, hair should be cut every four to six weeks by a professional hairdresser. Curly hair is best kept short so that it is manageable and does not tangle.

Long hair should have the ends trimmed every six weeks or so to encourage healthy growth and prevent ends splitting.

Styling

Select a style which suits your particular face. Avoid styles which emphasise facial points that might be better disguised.

Large face. Choose a medium length style. Avoid very short styles and bouffant styles which will give your head an over-large appearance.

Square face. Soften by wearing your hair in a smooth style, and fairly long so that it falls over the point of the jaw at each side.

Long thin face. Choose a style that bulks the hair out at the sides to give width. Avoid very short styles—longer hair makes the face look oval. Wear hair slightly down over forehead to help shorten the face.

Plump, round face. Keep side hair close to the head or swept upwards to slim the face.

Left: For a high forehead, wear the hair forward. Right: For a low forehead, sweep the hair back.

High forehead. Wear a style that calls for a fringe, or wear the hair dressed forward at the front.

Low forehead. Sweep hair upwards and back from the forehead. Avoid fringes.

Pear-shaped face. Build hair out at sides at ear level to balance shape.

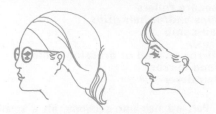

Left: Smooth hairstyle to go with spectacles. Right: Hairstyle to counterbalance prominent nose.

Prominent nose. Dress hair forward over the forehead to counterbalance.

If you wear glasses. Avoid heavy fringes or loose hanging hair at sides of face. Off-the-forehead smooth styles look best.

Colouring Your Hair

It is simple to change the colour of your hair, but before experimenting study the different types of colourant.

In that way you will know whether you have chosen something which will wash out next time you shampoo your hair, or whether you will have to wait until it grows out before you can return to your natural colouring.

Colour rinse. Washes out with next shampoo.

Semi-permanent rinse. Withstands washing, and takes 4–6 weeks to wash out.

Shampoo tints. Can be semi-permanent or permanent. The latter will take from six to eight months to grow out.

Tints. Permanent dyes. See above.

Hair cosmetics. Spray, stick or paint on. Used to produce highlights, streaks or tips. Will usually wash or brush off.

Coloured wave sets. Wash-out colouring available in lotion or cream form.

Bleaches. Remove some or all natural colour. Bleaching dark hair blonde requires several applications of strong bleach, and usually leaves hair lifeless unless fully compensated by conditioning creams. Full-scale bleaching should only be undertaken by a qualified hairdresser.

Above: Putting in a roller.
Below: Rollers in position and the resulting hairstyle.

Setting Your Hair

To set your hair at home you need:
8–12 rollers. The smaller the rollers, the tighter the waves or curls
Strong hair pins or special sticks to secure rollers
Clips and/or hair grips
Tail-comb
Brush
Mirror on wall or dressing table
Hand mirror
Hair dryer

Part off hair into sections; lift a small portion about 1 in. wide, and comb away from the scalp. Hold between thumb and finger of left hand at right angles to scalp.

Take roller in right hand, place it at the tip of the hair and smooth ends over it. Roll up towards roots until roller rests on scalp. Secure.

Place rollers either parallel in a line with the eyebrows, or vertical with hair rolled sideways in the direction in which it is to be brushed out.

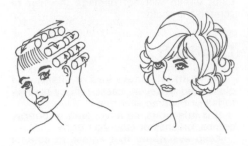

Leave to dry naturally (several hours) or;
Dry with hand dryer (about 1 hour) or;
Use a hood dryer—$\frac{1}{2}$ to $\frac{3}{4}$ hour.
Make sure the hair is absolutely dry before unrolling.
Brush out really hard in the direction you want it to lie.
Use tail of comb to lift and flick hair into position.

To back comb, hold the ends of the hair and comb upwards with very light strokes.

Hold spray can well away from head

Smooth back the top part with a brush.

To hold, set firmly in position and spray with lacquer. Keep canister well away from head so that a fine mist reaches hair—not a heavy wetting.

Permanent Wave

Even with straight styles, a light permanent wave helps to hold hair in position, and will give it life and bounce. If you have your hair permed professionally, the assistant will advise which type is most suitable for your hair.

TIPS FOR HOME PERMING
Even though you may have done a home perm before, **do** read the instructions on the package from start to finish before you begin.

Wind hair correctly. Wind firmly but not tightly, or you may damage the hair. When all curlers are in they should feel comfortable. Re-wind if they feel tight or uncomfortable.

Use plastic curlers and ball-fastening plastic rollers. Avoid metal curlers, pins or grips, because these may stain the hair.

It is important to have hair cut before you start to remove all traces of old perm. This way you can avoid frizzing. If hair is already short, trim ends which may be split or damaged.

Neutralising locks in the curl, so pay particular attention to this part of the perm. In some cases it will be necessary to apply a special solution; in others to allow slow drying.

Condition your hair before perming it. If your hair is dry, lifeless, bleached or tinted, this may mean two or three weeks' treatment before your perm, as well as the use of conditioning cream afterwards.

Your health and general condition affects the state of your hair. Do not perm your hair if you are feeling at all unwell.

If you want to colour *and* perm your hair, perm it first, then wait at least ten days before tinting. Perm lotion tends to lift artificial colour out of the hair.

To avoid 'fish-hook' ends, use end-tissues when perming. Fold tissue round the strand, and slide it down to the tip before rolling curler under.

Remember, for tight curls use small rollers. Do not wind the hair tightly.

A wig or hairpiece can give a real 'lift' on special occasions. Wigs when not in use should be kept on a proper wig stand.

Protect your hands with rubber gloves when perming and protect sensitive skin around eyes with cold cream.

If your hair is bleached or tinted, take special care. Do a test curl first.

Make a note of the date you do your perm. You should not do another perm for at least three months.

Hair Pieces

Switches, curls, half wigs and full wigs are all easy to buy and easy to wear. Do not scorn them because they are artificial—the more expensive pieces are made from real hair, and when properly matched to your own hair texture and colour, are barely discernible.

Switches and curls are an excellent way of improving your hair for special occasions. Use a half wig or full wig when your own hair is out of condition, and you need a super hair-do for a special occasion.

Makeup and hairstyles

Whatever the shape of your face the correct makeup technique can improve it. First identify its shape:

OVAL   ROUND   SQUARE   LONG

LIPS

For a too-small mouth use bold colour lipstick and carry to the edge of the natural lines, or just over.

For a too-large mouth use soft shades and keep within the natural lines.

EYES

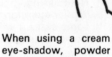

Apply eye-shadow with a brush or the cushion of the third finger.

When using a cream eye-shadow, powder after application.

NOSE

Too broad: Apply brown tint down sides.

Too flat: Use a cream tint down whole length of bridge.

Too narrow: Use a brown tint at sides, starting low down.

TOO BROAD   TOO FLAT   TOO NARROW

HAIR

WRONG: Very short or bouffant styles emphasise a large face.

RIGHT: A medium length style will slim down a large face.

WRONG: A very short style will make a square face look hard.

RIGHT: A fairly long smooth style will soften the outline of a square face. Make sure it falls over the point of the jaw at each side.

WRONG: Long hair style will emphasise an oval or long face.

RIGHT: Choose a style that provides fullness at the sides and is worn down over the forehead to help shorten the face.

WRONG: Hair styled close to the face will emphasise a pear-shaped face.

RIGHT: Dress hair out at the sides at ear level to balance shape.

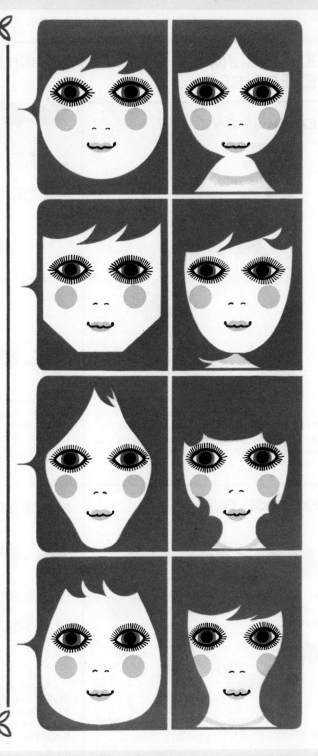

KEEP SLIM EXERCISES

EXERCISE ONE

1. Stand erect, feet together, arms outstretched, shoulders back, head up.
2. Keeping back straight and head up, bring arms back to hips and bend knees. Stand erect.

EXERCISE TWO

1. Lie face down on the floor, arms behind back, hands held loosely together. Relax.

2. Stretch arms and lift legs and head at same time. Relax.

EXERCISE THREE

1. Lie on floor on your back with arms at your side, legs straight out. Relax.

2. Keeping legs together, lift them in the air until they are at right angles to your body. Keep head and back on floor all the time. Relax slowly, lowering legs, still together, until they are straight out on the floor.

EXERCISE FOUR

From the starting position for Exercise Three, raise legs again, but this time swing them right over your head until your toes touch the floor behind your head. Keep your hands at your side.

EXERCISE FIVE

1. Lie on floor, legs together in the air, hands supporting hips, and feet pointing to the ceiling.

2. Move hands from hips, and place them flat on the floor. At the same time start pedalling in the air with your legs.

EXERCISE SIX

1. Lie on floor with your knees drawn up to your chest, hands clasped around your knees.

2. Keeping tightly rolled, rock from side to side.

EXERCISE SEVEN

Stand erect, head up, shoulders back, legs apart. Bend arms, hands on shoulders. Pull elbows back as far as possible. Relax and repeat.

EXERCISE EIGHT

Stand tall, legs apart. Stretch arms above head, and clasp hands lightly together. Bend sideways, first to right and then to left, keeping back straight.

EXERCISE TEN

Sit erect on a straight chair with legs stretched out straight in front of you. Place a large, light ball on your ankles, keeping legs straight. Toss ball in air, and let it return, using only your feet to balance it.

EXERCISE NINE

1. Stand tall, legs apart. Raise arms until they are level with your shoulders. Press back, relax.
2. With arms stretched out at shoulder level, bend from waist, making first, the right hand touch left toe, then the left hand touch right toe.

EXERCISE ELEVEN

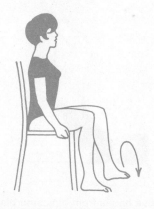

Sit upright on a chair. Cross one leg over the other, and rotate ankle in a circle. Repeat with other foot.

EXERCISE TWELVE

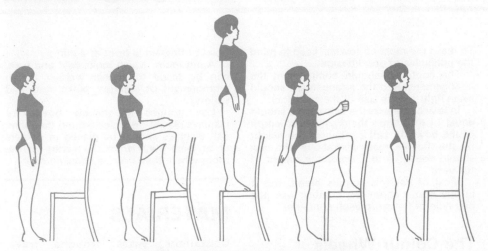

Stand in front of a straight chair, raise left leg and place foot firmly on chair-seat. Keeping back straight and head up, step on to the chair. Repeat, using right leg.

EXERCISE THIRTEEN

Stand behind a straight-back chair, hold top back of chair with one hand to help you balance, and swing the leg nearest the chair backwards and forwards six times. Turn round, use other hand for support and swing the other leg six times.

Flower Arranging

To make the most of flowers, keep in mind the principles of good design.

The container should complement the arrangement. And the arrangement should seem right for the size of the container.

In **low** containers the tallest stem should equal 1½ to 2 times the diameter or length of the bowl. In **tall** containers the height of the flower materials above the rim should equal 1½ to 2 times the height of the vase.

Most of nature's colours blend. But if in any doubt about the colours, use just one type of flower in each container.

The Colour Wheels

Blend the flowers to the colour of the container. If the container is neutral, then the colours should harmonise with the colours in the room. Foliage can be used to soften and blend any combination of colours.

The colour wheels might help in choosing the flowers for an arrangement. The first wheel shows the primary, or pure, colours: **yellow, red** and **blue.** The second wheel shows the shading which can result from blendings of the three primaries.

The colours opposite each other on this wheel are also opposite in the colour spectrum. Colours next to, or near to, each other, are those which will blend.

As a general rule, use the dark shades at the base of the container and the light shades at the top.

Settings

Choose the right flowers for the setting; dramatic arrangements need space to look effective. For the table, choose small low arrangements so that you can talk across them.

Small rooms call for dainty arrangements. They can be made to appear larger by placing an arrangement of blues and greens against the wall.

Lofty rooms need tall arrangements or the placing of bowls on top of a bookcase, or wall shelf. For added effect, stand the bowl of flowers in front of a mirror.

A big room, which looks cold and bare, can be made to appear warmer by an arrangement of oranges, pinks, reds and yellows.

Use troughs or shallow bowls for displays placed on tables around the room. Tall displays should be placed in corners or at least away from the centre of the room where they may be knocked over.

MATERIALS

Containers: vases, troughs, trays, jugs, bowls, saucepans, etc.
Strong scissors, secateurs or sharp knife
Pinholders in variety of shapes
Florists' sponges or pieces of foam rubber
Crumpled chicken wire
Modelling clay or waterproof plasticine

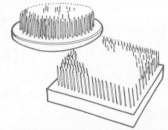

Pinholders, which can be bought in a variety of shapes, are used to hold the flower stems in place.

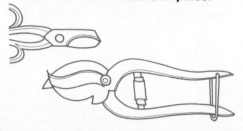

A pair of florist's scissors (top) and a pair of secateurs.

ARRANGING THE FLOWERS

The pinholders, which can be bought from florists in round, square or oblong shapes, hold the bottom of the flower stems in place. The stems are simply stuck on the pins. Heavy stems can be pushed between the pins.

Crumpled chicken wire can be used with, or instead of, the pinholders to hold more flowers.

The pieces of sponge or foam are used in shallow dishes where water might spill. The stems are stuck in the sponge, which has been soaked with water.

The modelling clay or plasticine is used for anchoring pinholders carrying tall or heavy blooms. It can be used also for sticking small containers on to bases or shallow dishes. Place three or four blobs of clay on the bottom of the pinholder or container, and press it down firmly on to the base.

Bases for containers can be made from any pleasing piece of flat stone or wood, or any large, shallow dish or tray.

The bases can be covered, if necessary, with twigs, dried leaves or flowers, as a surround for the fresh flowers in the container.

FLOWERS IN SEASON

JANUARY	Daffodil; Narcissus
FEBRUARY	Daffodil; Freesia; Narcissus; Tulip
MARCH	Anemone; Daffodil; Freesia; Iris; Narcissus; Tulip; Violet
APRIL	Anemone; Daffodil; Freesia; Iris; Lily of the Valley; Lily; Narcissus; Tulip; Violet
MAY	Anemone; Carnation; Iris; Lily of the Valley; Lily; Sweet Pea; Stock; Rose; Tulip; Violet
JUNE	Carnation; Lily of the Valley; Lily; Iris; Sweet Pea; Stock; Rose; Violet
JULY	Aster; Chrysanthemum; Dahlia; Carnation; Lily; Gladiolus; Sweet Pea; Stock; Rose
AUGUST	Aster; Carnation; Dahlia; Chrysanthemum; Sweet Pea; Gladiolus; Rose
SEPTEMBER	Aster; Carnation; Dahlia; Chrysanthemum; Rose; Gladiolus
OCTOBER	Anemone; Chrysanthemum; Aster; Carnation; Dahlia; Rose
NOVEMBER	Chrysanthemum; Violet
DECEMBER	Chrysanthemum

● *The flowers listed may all be obtained from florists. In their seasons (as above) they are reasonably priced, but at other times may cost rather more.*

267

The colour-key to flower arrangement

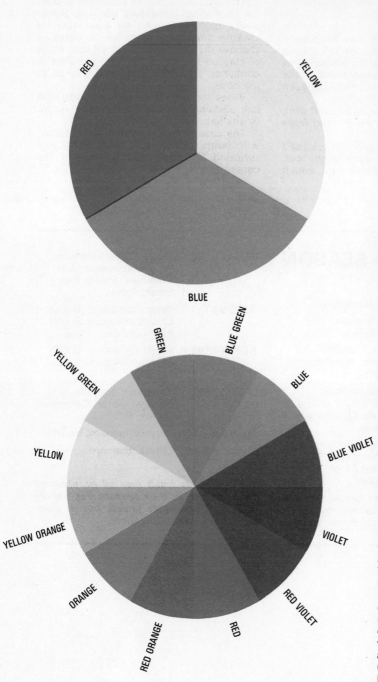

RED

YELLOW

BLUE

GREEN

BLUE GREEN

YELLOW GREEN

BLUE

YELLOW

BLUE VIOLET

YELLOW ORANGE

VIOLET

ORANGE

RED VIOLET

RED ORANGE

RED

Right: The flower arrangements here were made to decorate a banquet. They show particularly how the blending of colours goes to produce attractive displays. The simpler arrangements you make for home decoration need a similar 'eye' for colour. Flowers shown in these displays are:
Top
Chrysanthemums (*Galaxy*) all the year round; gladioli; euphorbia; chrysan- themums (*Shantung*); kalanchoë; cenera eucalyptus; tulips (*Appledorn*).
Middle
Yellow carnations; daffodils, chrysan- themums (yellow and bronze *Galaxy*) all the year round; roses (*Dr. Verharge*); tulips (*Appledorn*); pale blue hyacinth; euphorbia; kalanchoë, populus eucalyptus.
Bottom
Chrysanthemums (yellow *Galaxy*) all the year round; daffodils; tulips (*Golden Harvest*); tulips (*Appledorn*); gerbera; roses (*Dr. Verharge*); yellow freesia; kalanchoë; eucalyptus populus; flowering populus.
Left: These colour wheels will help you in selecting the flowers for your arrangements. Above: The three pure, or primary, colours, Below: How the primaries shade one into another; colours next to, or near to, each other are those which will blend best in your arrangements. Generally, use dark shades at the base of a container, light shades at the top.

CUTTING AND PREPARING FLOWERS

Flower	When to cut	How to treat
ANEMONE	$\frac{1}{2}$ to fully open	*Deep water*
ASTER	$\frac{3}{4}$ to fully open	*Scrape stems*
AZALEA	Bud to $\frac{3}{4}$ open	*Scrape stems and slice open*
BUDDLEIA	$\frac{1}{2}$ to fully open	*Scrape stems and slice open*
CALENDULA	$\frac{3}{4}$ to fully open	*Scrape stems*
CARNATION	Fully open	*Snap off ends, scrape*
CHRYSANTHEMUM	Fully open	*Scrape stems and slice $\frac{1}{2}$ to 1 inch*
CLEMATIS	$\frac{3}{4}$ to fully open	*Stand in shallow boiling water before arranging*
DAFFODIL	Full bud	*Remove white portion and rinse under warm running water*
DAHLIA	Fully open	*Stand in hot water before arranging*
DAISY	$\frac{1}{2}$ to fully open	*Scrape stems*
DELPHINIUM	$\frac{3}{4}$ to fully open	*Scrape stems*
GERANIUM	Fully open	*Slice ends*
GLADIOLUS	When second floret opens	*Scrape stems. Break off top buds*
HELIOTROPE	$\frac{3}{4}$ to fully open	*Stand in water before arranging*
HOLLYHOCK	$\frac{3}{4}$ to fully open	*Scrape stems. Hot water drink before arranging*
HYDRANGEA	Bud to fully open	*Stand in boiling water before arranging*
IRIS	When first bud opens	*Scrape stems. Rinse under warm running water*
LILAC	$\frac{1}{2}$ to fully open	*Scrape and crush stems. Remove leaves*
LARKSPUR	$\frac{3}{4}$ to fully open	*Scrape stems. Snap off top buds*
LILY	As first buds open	*Scrape stems*
MARIGOLD	$\frac{1}{2}$ to fully open	
MIGNONETTE	$\frac{3}{4}$ to fully open	*Shallow water drink before arranging*
NARCISSUS	As colour shows	*Rinse stems under warm running water*
NASTURTIUM	$\frac{1}{2}$ to fully open	
PAEONY	Bud to fully open	*Split stems*
ROSE	Full bud	*Split stems or scrape well. Stand in boiling water before arranging*
SNAPDRAGON	$\frac{3}{4}$ to fully open	*Split stems*
STOCK	$\frac{3}{4}$ to fully open	*Scrape stems and split*

Continued on next page.

270

CUTTING AND PREPARING FLOWERS

Flower	When to cut	How to treat
SWEET PEA	¾ to fully open	
TULIP	Bud to ½ open	Stand in deep water before arranging
VIOLET	½ to fully open	Soak in water before arranging
ZINNIA	Fully open	Stand in hot water before arranging

WILD FLOWERS

Flower	When to cut	How to treat
BLUEBELLS DAFFODILS FOXGLOVES	½ to fully open	Remove white portion, rinse stems under warm running water
HONEYSUCKLE	Any stage	Split stems
DOG ROSE	Bud to ½ open	Scrape and split stems
PRIMROSE VIOLETS COWSLIP etc.	½ to fully open	Warm water drink before arranging

BASIC SHAPES FOR FLOWER ARRANGEMENTS

Shape	Container	Comments
TRIANGLE	Trough or round container	Use tall flowers for centre, smaller flowers and foliage to fill in shape
ROUND	Round bowl	Large round bloom for centre. Work outwards mixing flowers and foliage
CRESCENT	Trough	Use flowers with pliable stems to achieve and hold curve
TORCH SHAPE	Deep vase	Ideal for tall flowers
FAN SHAPE	Trough	Keep arrangement low and symmetrical
S-CURVE	Tall vase	Pliable tall flowers, curved foliage
RIGHT ANGLE/ LEFT ANGLE	Trough	Tall flower or spray at right or left angles to container
ORIENTAL	Any shape	Triangle shape; tallest line to represent Heaven. Facing and looking to Heaven is Man. Looking up to both is Earth
MODERN AND ABSTRACT	Any type of container or collection of shapes	No rules or formulas. Use unusual shapes and materials. Results to please the individual

Basic flower arranging shapes

MODERN ELLIPTICAL

Corn husks; bleached bamboo; dried soya pods; bleached broom; split bamboo whirls; dried cycas leaves; dried phlomis; preserved magnolia; oak; dried hydrangea; dried ferns; grasses and barley

SCALENE TRIANGLE

Daffodils; narcissus Soleil d'Or variegated pittisporum

CRESCENT

Violets; freesias; roses 'Carole'; anemones

TRIANGLE

Euphorbia; orchid 'Hybrid'; gerberas, double; polyanthus; carnations 'Harvest Moon'; double yellow freesia 'Fantasy'; forsythia; single yellow freesia

FAN

White orchids; grape hyacinth 'Muscari'; freesias, mixed colours; pale blue hyacinths

MODERN TRIANGLE →

Delphinium florets; peach blossom; dried parsley; South African dried daisies; hares-tails; red sorgium, achillea, glixis; phalaris; breeze

MODERN ROUND

Blackberries; miniature lemons; red currants; dried South African daisies; artificial rose leaves; red and yellow immortelles miniature red currant spray

CRESCENT

White orchid; forsythia; narcissus 'Margaret Mitchell'; green hellebore; yellow freesia

For attractive displays arrange your flowers in these basic shapes
—shapes which show the different collections to their best advantage

BASIC SHAPES FOR FLOWER ARRANGEMENTS

TORCH SHAPE

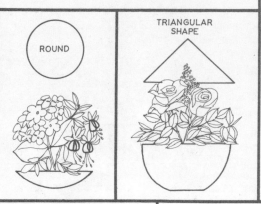

ROUND

TRIANGULAR SHAPE

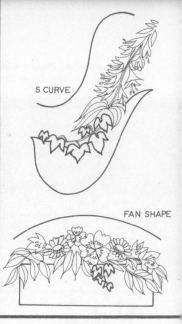

S CURVE

FAN SHAPE

CRESCENT SHAPE

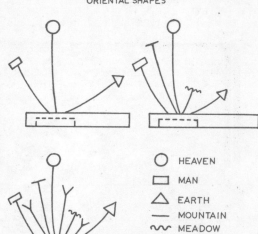

ORIENTAL SHAPES

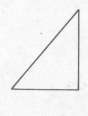

○ HEAVEN
□ MAN
△ EARTH
— MOUNTAIN
〜 MEADOW
∨ HELPERS

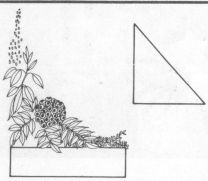

LEFT HAND OR RIGHT HAND TRIANGLES

Entertaining

Whether you are entertaining on a small or grand scale, formally or informally, in your own home or at a restaurant or hotel, the secret of success lies in making the people you have invited feel happy and at ease.

Making people feel relaxed is comparatively simple if you are genuinely pleased to see them. Let them sense the warmth in your welcome and feel themselves wanted.

1.   Have the room comfortably warm.

2.   Show guests where to leave their coats. Women also like the opportunity to tidy their hair and powder their noses.

3.   If the occasion is a party, do not leave newcomers on the fringe of things. Introduce them to those already present. Make a point of leaving them with someone who will talk to them and put them at their ease.

4.   Offer guests a drink and a cigarette. Carry on a light conversation while they adjust to their surroundings. Soft background music can help, but not a blaring radio or TV that makes conversation impossible.

Informal Entertaining

Entertaining should be fun and need not always be planned in advance. Informal gatherings can be extremely enjoyable and present themselves completely without warning. For example:

Mid-morning coffee with a friend or neighbour
Coffee morning for group of friends
Pot-luck lunch after shopping with a friend
Mid afternoon 'cuppa'
Evening drinks
Late night coffee with friends met at the local
Gathering of teenagers
Hen party
Group of children after school
Play group of under fives

A Dinner Party

Most women enjoy giving a dinner party once they get over the fear of its being a flop. To ensure success with a formal meal:

1.   Let it be small. Choose your guests carefully, making sure they have similar interests.

2.   Do not dominate the conversation, but steer it away from controversial topics should they threaten to get out of hand.

3.   Ensure that no one person dominates the conversation.

4.   Remember it is better to have three courses of good quality, well served food than an indifferent six course meal.

5.   If you are coping single handed, select manageable dishes.

6.   Prepare in advance. Have the table laid, flowers arranged, lighting set and kitchen cleared for the stacking of returned dishes.

7.   Do not fuss when the meal is over. Leave the dishes on the table and withdraw to another room if possible, rather than attempt to show your efficiency in clearing up.

8.   End the evening with coffee in the lounge.

A Wine and Cheese Party

When you owe hospitality to several people it is usually easier to have a buffet meal than a formal sit-down affair.

One of the most popular buffet meals is a wine and cheese party. It is also one of the easiest to organise. Cheese is extremely versatile and looks appetising whether you serve it:
In **WEDGES**,   leaving guests to cut for themselves.
In **DICED CUBES** that can be speared with a cocktail stick or picked up with the fingers and eaten with biscuits.
As a **FONDUE** or **DIP**. Serve with fingers of toast, biscuits, sticks of celery or sausages on sticks, all of which can be dunked into the cheese mixture.
Provide a good selection of cheeses. There are   some   delicious English and

Welsh varieties: **Cheddar, Derby, Caerphilly, Blue Stilton, Lancashire, Leicester, Wensleydale, Double Gloucester** and **Cheshire** are universal favourites and team well with wine, particularly with port.

Choose a variety of breads and biscuits to go with them and you'll be surprised how well the occasion goes.

Guests to stay

Extended entertaining—over a weekend or longer—calls for more detailed planning.

1. Make sure your guests know how long you are inviting them to stay.

2. Make up their bed. If the weather is cold, put a bottle or electric blanket in, or have extra blankets ready.

3. If they are bringing a small child or baby, borrow or hire a cot. A very small baby can sleep in a large drawer.

4. Serve their breakfast in bed, leaving yourself free to get your own family off to work and to do your chores.

5. If there is only one bathroom, tell the visitors when it is most convenient for them to use it.

6. If guests offer to make their own bed, dust the living room or wash up, accept their help.

7. Unexpected visits should not be allowed to disrupt your entire routine. If you have no spare room, then make it clear that the guests will have to sleep in the living room on the settee, or on a camp bed.

8. If you live in the country, remember guests from town will enjoy seeing something of the countryside.

9. If you live in town, guests from the country will enjoy visiting the theatre or having a meal at a restaurant.

10. Leave guests some free time to spend as they wish.

PARTY APPETISERS

CHEESE AND PINEAPPLE PORCUPINE

1 large grapefruit
6 oz. Leicester cheese
6 oz. Derby cheese
1 medium-sized can pineapple cubes, well-drained

1. Stand grapefruit on serving dish. (If necessary, cut small slice off base so it stands without toppling.) **2.** Cut both cheeses into ½-in. cubes. **3.** Put on to cocktail sticks alternately with pineapple, then spear into grapefruit.

HOT MUSHROOM TARTLETS

CHEESE PASTRY
4 oz. plain flour
¼ level teaspoon mustard powder
¼ level teaspoon salt
2½ oz. English or Welsh butter
2 oz. finely grated English Cheddar cheese
4–6 teaspoons cold water or egg yolk
MUSHROOM SAUCE
2–3 oz. button mushrooms
Butter for frying
½ oz. English or Welsh butter
½ oz. flour
¼ pint milk
Salt and pepper

1. Mix the flour with the mustard powder and salt, then 'rub-in' the butter until the mixture resembles fine breadcrumbs. Stir in the cheese and bind the pastry together with water or egg yolk. Roll out the cheese pastry and cut out rounds to line 10 to 12 bun tins. Prick the bottom of each tartlet case and line them with a piece of aluminium foil. Cook at Gas No. 7 or 425°F for five minutes, remove the foil and continue cooking the cases for a further 5 to 10 minutes. **2.** Select the best 12 mushrooms and lightly fry them. Chop the remaining mushrooms and fry them also. Melt the ½ oz. butter, stir in the flour and gradually blend in the milk; stir over a medium heat until the sauce is thick. Stir in the cooked chopped mushrooms and season to taste with salt and pepper. **3.** Pour the hot mushroom sauce into the cheese pastry tartlets and top each with a cooked button mushroom and a good shake of paprika pepper.

Party
appetisers

1. & 2. Hot mushroom tartlets;
    Cheese and olive balls
3. Hawaiian sandwiches
4. Cheddar cheese and celery dip
5. Onion dip
6. Potato crisps for dips

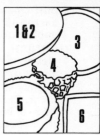

CHEESE AND OLIVE BALLS

$\frac{1}{4}$ lb. cream cheese
1 tablespoon fresh double cream
1 level tablespoon finely-chopped
    stuffed olives
$\frac{1}{4}$ level teaspoon paprika
Seasoning to taste
About 1 oz. finely-chopped shelled
    walnut halves

1. Beat cheese and cream together until smooth. Stir in olives and paprika. 2. Season to taste with salt and pepper. 3. Divide into 12 to 14 equal-sized pieces. Shape into balls. 4. Roll in chopped walnuts and chill. 5. Spear on to cocktail sticks just before serving.

TOASTED LANCASHIRE ROLLS

8 rashers streaky bacon
16 × $\frac{1}{2}$-in. cubes of Lancashire cheese

1. Cut bacon rashers in half. Wrap round cubes of cheese. 2. Secure with cocktail sticks. 3. Cook under hot grill until bacon is crisp and golden. 4. Serve straight away.

CREAMED YOGURT DIP

1 carton (5 oz.) natural yogurt
$\frac{1}{4}$ lb. cream cheese
2 level tablespoons finely-chopped
    peeled cucumber
1 level teaspoon paprika
$\frac{1}{2}$ to 1 level teaspoon salt
Good shake of pepper

1. Beat yogurt into cheese. Stir in cucumber and paprika. 2. Season to taste with salt and pepper. Chill. 3. Transfer to bowl before serving.

ONION DIP

$\frac{1}{4}$ pint fresh double cream
1 carton (5 oz.) natural yogurt
$\frac{1}{2}$ packet onion soup
GARNISH
1 level tablespoon finely-chopped
    chives or parsley

1. Lightly whip cream. 2. Stir yogurt and soup. 3. Chill for 2 or 3 hours. 4. Transfer to bowl or hollowed-out cabbage. Sprinkle with chopped chives or parsley.

LEEK DIP

$\frac{1}{4}$ pint fresh double cream
1 carton (5 oz.) natural yogurt
$\frac{1}{2}$ packet leek soup
2 oz. Caerphilly cheese, grated
GARNISH
Paprika

1. Lightly whip cream. 2. Stir in yogurt, soup and cheese. 3. Chill for 2 or 3 hours. 4. Transfer to bowl before serving. Sprinkle with paprika.

CHEDDAR CHEESE AND CELERY DIP

2 oz. English or Welsh butter, softened
$\frac{1}{2}$ lb. very finely grated English
    Cheddar cheese
2 level teaspoons made mustard
$\frac{1}{4}$ lb. very finely-chopped celery
$\frac{1}{4}$ pint fresh single cream
Seasoning to taste

1. Beat butter until creamy. Stir in cheese, mustard and celery. 2. Very gradually beat in cream. Season to taste with salt and pepper. 3. Before serving, transfer to bowl or a scooped-out pineapple. Sprinkle top lightly with chopped nuts.

HAWAIIAN OPEN SANDWICHES

4 slices freshly-made white or brown
    toast
English or Welsh butter
4 oz. grated Derby cheese
A little milk
4 small crisp lettuce leaves
4 pineapple rings
GARNISH
Mustard and cress

1. Spread the slices of toast with butter. 2. Mash the grated cheese to a stiff cream with a little milk. Spread it over the toast. 3. Top each slice with a lettuce leaf and a pineapple ring. Garnish with mustard and cress.

AFTERNOON TEA SANDWICHES

1. Spread very thin slices of white or brown bread with well-creamed English or Welsh butter. **2.** Sandwich together with choice of finely-chopped hard-boiled egg mixed with salad cream, thin slices of peeled cucumber, smoked salmon, well-seasoned cream cheese or fish or meat paste **3.** Remove crusts and cut each sandwich into 4 squares or triangles. **4.** Arrange attractively on serving plate. **5.** Sprinkle with mustard and cress. Allow 8 to 10 squares or triangles per person.

PIN WHEEL SANDWICHES

1. Remove crusts from very thin, very fresh, slices of white or brown bread. **2.** Stand on damp tea towel (this helps to prevent bread from cracking). **3.** Spread with well-creamed English or Welsh butter. **4.** Cover with choice of well-seasoned cream cheese, smoked cod's roe, smoked salmon, soft liver sausage, pâté or fish or meat paste. **5.** Roll up and hold in place with wooden cocktail sticks. **6.** Stand on plate or small serving tray. **7.** Cover with aluminium foil or sheet of polythene. **8.** Chill thoroughly. **9.** Just before serving, remove sticks and cut each roll into thin slices. Allow about 8 to 12 Pin Wheels per person.

ENTERTAINING CHILDREN

Keeping children happy and amused calls for careful planning. Do not expect them to sit quietly for more than a few minutes.

If you are having a children's party, plan every minute of the time so that something new is happening. If their interest and attention is retained, there is no fear of them teasing each other, fighting or generally getting out of hand.

When organising a children's party:

1. State on the invitations the time the party is to start and end, so that parents can collect their children on time.

2. Plan the meal so that it is easy to handle, colourful and tasty. Remember children often enjoy savoury foods more than sweet ones.

3. Keep drinks limited to milk-based ones—which all children enjoy—and fruit juices.

4. Plan the events in this order:
Games
Break for refreshments
Either a quiet game, a film show or a conjurer
More boisterous games

5. End at the stated time so that parents are not kept waiting for their children.

6. Give each child a small gift or balloon to take home.

PARTY MILK DRINKS

BANANA SHAKE

**1 pint milk
2 ripe bananas, thoroughly mashed
1 brickette ice cream cut into small pieces**

1. Put all the ingredients into a large bowl. **2.** Whisk until well blended and foamy. **3.** Serve in tall glasses.

ALMOND AND NUTMEG SHAKE

**1 pint milk
4–6 drops almond essence
2 brickettes ice cream cut into small pieces
Grated nutmeg**

1. Whisk ice cream, milk and essence together until very foamy. **2.** Pour into tall glasses. **3.** Sprinkle with nutmeg. **4.** Serve with straws.

CAFE AU LAIT

**1 pint of cold milky coffee
2 brickettes ice cream cut into small pieces
2–3 drops vanilla flavouring**

1. Whisk all ingredients in large bowl until very well blended and foamy. **2.** Pour into tall glasses. **3.** Serve with straws.

Milk drinks

1. Chocolate milk shake
2. Chilled milk
3. Café au lait
4. Orange milk shake
5. Strawberry and banana shake

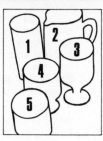

Home-made sweets

1. Toffee apples
2. Cornflake crackles
3. Coffee walnut wonders
4. Coconut clowns

CHOCOLATE MILK SHAKE

1 pint milk
8 chocolate peppermint creams
2 brickettes ice cream cut into small
  pieces
1. Melt the peppermint creams in small
basin over pan of hot water. 2. Remove
basin from heat and stir in milk gradually.
3. Add ice cream and whisk until well
blended. 4. Pour into tall glasses and
sprinkle with flakes of chocolate.

PARTY PUNCH

2 pints milk
1 pint canned pineapple juice
1 family brick ice cream cut into small
  pieces
A little crushed pineapple
1. Mix milk and pineapple juice in large
bowl. 2. Add ice cream. 3. Whisk vigorously
until all ingredients are smoothly blended
and foamy. Pour into punch bowl;
sprinkle with crushed pineapple, decorate
with sprigs of young mint.

STRAWBERRY AND BANANA SHAKE

1 pint milk
½ lb. ripe strawberries or 1 carton
  frozen
2 ripe bananas
1 family brick ice cream cut into small
  pieces
1. Sieve strawberries and bananas into
large bowl. 2. Add milk and ice cream.
3. Whisk until thoroughly blended and
frothy. 4. Pour into glasses.

ORANGE MILK SHAKE

1 pint milk
Strained, chilled juice of 3 large
  oranges
Sprig mint
Slice of orange
1. Chill milk well. 2. Mix thoroughly
with orange juice. 3. Serve topped with a
slice of orange.

PAM'S DELIGHT

1 pint milk
1 standard egg
Level dessertspoon cocoa powder
Sugar to taste (about 2 dessertspoons
  caster sugar)
1. Mix cocoa powder to smooth paste
with a little hot water. 2. Whisk up egg and
add to cocoa. 3. Top up with milk and
stir until blended together. 4. Sugar to
taste.

MARSHMALLOW MILK SHAKE

1 pint milk
1 brickette ice cream cut into pieces
2 tablespoons milk shake flavouring
6 marshmallows
1. Whisk milk, ice cream and flavouring
until frothy. 2. Pour into tall glasses. 3. Top
with marshmallows.

YOGURT FRUIT CUP

1 carton (5 oz.) pineapple fruit yogurt
½ pint pineapple juice
1. Whisk yogurt and pineapple juice well
together. 2. Chill before serving. Serves 2.

SWEET MAKING

Home-made sweets always go down
at a children's party. The following recipes
are delicious, but simple enough for your
children to help you make.

TOFFEE APPLES

8 medium-sized eating apples
8 thick wooden skewers
¼ pt. water
12 oz. granulated sugar
6 oz. golden syrup
2 oz. butter
Red food colouring
1. Wash and dry apples. Push a skewer
carefully into each apple at the stalk-ends.
2. Put water into tall-sided, heavy sauce-

pan, and bring to boil. Add sugar, syrup and butter, and heat slowly, stirring all the time, until sugar dissolves and butter melts. Bring to boil, cover saucepan with a lid and boil gently for 3 minutes. **3.** Uncover saucepan, and continue to boil hard, without stirring, for 8 to 10 minutes (or until a little trickle of mixture, dropped from wooden spoon into cup of cold water, separates into brittle threads). **4.** Move saucepan away from heat, and add about 1 teaspoon of red colouring. **5.** Lift up each apple by skewer and dip into hot toffee, swirling it round so that it is completely covered. Lift out, and stand on shallow, buttered tin. Leave until cold and set. **6.** If apples are not going to be eaten straight away, wrap each one separately in waxed or greaseproof paper.

COFFEE WALNUT WONDERS

1 lb. icing sugar
4 oz. shelled walnut halves
3 teaspoons instant coffee powder
2 oz. butter
2 tablespoons single cream or top of the milk
Extra shelled walnut halves

1. Sift icing sugar into bowl. Put nuts on board, and chop up into tiny little pieces. Add to sugar and coffee powder, and mix well. Put butter and cream into saucepan. **2.** Stand saucepan over a low heat, and leave until butter has melted, taking care not to let mixture boil. **3.** Leave on one side to cool slightly, then pour on to icing sugar, nuts and coffee and mix well. **4.** Lift out of bowl on to a board or table thickly covered with more icing sugar— which should be sifted first—and knead well. **5.** Break off small pieces and roll into balls, press a walnut half into centre of each.

CORNFLAKE CRACKLES

1 oz. butter
2 level tablespoons golden syrup or clear honey
1 level tablespoon cocoa powder, sifted
2 level tablespoons granulated sugar
7 rounded tablespoons cornflakes

1. Put 20 sweet-paper cases with fluted sides on flat plate or wooden board. **2.** Put

butter into a saucepan and add syrup. Leave over a low heat until butter melts. Stir in cocoa. **3.** Take saucepan away from heat, and add sugar. Sprinkle in cornflakes. Stir quickly with metal spoon until corn-flakes are well coated with cocoa mixture. **4.** Using 2 teaspoons, pile into paper cases. Leave in the cool to set.

COCONUT CLOWNS

1 oz. butter
1 heaped tablespoon lemon curd
½ teaspoon vanilla essence
1 heaped tablespoon icing sugar, sifted
4 heaped tablespoons desiccated coconut
Extra sifted icing sugar

1. Put butter into bowl. Add lemon curd and vanilla essence, and beat with wooden spoon until soft. Add icing sugar, and beat in well. Stir in coconut, and knead with hands until thoroughly mixed. **2.** Lift out of bowl, and put on table or board on which icing sugar has been sprinkled. Shape coconut mixture into long roll, and divide into 16 little pieces all the same size. Roll each into a ball, and toss in toasted coconut. Leave in cool place until firm.

For toasted coconut, put coconut into baking tin, and leave in warm oven until it turns light brown.

MILKY CANDY

¼ pt. milk
1 lb. granulated sugar
2 oz. butter
1 teaspoon vanilla essence

1. Put milk into tall-sided, heavy saucepan, and bring it to boil. Add sugar and butter, and heat slowly, stirring all the time, until sugar dissolves and butter melts. Bring mixture to boil, cover pan with a lid and boil gently for 3 minutes. Take off lid, then boil a little more quickly, stirring often, for about 10 minutes (or until trickle of mixture, dropped from wooden spoon into cup of cold water, forms fairly hard ball when picked up and rolled between finger and thumb). **2.** Take saucepan away from heat, and add vanilla essence. Stir candy briskly for ½ minute, then pour into a buttered tin. Cut into squares when set, and keep in air-tight tin.

Home Winemaking

Home winemaking always used to be associated with country folk, but now amateurs everywhere are trying it, with quite professional results. To make these wines for your own use—not for sale—a licence is not needed.

BASIC ESSENTIALS

Start by choosing a basis for the wine. In its true sense, wine is the fermented juice of freshly-gathered grapes. Fermentation occurs when yeast 'feeds' on sugar to produce alcohol and carbon dioxide. The alcohol remains in the liquid; the carbon dioxide escapes into the air. For homemade wine, however, almost any edible fruit or vegetable, cereals and some flowers can be used. Leaves need not be considered.

The juices are extracted in water. Other ingredients are then put into the liquid, and the whole allowed to work together to build up the wine, improve the taste and keeping qualities, and infuse it with an alcohol content.

When choosing the basic ingredient, keep to the types most generally used, bearing in mind that not every berry or flower is suitable. The following list, though not exhaustive, indicates some favourite varieties—and some to avoid:

Use: Apple, apricot, bilberry, blackberry, blackcurrant, cherry, clover, coltsfoot, cowslip, damson, dandelion, elderberry, elderflower, gooseberry, grape, hawthorn berries, marigold, marrow, mint, parsley, raspberry, rhubarb, rose hips, sage, sloe, strawberry, rice, white lilac, beetroot, carrot, turnip—the three last-named usually being boiled to help juice extraction.

Avoid: Arum, bryony, buttercup, foxglove, ivy, laburnum, laurel, nightshade, privet, poppy, rhubarb leaves, yew—and any you are not sure about.

Fresh materials are preferred, though several can be obtained in dried form. There is also concentrated grape juice.

All the other ingredients are the everyday sort kept in the house or readily bought. Some large chemists stock materials and equipment for winemaking, and there are a number of firms who specialise in this line and who can supply everything you need.

EQUIPMENT

For regular winemaking, try to get together a set of equipment and keep it exclusively for that purpose.

In the meantime, some household utensils may have to be used. They must be perfectly clean and undamaged, not even chipped. Stick to polythene, glass, wood, or earthenware, avoiding metal except for boiling pans, which may be of good quality enamel, stainless steel or heavy aluminium. For most wines it is not necessary to boil anything at all.

Here is a list of what you need:

1. **Storage jar**
2. **Large pail or bowl**
3. **Spare pails**
4. **Jug or ladle**
5. **Funnel**
6. **Fine nylon-mesh sieve**
7. **Stirring stick**
8. **Fermentation lock**
9. **Bottles, corks and possibly paraffin wax**

You may also need:

10. **Siphon**

The first item of equipment is the storage jar in which the wine spends most of its time, first fermenting, then maturing for a long period.

Oak casks are the traditional containers, but for home use there are now small polythene barrels which are light to handle, easy to clean and inexpensive. Large glass and stone jars are also used extensively. Ideally, these containers should have a tap.

As it is best to fill the storage jar right up, its size will determine the quantity you make—one or two gallons perhaps being sufficient for a start. You can reckon on getting about 50 wineglassfuls from a gallon.

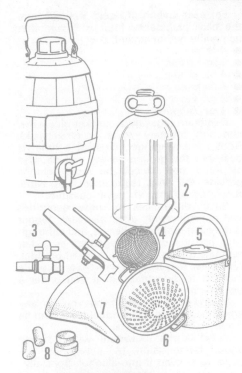

finished wine goes into the storage jar. Its purpose is to enable gases to escape from the fermenting liquor without allowing harmful elements to enter it.

One popular type consists of two small bulbs joined by a U-shaped bend, and a stem which is pushed through the centre of a bored cork fitting firmly into the bunghole or mouth of the jar. Corks are made in many sizes, to fit the smallest bunghole or the much wider opening at the top of polythene barrels.

In use, the bend (not the bulbs) has to be filled with water, which is pushed up the outlet side when fermentation is in progress, and drops level again when it subsides. Make sure there is a little space inside the jar between the wine and the bottom of the lock.

Eventually sediment will settle at the bottom of the storage jar, and the clear wine has to be drawn off. When the container is provided with a tap, this presents no problem. Otherwise, the liquid will have to be siphoned out.

In its simplest form, a siphon is a length of rubber or plastic tubing. One end is lowered into the jar to within an inch or

SOME BASIC EQUIPMENT

1. Polythene barrel
2. Glass Storage jar
3. Wood and brass taps
4. Sieve
5. Lidded pail
6. Colander
7. Funnel
8. Corks

The large pail or bowl is for use when preparing the *must*, which is what wine in its earliest stages is called. Since this will contain ingredients as well as water, it should have twice the capacity of the finishing-off jar, polythene dustbins sometimes being used for extra large quantities. A cloth or board to cover it should be available.

Spare pails are for temporary use when straining out the ingredients.

A colander lined with muslin would serve for straining. The stirring stick ought to be wide and strong, so that it can be used for crushing the fruit as well.

A fermentation lock, made of glass or plastic, comes into use when the partly

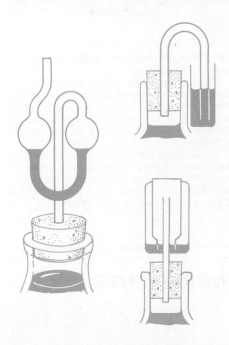

Three types of fermentation lock.

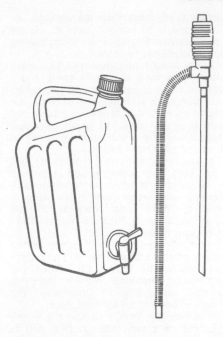

Easily-stored plastic container and plastic siphon.

so of the sediment, the other hangs to a lower level outside.

To draw out the wine, first suction it through the tube with a starter bulb. When this is removed, the flow can be stopped or started with a small clip at the end. A complete, well-made little siphon is not expensive.

Good wine can be made with modest equipment. Extras, such as a hydrometer for testing the sugar content and measuring the alcoholic strength, need only be added if you are inclined to experiment.

INGREDIENTS

The additional ingredients may be varied a little in different recipes. Special flavourings can be bought, but for most wines beginners will find the following a good general guide to the items and quantities to put in.

For each gallon of liquid strained from the basic vegetable, fruit or flower after its preliminary treatment, use:

- *4 lb. sugar*
- *¼ lb. raisins*
- *½ oz. ginger*
- *1 lemon*
- *½ oz. yeast*
- *⅛ oz. isinglass*

Demerara sugar always makes nice wine, although ordinary white is often used. Root (whole) ginger, crushed a little, is best, but the ground variety will do. Use all the lemon except the pips. Lemons provide the acid requirements of wine. Rinse ingredients whenever possible.

Small differences in these quantities will not noticeably affect the taste. Sugar is the most difficult to decide, and although four pounds may be regarded as a fair estimate for a nice medium-sweet product, rather less may be used with fruits naturally inclined to sweetness, or if you prefer a dry type of wine.

If you keep a record of what you use, any adjustments to suit individual tastes can be made on later occasions.

Yeast is the ingredient which brings about fermentation by acting on the sugar to convert it into alcohol. Specially-prepared wine yeasts, in dry or liquid form, are best. Follow their directions for use.

The sort the grocer sells for home baking will also do quite well. This is prepared by covering with a teaspoonful of sugar. Press into a paste with the back of a spoon. Spread the paste on a piece of toast and drop it lightly into the mixture after the other ingredients, making sure that the liquid is not more than lukewarm.

Optional Extras

The following items are mentioned, not necessarily for inclusion in your wines, but to indicate their purpose:

1. **Campden tablets** serve as a preservative to counteract bacteria and mould.

2. **Enzymes** (such as Pectolase and Pectozyme) help to break down the fruit, releasing more juice and destroying matter which tends to make wine cloudy.

3. **Nutrients** are put in with the yeast to assist fermentation.

4. **Tannin** (strong tea is sometimes used) may be added if there is a deficiency. Most fruits contain enough already.

5. Cloves and bay leaves can be added (about half a dozen of each) if you like the flavour.

THE DIFFERENT STAGES

Winemaking is best done in a medium-to-warm temperature, extremes tending either to slow down the process of fermentation, or to make it work too actively. A rather cool place is best for storing the finished product. Garages and workshops where fumes might be present should be avoided at all stages.

Rhubarb, flowers and the juicy fruits such as blackberries and gooseberries, are perhaps the easiest winemakers, because their goodness can simply be soaked out in water. Vegetables such as parsnips and beetroot are best boiled to extract as much goodness as possible. Use three to four pounds of the fruit or vegetable to a gallon of water.

The whole process, from raw material to finished wine, progresses in stages.

Preliminary Treatment

Scrub vegetables and remove unsound pieces. Then cut into slices without peeling, and simmer till tender.

Fruit or flowers (petals only, no stems or greenstuff) need only be put uncooked into the pail, covered with hot water, and soaked for three to seven days. Stir and press out the juice every day.

Fermentation in Pail

After this initial treatment, strain through a fine sieve and throw the pulp away. Measure liquid into the pail, and put in all the other ingredients except the isinglass. The yeast, added when the liquid is lukewarm, will make it ferment, and it should be allowed to work for about 10 days. Give it a good stir every day. Keep the vessel covered, because wine in the making must be exposed to the air as little as possible.

Fermentation in Barrel

After this first period of fermentation, strain through the sieve again, and throw away the solids. Pour the liquid into the storage barrel or jar, and bung down with a cork containing the fermentation lock. Any surplus can be put aside in a lightly-corked bottle. The liquid will start to ferment again, and continue for many weeks.

Finishing Off

When the wine has *quite finished* fermenting, draw it off through the tap or siphon, leaving the sediment behind. Rinse out the jar, then put the wine back, filling it right up with the surplus you put aside, if any.

Dissolve the isinglass (a clearing agent) in two or three spoonfuls of hot water, then shake it up thoroughly with some wine in a bottle, pour into the jar and stir it up inside with a stick. Bung down tight.

To make sure the wine has finished working, take out the bung and listen carefully. All should be perfectly quiet inside—fermenting wine makes a slight hissing noise.

Leave the wine undisturbed for at least six months to clear and mature. Then it is ready to be bottled off for use, though the longer it is kept, particularly in bulk, the better.

Bottling Your Wine

Proper wine bottles, attractively labelled, give a good finish to your products. It is worth buying a few (six to the gallon) which you can always use, and know to be perfectly clean.

Second-hand ones need to be thoroughly washed out in fairly hot water. Throw out any that cannot be cleaned by this method, and disregard altogether bottles that may have contained anything other than foodstuffs.

Remove the bung from the top of the barrel or jar before turning on the tap. The wine will be clear enough to run straight into the bottles, but keep an eye on it as you near the bottom of the barrel in case sediment starts to stir up and make it cloudy. Fill the bottles to about half-way up the neck.

Some bottles have screw caps. These will be airtight and should be stood upright when filled. Ordinary corks are more likely to be used, preferably those of the stopper pattern with a large head, which can be extracted later on without a corkscrew.

Scrub them lightly in hot water, and just before use sterilise and soften them by soaking them in boiling water for five minutes. Hold the bottle in a tea cloth, and knock the cork in with a flat piece of wood.

Let the wine come into contact with these corks, to keep them swelled and airtight, by laying the bottles on their side in a rack or between layers of paper. Faulty corks can be made airtight, after they have been knocked in and the top dried, by dipping the corked part of the bottle in melted paraffin wax.

SELECTED RECIPES

The description red wine explains itself. White wine refers to the light colours, including yellow. These recipes include both. Here is a varied selection for beginners who do not want to devote too much time to winemaking.

Blackberry

Use sound, ripe berries, preferably gathered on a dry day, or used straight-away if damp. Three to four pounds for each gallon of water. Pour boiling water over them, and help extraction of juice by pressing with stick. Steep for six days, stirring daily. Strain, then ferment for 10 days with all ingredients added. Strain again and proceed in usual way. Other soft fruits can be treated like this.

Rhubarb

First-class wine, quite easy to make. About five pounds to gallon. Trim off leaves (which must not be used) and

stumps, wipe and cut sticks into short lengths without skinning. Steep in cold water. After 10 days strain off liquid, mix in all other ingredients and give usual 10 days fermentation.

Beetroot

Wash and trim, cut into slices without peeling and boil gently till tender, adding boiling water if necessary from time to time to make up for any lost as steam. Treat liquid as before. Four pounds of beetroot to gallon. Make parsnip wine in same way.

Wheat

Basic ingredients are 1 lb. good-quality wheat (thoroughly rinsed) and 1 lb. potatoes (cut into chips). Do not use potatoes with green on them. Add boiling water, putting all ingredients in at same time (yeast when lukewarm). Ferment as described in The Different Stages. Quantities given are to each gallon of water.

Wine from Flowers

Dandelion and elderflower are the most popular. A quart measure tightly packed with prepared flowers is about the right quantity for each gallon of boiling water. Allow them to steep as described in Preliminary Treatment, then strain off liquid and proceed to other stages as described.

Concentrated Grape Juice

This can be substituted for the fruit as the basic ingredient. Use two pints of juice to the gallon. Sugar can be reduced to 3½ lb. or 2 lb. Ferment it along with the other ingredients. Grape juice can also be used as an *addition* to other wines—up to ½ pint in each gallon.

● *Do not judge your wine by what it looks or tastes like in the earlier stages. Good wine needs plenty of time to mature.*

Commercial Wines

Commercial wine is the fermented juice of the grape: **red** when crushed with the skins on, **rosé** when the skins are withdrawn as the right colouration is reached or **white** when the grapes are crushed and pressed away from their skins.

White wines are made from white grapes, or red grapes with colourless juice.

Sparkling wines are made by a special process from still wine.

Fortified wines (e.g. port and sherry) have added brandy.

Wines vary because of the many varieties of grape, the location, climate and soil of the vineyard and the method of vinification; hence the very large number of flavours to choose from.

GERMAN HOCK
BURGUNDY   BORDEAUX

Above: Three standard bottle shapes. Below: Glasses for different kinds of wines and spirits.

SERVING AND STORING

Red wines should be served at room temperature. In warm weather, **rosé** and young **Beaujolais** should be slightly chilled.

White and **sparkling wines** are served lightly chilled (the sweeter, the colder).

Fortified wines are served at room temperature, except (especially in summer) **dry sherries** and **white port** which can be chilled as aperitifs.

BOTTLES AND GLASSES

Standard shapes of bottles are generally used.

As a rule there are six glasses to a bottle of **still table** or **sparkling wine** and 12 to **fortified wines**.

The glass should never be filled right to the top. Room should be left to allow the drinker to roll the wine round the glass for better tasting.

Wine bottles when full should be stored on their sides to keep the cork moist, but **spirits** are kept upright.

SHERRY   COCKTAIL   WHISKY

TABLE WINES   BRANDY

HOCK

CHAMPAGNE

GUIDE TO WINES

Wine is produced wherever grapes are grown, but French wine is acknowledged to be the best. Here is a list of wine-producing countries and their different sorts of wine.

France

ALSACE
White and mostly dry.
Sylvaner. Light and mellow.
Riesling. Dry but a little heavier.
Traminer. Fruity and less dry.
Muscat. Dry but very grapy.
Pinot. Dry and spicy.
● *All should be served chilled and are excellent with fish and shellfish, pork, poultry and salads.*

BORDEAUX, RED
Lighter than Burgundy.
Claret. Pleasantly light and dry, ranging to the finest of all red wines.
Principal districts: **Medoc, Graves, Saint Emilion, Pomerol Fronsac, Bourg and Blaye.**
● *Serve at room temperature with plainly cooked meat, poultry and cold meats and the milder cheeses.*

BORDEAUX, WHITE
Dry, medium dry or sweet.
Dry or medium dry: **Graves, Entre deux Mers, Côtes de Bordeaux.**
Sweet and medium sweet: **Sauternes** and **Barsac** most famous wines of former **Château d'Yquem.**
● *Serve dry with fish, poultry and veal: sweet with fruit and dessert.*

BURGUNDY, RED
Full-bodied and soft.
Districts: **Côte de Nuits; Côte de Beaune; Côtes Chalonnais, Mâconnais, Beaujolais.**
● *Serve lighter wines with all meats and cheeses: fuller wines with rich meat dishes, game and stronger cheeses. Serve at room temperature.*

BURGUNDY, WHITE
Dry.
Districts: **Chablis; Côte de Beaune; Côte Chalonnais; Mâconnais; (e.g. Pouilly Fuissé).**
● *Serve chilled with fish, shellfish, poultry and salads.*

CHAMPAGNE
Usually dry.
Shown on labels as dry, extra dry, extra **sec** or **brut.** There is a sweeter **demi-sec** and pink champagne is sometimes obtainable. Other sparkling French wines are labelled **vin mousseux.** There is a German equivalent, **Sekt,** and a Spanish, **Perelada.**

LOIRE WINES
Pouilly-sur-Loire-fumé. Light and dry (not to be confused with Pouilly Fuissé).
Vouvray. Medium dry or medium sweet, also sometimes sparkling.
Chinon and **Bourgeuil.** Strong red wine.
Anjou. Medium dry, white or **rosé.**
Muscadet. (Nothing to do with muscat flavour) white, light and dry.
● *Serve these with any kind of meat, cheese and sometimes fish and as a change from other French wines.*

RHÔNE WINES
Resembling Burgundy in body.
Best known: **Châteauneuf-du-Pape, Hermitage, Côtes du Rhônes** and **Tavel (rosé).**
● *The red wines go with meat, game, cheese and highly-seasoned dishes: serve white chilled with fish, meat or poultry.*

OTHER FRENCH WINES
Bergerac. Not unlike sauternes.
Gaillac. Full sweet.
Jura. Red, rosé and white.
Languedoc and **Roussillon.** Red and white wines.
Provence. Mainly rosé but also red and white wines.

European Wines

GERMAN WINES
White and very little red.
Hock. Sweeter than dry, sometimes very sweet, in reddish-brown tall bottles.
Moselle. Dry or medium-dry in greenish bottles.
● *Serve both chilled with fish, plainly cooked meat and the milder cheeses.*

ITALIAN WINES
Chianti and **Orvieto.** In straw-bound flasks.
Barolo, Barbaresco. Full red wines.
Lacrima cristi and **Valpolicella.** Light, white and red.

Soave and **Frascati**. Dry white.

Secco means dry, **abbocato** fairly sweet.

● *Serve red wine at room temperature, white wine chilled, with any rich food or pasta. Marsala is a fortified sweet dessert wine.*

PORTUGUESE WINES

Port wine. Vintage or wood.

The wood ports are: **Ruby, Tawny** and **White Port**. White Port can be served as an aperitif when chilled; otherwise at room temperature.

Vinhos verdes (green wines) : Medium-dry, white and rosé.

Dao. Red and white.

Colares. Red.

Setubal. Sweet rich dessert.

Madeira. Dry, medium and sweet, all with a lightly burnt taste, otherwise slightly reminiscent of sherry. Keeps longer than any other wine once the bottle is opened.

SPANISH WINES

Sherries.

Fino. Dry.

Amontillado. A medium-sweet nutty wine.

Oloroso. A full, sweet, dark and nutty wine.

Golden. Golden, sweet and rich.

Brown. Medium-sweet or sweet, full and nutty.

Table wine districts.

Rioja red and white; **Valdepeñas** red and white; **Montilla** dry and sherry-like.

Other European Wines

AUSTRIAN WINES

Mostly light, dry spicy white wines and a few reds.

BULGARIAN AND ROMANIAN WINES

Red wines with much body.

GREEK WINES

Retsina. Dry, white (flavoured with pine resin).

Samos. Dry, medium or sweet.

Mavrodaphne. Sweet red fortified wine.

HUNGARIAN WINES

Red and white.

Balaton Riesling. Medium dry white.

Egri Bikaver (Bull's Blood). Aromatic and full-bodied red.

Tokay. Sweet dessert wine.

SWISS WINES

Fendant. White, light and dry.

Johannisberger. White but fuller.

Dôle. Red, soft but full bodied.

YUGOSLAVIAN WINES

Riesling. Medium-dry white wine.

Traminer. More fruity.

Tiger Milk. Sweetish white.

Brda. Generous red.

Other Wines

AUSTRALIAN WINES

Many European-style red and white table wines, port and sherry.

CYPRUS WINES

Red and white table wines and especially sherry.

Commandaria. Fortified wine.

SOUTH AFRICAN WINES

Excellent red and white table wines, especially Hock type, sweet port-type dessert wines and a good range of sherries.

Sound wines are also produced in the following countries:

RUSSIA

Red, white and sparkling.

ISRAEL

ALGERIA

TUNISIA

Coarse red and white

UNITED STATES

A little red and white wine is imported from California, but it is expensive by British standards.

CHILE

Excellent red wine and comparatively cheap.

291

Care of the Car

Just as your home benefits from regular cleaning and maintenance, so your car needs routine and regular attention, with servicing—the equivalent of a Spring Clean—at least twice a year, or every 2,000 miles.

Major troubles frequently stem from minor initial causes. By checking the trivial faults without delay you may avoid the more serious ones.

The golden rule is to look for the **simple** causes first.

Before a drive

Make a walk-around check:
Are all the tyres correctly inflated?
Are there any dangling wires or loose pieces?
Are there new scratches on the paintwork?
Are both bonnet and boot securely closed?

Take immediate remedial action for any observed fault.

Before a Long Drive

BATTERY
Check water level. Top up **only with distilled water,** covering the internal plates by no more than $\frac{1}{4}$ in. of water. Ensure the terminals are free from dirt.

RADIATOR
Check water level (unnecessary with sealed radiator systems).

Check for leaks on the honeycomb.

After the winter, be sure to remove the cold weather radiator muff or screening.

PLUGS
Check the leads are secure.

OIL
Check level with dipstick. Too much oil is almost as bad as too little oil.

If the dipstick shows a black sludge instead of clear oil, a change is urgently needed. If there are tiny specks of white metal on the dipstick oil, that means an engine bearing is wearing badly and needs immediate attention.

GENERAL INSPECTION

Touch as many parts and pieces as you can.

Tighten up any loose nuts.

Feel for broken hosepiping.

Check for a slack fan-belt and for disconnected electrical leads.

Look for leaks anywhere along the fuel, water and oil pipes. Tighten up union-nuts. Insulating tape can check a minor leak.

WEAR AND TEAR SCALE

A rule-of-thumb working scale for replacement of vital parts is:
New sparking plugs every 5,000 miles
New tyres at 20,000 miles, often less
New windscreen wiper rubbers every 8,000 miles
New battery after $2\frac{1}{2}$ years
These are not firm figures: too many factors are involved to generalise effectively. But:

Good **plugs** will cut your fuel consumption and improve car performance.

Good **tyres** are an insurance for safety—and give better travel.

Windscreen wipers are useless if they do not make a clean sweep.

The **battery** is the heart of the engine—treat it as such.

CORROSION

A scratch on the paintwork leaves the metal beneath open to corrosion attack. Any deep scratch should without delay be delicately brushed over with touching-up paint (sold with a hair brush affixed to the lid of the tin).

Do NOT trust your eye to match the car colour: use only the colour recommended by the car manufacturer.

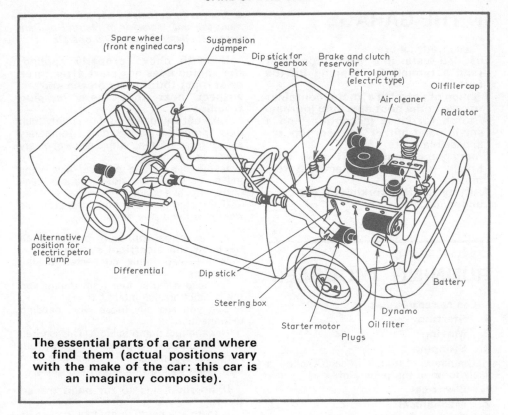

The essential parts of a car and where to find them (actual positions vary with the make of the car: this car is an imaginary composite).

Labels: Spare wheel (front engined cars), Suspension damper, Dip stick for gearbox, Brake and clutch reservoir, Petrol pump (electric type), Oil filler cap, Air cleaner, Radiator, Alternative position for electric petrol pump, Differential, Dip stick, Steering box, Starter motor, Plugs, Oil filter, Dynamo, Battery

Salt damage

Corrosion can attack the unseen under-parts of your car. Especially after driving on roads treated with snow-dispersing commercial salt. A thorough underside hosing will well repay the effort.

A windy day by the sea may give a corrosive coating of salt spray. As soon as convenient, clean all exposed metal parts—bumpers, wipers, handles, etc.—with a branded polish. Do this thoroughly: one neglected spot could lead to trouble.

CLEANING

Housing in a garage or even a car port definitely prolongs the life—and second hand value—of a car. Where a car has to be left in the open, regular cleaning is recommended—a detergent wash-down once a week is the minimum treatment, with a silicone polish once a month after the wash-down.

A car is NOT cleaned by heavy rain. Rain is ineffective as a washing agent and often carries its own corrosive salts.

Clean glasswork with two rags—one to remove the surface dirt, one to polish off. Do NOT rub forcibly—that could cause particles of dirt to scratch the glass. The polishing rag should be clean before use—and cleaned after use.

Chamois leather, though more costly, is the best cleaning article for metal, glass and paintwork. To clean a 'chammy' use only warm water with a minimum of soap flakes: hot water with detergents will ruin it.

● **Caution:** *On artificial leatherwork, plastic seats, etc. use only warm water with soap. Do NOT use detergents or, especially, petrol or spirit to clean off spots.*

IN THE GARAGE

Keep ready for use:

Distilled water in a plastic container (and a funnel) for topping up the battery.

1 gallon of petrol in a metal container to take in the boot on a long journey.

A torch for close inspection, and a small hand-mirror to see the inaccessible parts.

Emery paper and a stiff steel wire brush, for cleaning electrical terminals.

A utility rug for working on the car's underside.

RUNNING TROUBLES

Can be separated as:
1. **Starting**
2. **Moving**
3. **Stopping**

The nature of trouble in each section is likely to be in the priority of:
1. **Electrical**
2. **Mechanical**
3. **Fuel**

● **Remember:** *Look for the simple explanation first.*

Starting

If, when the starter button is pressed or pulled, the engine does not come to life, think first of a possible electrical failure:

Have you switched the ignition ON?

Is the battery working? Turn on full headlights, and try the starter again. If the dashboard indicator shows a heavy discharge, your battery is low. It may need some distilled water.

Has the starter motor jammed? This may be an electrical fault—but a common cause of trouble is dirt on the starter shaft. A smart rap on the starter motor casing with a spanner may free the shaft, or a spanner can be used to turn the squared end of the armature shaft.

● Cars with automatic transmission must have the gear selector in Neutral or Park before the starter motor will operate.

If, with choke properly applied, the engine does not start after three or at most four bursts on the starter, suspect next that there is plug trouble.

Take out any one plug. If it is dirty then most probably all are dirty. Temporary cleaning can be done with a piece of emery paper, or a penknife.

Is the gap setting correct? Too wide means no spark; too close means a weak and ineffective spark.

If the plug points are oily, the probable trouble is the piston rings.

If the plugs appear in order, track back on the electrical system:

Is the lead firmly connected to the distributor?

Is the distributor free from damp, and the contact breaker intact?

Can you see any loose wire, needing reconnection?

Has the fuel pump failed? (This is often in the boot, near the petrol tank.) Put your hand on the pump: if it feels hot, then that could be the source of the trouble.

If no fault has so far been traced then:

Is there any petrol in the tank?

Is the fuel gauge reading properly? Test for petrol quantity by getting out of the car and rocking it—you should hear petrol sloshing about in the tank.

Is the petrol filter blocked? Test by disconnecting the feed pipe to the carburettor, and then use the starter button to pump fuel along that pipe. If no fuel emerges, the pipe is clogged or the pump has failed. Clear the pipe by blowing down it—but have a large rag at hand to mop up petrol discharged along the disconnected pipe.

If no success after all that, return to the electrical system.

Check closely the high tension lead (the thick cable to the distributor). Vibration may have caused this to work loose, or acid may have burned through the cable.

Check the battery terminals: they must be truly clean to make an efficient electrical flow.

The battery may simply have outworn its useful life which is generally about $2\frac{1}{2}$ years.

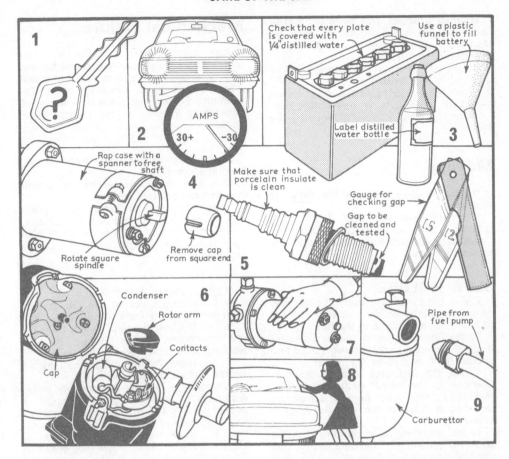

1. **Always carry a spare ignition key.**
2. **Keep an eye on your instrument dials—especially the ammeter.** A heavy discharge (as shown) indicates an electrical fault needing immediate attention. The immediate action is to switch the ignition OFF if the car is stationary. If the car is moving, stop as soon as possible and switch OFF.
3. **Battery maintenance well repays any trouble taken—use only DISTILLED water to top up the individual cells.**
4. **If the starter fails to work when you operate the dashboard button:**
   (a) a smart rap on the starter motor casing may free the shaft;
   (b) rotation of the shaft, as shown, may be necessary, using a spanner on the square spindle head.

5. **Clean plugs mean better running and more miles to the gallon. Use feeler gauge for correct gap setting.** The spark point is of soft metal, easily moved to increase or decrease the gap.
6. **The distributor feeds electricity to the spark plugs: keep it clean and, especially, free from moisture caused by condensation.**
7. **If the petrol pump is hot to the touch, it may be the source of petrol supply trouble.**
8. **To avoid scratching when cleaning windows, remember:**
   (a) not to rub hard;
   (b) not to use dry rags.
9. **Diagram shows the union nut which connects the fuel pump to the carburettor (see Page 294).**

Having started the engine, listen for any untoward noise. It may be that something is loose, but it may be mechanical trouble.

Check on whether the rotating fan is touching any other part.

Check the exhaust pipe securing bracket —and for loose nuts on any visible part.

Listen for any 'knocking' sound—*see below.*

Moving

If the engine fails, note <u>how</u> it stops:

If it peters out and 'dies' on you, the chances are it is a fuel supply failure.

If it stops *abruptly* then there is probably an electrical fault.

SLOW FAILURE

Check the petrol. The fuel indicator may be giving a false reading so rock the car to hear if there is liquid in the tank.

Is the (electric) petrol pump working? It should make a click-clicking sound and should NOT be hot to the touch.

Check the fuel pipe lead to the carburettor. Is the petrol getting through? Insulating tape may give a temporary repair to a crack in the pipe or a worn union nut.

In hot weather, or in prolonged traffic jams, the engine may become so hot that the fuel vaporises in the supply pipe, thus starving the engine. Draw out of the traffic and allow the engine to cool down. A cold compress of wet rags on the fuel pipe may help.

Another possibility is water in the fuel tank, especially if the fuel is very low. By putting in more petrol the immediate trouble may be cleared, but the real answer is a thorough clean-through of the fuel system.

Finally, the cause may be a grain of dirt in the carburettor.

SUDDEN FAILURE

Almost certainly an electrical fault. Test by turning on the windscreen wipers. If they work, the battery is obviously supplying power.

Open the bonnet and inspect for a loose lead, in particular the thick high tension cable to the distributor.

Inspect the fuses. Replace any blown fuse.

Mechanical Failure

Any moving part can fracture: the nature of the noise may help quick tracing of such a failure. A broken piston rod will make an ominous clanking noise, for example. But usually there is warning of impending trouble by the engine overheating:

If the engine becomes excessively hot, stop and

Check the radiator water (on cars which do not have a sealed system).

Check for radiator leaks. Take great care in removing the cap of a hot radiator. Cover the cap with a large rag to protect your hands from steam when the cap is removed.

If the radiator water is in order:

Is something blocking the cooling air from getting to the radiator honeycomb?

Is the fan belt broken? A red light on the dashboard should show ignition warning. Could be a broken fan belt.

Is the water hosepipe from radiator to engine broken or cracked?

● *Note that a radiator can lose its water without any outward sign of a leak. If a gasket has 'blown', the seal thus destroyed will admit water to the oil sump. Test for this by examining the oil dipstick: if there is water in the oil it will look grey and have numerous tiny bubbles . . . and the dipstick level will be above the 'full' mark.*

A hot radiator should be replenished with water a little at a time. A sudden input of cold water in quantity could crack the engine casing.

If the radiator has a visible leak, with water dripping away, a handful of any flour-type substance (even mustard) may clog the pinhole leak—simply put the substance in at the top, with the water. A raw egg broken into the radiator water can make a good seal.

More serious causes of engine overheating can be bearings, in particular the Small End and Big End.

The symptoms are audible 'knocking' when the engine is running, whether you are moving or stationary. On hearing such a noise:

Stop. Check the oil level with the dipstick. Insufficient oil will give overheating and, if the level is very low, will cause a knocking sound.

A badly-worn Small End gives a smart tap-tap-tapping sound when the engine is at slow speed. A Big End gives a much deeper knock-knock sound. Repair of either is a garage job.

These sounds should not be confused with another type of knock, generally called 'pinking'—caused by the ignition being too far advanced. The car's handbook will show you how to retard the spark, usually by a simple turn of a thumb screw.

● *'NURSE' A KNOCKING ENGINE. DRIVE SLOWLY. DO NOT ACCELERATE SHARPLY. CODDLE THE CAR BACK TO A GARAGE FOR PROFESSIONAL EXAMINATION.*

LOSS OF POWER

Suspect first of all failure of a plug: it may be very dirty and simply not firing, thus cutting out at least 25 per cent of the power of a 4-cyl. engine.

If the car does not travel as quickly as the engine speed would appear to justify, you may have a slipping clutch—caused by worn plates, lack of free play in the linkage, or oil on the friction surfaces. This is a garage job.

STEERING WHEEL SHAKES

Wheel wobble, caused by tyre faults, bad alignment or mechanical linkage wear, gives a shaking tremor on the steering wheel.

The most simple cause is a front-wheel slow puncture, which sets up an imbalance. Examine tyre treads for uneven wear. If the outside of the treads show more wear than the inside the tyre pressures are too low. But uneven wear on any one side, with 'ripples' means the steering is faulty.

If wheel wobble occurs only at certain speeds, then:
The mechanical linkage is worn, or loose.

At least one wheel is out of true fore-and-aft alignment.

Both these troubles can be cured at a garage, where the wheels should also be dynamically 'balanced' (rotated on a machine, and small balance weights added to give smooth rotation).

More sophisticated reasons for wheel wobble are suspension or damper faults, needing garage attention.

CHANGING A WHEEL

Regular maintenance should have ensured that the spare wheel tyre in the boot (or sometimes bonnet) should have been kept at the correct pressure *for a front wheel change.*

1. Position the car on level ground. Put the hand-brake firmly ON. Use a brick (or other block) as a wedge under at least one tyre to prevent the car inadvertently moving during a wheel change.
2. Remove hub cover (a screw driver can lever it off).
3. Unscrew the securing nuts to a point where they are free from pressure BUT NOT OFF.
4. Operate the lifting device—there are many types—until the wheel to be changed is clear of the ground.
5. Now remove the wheel securing nuts —a hand operation.
6. Take off the wheel. Replace it by the change wheel. Replace the securing nuts, which should be tightened up by hand.
7. Lower the lifting device until the replaced wheel just catches firmly on the ground—then tighten up the securing nuts. (If there are, say, five nuts then tighten in sequence of 'opposites', for example in the order 1, 3, 5, 2 and 4 . . . and then go round in the sequence for a final tightening.
8. Lower the lifting device; replace hub cap. Remove security brick or block from the other wheels. Release hand-brake.

LAYING UP A CAR

The most important thing is:
DISCONNECT THE BATTERY. (A dashboard clock will, in time, run a battery completely flat.)

If the lay-up is for a short period—say three of four months—no draining of water is necessary. But care **must** be taken to keep any damp at bay.

A sophisticated precaution is to remove the plugs from the engine and block the apertures with an oily wad. Routine inspection should ensure that the rest of the engine and tarnishable parts are wiped over to remove condensation moisture.

If a prolonged lay-up is planned, the tyres need attention: it is bad for the rubber to have a sustained weight for months on end. Either:

Remove the wheels and lay them out flat on their sides, or

Arrange to have the car shunted in and out of the garage, by hand if necessary, to revive the elasticity of the tyres.

If only to keep off dust spoilation from the **inside** upholstery, cover the whole car with a sheet or aluminium cloth spread.

NEVER run the engine in the garage with the garage door shut. Exhaust fumes are insidious—and quickly fatal.

ANTIFREEZE

This operation combines two tasks in one:
● *To give the coolant system a good flush through, and*
● *To put in anti freeze mixture which is a preventive against modest frost but NOT AGAINST VERY SEVERE ICING.*
1. Set the air conditioning lever at maximum warm to ensure full drainage.
2. Consult the car manual for the position of the two drainage taps—one at the rear of the engine, one at the base of the radiator.
3. Open both taps. Remember a considerable quantity of water will be drained off. It may be discoloured: after the flow has ceased put a water hose in the radiator cap and flush the system through with clean water.
4. After flushing, close the drain cocks, and then pour in the anti freeze mixture. You may have to top up the radiator water. DO NOT FILL UP COMPLETELY: stop short about 1½ in. from the top. A full radiator will only mean wastage because anti freeze expands as the engine warms up. THE ENGINE SHOULD BE RUNNING SLOWLY TO CIRCULATE THE LIQUID AS YOU PUT THE MIXTURE IN.

ROAD HAZARDS

Shattered Windscreen

Most common cause—a flying stone. It will happen in a fraction of a second. Be prepared for instant action:
1. With the right hand hold the steering wheel firm and steady
2. With the left hand, punch the shattered glass hard. This will instantly make a hole for you to see through. The glass will be in globules which will not harm you, at worst give a minor scratch.

Burst Tyre

Sounds like a large paper bag bursting. **Brake at once, not fiercely but firmly and with gradually increasing pressure all the while gripping the steering wheel to retain control. The car will tend to sway from side to side, and must be checked.**
● *A deep pool of roadside water has a similar effect to a burst tyre—it will cause a drag, tending to pull you to one side. This must be firmly counteracted on the steering wheel.*

Engine Stall

Often caused by running with the choke out. This gives a too rich mixture.

But the choke cable may have become twisted, or improperly secured at the carburettor end.

A choked engine symptom is engine stall when the car is stopped.

Skidding

1. DO NOT BRAKE—that will increase the skid. Use the engine power to slow down, by changing gear down.
2. Turn the steering wheel INTO THE DIRECTION OF THE SKID. Thus if the rear wheels skid to the left, turn your steering wheel left.

Towing

If with failed brakes you accept a tow,

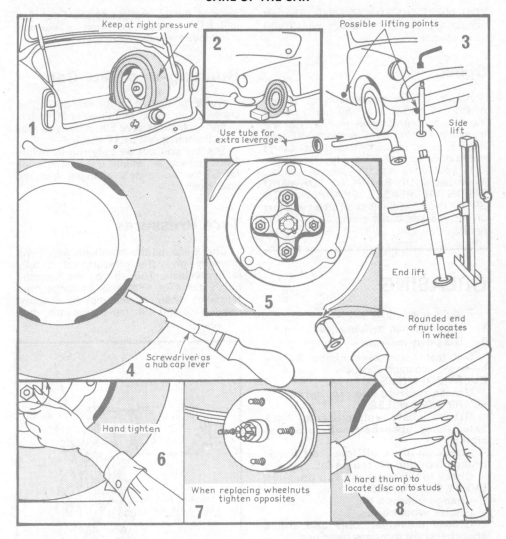

1. You may need the spare tyre urgently: maintain it at right pressure for an immediate change.

2. Use any available chocks to prevent car moving during a wheel change.

3. Make sure the lifting jack is fully engaged with the correct slot or point.

4. Use a blunt tool (not a sharp chisel) to prise off a wheel hub cap or cover disc.

5. The leverage power of a wheel nut spanner can be increased by slotting a metal tube over the spanner handle.

6. On replacing the wheel nuts, first tighten by hand. Complete the tightening with a spanner.

7. To make an even pressure all round, tighten the wheel nuts in rotation but tightening 'opposites'. With four nuts the sequence would be 1, 3, 2 and 4.

8. The wheel cover disc (removed as in 4 above) can be restored in position by a smart tap of the hand. It is self-securing.

YOU MUST DO THE TOWING. The car behind can apply the brakes which you have not got.

Speed

Above a reasonable cruising speed, which can be set at 40/50 m.p.h., every increase gives an entirely disproportionate increase of petrol consumption AND tyre wear. From an economy viewpoint, it pays not to drive beyond 50 m.p.h.

If you drive at the higher speeds, remember YOUR RANGE OF FORWARD VISION DECREASES SHARPLY WITH SPEED INCREASE. This can affect whether or not you see traffic emerging from side roads.

GREASING

Regular greasing:
1. Improves road performance.
2. Is a safety measure.

See that your car conforms to the following minimum schedule.
EVERY 500 MILES
Grease steering and rear springs.
EVERY 2,000 MILES
Grease shaft splined end, back axle, shock absorbers where accessible.
Check gearbox oil level, oil handbrake pivot and clutch pedal.
Check brake fluid and top up.
EVERY 5,000 MILES
Change gearbox oil.
Grease wheel hubs.
Grease universal joint and shock absorbers; oil dynamo bearings.
● *If you take your car to a garage for servicing it will help if you stipulate what service you want in terms of mileage run (i.e. ask for a 2,000 miles service, or whatever is the correct distance run figure).*

POINTS TO NOTE

Petrol

It is a waste of money to buy petrol of higher octane rating than that recommended by the manufacturers. Such fuel will NOT increase performance nor will it improve the miles per gallon figure.

Running-in a New Car

Nurse the engine for the first 500 miles. Usually, top speed permitted is 30 m.p.h.

For each successive 500 miles you may raise the top speed by 10 m.p.h.

The car will not be truly run-in before 6,000 miles, at which distance the oil MUST be completely changed and the filter cleaned.

Tyre Pressures

Check against the handbook which will normally give the pressure for a fully loaded vehicle. Thus, if you are normally riding alone or with one passenger, the pressures recommended may be dropped between 2 and 4 lb. per square inch.

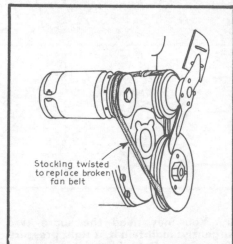

Stocking twisted to replace broken fan belt

A tightly twisted nylon stocking or plaited cord will make a temporary replacement for a broken fan belt. It must be *tightly* twisted to work effectively.

Emergency Etceteras

A sliced potato rubbed on a windscreen gives reasonable clearance from rain.

A twisted nylon stocking can act as a temporary fan belt.

A small coin is useful for turning some screws, especially the jet of the carburettor.

Any towing rope or cable used should be made fast to the structural part of the car chassis—DO NOT FIX IT TO A BUMPER OR NUMBER PLATE.

A darkened electric bulb indicates it is nearing the end of its service life.

Useful Etceteras

Tyre pressure gauge
Spark gap feelers
Small mirror for inspecting awkward places
Breakdown red triangle sign
Ball of string
Insulating tape
Torch, with bracket to suspend it over the engine

Useful Spares to Carry

2 spare light bulbs
2 spare fuses
Fan belt
Windscreen wiper
Water container, for radiator
Small reserve supply of petrol in closely sealed container

First Aid

THE FIRST AID CABINET

The First Aid cabinet, or box, should be clearly marked and kept in a warm, dry place which is easily accessible though out of reach of small children and known to members of the family.

It should be clearly marked with a Red Cross.

It is better if it is waterproof, but need not necessarily be airtight, and should have compartments. It should shut with a firm lid or door, so that it cannot be penetrated by damp or insects, and should be childproof.

If it is to be transported, breakable containers should be adequately protected. If possible, containers should be of plastic or metal to reduce chance of breakage.

A wide range of supplies can be included in the Home First Aid Box. The basic necessities are:

1. Tube or bottle of antiseptic lotion
2. Soluble aspirin, or Paracetamol, for relieving pain
3. 6×1 in. finger bandages
4. 6×2 in. bandages
5. 6×4 in. bandages
6. 2×3 in. crepe bandages
7. 1×½ in. tin zinc oxide plaster
8. 1×3 in. Elastoplast
9. 1 pkt. assorted sticking plaster dressings
10. 1 bottle of bicarbonate of soda
11. 1 pair scissors
12. 1 pair tweezers
13. Torch
14. 1 triangular bandage
15. Cotton wool
16. Assorted safety pins

Useful extras are:

1. Bottle old-fashioned smelling salts
2. Sterile pack dressings (attached to bandages and broken open for use)
3. 1 plastic water-bottle
4. Assorted splints, preferably inflatable ones
5. 1 indelible pencil
6. 1 jar 'Vaseline' petroleum jelly
7. 1 roll gauze

HOME FIRST AID TREATMENT

Burns and Scalds

● *Burns caused by dry heat and corrosive chemical substances.*
● *Scalds caused by moist heat, steam and hot liquids.*

1. Remove from source of injury (i.e., quench flames, remove from scalding liquids, burning chemicals, etc.).
2. Take out heat by cooling tissues with cold water.
3. For chemical burns, bathe the area of the injury with large amounts of water and remove contaminated clothing. Avoid burning yourself while removing clothing.
4. Reassure patient. Depending on area burnt, treat for shock.
5. Cover burnt area with sterile dressings or, if not available, clean linen. If burns or scalds cover a large area of skin, hospital treatment is required **IMMEDIATELY.**
6. Do not prick blisters, or apply grease or lotion to burns or scalds.
7. Remove constricting clothing, rings, belts, etc., that could be causing the burnt area to swell.
8. Aim to handle burnt areas as little as possible in dressing.
9. Keep surface sterile and clean.

ELECTRICAL BURNS
1. Make sure patient is not still in contact with electricity.
2. Turn off electricity before treating.
3. Treat for shock (see this section under **Shock.**)

4. Treat burns as before.

● *For large burnt areas give fluids by mouth on way to hospital to make up for fluid lost through burns and scalds.*

Cuts and Bleeding

MINOR CUTS
1. Stop bleeding by direct pressure.
2. Clean area with antiseptic solution.
3. Apply firm dressing that does not interfere with circulation of limb.

● *If limb is involved, raise limb. If trunk of body, keep still till no evidence of further bleeding.*

HEAVY BLEEDING
Apply direct pressure on wound and if necessary above wound.

ARTERIAL BLEEDING
Arterial bleeding can be recognised by its spurting nature. Apply pressure to the nearest pressure point as well as direct pressure.

Penknife, stick, tablespoon etc.

A tourniquet will be needed sometimes to stop arterial bleeding from a limb. Twist until bleeding is controlled. Release every 20 minutes to allow blood to reach the extremities and re-apply after two minutes.

VARICOSE VEINS
For bleeding from varicose veins, apply pressure above and below wound.

POINTS TO WATCH
● *Deep cuts over half an inch long will probably need stitching.*
● *When cleaning cuts and abrasions, always clean* **outward** *from wound, taking sepsis away from area. Do* **not** *clean skin towards wound.*
● *Check that anyone who is cut has had a* **tetanus** *immunisation.*

Internal Bleeding

● *Internal bleeding caused by either injury or erosion of a blood vessel.*
● *Patient is shocked, pale, sweating, with increasing weakness.*

1. Do not give fluids by mouth.
2. Place in position of absolute rest.
3. Loosen all tight clothing.
4. Reassure, send for medical aid immediately, or get to hospital.

● *For penetrating wounds, cover area of penetration with sterile dressing, treat as for internal bleeding. Do not attempt to remove foreign bodies.*

Bruises

1. Immobilise bruised areas.
2. Bathe with cool lotions or soft wet cool pads.

Stings

1. Look for remaining sting in flesh. Remove with tweezers.
2. Apply antiseptic to skin.
3. Immobilise stung portion.
4. Do **not** squeeze swollen area.

Shock

SIGNS AND SYMPTOMS
Blanching of the face
Sweating
Blurring of vision
Feelings of giddiness
Rapid shallow breathing
Anxious, stunned appearance
Initial increase in pulse rate, followed
  by weak thready pulse

CAUSES
Heart attack
Coronary obstruction
Abdominal emergencies
Burst appendix
Perforated stomach
Severe bleeding
Electric shock
Loss of body fluid
Severe infections
Emotional upset

TREATMENT
1. Reassure patient.
2. Make as comfortable as possible.
3. Warm, without over-heating.
4. Ascertain cause of shock. See if any local remedy such as stopping bleeding from artery.
5. Summon medical aid or get to hospital.
6. Keep check on pulse and respiration.

Snake Bite

● *The only poisonous snake in the British Isles is the* **adder**.

TREATMENT
1. Tie a ligature firmly around the arm or leg between where the snake has bitten and the rest of the body. Binding should not be as tight as a tourniquet, but should be sufficient to stop the poisoned blood going back in the body.
2. Wash the area of the bite without rubbing. Move the bitten part as little as possible.
3. Keep patient quiet with complete rest until either medical or hospital aid is available.

● *Do not walk the patient.*

Nose Bleed

● *Nose bleeding is of little significance. The only thing important is to stop it.*

1. Have the patient in a half sitting position with the head tilted slightly back and breathing through the mouth.
2. Apply a cold or ice pack to nose.
3. If bleeding still persists, block both nostrils firmly with cotton wool and apply pressure to nose with finger and thumb.

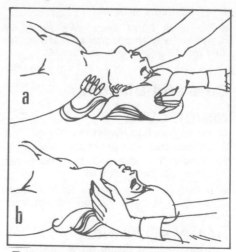

Two ways of tilting back the head of an unconscious patient to ensure that the breathing airway is open.

Above, left: The breathing airway of an unconscious patient blocked by the tongue. Above, right: The tongue moved clear of the airway by tilting back the head and lifting the angle of the jaw.

Unconsciousness

1. Try to ascertain whether this has been caused by a blow or is for some other medical reason.
2. If obvious blow, treat injured area.
3. See that no false teeth or chewing gum are loose in the mouth, and that the breathing airway is not obstructed in any way.
4. Watch the patient's face for colour sign or change of breathing rate: this will indicate there is some obstruction in the breathing.
5. Seek medical aid.

● *If one can be certain that movement will not harm the patient, put in coma position (see illustration) to aid drainage of saliva, vomit, etc., from mouth.*

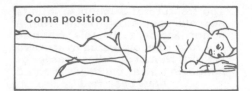
Coma position

Concussion

Any unconsciousness following a blow to the head other than fractional loss of consciousness must be treated as a case of concussion. Keep the patient lying down, cushion the head and observe pulse, respiration and level of consciousness until medical help arrives.

Injuries to limbs

● *A limb that is in a distorted position or unusual position is likely to be broken.*

Treatment for the fracture of any limb:

1. Put limb into as comfortable a position as possible.
2. Immobilise it with whatever materials you have available.

● *Sometimes it is convenient to make a wooden splint. Often the body or the opposite limb is an ideal splint and the injured limb can be anchored until further aid is available. The aim is to relieve pain and prevent movement of the injured part.*

Use rolled up newspaper as splint

Three splinting techniques. Above: Using a sling and a rolled newspaper. Below: Using the body to immobilise the arm. Right: Using a padded board. Numbers indicate the order of bandaging.

Padding against body

Bandages drawn firmly but not tight

Padding against body

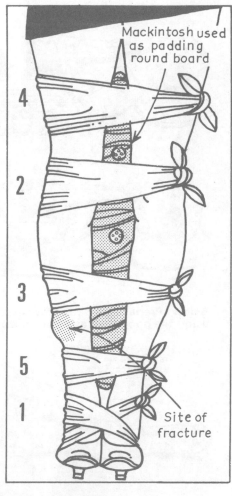

Mackintosh used as padding round board

4

2

3

5

1

Site of fracture

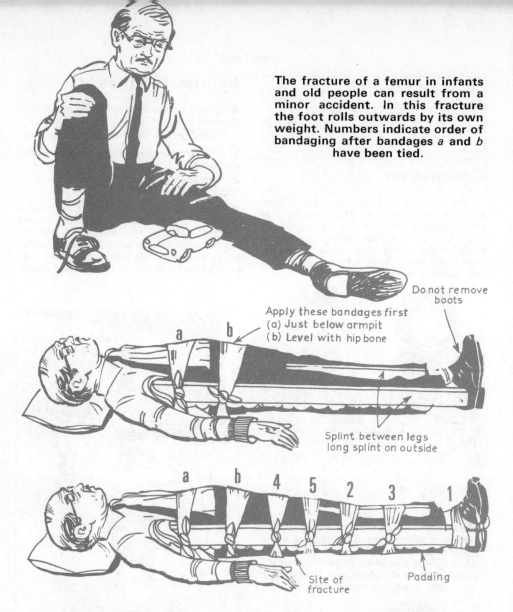

The fracture of a femur in infants and old people can result from a minor accident. In this fracture the foot rolls outwards by its own weight. Numbers indicate order of bandaging after bandages *a* and *b* have been tied.

Do not remove boots

Apply these bandages first
(a) Just below armpit
(b) Level with hip bone

Splint between legs
long splint on outside

a b 4 5 2 3 1

Site of fracture

Padding

Below: Preparing a patient with a fractured leg for transport to hospital, using the good limb as a splint. Numbers indicate order of bandaging.

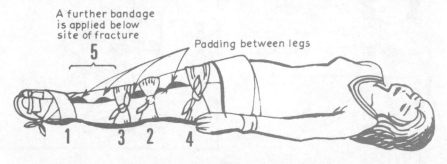

A further bandage is applied below site of fracture

5

Padding between legs

1 3 2 4

Broken back, fracture of spine

● *Pain in the region of back with some associated loss of sensation in limbs.*

1. Move as little as possible.
2. Put in comfortable position.
3. Support with pillows, pad to stop movement, summon medical aid.

Road Accident or similar serious injury

1. Give adequate warning to oncoming traffic.
2. Where there is fire risk, remove victims with all possible speed.
3. Look for signs of external bleeding. Control by direct pressure where possible, or by tourniquet.
4. If victim is not in immediate danger from fire or further road accident, do not move.
5. Make as comfortable as possible in position found.
6. Do not attempt to straighten twisted limbs.
7. Treat for shock, keep warm, reassure.
8. Do not give fluids by mouth if there is a suspicion of serious injury.
9. Protect from weather.
10. Get medical aid by telephone or by stopping passing vehicle.

● *A car First Aid kit is a valuable investment.*

Poisoning

● *Avoid poisoning by keeping all poisons safely locked away in cupboards and out of reach of children.*

1. If the patient is unconscious, move to hospital with all possible speed.
2. If possible, send sample of poison that has been taken.
3. If the patient is conscious and there is no sign of burning around the mouth, induce to vomit by either putting fingers down throat, or drinking large quantities of salt water. Send to hospital immediately.
4. If poisoning has caused burning of mouth and lips, do not give anything by mouth, but send to hospital.
5. For gas poisoning, remove from gaseous area, commence artificial respiration as required.

Drowning

● *Resuscitation can start while victim is still being brought out of the water.*

1. Clear the mouth of weed and false teeth as soon as possible.
2. With the victim's head held downwards, drain water from lungs.
3. Start mouth to mouth resuscitation:

(a) If the patient is lying on his back, pull the head back and pinch his nose.

(b) Put your mouth on his and blow up as if you were blowing a balloon with one breath.

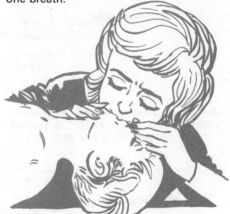

Mouth to mouth resuscitation. The patient's nose is pinched and the head pulled back.

(c) Remove your mouth and let the chest deflate.

(d) Repeat this procedure until the victim can breathe on his own. If someone can collaborate by pushing gently on his chest after you have removed your mouth, it will help empty the chest of air before you blow it up again.

● *If the non-breathing victim is a child do remember to blow gently into the mouth and watch carefully the rise and fall of the chest.*

ALTERNATIVE METHOD

1. Lay the patient on his back.

2. Raise his shoulders on a folded blanket or some other convenient material.

3. Kneel astride the patient's head with the head turned to one side.

4. Grasp his wrists and cross them over the lower part of his chest.

5. Keep your body forward and press down on the patient's chest.

6. Release the pressure. With a sweeping movement, draw the patient's arm backwards and outwards as far as possible.

7. Repeat this procedure twelve times per minute, keep the mouth clear.

Ears

● *A discharging ear needs medical inspection.*

BLEEDING FROM EARS

Bleeding from ears associated with head injuries can indicate that there has been a fractured base of the skull.

Eyes

FOREIGN BODIES

1. Attempt to move gently with twist of cotton wool or corner of clean linen.

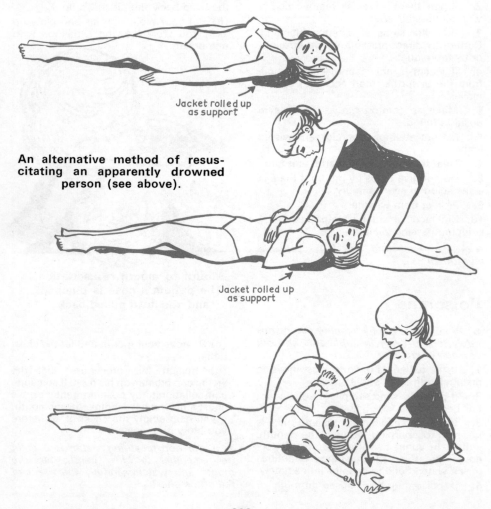

Jacket rolled up as support

An alternative method of resuscitating an apparently drowned person (see above).

Jacket rolled up as support

2. Wash out eye with cold boiled water or simple eye solution.

3. If foreign body will not come out easily do not push or probe, but seek medical aid.

● *For penetrating injuries to the eye, or injuries to the eye that interfere with vision—cover the eye with a sterile pad and seek hospital treatment.*

Foreign Bodies

BONES IN THROAT

1. Do not attempt to remove fish, or other bones from throat.

2. Reassure until proper medical aid available.

FOREIGN BODY IN NOSE

1. Do not interfere with foreign body.

2. Tell victim to breathe through mouth.

3. Get medical aid.

SWALLOWING OF FOREIGN BODIES

● *Smooth objects are not usually of concern. Sharp metallic objects can be dangerous.*

1. Do not give anything by mouth.

2. Seek medical aid.

Animal Bites

1. Clean wound well with antiseptic.

2. Make sure that victim has had an anti-tetanus injection.

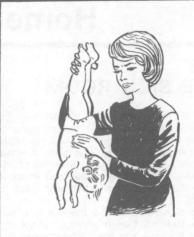

Dealing with choking children. Above: Position for a baby. Below: Position for an older child.

Give firm pats on the back if breathing does not return to normal after the child has been turned upside down.

Do *not* treat for swallowed bones in this way *(see Bones In Throat).*

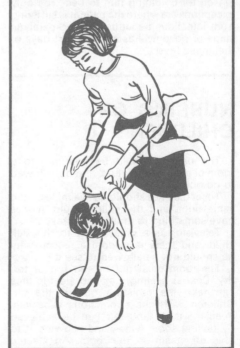

Home Nursing

THE SICK ROOM

One of the commonest treatments for illness in the past has been putting patients to bed, but present medical views indicate that confinement to bed has many dangers and few advantages, particularly for children. The only treatment that bed offers is rest—and is bed always the best place to rest in?

The sick room in the modern home is not an isolated, barren bedroom at the top of the house—it is the bed-settee in the sitting-room where the patient can be supervised, but can also take part in what is going on.

It is important for sick children not to get bored, and isolation and a feeling of being out of touch with the everyday events of the household lead to boredom. If a child feels well enough to sit in a chair by the fireside, even if his temperature is higher than it should be, there is no reason for confining him to bed. The only exceptions are where the patient is suffering from infectious hepatitis, the pre-paralytic stage of poliomyelitis and the first days of rheumatic fever.

NURSING OF CHILDREN

The patient should be confined to a room of even temperature, and not allowed to go out.

Toilet facilities should be available on the same floor, and the child should always have something to drink within reach.

Television is a great boon to the sick child, and there is seldom a reason why he should not be allowed to see it.

The room must not be too hot or too dry. Central heating, gas and electric fires can take the moisture out of the air. Children with chest infections especially need moist air, and this can be achieved by boiling some water, and allowing it to give off steam, in the room. An electric kettle will do.

NURSING OF ADULTS

Adults, though they need less amusing than children, should not be left out of things too much. Television and radio help. There are several conditions that adults suffer from which necessitate long periods in bed, particularly coronary thrombosis, heart and chest conditions and infectious hepatitis.

Patients requiring long bed treatment at home need special nursing attention.

Toilet

If possible, give the patient an all-over wash (a blanket bath) each day. Bathing should not take too long, or the patient will become tired, and it is best if two people can do it. The room should be warm and free from draughts. You require:
● *Adequate supply of hot and cold water.*
● *Soap and flannels.*
● *Towels.*
● *Dusting powder.*
Then set about the task of blanket bathing this way:

1. Strip bed and leave patient between two blankets, warmed if possible.

2. Remove night attire.

3. Wash face and neck. Take care of areas round nose, eyes, ears and mouth. Rinse and dry carefully.

4. Wash arms one at a time, using long, slow strokes. Rinse and dry. Inspect finger-nails.

5. Turn blanket down to waist, and wash whole of front of chest, particularly under arms. Rinse, dry and powder.

6. Lift blanket to cover chest, then wash exposed abdomen, groins, genitalia. Dry, powder groins. Cover abdomen.

7. Wash legs similarly, paying particular attention in between toes, and to toe-nails. Rinse, dry and cover.

8. Roll patient on side towards you.

9. Wash back from the shoulder to the buttocks. Rinse and dry.

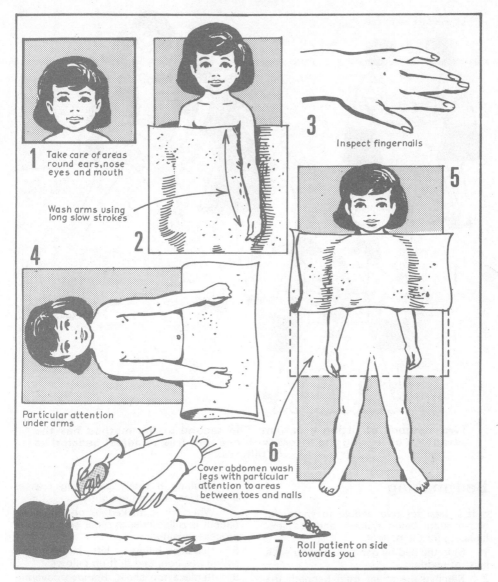

1 Take care of areas round ears, nose eyes and mouth

Wash arms using long slow strokes

2

3 Inspect fingernails

4 Particular attention under arms

5

6 Cover abdomen wash legs with particular attention to areas between toes and nails

7 Roll patient on side towards you

Give the patient—whether child or adult—a blanket bath every day if possible.

10. Attend to pressure areas on shoulder, buttocks and hip. These require extra vigorous rubbing. Inspect carefully for broken skin.

11. Dry the half just washed, then move round to other side and roll patient over to other side. Dry carefully. Powder.

12. Allow patient to brush teeth, clean nails and gargle if possible.

13. Put on night attire.

14. Re-make bed.

15. Give patient hot drink, if this is allowed in treatment.

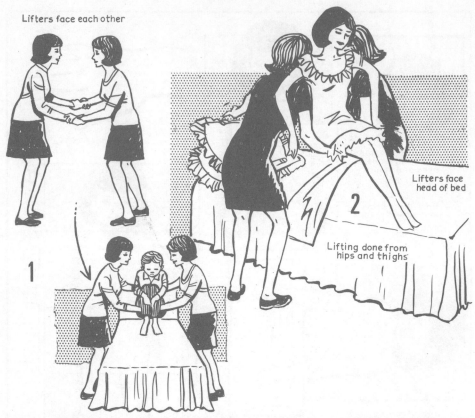

Lifters face each other

Lifters face head of bed

1

2

Lifting done from hips and thighs

Two methods of lifting a patient. The second lifting method has the advantage of leaving the lifters with one arm free to adjust bedclothes or pillows.

Bed-making

It is best for two people to share the bed-making, being quicker and less exhausting for the patient.

1. Strip the bed by gently removing each layer of bedding.

2. Remove the sheet from beneath the blanket, leaving patient covered by blanket.

3. Loosen the under-sheet all round.

4. Remove all pillows except perhaps one.

5. Roll patient on side, giving support across shoulders and buttock. See head is supported, and patient is covered.

6. With patient in this position, other bedmaker brushes out any crumbs, rolls the clothes close to the patient's back then attends to each piece of bed-linen in turn, pulling it firmly, removing creases and ruckles, tucking in tightly.

7. When all is tucked in on one side, patient is rolled over to other side and the process repeated.

8. Replace pillows. Lift patient into sitting position, and fluff up pillows.

9. Replace top sheet. Remove covering blanket, then proceed to make bed normally, tucking in blankets.

Lifting

To lift the patient in a sitting position, two people should first adopt a correct posture of straight-back bending entirely from hips to knees. Then they stand facing each other with feet apart. They grasp each other's wrists, with the lower arm under the thighs near the patient's buttocks, and the other arm low against the back, with the patient sitting in the well.

The patient puts his hands on his knees with his head forward to allow his weight to rest against the arms at his back. He is lifted in one movement, then back up the bed.

Alternatively, use the shoulder lift. Again with the patient in a sitting position, two people stand facing towards the head of the bed, and join wrists under the buttocks. The patient puts his arms on the shoulders of the lifters, and again he is lifted in one movement.

For the heavy and awkward patient there are many lifts and hoists that can be attached to the bed to aid his movement and management.

Bed-pans

A bed-pan is not often necessary. It usually involves less physical effort to get on to a commode beside the bed, or be wheeled to a lavatory, than for the patient to have to balance in bed on a cold bed-pan.

Bottles

A plastic urinal bottle is essential for the male sickroom.

NURSING OF THE ELDERLY

Nursing the elderly varies little from that of the ordinary adult, except that there are special conditions which arise in nursing fatal illnesses and conditions such as strokes, where part of the body is paralysed and the possibility of pressure sores arising is greatly increased.

Bed sores are caused mainly by pressure against a rigid surface for too long, but are aggravated by moisture through inadequate washing or incontinence.

Paralysed limbs should be protected from the weight of the bed-clothes, and massaged and inspected daily. Over any bony prominence, the skin should be rubbed vigorously with flannel and soap, dried and dusted. If the skin breaks down, and a bed-sore appears in spite of this treatment, seek help from a trained nurse or your doctor rather than pursue the treatment yourself.

In the care of the elderly, particularly in the case of fatal illness, the need is more for peace and quiet well away from telephone, TV or radio.

Incontinence

Use a rubber draw-sheet and Gamgee incontinence pads, which should be changed frequently. The patient's buttocks lie on this square of absorbable material. There are various aids now available which patients, both male and female, can wear to control their incontinent secretions. These can be worn in bed at home.

DIET FOR INVALIDS AND CONVALESCENTS

See Section **Diets for Healthy Living.**

COMMON COMPLAINTS

Coughs and colds

Drink plenty of fluids. Take aspirin or similar preparation as required. Stock up with tissues. Stop smoking. Avoid places where the air is very dry.

Influenza

Similar treatment as for coughs and colds. Keep check on temperature. If after 48 hours temperature is not settling, and the patient is bringing up phlegm, particularly if it is green in colour, seek medical aid.

Bronchitis

If patient has cough and brings up sputum, try simple cough medicine. If this does not bring relief, and particularly if there is green-coloured sputum, seek medical aid.

Pneumonia

Pneumonia sometimes follows bronchitis. Chest infection with high temperature. Pain usually in one side or the other of the chest. Rapid, shallow respiration. Productive cough. Medical aid should be sought. Usually responds rapidly to antibiotics.

Abdominal Pain

The commonest cause of abdominal discomfort or colic is distension from wind. This usually lasts a short time, and is passed itself. Conditions to be aware of:

Appendicitis. Starts with discomfort in the upper abdomen, spreading down to right groin. Tender when pressure is applied to that area. Associated with nausea and vomiting and raised temperature (99–100°F.)

Perforated ulcer. Acute onset of abdominal pain, with board-like rigidity of the stomach. Sometimes vomiting. Patient in severe pain, shocked and in distress. Summon medical aid immediately.

Gall bladder colic. Pain, vomiting and raised temperature, with pain and tenderness in right upper abdomen, particularly just below the ribs. Sometimes pain in right shoulder. There is usually some history of this condition, with an aversion to fatty foods, and it can be associated with jaundice.

Renal colic. Caused by a stone or infection in the kidney. Severe pain on either side of the small of the back, radiating down side of abdomen, frequency of passing water, possibly blood in water, may be some vomiting. Renal colic is difficult to distinguish from cystitis.

Cystitis. Inflammation of the bladder, which shows in too-frequent and painful passing of urine, possibly with blood.

Bleeding Ulcer. Usually some history of indigestion. Recognised by vomiting of dark coffee-ground material (altered blood) and the passing of black, shiny (malena) stool. This is an emergency condition, and needs hospitalisation soon to determine the extent of the bleeding.

● *No attempt should be made to treat these conditions in the home, but the symtoms listed are useful in describing the character of the abdominal pain to your doctor.*

Diarrhoea. Most diarrhoea can be cured by simple starvation dieting. Take glucose, not milky, drinks. Eat well-done toast, properly chewed. Obtain simple diarrhoea mixtures from chemist. Diarrhoea in babies is a potentially dangerous condition, and should not be treated lightly. Seek medical aid early. Diarrhoea may be caused by food-poisoning or gastro-enteritis, for which you should consult a doctor.

Constipation. There are many preparations for the treatment of constipation. A suppository which unplugs the lower end of the blockage is often more effective than drastic purgers.

Indigestion. If you are sure that the discomfort and flatulence felt after meals is indigestion, relief can be obtained by taking simple antacid mixtures, such as bicarbonate or proprietary preparations.

Cerebral conditions

These include cerebral haemorrhage, cerebral thrombosis, poliomyelitis and meningitis. With most of these, victim has stiff neck, desire to avoid the light, headache, vomiting, possible unconsciousness and resistance to straight-leg raising. Contact doctor as soon as possible.

Stroke. This is usually caused by a cerebral thrombosis (clotting of a blood vessel in the head), and may result in the loss of use of one or more limbs on one side, slurring or loss of speech and distortion of the shape of the mouth.

Coronary thrombosis

Most common in 45–65 age group. Gripping pain round chest and under chest-bone, with perhaps pain radiating down left arm. Keep patient at absolute rest. Loosen restrictive clothing. Seek medical aid. Do not allow patient to walk downstairs. The onset of cerebral and coronary thrombosis may be accompanied by the involuntary incontinence of faeces and urine.

Ear trouble

Discharging and painful ears require medical inspection before treatment. Do not drop warm olive oil into painful ears, as you are introducing a non-sterile substance into an inflamed area.

Fits

Patient may become unconscious, possibly with foaming of the mouth, and tendency to bite tongue. Loosen restrictive clothing to prevent patient from damaging himself. Place padded spoon-handle in mouth to prevent tongue-biting. See that airways are clear. Patient may be incontinent while fit is on, and this will tend to distinguish it from an ordinary faint.

Jaundice

Can mean one of several things, which include stones in the gall-bladder, or catarrhal jaundice (infectious hepatitis). Do not try to make the diagnosis yourself, but go to the doctor. Just because your next-door neighbour has recovered from his infectious hepatitis by taking a long rest in bed, it does not follow that your jaundice will benefit from similar treatment. It could easily be a gall-stone, and require an operation.

Shingles

Caused by the chicken-pox virus attacking a group of nerve fibres. Blistery spots start somewhere in the back, from the head downwards, and spread in a circling arc to reach the midriff much lower than they started in the back. They look like chicken-pox spots, and are extremely painful. Take simple analgesics. Dab with calamine. If attack is severe, or if face and eyes are effected seek medical aid.

Sugar Diabetes

Any member of the family who has excessive thirst and frequent passing of urine with acetone (peardrop) smell, should have urine tested for sugar.

Tonsillitis

Headache, temperature, soreness in swallowing. Large red swellings at back of throat. Plenty of fluids, plus aspirin, and simple lozenges may be sufficient to conquer the infection, but if temperature and swelling increase, medical aid should be sought.

Pregnancy

Pregnancy is caused by the fertilisation of the female ovum by the male spermatozoa. It can take place at any period of the menstrual cycle, but is most likely when insemination takes place 14 days before the next menstruation is due.

Conception can occur without penetration if spermatazoa are ejaculated into the vaginal orifice.

Ovulation usually takes place between the 11th and 16th days of the menstrual cycle. Ovulation time can be determined in the individual by taking daily temperatures through the cycle, a temperature rise of one degree in mid-cycle being the likely day of ovulation.

Signs and Symptoms of Pregnancy

The commonest symptom of pregnancy is cessation of menstruation, and similarly the commonest cause of cessation of menstruation up to the age of 40 is pregnancy.

Signs that appear after missing the first period.

1. Swelling and tenderness of the breasts, darkening of the nipples.
2. Morning nausea and vomiting (not usual until after the first month).
3. Hyper-acute sense smell, and desire for strange foods like sardines with peach jam.
4. Aversion to everyday food and drink, and to habits like smoking.

Confirmation of pregnancy

Manual Examination. Detection of an enlarged uterus by internal examination. This cannot usually be ascertained before the eighth or 12th week.

Hogben Pregnancy Test. A test carried out on the urine. Not accurate unless the specimen has been taken at least 40 days after the last period.

Hormone Test. If a course of Oestrogen tablets, is taken, vaginal bleeding within two weeks of stopping taking the tablets indicates that pregnancy is unlikely. No vaginal bleeding on stopping taking the tablets could indicate pregnancy. This is the least satisfactory of the three methods.

Phantom Pregnancy

One of the unkindest tricks that the mind can play on any woman is to convince her that she is pregnant when she is not; and to convince her so completely that her body starts imitating pregnancy. She loses her period and gains weight, and her stomach and breasts enlarge. This is a recognised medical condition called pseudocyesis—a phantom or false pregnancy.

The condition is not uncommon, and is known throughout the world. It has been reported among primitive peoples, and Queen Mary, half-sister to Queen Elizabeth I, suffered from it. Even dogs have it.

The commonest cause is the unsatisfied desire for a child by a childless woman. She may lose her periods through this desire, or her periods already having stopped for some other reason, she may start to put on weight and her abdomen enlarge. Often the size of her abdomen is related fairly accurately to the size she would be if she was pregnant.

Phantom pregnancy also occurs in women who continue to menstruate, and in spite of the fact that they have monthly evidence to show they are not pregnant, they still believe they are. It can also occur in women who have never had intercourse. It is even possible for the condition to reach the stage of simulated labour pains.

In the thin person, a phantom pregnancy is not difficult to diagnose, in the obese woman it may require an examination under anaesthetic or X-rays to confirm that pregnancy is not established.

When to go to the doctor

No pregnancy can be considered a going pregnancy unless two periods have been missed. One fifth of all first pregnancies miscarry between the first and 12th weeks, and this in no way indicates that the mother is going to have trouble in future pregnancies.

Unless there is some medical, social or economic factor, there is little point in presenting yourself to your doctor unless you have missed two periods. Do not start buying prams, cots and other baby things until the pregnancy is 16 weeks established.

Once pregnancy has been confirmed you will need to attend your doctor, midwife or ante-natal clinic at least once a month from confirmation of pregnancy until the 32nd week; fortnightly from the 32nd week to the 36th week; then weekly until delivery of the baby.

WHERE TO HAVE YOUR BABY

The most important factor in deciding is where you want to have it. If you can be delivered in the place of your choice, by the person of your choice, you are much more likely to be relaxed, and you will then have a much better chance of an easy labour than you would if you were unhappy about your surroundings, and tense and strung up.

Babies can be born anywhere, and there are records of births in taxis, aeroplanes, trains, and pretty well anywhere where anything else can happen. Generally there are three choices:

1. A specialised hospital obstetric unit with operating theatre facilities and a large comprehensive midwifery-trained staff.

2. A general practitioner maternity unit or nursing home, where there is a resident maternity staff with probably anaesthetic facilities, and equipment for doing minor surgery, but not as a rule true operating facilities.

3. The home confinement, where you are attended by the district midwife and your own doctor.

If you live in an area where there are a reasonable number of maternity beds available, and you are expecting a first, fourth or subsequent baby, then it is desirable that you have a hospital confinement. There are only a few areas now where hospital beds are not available for first confinements and confinements for the fourth child onwards.

Difficulties that might arise during labour are anticipated during your ante-natal examinations. From these examinations, which increase in frequency as the pregnancy goes on, the doctor and midwife will get the information which helps them to decide how you will get on in labour. Unless from their examinations they find some particular reason why you should go to one of the three choices other than your own, the choice of where you have your baby rests with you.

Unmarried Mothers

There are special maternity homes for unmarried mothers, and information about these can be obtained through your doctor and the local welfare services. If booked for one of these homes, it is usual for the expectant mother to be admitted six weeks before confinement is due, and to remain in the home for six weeks after baby is delivered.

MANAGEMENT OF PREGNANCY

Pregnancy is not an illness. You are often fitter during your pregnancy than at any other time, and some conditions, like rheumatoid arthritis, disappear whilst the pregnancy lasts. If you have a job it is best to keep working unless for some particular reason your doctor advises otherwise. Do not change your normal routine.

Ante-Natal Clinics

By far the most important aspect of ante-natal care during pregnancy is attendance at ante-natal clinics. At the clinic

HOW TO KEEP FIT IN PREGNANCY

STANDING
1. Stand with heels and shoulders against the wall. 2. Put hand into the hollow of your back. 3 Push bottom down along the wall without bending your knees more than you have to.

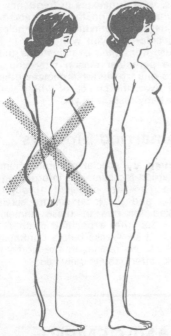

WALKING
Now learn to walk with your tummy bulge held up and your bottom held down.

SITTING
Next, sit on a chair in the same way as you have learned to walk and stand. Do this, and the ache across the shoulders and back will gradually vanish as the muscles are used properly to support the tummy bulge. Wear medium sized heels while you do these exercises.

BENDING AND LIFTING
It is not *what* but *how* you lift that matters. The *how* is very simple:

1. Put one foot in front of the other bending both knees. 2. Pick up an object off the floor. Practice with a matchbox on the floor. As you get back into an upright position you will feel your thigh muscles—not your tummy muscles—pulling your weight. Use the same method for lifting a shopping basket, or a chair. You will find your thigh muscles will lift you *and* the shopping basket.

RESTING
A good night's rest is essential— and a good night begins at 11 pm at latest. You should also rest for a short period during a busy day. At home, after lunch is a good time; half-an-hour is enough. If you are working lie down when you come home, before you start cooking:

1. Lie on the floor or on a hard mattress. 2. Have two pillows under your head and shoulders and one or two thick pillows or cushions, rolled up to form a sausage, under your thighs as close to your bottom as possible. 3. When you are comfortable, close your eyes.
Warning: Do not jump up from

your resting position quickly. It could make you feel faint. Use this method:

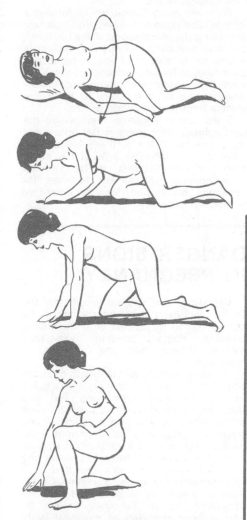

1. Lie on your side with two pillows under your head and shoulders and your underneath arm pulled through to the front so that your hand lies in front of your face. 2. Use the cushion you had behind your knees in front of your tummy bulge and put your top thigh on it with the knee bent comfortably.

you will be checked for blood pressure levels, weight gain, blood levels, blood group, progressive development of the baby, its position and presentation. This will enable the doctor and nurse to assess how your confinement will go.

Relaxation Classes

Associated with ante-natal clinics are relaxation classes where the muscles that are useful in labour can be built up, and where you can become familiar with the stages and events of labour.

Eating Habits

As the uterus enlarges in the abdomen and presses up, causing pressure to the stomach, indigestion can make life uncomfortable. This is particularly so at night, and can be best avoided by having small, frequent meals as opposed to large, heavy ones. Sleep on three or four pillows so that the weight of the uterus is pressing downwards rather than upwards. Simple antacid mixtures taken after meals will also help to relieve discomfort.

Diet

See *Diets for Expectant Mothers* in **Diets for Healthy Living**

SLEEPING AT NIGHT
As you get closer to the end of your pregnancy you must support your body properly for sleeping in order to have a good night's rest. If the 'resting' position is comfortable and you can sleep on your back easily all well and good, if not try this way:

Sleep

Make sure you have at least eight hours' sleep at night. If you cannot sleep, and you are not getting adequate rest, take medical advice.

Sexual Intercourse

Sexual intercourse is best avoided until after the third month after conception, and again after the seventh month, until the post-natal examination has taken place six weeks after birth.

Exercise

Take plenty of exercise, but do not become fatigued. Walking is one of the best and most suitable forms, golf and bathing are also excellent, but avoid bumpy sports like pillion riding or horse riding, and diving into swimming pools.

Bowels

Aim at establishing a regular, comfortable bowel habit. This is best achieved by a good fluid intake, and plenty of roughage. Aperients should be avoided, as they irritate the gut. See your doctor if you are constipated.

Teeth

If you have any troublesome teeth, get them attended to early on. Dental care in the later stages of pregnancy may not be advisable.

Clothing

When pregnant you should avoid wearing any constricting clothing and maternity corsets unless you have some abdominal muscle weakness.

THE RHESUS FACTOR

In some mothers whose blood group carries the Rhesus Negative Factor, it is possible that the mother will develop antibodies against her baby's blood, and the child will need replacement transfusion after birth. This never occurs with the first pregnancy unless the mother has previously been transfused with Rhesus incompatible blood.

There are many factors which influence whether this condition arises, the important one being the blood group of the husband, but only one child in every 400 deliveries is affected by this condition. A blood test on a Rhesus Negative mother at the 32nd week of pregnancy will determine definitely whether the baby is likely to have any trouble from this condition or not.

If the test is negative, then where the confinement takes place is not influenced by this factor. If the mother's blood does show some antibodies against her child, then it is essential that she be confined in a hospital unit where facilities for exchange transfusion for her baby are available if necessary.

DANGER SIGNS IN PREGNANCY

Bleeding. Any vaginal loss before the fourth month of pregnancy must be considered to be a sign of a threatened abortion. Vaginal bleeding with pain usually means that the abortion is inevitable.

Bleeding from the fourth month onwards suggests that not only is there a possibility of the pregnancy miscarrying, but also that part of the afterbirth is over the neck of the womb. Any vaginal bleeding at any stage of pregnancy is important, and medical aid should be summoned straight away. Immediate rest helps to prevent any potential condition being aggravated.

Excessive sickness. Sometimes sickness of pregnancy is so severe that the expectant mother becomes unwell by having been deprived of essential body fluids. If this cannot be controlled with tablets and bed rest at home, occasionally it is necessary to admit patients to hospital for intravenous fluids to replace the ones that are lost by vomiting.

There is no particular reason for this severe sickness of pregnancy. Some mothers are more sensitive to upset than others. Excessive sickness in one pregnancy does not indicate that there will be excessive sickness in future pregnancies.

Toxaemia of pregnancy. By far the most important reason for attending ante-natal examinations is to detect early signs of mother's reaction against her own pregnancy. This condition is known as toxaemia of pregnancy. Before strict ante-natal care was practised in this country, the condition was often missed, and mothers were then exposed to the risk of the condition known as eclamptic fit.

The symptoms of toxaemia of pregnancy are:

1. Protein in the urine. This is why a urine specimen is required at every ante-natal clinic.

2. A rise in blood pressure, which the doctor records when he examines you in the ante-natal clinic.

3. Swelling of the feet or hands, or both. One can have some swelling of the legs without it being toxaemia of pregnancy. This is either because the baby is pressing on the veins at the top of the legs, or that varicose veins that were present before pregnancy become worse.

4. Excessive weight gain, headache and change in vision. These signs and symptoms can come on quite rapidly in the middle and at the end of, the pregnancy.

If four days or a week after you have seen your doctor in the ante-natal clinic you do not feel well, and any of these signs are present, do not wait until the next clinic, but get in touch with him.

PREPARATION FOR BREAST FEEDING

Preparation for breast feeding begins early in pregnancy with care and treatment of the nipples. They should be kept clean, and well supported, and a well-fitting brassiere should be worn.

If either nipple is inverted or retracted, this can be put right by gentle massaging, and if necessary by the wearing of nipple shields under the brassiere. By pressing on the tissue round the nipple, this helps to push the nipple outwards. If care is taken from the beginning, even severely retracted nipples can be everted.

DISCOMFORTS IN PREGNANCY

Heartburn. See Eating Habits in this Section.

Varicose veins and haemorrhoids. Pressure of baby on the pelvis gives rise to varicose veins in the legs and haemorrhoids (or piles), which are really varicose veins in the rectal passage. With varicose veins will be some accompanying leg and ankle swelling. This can all be reduced by taking adequate rest. It is advisable for expectant mothers after seven months, as well as having a good night's sleep, to have an hour on the bed after lunch.

Varicose veins can be helped by the wearing of elastic stockings. These should be put on before getting out of bed in the morning, and removed before going to bed at night. Piles are kept to the minimum by a regular, smooth bowel action, and the use of suppositories.

Cramp. This is a common occurrence at night in the later stages of pregnancy, and may be relieved by a sympathetic husband stretching your foot and rubbing your leg. There is no medical preparation that will clear it.

REQUIREMENTS FOR HOME CONFINEMENT

1. Well-lit airy room, with adequate heating (preferably gas or electricity) near a supply of constant hot water.

2. Bed (preferably a single bed) high from the ground with firm mattress.

3. Sterilised pack (from your local council). This will be given by your midwife, who inspects the lay-out and the room in which you are to be confined.

4. Two hand bowls and one large bowl.

5. Large sheet of brown paper, and plenty of clean newspaper.

6. Small table.

7. One plastic or mackintosh sheet.

8. Clean old boiled linen.

9. Pail.

10. Bedpan.

11. Large jug.

12. Two bath-towels.

13. Two hand-towels.
14. Two face flannels.
15. Sanitary belt.
16. Two dozen sanitary towels.
17. 'Vaseline' petroleum jelly.
18. Bottle of disinfectant.
19. Nail brush.
20. Toilet soap.
21. Toilet roll.
22. Nightgowns and dressing gowns.

If there is no lavatory on the same floor, a commode in the bedroom for the first few days is very helpful.

LAYETTE FOR BABY

1. A cot or basket with three blankets.
2. Two underblankets.
3. Four sheets.
4. Mackintosh sheet.
5. Two dozen towelling nappies.
6. Two dozen muslin nappies.
7. Three soft towels.
8. A 3 in. crêpe bandage for binding.
9. Hot water-bottle and cover—for warming cot, not to be applied directly to baby.
10. Three nightgowns.
11. Three soft vests.
12. Three warm matinee coats.
13. Three pairs of bootees.
14. Shawl.
15. Pail for napkins, with lid.
16. Safety pins.
17. Small chest of drawers.
18. Baby bath.
19. Baby soap and powder.
20. Potty.

ONSET OF LABOUR

Onset of Labour. Backache is usually the first sign of labour. This is constant in the background, with at first irregular contractions or pains beginning in the lower back, and extending to the abdomen. These pains, which are intermittent, infrequent and irregular to begin with, increase in frequency and strength as labour progresses. The baby's head descending into the mother's pelvis will sometimes imitate the onset of labour, with backache and discomfort and contractions, but instead of continuing the pain will die away.

Confirmative signs of labour are the classical 'show', and the passing of a plug of mucus and blood associated with pains. This shows that the neck of the womb has begun to open, and that labour has started.

For first pregnancies it is safe for mothers to wait until they have regularly timed pains before they go to their place of confinement. Any excessive bleeding at this stage is a medical emergency, and help should be sought straight away.

For other than first babies, the mother should go to her place of confinement as soon as she has any sign that labour is commencing.

Labour may also start with a spontaneous rupture of membranes, with a loss of fluid from the vagina. This is uncommon with first babies, but becomes increasingly common with subsequent pregnancies. Labour is divided into three stages.

1. **The first stage lasts from the onset of labour until the full dilatation of the cervix.**
2. **The second stage is from full dilatation of the cervix to the birth of the child.**
3. **The third stage lasts from the birth of the child to the delivery of the placenta.**

Child Care

Infant feeding is restricted to breast and bottle feeding, or a combination of both. Although there are many excellent artificial milks now on the market, there is nothing to beat the maternal product. As well as being excellent foodstuff, it passes on some of the mother's acquired immunity to diseases, particularly childhood ones, to her infant.

BREAST FEEDING

Essential requirements for breast feeding are:

1. Normal breast tissue and everted nipples.

2. Adequate maternal fluid intake. Minimum of two to three pints a day with no maximum limit.

3. Adequate maternal diet. Inadequate diet means that the consistency of breast milk will be maintained at the expense of the mother's health and reserves of body foodstuff.

4. Adequate rest for both baby and mother, baby's foodstuff being much more important than routine domestic duties. Sometimes adjustment in feed times. For example, changing from three- to four-hourly feeds can make both mother and baby more rested.

5. The mother's freedom from intercurrent disease, such as tuberculosis.

INFANT FEEDING

After delivery, a baby is put to the breast eight-hourly. This helps to develop the sucking reflex, and at this time the baby obtains fluid called colostrum from the breast. The milk supply is not established until the third or fourth day, when three- or four-hourly feeding should commence.

The way the baby is held at the breast during feeding needs to be worked out by each mother, under the guidance of her own midwife.

The common position for breast feeding is for the mother sitting up supporting baby's head with one arm, and controlling the breast with the other hand.

Nipples should be washed and dried carefully before and after each feed. Baby should not be allowed to suck at an empty breast, or chew the nipple as this leads to it becoming sore.

At each feed, alternate breasts should be used first—with the baby given 10–15 minutes on each side. The first breast should be emptied before the baby is put to the second.

Each mother and each baby has different characteristics, and as the baby progresses a suitable feeding routine should be established, which should be a mixture of feeding on demand and commonsense.

If you have a contented baby who is gaining weight, you know that breast feeding is going satisfactorily. If, however, your baby is not gaining weight, and is discontented as well, then you need help with your regime.

Generally, breast feeding is kept up for six or nine months. At between six and nine months there is an adequate supply of mixed food from other sources, and with the reduction of the number of feeds, the breast milk tends to dry up. If the milk comes in greater quantities than is actually required, tablets to suppress lactation can be obtained from your doctor.

BOTTLE FEEDING

Having decided to bottle feed your baby, you will need dried or evaporated milk, bottles and teats, and a container for sterilising them in. It is most important to observe the elementary laws of hygiene. Wash the bottle and teat thoroughly after each feed, then leave them soaking until the next feed in some antiseptic solution such as Milton.

Selection of Teat

Choose a teat that will give a flow of milk that does not require too much effort from the baby, yet does not drown him. You will find the right one by experimenting with several teats and your own baby.

Nearly all artificial milk feeds are of modified cow's milk. Ordinary cow's milk in its undiluted form is not suitable for feeding new babies. The casein content is too high, and the sugar content is too low. If you use cow's milk, it must be boiled, diluted according to the age of the baby and sweetened with sugar.

The various artificial milks available for babies vary very little. The important thing is that, once having settled on a particular brand, you should stick to it. Difficulties that arise are more likely to be due to feeding techniques than to the variety of milk chosen.

There are differences of opinion on the advantages of starting feeding on half-cream milks (low fat content) or full-cream. There is no right or wrong—most babies will tolerate full-cream milk from birth, most will thrive satisfactorily on half-cream for the first six or eight weeks of life, gradually changing over to full-cream over a period of two weeks.

If a baby is bringing back its full-cream feed, this is a warning to change back to half-cream. Similarly, if at a week old half-cream is not satisfying baby, put him on to full-cream. The quantity of food given to a baby will depend to some extent on his demand.

From about three ounces of made-up mixture at each three-hourly feed at a week old, he will build up gradually to about seven ounces at each four-hourly feed at five months. The general average is $2\frac{1}{2}$ ounces of feed per pound of body weight per day.

Bottle-fed babies require extra vitamins, and should be given daily cod-liver oil or its equivalent. This should be given separately, and not mixed with feeds. Vitamin C, can be given as diluted orange juice from three to four weeks onwards.

All feeds should be mixed just before they are needed. It is wrong to warm up a feed that has been prepared in advance. Prepared feeds should not be left in vacuum flasks, as they are breeding grounds for bacteria.

Routine Feeding

Start with three- or four-hourly feeds when baby is first born, then follow the pattern as described for breast-fed babies. The earlier the 2 a.m. feed can be omitted, the better the chance of a good night's sleep for both baby and mother.

The baby who can do without it at the third week is not any better than the baby who is still having it at five months; he is just a different baby, and the fact is no more relevant than that he has different colour hair and eyes and a different-shaped nose from other babies.

For the first four or five months, baby's main feeding will be from the bottle, from then on, bottle feeds will be decreased as mixed feeding takes over.

FEEDING A BABY

Support the child's head, with its body cradled in your arms, and tilt the bottle so that the teat is continually full of milk.

The rate at which baby feeds from a

Holding a baby for bottle feeding.

bottle will be to some extent determined by the size of the nipple. Do not have a nipple so big that the baby is swamped by milk, or so small that he has to work too hard at getting the feed out.

Most babies regurgitate some milk at the end of feeds when they bring up wind. Hold the baby upright over your shoulder or in your lap, gently patting his back or rubbing his stomach. Do not place baby flat with the head down immediately after feeding. Do not give baby a bottle to suck when he is lying down, as there is a risk of inhalation of food.

Mixed Feeding

Mixed feeding or weaning consists of the addition of non-milk food to the baby's feeding routine. This is usually begun between the third and fourth month, and is started with small quantities of cereal. The changeover from breast or bottle to spoon is sometimes resented, and it is best to start feeding with a small quantity of cereal before the baby is put to the breast or bottle.

The addition of solids and semi-solids should start at one feed in the day to begin with, with little more than a taste of whichever cereal you give first. No particular feeding time is better than any other at this stage.

Begin with very small quantities of cereal of very fluid content, perhaps made up with the usual milk for just one feed a day. Then gradually decrease the fluid of the cereal, and increase the number of feeds in which it is being given. Once baby has become accustomed to increased amounts of cereal, the solid matter of his diet can be added to.

Fruits and vegetables are usually the next in order, and there are many excellent fruit and vegetable preparations specially prepared for infants.

If giving baby fresh vegetables or fruit, it is important that they should be puréed. Banana which is a good, comforting filler, can be mashed to a fine consistency, and mixed with milk and sugar.

It is important to give ripe fruit, as unripe fruit easily leads to colic. From five or six months old, egg can be given, again in a very soft and diluted form. It is no good giving a baby anything that he needs to chew until he has got the apparatus for chewing. By the time he is about six months old, his gums are generally hard

Two ways of getting wind up after a feed. Top: Rubbing the baby's stomach. Bottom: Patting the baby's back with his head over your shoulder.

enough to chew with, although he may not have any teeth.

At six months a baby should be taking, in addition to milk, a fairly comprehensive diet of cereal, egg, fruit, strained vegetables and a meat extract. From then on the diet will increase progressively.

A hungry baby can be satisfied by giving additional amounts of starches, such as bread and potatoes. At about a year, meat can be varied with fish.

Once baby has acquired a set of teeth, and can chew and suck fairly well, it is no longer necessary to purée preparations and mashed food can be given.

From a year onwards, the food baby has is a small-scale replica of the parents' diet. It is extremely important that it should not be lumpy, it should consist of small, easily-digested particles, and there should be no lumps of meat or potato that can choke him.

Diets for infants up to five years and growing children

See **Diets for Healthy Living.**

TEETHING

Before you decide that baby's pain and distress is due to teething, look for some evidence that this really is the cause. Signs can be:

Reddening or bleeding of the gums.
The anticipated arrival of the tooth when its brother on the opposite side of the mouth has already appeared.
Reddening of the cheek.
A tendency to bite hard objects.
Continual putting of fingers in the mouth.
Excessive amount of saliva.

You can relieve teething trouble by comforting baby. Teething is not going to go on for ever, and all pain is made easier to bear by comforting.

Firm pressure of your fingers (make sure they are clean) on the gums will give some relief. Similarly, hard, suitable things to chew can be comforting.

If the pain is still not relieved, many commercial pain-relievers are available. The commonest is aspirin. Be careful to check how much a child of this age can be given.

Teething mixtures can be obtained from your doctor. They usually consist of a sedative, with perhaps some pain-relieving substance. Again, it is important not to exceed the prescribed dose.

Do not give baby teething powders— some may be seriously harmful. Those which contain mercury may cause Pinks Disease.

Lancing or cutting of the gums is no help, and it is dangerous, as it can lead to bleeding and infection. Teething is a natural process we all have to go through, and we all manage it.

During the time a baby is teething, as at other times, he is quite likely to have upsets of the stomach, diarrhoea, cough and skin rashes. These may be in no way connected with the coming of teeth, and should be treated in their own right.

BATHING A BABY

It is important in bathing a baby to test the temperature of the water, and it is easier to warm cold water than it is to cool warm water. A sensitive test for water temperature is with the bare elbow. The skin of the adult hand is not sensitive enough.

Hold the baby firmly all the time with one arm around the back under the baby's

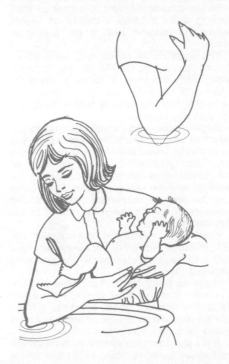

Test the baby's bath water first with your elbow (top). Make doubly sure (bottom) by dipping in your elbow again when putting the baby in the bath.

Holding baby in the water.

armpit, and the other hand supporting the buttock.

In the bath, keep the baby's head out of the water with one arm placed under the head while the hand gently grips baby's shoulder.

Do not leave baby alone in the bath, however secure he looks.

Soap with soft baby-soap, rinse well and dry with soft, clean towelling. Powder the skin-creases.

DUMMIES

Dummies are not recommended. It means introducing a non-sterile object into the mouth of an infant who is still building up his immunities to infectious diseases.

The only justification for the use of a dummy is if all other remedies to quieten a crying baby have failed and the household is kept awake at night with baby getting no rest either.

COLIC

The two commonest causes of pain and discomfort in small babies are teething and colic. It is not always possible to decide which is causing the trouble, but as a rule colic is associated with distension and hardness of the abdomen. The pain comes in spasms, with the baby drawing up his feet.

Some relief can be given by comforting, gripe-water and the bringing up of wind. The most effective treatment is to remove the

cause of colic, which is most likely feeding. A baby is much more likely to take in air if he is lying down than if he is upright. If he is crying when he feeds, he will fill up with air and be tired before he starts.

For feeding, both breast and bottle, see that he does not gulp his food too quickly. Colic is more common in the bottle-fed baby. The right-size teat, giving neither too quick nor too slow a flow, will reduce the amount of air taken in with the feed.

Too sudden a change to mixed food can cause irritation to the intestine. All changes in foodstuffs should be gradually and slowly introduced.

Three-month Colic

The phenomenon of three-month colic has never been satisfactorily explained, but many babies up to the age of three months scream for about four hours a day with signs of colic which tend not to be relieved by correct feeding, or the bringing up of wind. The trouble usually passes after the third month. Again, it is important not to assume that baby has got colic, but to look for other causes.

The colicky baby eventually passes out of this phase. It may be speeded by varying the routine. Provided the baby is thriving, too much notice need not be taken of it. But colic with a baby that is not thriving calls for further medical investigation.

INFECTIOUS DISEASES OF CHILDHOOD

For childhood infections, there is no need to keep the patient in bed unless he feels that he is too unwell to get up. The sickroom has now been replaced by a bed in the lounge in front of the television.

There is no benefit in keeping a child with an infectious disease in bed if he feels he is well enough to get up. This does not mean that he should go outside, where he is exposed to temperature changes and a risk of catching further secondary infections.

Immunisations

Children can be protected from many diseases. The present recommended schedule of immunisations is listed below. In addition, there is now a vaccination against measles which is available on demand from your own doctor or from the school doctor.

Measles

The characteristics are sore eyes, a coarse red rash covering the face and body, high fever and cough.

The interval between the onset and appearance of rash is three or four days. The incubation period is 10 to 15 days.

The child is isolated for about a week after the rash has disappeared. Measles is a notifiable disease—there is now an injection against it. (Your doctor will notify the local Medical Officer of Health.)

German Measles

This is usually a red rash that lasts between 24 and 48 hours, and is accompanied by swollen glands behind the ears. Children should be isolated for seven days from the appearance of the rash.

Contacts should take great care to keep away from pregnant mothers, particularly women who are in the first three months of pregnancy. Damage may be done to the

VACCINATION AND IMMUNISATION SCHEDULE

During the 1st year of life	Diphtheria, tetanus, whooping cough and oral polio vaccine (1st dose)		The earliest age at which the 1st dose should be given is 3 months, but better results can be expected if the 1st dose is delayed until 6 months
	Diphtheria, tetanus, whooping cough and oral polio vaccine (2nd dose)	Preferably after an interval of 6–8 weeks	
	Diphtheria, tetanus, whooping cough and oral polio vaccine (3rd dose)	Preferably after an interval of 6 months	
During the 2nd year of life	Smallpox vaccination		While the 2nd year is recommended for routine vaccination, if special circumstances call for it, vaccination may be carried out during the 1st year
At 5 years or school entry	Diphtheria, tetanus and oral polio vaccine or diphtheria, tetanus, polio vaccine, smallpox re-vaccination		With the exception of smallpox re-vaccination these may be given if desired, at nursery-school entry at 3 years
Between 10 and 13 years	B.C.G. vaccine		For tuberculin negative children
At 15–19 years or on leaving school	Polio vaccine (oral or inactivated), tetanus toxoid and smallpox re-vaccination		

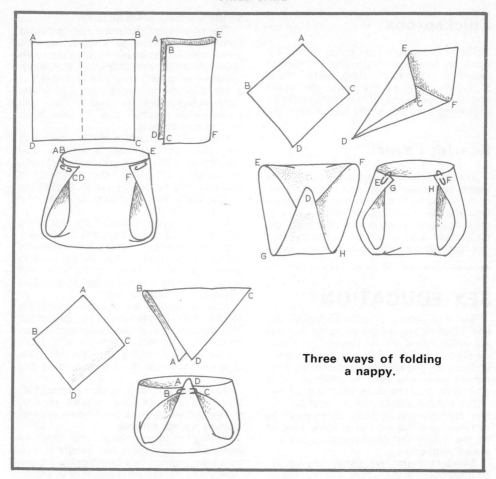

Three ways of folding a nappy.

baby she is carrying if she catches German measles.

Any expectant mother under three months pregnant who has been in contact with German measles should immediately, through her doctor, obtain an injection of Gammaglobulin—which will prevent her becoming infected.

Whooping-cough

The symptoms are a cough with the characteristic whoop, sometimes followed by sickness. Since immunisation, it may be less easy to diagnose, because immunisation may not prevent a child from getting the disease—merely cut down the severity of it.

Patients should be isolated for 28 days from the beginning of the cough. Children who live in the same house should be kept away from children who have not had whooping cough until three weeks after the house is free from infection.

Mumps

Symptoms are swelling of the angle of the jaws, and difficulty in opening the mouth or chewing. The incubation period is 12 to 28 days. The child should be isolated until seven days after the swelling has disappeared.

Chicken-pox

The characteristics are crops of blistery spots on face and body. The incubation period is 11 to 21 days, with about a two-day interval between the onset and the appearance of the rash. Isolation should be until the scabs have fallen off.

Scarlet Fever

The characteristics are a fine rash, sore throat and some fever. Incubation period is from two to five days, and the interval between the onset and the appearance of the rash is one or two days. Patients should be isolated until seven days after the rash has disappeared. Scarlet fever is notifiable.

SEX EDUCATION

Sex is a natural functional happening, and children should grow up to become naturally aware of it. Usually, curiosity awakens during the nursery stage—children are sometimes fascinated by their private parts and their by-products. It is normal for them to experiment with these.

If a mother shows she is upset by this, she distinguishes it from other playtime activities, and this kind of reaction focuses on the wrong sort of attention to sex and sexual differences.

Small brothers and sisters should not be segregated at bath-time. Let them grow up accepting each other as they are—it is probably the most important thing not to fuss about. Nor should parents themselves worry about appearing unclothed in front of their children. This does not mean that we have to parade about naked in front of each other at any age. The right attitude is to avoid making a thing about either being dressed or undressed.

If you have not worried about whether you have been undressed or not in front of the children since they were toddlers, it will not matter if your child sees you in the bath. But it might matter if he sees you

for the first time when he is 12.

The keeping of domestic pets provides splendid instruction, as children can be given simple explanations of their own observations as they occur. If they keep hamsters or rabbits they will probably get a practical demonstration of the whole cycle about every six weeks. They will accept it as normal, and in time even tend to lose interest.

If the children never show interest in sex, and do not ask questions, use opportunities like the reproduction of pets, or suitable television programmes, to explain in the same way as you might how an aeroplane flies, a jet engine works or a ship stays afloat.

Use the proper names when describing parts and functions of the body to 10-year-olds and upwards. If baby talk is continued for too long, children may be exposed to embarrassment. Johnny, at 12, does not want to find he is the only boy in the class referring to a 'little winkle'.

School lectures are not the ideal place for the older child to receive sex education. The atmosphere in the classroom is too impersonal. School is the place to learn simple biology dealing with the life cycle of lower mammals, their reproduction and birth.

Sex education should come principally from the parents, and school is only something to fall back on if home circumstances are not suitable.

Young children notice and take an interest in pregnancy, particularly if it is their own mother, or a friend or neighbour. When they do, tell them about baby inside, and that it is going to come out of Mummy's tummy. If they are very young, they will probably forget about it but some remnants of the information will stick, and in later years they will remember, and relate it to the facts they have learned subsequently.

There is never an exactly right time or age to begin a child's sex education. It can be early or late. It can start at any time, but it does not begin with a formal lecture on the lines of: 'I feel it's about time you knew . . .' It should be an explanation of happenings as they crop up in everyday life.

Knitting

Everyone can learn to knit even if they do not at first know the difference between a purl and a knit stitch. It is the most simple of all crafts to learn, but it does need practice to make it perfect.

There are only two basic stitches—knit and purl. These make all the knitted fabric there is by being used in various sequences. Remember:

1. The correct size of needle must always be used with the matching ply of wool. This will give you a knitted piece of work that will be neither too loose nor too taut, and the whole effect will be good.

2. Always check your tension before you start to knit the article. It is your tension which determines the correct size of your knitting.

Some people tend to be loose knitters; some are tight knitters. But there are not many knitters who work to the average tension. This is why it is so necessary to check the tension. If you do not do so, you may end up with a garment which is too small or too large.

NEEDLES

It is a good idea to have a stock of needles of various sizes. If you are keen on working with thick wools, the most popular sizes will be Nos. 6, 7, 8, 9 and 10. For the classic garment in 3- or 4-ply wool, you will need Nos. 9, 10, 11, 12 and 13 needles.

Always buy the best make of needle you can afford, and make sure that the ends taper off smoothly.

The Tension Chart shows the number of stitches and rows to one inch obtained with the correct size of needle and wool when worked over stocking stitch.

This is a guide for the average knitter. However, if the wool and needles quoted do not give you the stated tension, the needle size must be changed, and the tension checked, until the correct one is obtained. Our Tension Chart helps you to know whether or not you are an average knitter.

CASTING ON

To knit, you need a row of loops along the needle. The two most popular methods of doing this are by the thumb cast-on and/or the two-needle method. Casting on stitches by the thumb gives a good firm edge, and matches it in well with the rest of the knitting.

To do this, for a large garment like a sweater, leave a long length of wool (about 30 to 36 in.) free from the beginning of the wool. Make a slip loop, and put over one knitting needle and hold needle in right hand, together with the wool from the ball. With the free length of wool in left hand make a loop over the thumb (Figs. 1 and 1A).

Fig. 1

Fig. 1A

Place the point of the needle (which is still held in right hand) into loop on thumb. Take wool held in right hand over the point of the needle, and draw it through the thumb loop, making a stitch on right-hand needle by letting thumb loop tighten on the needle. Continue to make a loop on the thumb, and to knit it on to the right hand needle in this way, until you have the stitches required on needle (Fig.2).

Fig. 2

For the two-needle method, take the free end of wool and make a slip loop and place it on one of a pair of needles. Hold this needle in your left hand. Take the other

Fig. 3

needle in your right hand, and put the point of it into the slip loop (Fig. 3). Take the wool over the point of right-hand needle, and draw it through to make a loop on right-hand needle (Fig. 3A). Place the loop back on to the left-hand needle

Fig. 3A

beside the slip loop, place right-hand needle point into this second loop and put wool over to make a loop as before (Fig. 3B).

Fig. 3B

Continue to make loops in this way until you have the number required. With a row of loop stitches on the needle, you are now ready to start to knit.

TO KNIT

With the left hand, hold the needle with the loop stitches on it. With the right hand, hold the other needle pencil-wise, and take the wool in the right hand, passing it over the first finger, under the second and over the third finger. Put right-hand needle-point through first loop stitch on left-hand needle, now take wool under and over right-hand needle-point (Fig. 4).

Draw through to make a loop, letting the left-hand needle-stitch fall off at the same time. A stitch is now formed on the right-hand needle. Work across the left-

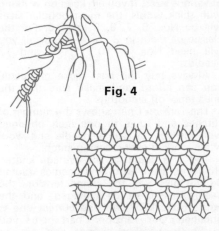

Fig. 4

Fig. 4A

Fig. 5

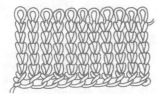

Fig. 6

hand loop stitches in this way. The first row of knitting is complete.

Garter Stitch

This consists of knitting every row in the way just described (Fig. 4A).

Stocking Stitch

This means one row is knitted, and the return row is purled. The knit side is the right side of work (Fig. 6).

To Work Purl Stitch

Take the point of the right-hand needle, and place it in the front of the stitch—it will be at an angle. The wool is taken over and round the needle-point, and drawn through the loop, then slipped off to leave a stitch on the right-hand needle.

This is repeated along the row of stitches. Always remember to keep the wool at the front of the work (Fig. 5).

Ribbing

For single ribbing, which is mostly used for welts of garments, cast on a number of stitches divisible by two. The first stitch is worked as a knit stitch, and the second stitch as purl stitch. Repeat this across row, ending with a purl stitch.

On the next row, work in the same way. It will now be seen that the knit stitch on one row is the purl stitch on the wrong side of row.

Ribbing can be worked in different widths. It can be knit 2, purl 2, but always on the same principle that the knit stitches on the right side of work will be the purl stitches on the wrong side of row (Fig. 7).

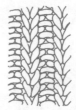

Fig. 7

Moss Stitch

This means ribbing worked over an odd number of stitches. Every row will then be worked as knit 1, purl 1 across all stitches (Fig. 8).

Fig. 8

To Work Decrease

This is generally worked by taking two stitches together when knitting or purling stitches. The point of the needle is put through two stitch loops of the left-hand needle instead of one loop, and the two loops are knitted together (Fig. 9). This

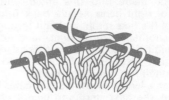

Fig. 9

means there will be one stitch fewer on needle.

Sometimes a decrease is worked in lacy-pattern instructions by passing a slipped stitch over a knitted stitch. For this, do not knit a stitch, but slip it on to the right-hand needle. Knit the next stitch in the usual way, then slip the unknitted stitch over the knitted stitch, lifting it with the point of the left-hand needle. It can then be pulled over the knitted stitch.

This is always known as 'pass slip stitch over'. It is never worked as a decrease unless stated in this way (Figs. 9A and 9B).

Fig. 10   Fig. 10A

we have a method of casting off the stitches securely.

TO CAST OFF

Knit the first two stitches in the usual way on to the right-hand needle. With the left-hand needle, put point through the first stitch knitted on right-hand needle, and draw this stitch by lifting it over the second stitch on right-hand needle and letting it fall. Knit the next stitch on left-hand needle making two stitches on right-hand needle again. Work in same way as before (Figs. 11 and 11A).

When all stitches have been worked in this way, and the end stitch remains on needle, break off wool and slip end of it through the stitch and draw up.

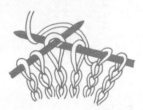

Fig. 9A

Fig. 9B

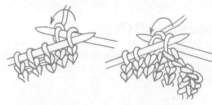

Fig. 11   Fig. 11A

Working Lacy Stitch Patterns

Unless you are an experienced knitter, it is best not to choose a lacy pattern with many rows forming the pattern, as this can be confusing to the beginner.

You will need to have a mental picture of the working of the lacy pattern, as most of these lacy effects are produced by working 'wool overs'. It is necessary, therefore, to begin with a fairly simple pattern. The instructions for the Matinee Coat (Fig.13) are quite good to start with, and not too difficult.

Some of the instructions given in a knitting pattern are written in an abbreviated form. This is quite usual and the

Working an increase

This is usually done at the side edges of a garment. To increase, knit the first stitch in the usual way, but do not let stitch fall off needle, as a second stitch must be made into this stitch. Put the point of right-hand needle back into the back of the first stitch, and knit through to make another stitch on right-hand needle. The original stitch is then slipped off in the usual way (Figs. 10 and 10A). An extra stitch has now been made.

When a length of knitted fabric has been worked, the next step is to take it off the needles without its unravelling. To do this,

terms are always given under a special heading, thus;

ABBREVIATIONS

K., knit; p., purl; st(s)., stitch(es); st-st., stocking stitch; alt., alternate; beg., beginning; cont., continue; dec., decrease; inc., increase; M.st., Moss st; G. st.,Garter st; rem., remain(ing); rep., repeat; patt., pattern; sl., slip; tog., together; w.fwd., wool forward; w.b., wool back; w.f., wool to front of needle; k.b., knit to back of stitch.

P.b., purl into back of stitch; t.b.l., through back of loop; m.l., make one, by picking up the thread between stitches and knitting it; w.r.n., wool round needle; p.s.s.o., pass slip stitch over; in., inch(es); tw., twist; C2.f., cable 2 front, by slipping 2 stitches on to cable needle and leaving at front of work, k next 2 stitches, then k stitches from cable needle; C2 B., cable needle is kept at back of work.

An asterisk is used in knitting patterns to indicate that figures are worked in repetition as many times as stated.

CHECKING TENSION

To check tension, work up a sample square of stocking stitch measuring 4 in. Choose the size of needles and ply of wool which you wish to work on. For example, using No. 10 needles with 4-ply wool, to get a 4-in. square you will need (at seven stitches to 1 in.) 4×7 stitches. This means 28 stitches will be cast on.

At nine rows to 1 in. you will need to work 36 rows to get 4 in. in depth. Cast on the 28 stitches as shown in Fig. 1 and work in stocking stitch. This is worked by knitting over the loops on one row, and purling over the stitches on the return row. (Figs. 4, 5 and 6).

When 36 rows have been worked, cast the stitches off as shown in Figs. 11 and 11A. Lightly press the work, then mark off 1 in. with the tape measure as shown (Fig. A). Now count the stitches between the inch. There should be seven. Now place the tape measure lengthways on the knitting, and count the rows between the inch (Fig. B). The knitted piece should measure 4 in. square exactly. If the square has worked up smaller, then try knitting it again on a size larger needle. If the square is larger than

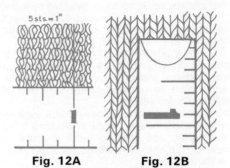

Fig. 12A   **Fig. 12B**

4 in., work on a finer sized needle.

You must do this by changing the needle until the correct tension is obtained. Only then can you begin to knit a garment.

TENSION CHART

NEEDLES	2-ply STS	ROWS	3-ply STS	ROWS
No. 5	5½	7½	5	7
No. 6	6	8	5½	7½
No. 7	6½	8½	6	8
No. 8	7	9	6½	8½
No. 9	7½	9½	7	9
No. 10	8	10	7½	9½
No. 11	8½	10½	8	10
No. 12	9	11	8½	10½
No. 13	9½	11½	9	11
No. 14	10	12	9½	11½

NEEDLES	4-ply STS	ROWS	Double Knitting STS	ROWS
No. 5	4½	6½	4	6
No. 6	5	7	4½	6½
No. 7	5½	7½	5	7
No. 8	6	8	5½	7½
No. 9	6½	8½	6	8
No. 10	7	9	6½	8½
No. 11	7½	9½	7	9
No. 12	8	10	7½	9½
No. 13	8½	10½	–	–
No. 14	9	11	–	–

WOOLS

For the best results, always use a well-known branded wool. The non-branded ones are often of shorter yardage, and do not always work up to a standard tension.

The ply of the wool means the thickness of it. Several strands of wool are stranded together in 3- 4-ply and double knitting.

Always buy the wool recommended for the pattern you wish to knit. Read through the pattern instructions before starting, and if you do not understand any part of them, ask for advice.

If the pattern stitch is new to you, cast on a few stitches and practice working it so that when you have to work it across a row of stitches you will be able to knit it without difficulty.

If you use the following wools for the garments recommended you cannot go wrong.

BABY WOOLS: 2-, 3-, 4-ply for all baby garments. **Quickerknits:** for outer baby garments.

DOUBLE KNITTINGS: Popular for patterned sweaters and cardigans for men and women.

2-, 3-, 4-PLY WOOL: For all classics for men and women.

THICKER KNITTINGS AND OILED WOOLS: For Aran designs, sailing garments, socks, sea boots, caps.

PATTERNS FOR BABY

Matinee Coat

Materials: 4 oz. 4-ply baby wool. A pair each of Nos. 10 and 12 knitting needles. 1¾ yd. of baby ribbon.
Measurements: width round underarm 20 in. Length from top of shoulders 9 in. Sleeve seam 5½ in.
Tension: 7 sts. and 9 rows to 1 in. over stocking stitch or 7½ sts. and 9½ rows to 1 in. over the lacy pattern.
Abbreviations: see general list.

BACK:

With No. 10 needles, cast on 78 sts. and work 8 rows garter st. (knit every row). **Next row:** right side k. 2, * w.f., sl. 1, k. 2, p.s.s.o., the k. 2 sts., rep. from * to last st., k. 1. **2nd row:** sl. 1, p. to end. **3rd row:** k. 1, * sl. 1, k. 2, p.s.s.o., the k. 2 sts., w.f., rep. from * to last 2 sts., k. 2. **4th row:** work as 2nd row. **5th row:** k. **6th row:** p. These 6 rows form the patt. throughout and are repeated. Pattern until

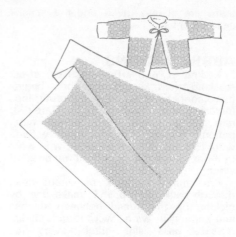

Fig. 13: The matinee coat and shawl

back measures 5½ in. from cast-on edge ending on a wrong-side row.

Shape armholes: at beg. of next 2 rows cast off 5 sts. then dec. 1 st. at beg. and end of next and alt. rows until 60 sts. rem. Work straight in patt. until Back measures 9 in. measured from centre back (armholes will measure 3½ in. from beg. of shaping). **Shape shoulders:** work stocking stitch throughout. At beg. of next 2 rows cast off 6 sts. At beg. of next 4 rows cast off 7 sts. Leave rem. 20 sts. on spare needle.

LEFT FRONT:

With No. 10 needles cast on 42 sts. and work in garter st. as for Back. Then work in the patt. rows, but begin each wrong-side row with k. 3 sts. to form the centre front band, and at the end of the right-side rows keep the last 3 sts. in k. Work straight in patt. until Front measures 5½ in. from beg. ending at side edge.

Shape armhole: at beg. of next row cast off 5 sts. then dec. 1 st. at beg. of every alt. row until 33 sts. rem. Work straight in patt. until Front measures 8 in. from cast on edge ending at front edge.

Shape neck: at beg. of next row cast off 6 sts. then at neck edge of every row dec. 1 st. until 20 sts. rem. Work 1 row to side edge. Armhole should now measure 3½ in. from beg. of armhole shaping and match the Back up to the shoulder.

If not, work a row or so more until it matches the Back. With right side of work facing, **shape shoulder:** Work stocking stitch throughout. Cast off 6 sts. at beg.

of next row. On next alt. row cast off 7 sts. Work 1 row. Cast off.

RIGHT FRONT:

Work as for Left Front, but reverse shapings. When working the patt. rows the garter st. border of 3 sts. will be worked at the beg. of the right-side rows and the end of the wrong-side rows.

SLEEVES:

With No. 12 needles, cast on 42 sts. and work in garter st. for 1 in. Change to No. 10 needles, and work the patt. rows and inc. 1 st. at beg. and end of 5th and then every following 6th row until 50 sts. are on needle. Now inc. every 4th row until 58 sts. are on needle. Work straight until sleeve measures $5\frac{1}{2}$ in. from cast on edge.

Shape top: at beg. of next 2 rows, cast off 5 sts. then dec. 1 st. at both ends of next alt. rows until 40 rem. Then dec. at both ends of every row until 30 sts. rem. Cast off.

TO MAKE UP:

Press lightly on wrong side, using a warm iron over damp cloth. With neat back-stitch seam, join side and shoulder seams. Join sleeve seams and set in sleeves. With No. 12 needles and right side of work facing, work neck border. Pick up and k. 19 sts. up right side of neck, 20 sts. from spare needle at back neck, and 20 down left Front neck. 59 sts. Rib k. 1, p. 1 for 1 row.

Next row: Rib 3 sts., X w.r.n. p. 2 tog., k. 1, w. 1 fwd., k. 2 tog., p. 1, rep. from X to last 2 sts., rib 2. Rib 1 row. Work 1 row in k. Cast off.

BOOTEES

Materials: 1 oz. 4-ply wool, a pair each of Nos. 8 and 10 knitting needles. 1 yd. baby ribbon.

TO MAKE:

With No. 8 needles, cast on 38 sts. and work in rib k. 1, p. 1, for 4 rows, inc. 1 st. at end of 4th row. 39 sts. Change to No. 10 needles and work in the patt. as for Matinee Coat for 2 in. ending 6th patt. row. Work 2 rows garter st.

Next row: make ribbon holes. k. 2, * k. 1, w. fwd., k. 2 tog., k. 1, rep. from * to last st., k. 1. Work 1 row garter st. **Shape foot:** k. 26 sts., turn.

Fig. 14: The finished bootee

Next row: k. 13 sts., turn. Work on these 13 sts., k. 20 rows end wrong side row. Break wool and leave. Rejoin wool to end of the first 13 sts. left and on the same needle k. up 11 sts. along instep, then work across the 13 sts. of instep and pick up and k. 11 sts. along second side of instep, then k. rem. 13 sts., 61 sts. Work 9 rows in garter st. With right side facing shape thus:

1st row: k. 2 tog., k. 21, take 3 tog., k. 9, k. 3 tog., k. 21, k. 2 tog., 55 sts rem. **2nd and alt. rows:** k. to end. **3rd row:** k. 2 tog., k. to last 2 sts., k. 2 tog. **5th row:** k. 2 tog., k. 17, k. 3 tog., k. 9, k. 3 tog., k. 17, k. 2 tog. 47 sts. **6th row:** as 2nd row. K. 1 row. Cast off. Make another bootee in same way. Join back seam and underfoot seam. Thread ribbon in holes.

To make a longer bootee, work until 4 in. before making ribbon holes.

Shawl in openwork stitch with garter stitch border

(See Fig.13)
Materials: 10 oz. 3-ply baby wool; a pair of No. 9 knitting needles.
Measurements: 40 in. square before pressing.
Tension: $7\frac{1}{2}$ sts. and $9\frac{1}{2}$ rows to 1 in. over the pattern.

THE CENTRE:

With No. 9 needles cast on 210 sts. and p. 1 row.

Now work in the patt. rows as given

for Matinee Coat until 28 in. from beg. and the knitting forms a square, ending on a p. row. Cast off.

GARTER ST. BORDER:

With No. 9 needles cast on 42 sts. and work in G. st. slipping the first st. of every row until it measures 14 in. from beg.

Shape corner: sl. 1, k. 40, turn, sl. 1, k. to end. **3rd row:** sl. 1, k. 39, turn, sl. 1, k. to end. **5th row:** sl. 1, k. 38, turn, sl. 1, k. to end. **7th row:** sl. 1, k. 37, turn, sl. 1, k. to end. Cont. to work in this way until rows sl. 1, k. 2, turn, sl. 1, k. to end have been worked.

Now work the rows backwards. Next row will be worked, sl. 1, k. 3, turn. Next row: sl. 1, k. to end. Next row: sl. 1 k. 4, turn. Then sl. 1, k. to end. Cont. in this way until row sl. 1, k. 41 is worked. K. across all 42 sts. for 28 in. ending at outside edge.**

Rep. from ** to ** twice more then work 4th corner. Work 14 in. straight across all sts. Cast off.

TO COMPLETE:

Sew border all round centre square joining the cast on and off edges together with a neat seam. Press lightly with a warm iron over damp cloth.

Make up of Knitted Garments

Never hurry over the making up of your knitted garment. Time must be allowed for this if you wish to have a neat and professional finish. Care in the details of pressing correctly and blocking to size is worthwhile.

Pin the knitted pieces out on to an ironing board or table. They should have a soft padding of blanket under the knitting. Always press on the wrong side of work. Pin out as shown in Fig. 15 Measure the bustline width, and pin to size, then pin down each side measuring from armhole to welt.

Do not pin the welt, as this will take away the elasticity in stretching it. Pin sleeves in same way. Use a hot iron over a damp cloth unless it states otherwise in the pattern instructions. Move the iron lightly over it, lifting it as you work. Leave the pieces pinned out flat until all steam has evaporated. Do not overpress.

A garment knitted entirely in ribbing

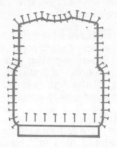

Fig. 15

should only be pressed with a warm iron, and the rib must not be opened.

TO JOIN SEAMS

Before doing the seams, make sure that all pattern rows match on Back and Front. Start at the shoulder seams; pin the pieces together on the wrong side about ¼ in. from the edges. With the same colour and ply wool as the garment, use a wool needle (having a blunt end) to make a neat back-stitch along the shoulder seam taking away the pins as the work progresses.

Pin side seams in same way, but at the welt make a flat seam by taking one loop of a stitch from each side of the welt alternately. This makes an invisible seam and it will remain flat.

For the sleeves, flat seam the welt and join seams with back stitch as for main part. With warm iron, press open all the seams as you work, use the tip of the iron to do so.

SETTING IN SLEEVES

Find the exact half of sleeve top by folding in half and marking it with a pin. Place this to the shoulder seam of armhole, and pin sleeve top into armhole. Take care not to stretch armhole when working. Now back-stitch all round armhole edge setting in the sleeve and making a neat ¼-in. seam. Press open seam very carefully.

When making up a cardigan, the front bands will be sewn on. Pin the band to front, slightly stretching the band as you do so. Oversew band to front, avoiding a hard ridge on the fronts. Buttons should be sewn on with wool never use cotton. If the buttonholes need to be neatened, work buttonhole stitch over them. Finally, press all seams.

Basic Sewing

You do not have to be expert at dress-making to be able to meet an emergency. If you can do more than that, then sewing can be a money-saving and satisfying hobby.

Basic tools and materials are:
Needles: large (darning) and small
Pins
A pair of scissors
A thimble
A tape measure
Reels of cotton: black, white and coloured
Button thread (grey and black are the most useful)
Darning wool: brown, black and grey
Knicker elastic
Card of medium sized press-studs
Card of hooks and eyes
Old buttons
A seam ripper
A box to keep them all in

As you cannot buy in supplies of odd pieces for patching, or even anticipate what will be needed next for a sewing job, collect what you can as you go along.

1. Take usable zips out of old garments before you throw them away.

2. Keep buttons, particularly from discarded trousers, waistcoats, jackets and shirts.

3. Keep any piece of material left over from shortening or altering jobs.

4. Cut out the good parts of old garments before throwing them away.

5. Sort the collection out from time to time and discard what is obviously no longer needed.

This will help meet an emergency, but if you aspire to dressmaking or soft furnishing you will need a few more things:
A sewing machine
Hem measure
Some really good scissors or pinking shears
Any left-over cotton reels with cotton left on them
Plenty of non-rust pins
Tailor's chalk
An iron
An ironing board with, if possible a sleeve board
A good light and plenty of room

There are also a few basic things you should know:

1. The most important thing about sewing is to get a neat result.

2. Do not use a sewing machine for fiddling jobs unless you are really expert.

3. Practise on spare pieces of material if you are at all nervous about starting on a garment.

4. Pin first to test for fitting and effect before sewing in place.

5. Match your sewing cotton or zip fast-ener with the material whenever possible. If an exact match is impossible, use the next darker shade.

6. When you unpick and alter a garment, note how the expert did the job in the first place. If necessary, make notes or draw rough sketches of what has to be done to get the pieces back in place.

7. Remember that materials like silk are slippery and that it is unsafe to rely entirely on pins to hold the material in place. Tack these materials before finally sewing. This is how it is done:

Tacking stitches—for which you use odd reels of cotton—pull out very easily afterwards.

HAND SEWING

Basic stitches

RUNNING STITCH
Insert the point of the needle into the material and out again, pull the cotton through, but do not pucker.

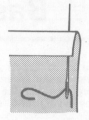

BACK STITCH

Neatly done, a good substitute for machine sewing. When you have made one running stitch, do not go forward to make the next. Go backwards and insert the needle into the material against the last stitch you made.

2. Push the needle through from the back of the material to the front, just under the lower edge of the flap. At the same time, hold the cotton down with your left thumb so that the needle passes over it.

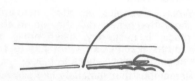

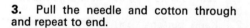

HEM STITCH

Sometimes called 'felling'. This is used for sewing down one piece of material on to another.

1. Start just above the fold.

2. Insert the needle into the material immediately below the fold.

3. Bring it out above the fold again.

3. Pull the needle and cotton through and repeat to end.

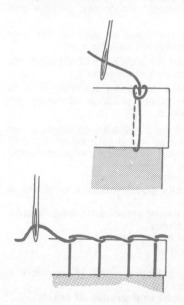

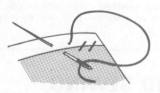

BLANKET STITCH

1. Push the needle under the flap and out through the outside edge of the fold.

BUTTONHOLE STITCH

This is done in the same way as blanket stitch but much smaller, closer together and often on a raw edge.

OVERSEWING

Used for joining knitting, joining two pieces of material or for neatening raw edges. Pass the needle and cotton from the back to the front of the material, over and into the back again. Do not pull tight.

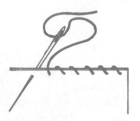

Seams

There are three basic seams, *plain running, french seam and run and fell.*

PLAIN RUNNING SEAM

This is the most frequently used and is suitable for everything where the inside will not be seen or where it will not be subjected to more than normal wear and tear.

1. Work on the wrong side of the material.
2. Sew about $\frac{1}{2}$ in. from the edge.
3. Open out and press flat.

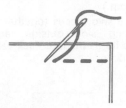

RUN AND FELL

This consists of two lines of sewing. It is used on garments where the seam has to be flat but where folded back turnings would look untidy, such as shirts, blouses, slips, briefs and blazers.

1. Work on the wrong side of the material.

2. Place one edge of material about $\frac{1}{4}$ in. below the other. Hold with the lower edge uppermost.
3. Make a running seam all the way along.
4. Fold the material out flat, wrong side uppermost.
5. Turn the top edge in and fold it over to make a hem.
6. Sew by machine or hem by hand.

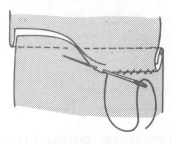

FRENCH SEAM

Can be hand sewn or by machine. This seam is used on pillowcases and similar articles subjected to constant putting on and taking off but where only one line of sewing should be visible.

It is worked with the right sides of the material outwards to begin with.

1. With the wrong sides of the material facing inwards, sew a running seam about $\frac{1}{4}$ in. in from the edge.
2. Turn inside out and fold along the seam just sewn.
3. Do another plain line of sewing far enough from the edge to take in the previous $\frac{1}{4}$ in. seam allowance.

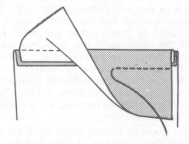

GATHERING

This is neither stitch nor seam, but is a very necessary technique. Use running stitches.

1. Use double cotton in a sufficient length to complete each stretch of gathering without a join.

2. Secure the cotton firmly before starting the running stitches.

3. After sewing as far as you need, pull the cotton gently and ease the material into even gathers.

4. Fasten off securely.

MACHINE SEWING

1. Do a test run on the material to be made up to ensure that needle and tension are correct.

2. A fine material generally needs a fine needle. If, when the needle goes down into the material, it pulls a thread or causes the material to jump, then it is too thick. It could also be blunt or bent at the point. Either way, change it.

3. If the sewing puckers without the needle actually breaking any threads, then the tension must be loosened. For this, follow the instructions given with the machine.

4. If the stitches are loose or too big, tighten the tension slightly.

5. If the stitches don't lock and you get masses of tangled cotton underneath, the machine is either not threaded properly or the shuttle is not turning properly. Re-thread the machine. If this does not work, take out the shuttle and replace it, making sure the cotton is fed out correctly.

If all else fails, use different gauges of cotton for the needle and the shuttle. (This is not in any book of instruction, but it has been known to work.)

6. All ends of cotton must be fastened off. Sew them down or, if time is short, tie in a knot.

7. Oil the machine only as instructed in the manual. After oiling, wipe well wherever the material could get marked by seeping oil.

8. Unless you are expert do not use the machine at all for tricky jobs. Bound buttonholes, for instance, would be better done by hand than on the machine if you are not used to it.

Simple sewing jobs

SEWING AROUND CURVES

1. Sew about half an inch from the edge.

2. Cut little V-shaped notches into the seam allowance.

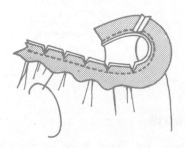

SEWING A STRAIGHT LENGTH OF MATERIAL AROUND THE CORNER OF ANOTHER PIECE:

1. On the straight piece, make a small cut the depth of the seam allowance at the point where the corner will come.

2. Hand sew a few little stitches at the end of the cut to reinforce. (You will have to open it out.)

3. Lay the two pieces together edge to edge, wrong side outside, and tack together as far as the cut. Tack very firmly at this point.

4. Open out the cut and lay the other two edges together and tack.

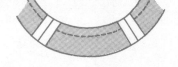

5. Turn inside out and make sure the corner is quite square, then machine on the wrong side.

BINDING ROUND CURVES:
● *Use bias binding which can be bought in all haberdashery departments, or make your own.*

MAKING YOUR OWN BINDING
1. The binding must stretch, so must be cut across the weave of the material.
2. The ends of each piece must slope and not be cut straight across.
3. Lay the material straight and cut 1-in. strips diagonally across it.

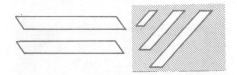

4. Join the pieces by sewing them on the wrong side with the slanting ends slightly overlapping each other.
5. Fold open and press flat.

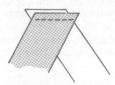

ATTACHING THE BINDING
1. Tack the binding wrong side outwards to the right side of the article. Sew about a ¼ in. in from the edge.

2. Fold over the binding to the wrong side, turn under the edge and hem it down.

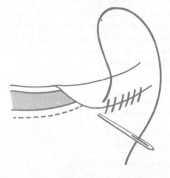

BINDING STRAIGHT EDGES
1. You can use binding tape bought in haberdashery departments, or make your own.
2. It does not have to be cut on the cross. The ends of the strips need not be cut diagonally.
3. Attach as above.

BOUND BUTTONHOLES
1. These must be at least the same width as the button.
2. They must be made before the facing is sewn on.
3. Start working on the right side of the garment.
4. Mark a small vertical line with tailor's chalk at each end of each buttonhole.
5. Mark a horizontal line between these two exactly where your buttonhole should come.
6. According to the thickness of the material (the thicker the material the wider the space) mark another line either side of the existing horizontal one. The space either side of the centre line will be the seam allowance round the buttonhole. You will not need too much of this, so leave just enough to ensure that it will not fray.

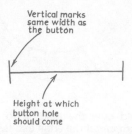

Vertical marks
same width as
the button

Height at which
button hole
should come

7. For the binding, cut two pieces of material for each buttonhole, not less than 1 in. wide and long enough to extend at least ½ in. beyond the ends of the buttonhole. Fold each piece in half, right side outwards, and press.

Material not less than 1″ wide

This space varies with the thickness of material

Right side out

½″ longer than button hole

8. Working each side of the buttonhole separately, lay the binding over the buttonhole. The folded edge should face away from the centre line and extend beyond the outer line the same amount as the space between the centre and outer line. Pin in place and sew along the outer line between the two vertical marks.

9. Bind the other side of the buttonhole in the same way so that the two pieces of binding are back to back.

10. Fold back the two pieces of binding. With very sharp scissors snip a small

Sewn on outer margin

V at each end of the buttonhole with the point on the centre line. Cut along the centre line.

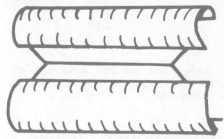

11. Turn the binding through to the back of the buttonhole. Tuck the ends in neatly to form good square corners.

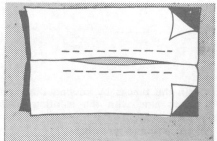

12. Working on the back of the garment, cut away any excess binding and tack down.

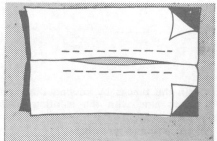

13. On the right side of the garment again, neatly hem all round the buttonhole.

14. When the facing (and interfacing if used) is sewn down, make a corresponding cut for each buttonhole. Turn in the edges

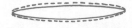

all round the buttonhole and hem down.

● *This is not the only method of binding buttonholes, but is a particularly neat and easy way.*

STITCHED BUTTONHOLES

These can be made after the facing has been sewn down by taking in the two thicknesses of material.

Measure and mark the buttonholes as for **Bound Buttonholes** but omit item No. 6.

1. Use a heavy gauge thread or double sewing cotton.

2. Work on the right side of the material.

3. Starting at the end farthest from the edge, buttonhole stitch along one side, round the end and back along the other side.

4. When you get back to where you started, oversew four stitches across that end of the buttonhole. Then buttonhole stitch across these, with the head of the stitch facing inwards.

● *Alternatively, use the buttonhole attachment for your sewing machine.*

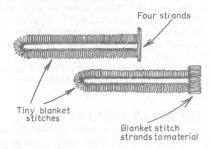

Four strands

Tiny blanket stitches

Blanket stitch strands to material

BLIND HEMMING

This is the method used for sewing up hems without any trace of stitches on the outside.

1. Either bind, oversew or blanket stitch the raw edge.

2. Turn one fold only. Do not tuck the edge under.

3. Tack a good ½ in. from the edge.

4. Slip stitch the underside of the hem to the outer piece by folding back the edge by about ½ in. and catching the underside to the threads of the outer piece.

5. Press.

STRAIGHTENING BADLY CUT ENDS OF MATERIAL

1. At a point just clear of the jagged end, snip a crosswise thread at the selvage edge of the material.

2. Pull this thread gently and cut along it all the way across.

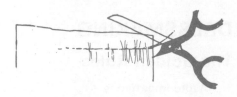

FITTING YOURSELF

● *Do not think this cannot be done.*

1. Have the garment inside out.

2. Pin one side only and put it on. By looking in a mirror it is possible to pin the other side.

3. This will give a guide as to whether it is too big or too small, and by how much. If, for instance, the skirt is 2 in. too wide on the hip, you will know that you must adjust it by 1 in. either side.

4. Get as near as you can to the correct length by checking against another garment and then by trying on in front of a long mirror. Stand fairly well back from the mirror to get the right effect.

5. As a final check see *Make Do and Mend, Making Up.*

MAKE THE MOST OF SEWING AIDS

Whenever you buy any kind of sewing aids, whether on a card or in a packet, never throw away the card or packet without first reading the instructions or information.

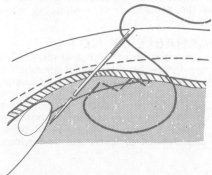

Dressmaking
& Household Sewing

A little success here can turn a chore into a pleasurable hobby and save pounds of housekeeping money.

DRESSMAKING

The Golden Rules

1. Avoid impatience.
2. Read instructions.
3. Measure the pattern before cutting and make any adjustments according to the instructions given with the pattern.
4. Fit everything before sewing.
5. Press all seams as you go along while the pieces are flat and easy to handle. It will not be so easy once the garment is made up

Buying materials

STANDARD WIDTHS

Woven cloth is sold in several different widths, generally 36 in., 48 in. and 54 in., but there are intermediate widths, for instance 35 in. or 58 in. So make absolutely sure of what you are buying.

Some popular paper patterns give American and Continental widths such as 35 in., 39 in. and 45 in. as well as our 54 in., and tell you how much material you will need of the various widths according to size. To calculate how much to buy take their 35 in. as our 36 in., and their 45 in. as our 48 in.

Dress fabrics like cotton, silk, taffeta, tricel, rayon, etc. are nearly always 36 in. wide.

Woollen materials generally come in the wider ranges of 48 in. and 54 in., sometimes 58 in. or even 60 in.

Make sure you buy enough by checking with the table given on the pattern envelope. If in doubt ask the shop assistant.

WHAT IS MEANT BY 'NAP'

Nap is another word for pile. Velvet is a good example. Care must be taken to have the nap or pile going in the same direction throughout.

If the pattern tells you how much to use of a material with a nap, buy what it says, but if you have no guide allow a little more than you would otherwise use. You will not be able to turn your pattern pieces around—they must all face in the same direction.

PATTERNED MATERIALS

If you are buying a material with any pattern where one side of a garment must match up with the other, allow for this when buying. You will have to lay your pattern pieces to suit the design on the material rather than the more economical way shown on the pattern instructions.

STRIPED MATERIALS

It is most important that stripes should match, specially at the side seams of skirts, sleeves, etc. and this must be allowed for when buying. Here again, you may not be able to cut economically, so buy more than the minimum requirement, unless the pattern gives you the amount for striped material.

RIGHT AND WRONG SIDES

There is always a right and wrong side to materials. Sometimes it is obvious, sometimes not. Any tufts or imperfections in the weave show on the wrong side, particularly near the selvage. If in doubt take the precaution of asking the shop assistant.

WASHABLE OR NOT

It is a good idea to check at the time of buying on whether the material is washable.

If in doubt, take a snippet of the material, place it on a piece of paper, draw a line round it and cut it out. Then wash the snippet and iron it as you would normally do. Check it against the piece of paper for size. Any other faults will be obvious.

FACING AND INTERFACING

Facing is most often done in the same fabric as the garment, except if you want toning or contrasting reveres, for instance. Only then would you buy a separate piece —it is allowed for in most patterns.

Interfacing—stiffening material—is bought separately. Any shop which sells dress materials sells interfacing. It can be stiffened muslin or hessian, or more popularly now, Vilene. The pattern will tell you how much for any particular garment but normally only small amounts are used. Interfacing is something to keep if you have any left over.

Paper patterns

All paper patterns give sewing instructions. If you follow them, you cannot go wrong. They do, however, carry sewing terms with which you may not be familiar. Here are some of them:

Baste	Tack
Bias	On the cross; diagonally across the weave of the material
Catch-stitch	Slip stitch. Lightly catch the sewing cotton in the threads of the material
Clip	Cut small V's into the seam allowance.
Fabric buttonhole	Bound buttonhole
Facing	Backing. Generally sewn on the front and turned to the back to form a double thickness
Interfacing	Stiffening which goes between the inner and the outer piece of material
Lap	One edge on top of the other instead of edge to edge
Notches	The V marks cut into the outer edges of paper patterns
Overcast	Oversew
Perforations	Holes in the pattern in the form of small o's, large O's, triangles and squares
Pink	To cut with pinking shears
Slash	Cut with scissors
Trim	Cut a little off

Some patterns are printed with clear lines and instructions, in which case lay all the pieces with the printed side uppermost.

If you lay one piece upside down and you have a patterned material, you may have one panel which does not match.

Other patterns are not printed but instead are marked off with small holes, large holes, triangles and squares. The small holes, regularly placed about ½ in. in from the edge all the way round indicate the sewing line. As the paper is smooth on one side and rough on the other, consider the smooth side the outside. Keep all your pieces this side uppermost, unless the instructions say otherwise.

Compare your pieces carefully with the sewing instructions to make sure you have the right piece against the fold.

Sleeves are tricky and will be marked with either some big holes or a line both of which should be straight on the material. For positioning on the material follow the diagram contained in the sewing instructions.

CUTTING OUT

If using a patterned material, make sure the pattern will be the right way up when the garment is finished.

To make sure the pattern or stripes line up all the way round the garment, use the notches on the pattern as a guide (you have to match the notches anyway).

If you are working without a diagram, make sure that you get the right edge against the fold. If you cut any pieces singly instead of through a double thickness of material, make sure to reverse the pattern piece *(see Reversing, Page 348)*.

NOTCHES

It is a mistake to cut a V in your material. You may cut too far. Better to cut outwards, like this

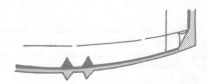

Pin the pattern securely to the material before cutting.

Do not remove the pattern until you

have marked all the holes, squares, triangles and dots. This is done with tailor's tacks, like this:

1. Use double thread—it clings better—in a contrasting colour.

2. Sew very loose loops from one hole to another, going in and out of each hole then across the paper to the next one.

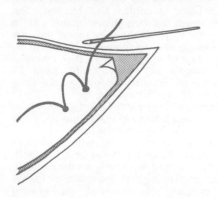

3. Cut all the loose loops and remove the pattern.

4. Carefully part the two thicknesses of material and cut the threads of the loops midway between the two.

5. Work with these pieces of cotton stuck in the material. They pull out very easily afterwards. Meanwhile, they are your markers for matching one piece to another.

On printed patterns, large and small dots, squares and triangles are marked in ink. They have, however, to be treated in the same way as perforations for the purpose of marking your material.

With plain patterns, cut against the edge of the paper. With printed patterns, cut along the cutting line, which will be clearly marked.

REVERSING PATTERNED PIECES

Sometimes the instructions will tell you to cut, for instance, two bodice pieces, separately instead of once through a double thickness of material. When this happens, you must reverse one of the pieces, i.e., cut one piece with the right side of the pattern uppermost and the other with the wrong side of the pattern uppermost. If you do not, you will have two left bodices instead of a right and a left, or vice versa. The same applies to sleeves or skirt panels.

Raw edges

If you cut your material with pinking shears you needn't worry any more.

If you have no pinking shears, you can deal with raw edges in one of three ways:

1. Use the zig-zag gadget on your machine if there is one. Do the job before any other sewing.

2. Oversew the edges. This can be done now or when the garment is finished. In the absence of a special gadget, this method gives the best overall effect after pressing.

3. Turn a tiny single hem round the edges of all your pieces and sew them on the machine. This is neat, but care must be taken when pressing to avoid a ridge showing on the outside.

Making up

Follow the instructions included with the pattern.

Sew on the wrong side of the material unless instructed to do otherwise.

Fasten off all loose ends of cotton by sewing them down, particularly at the ends of darts.

When the pattern says 'match large Os' it means you must take the mark you made for the large O on one piece and pin it to the mark you made for the large O on the other piece. The same applies to the other markings, i.e., small Os, triangles, squares or dots.

When the instructions say 'slash to large O' it means cut the material from the edge to the large O.

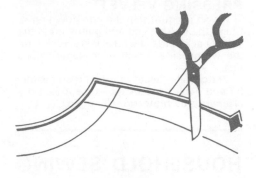

● LARGE 'O'

To prevent the material fraying when it is cut in this way, do a few little stitches by hand at the end of the cut.

If you find any particular operation awkward to do on the machine, do not be afraid to sew just that part by hand—it will probably be neater.

If the instructions tell you to make the buttonholes first before sewing the coat, then you must do this *(see Bound Buttonholes, Page* 343*).*

Fit the garment as you go along *(see Fitting Yourself, Page* 345*).*

Adjustments will be more easily made at this stage *(see Letting Out Garments, and Taking In Garments in*

MAKE DO AND MEND section.

Snip curves before pressing *(see Sewing Around Curves, Page* 342*)* but not so savagely that you cut the seam.

Press all seams on the wrong side.

For woollen materials press over a damp cloth.

SEWING ZIP FASTENERS

The zip must not show when the garment is fastened, so have it slightly to one side of the opening.

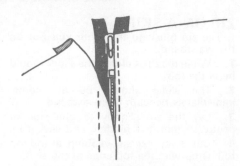

It must be anchored very securely top and bottom or it will not slide.

The 'home' of the slider is at the top when the zip is closed. Provided you have it this way up, you can sew it in either open or closed, whichever is easiest.

Use the special foot on your sewing machine if you have one. If not you may get a better result by hand.

When the top of the zip comes at the neck edge it should fit under the facing to get a neat finish.

1. Leave the facing open until the zip is in.

2. Cut away excess webbing and leave only a small amount to turn over.

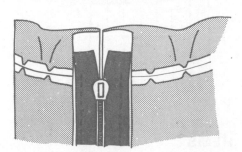

3. Turn in the ends of the facing and fold over to lie flat.

4. Slip-stitch the ends of the facing to the webbing of the zip, keeping them clear of the slider.

5. Put a small hook and eye at the top of the opening.

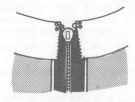

ZIP ON A SKIRT

The zip must go in before you put on the waistband.

1. When the zip is closed the slider should be at the top.

2. The slider should be at 'home' immediately beneath the waistband.

3. Lay the zip slightly to one side of centre so that it is hidden, and sew it in.

4. Cut away excess webbing at the top to line up with the top edge of the skirt.

5. Sew on the waistband.

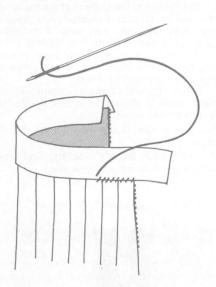

HEMS

1. Straighten the lower edge and oversew it *(see Oversewing, Page 341).*

2. Get someone to turn up the hem while you wear the garment if possible.

3. If you are on your own, measure the garment against another one which is the right length.

4. Try it on and inspect in a long mirror.

5. If it is a dress, put on a coat to see if the dress shows below it anywhere. If it is a coat, wear a dress underneath it.

6. Tack the hem about three-quarters of an inch in from the edge.

7. Blind hem as in *Blind Hemming, Page 345.*

8. Remove pins and tacking. Press.

BINDING TAPES

If you use binding tape anywhere inside a dress, make sure it is pre-shrunk by washing it before using.

PRESSING

Remove all tacking stitches and pins before pressing, especially thick materials. If this is not done, there will be marks where the pins or stitches were.

Use a cool iron for delicate materials and wools. Always iron on the wrong side.

PRESSING VELVET

On no account slap the iron down on it. Stand the iron on end and gently press the velvet backwards and forwards across it, on the wrong side. Practise on some scraps first.

Better still—because velvet is so beautiful and liable to damage—take it to a dry cleaner to be professionally done.

HOUSEHOLD SEWING

This is not necessarily just mending. It can be something creative and very rewarding and, for the most useful items, you do not have to be an expert.

Buying materials

These are known as soft furnishings and comprise curtaining, loose cover and upholstery materials, curtain linings and nets.

Most materials are 48 in. wide, some cottons are 36 in. wide and the more expensive, heavy materials are 60 in. wide.

Curtain lining is sold in the same widths as curtaining, but if you cannot buy the correct width it is easy to join linings.

TERYLENE AND NET CURTAINING

These come in two categories:

1. The standard widths, bought by the yard, for making up at home.

2. Made-up curtains in varying lengths, sold by the yard width.

POINTS TO WATCH

● *The pile of velvet curtaining must go in the same direction throughout. If you have one curtain with the pile facing upwards and the other downwards, you will have one curtain dark and the other light.*

● *If you are buying curtaining with a large pattern, remember that the pattern must match right across the two curtains when drawn. So allow for some wastage.*
● *Consult the sales assistant if in doubt.*

Making curtains

MEASURING UP

For ordinary curtains, the pair side by side must be at least the width of the window plus half as much again.

For a full, rich curtain allow at least twice the width of the window.

Some curtain fitting manufacturers give recommended widths to suit their fittings. Do not buy less than the recommendation.

Curtains can either fall right to the floor or well below the window-sill or, for utility rooms like kitchens and bathrooms, can rest on the window-sill.

Measure the length according to preference. Add to each curtain a further few inches for turnings at the top and bottom.

Allow the same amount for lining.

If curtaining or lining is joined, the join must not be obvious.

JOINING PATTERNED MATERIALS

Be careful to match the pattern so that it remains unbroken right across.

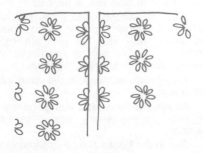

JOINING VELVET

To make sure that the pile on joined velvet all runs the same way, draw arrows down both selvages with tailor's chalk, following the run of the pile, before you start cutting.

MAKING UP

1.　Straighten the top and bottom edges.

2.　Lay the curtain out flat, on the floor if necessary, wrong side uppermost.

3.　Having first hemmed the lining at the bottom, lay this on the wrong side of the curtain, with the turning facing inwards.

4.　Cut away any excess lining.

5.　Place the top edge of the lining just far enough below the top of the curtain for it to fit under the hem when it is turned down. Pin in place.

6.　DO NOT TURN DOWN THE HEM AT THIS STAGE.

7.　If you are using Rufflette tape, this top hem must be wider than the Rufflette tape to create a small frill at the top.

8.　Place the side edge of the lining about 1 in. in from the edge of the curtain.

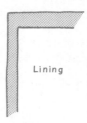

Lining

9.　Make a small box pleat in the lining at the top centre, to absorb excess width.

10.　Fold over the 1 in. of curtain each side, all the way from top to bottom. Sew it to the lining to within about 1 in. of where the lower hem will come. At that point continue sewing to the curtain but do not take in the lining.

11.　Turn over the top hem and tack in position.

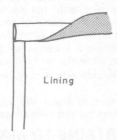

Lining

12.　If you are using Rufflette tape, tack this in position with the lower edge level with the hem. The Rufflette tape and the hem can be sewn at the same time.

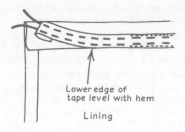

Lower edge of
tape level with hem

Lining

13. When sewing Rufflette tape in position, tuck the ends under but leave the strings free to pull.

14. Turn up the bottom and blind hem it *(see Blind Hemming, Page* 345*)*. The last inch or so of the lining should hang loose over the hem.

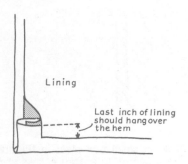

Lining

Last inch of lining
should hang over
the hem

A GOOD FINISH THE EASY WAY

To get a good, firm finish down the sides of curtains insert a strip of Vilene under the turning.

MADE-UP NET CURTAINS

1. Net curtains only fall as far as the sill, so measure the depth of the window and choose a net of the same depth.

2. Buy sufficient yardage to go across the window, allowing for fullness.

3. Sew the side edges only, with a tiny hem.

4. Remember to leave the space open in the top hem for the wire to go through.

NET CURTAINS TO MAKE YOURSELF

1. If there is a pattern, make sure it runs straight across the two curtains.

2. Take a turning at the top about 1½ in. wide.

3. After sewing down this hem, sew another line ½ in. above it. This will leave a space through which to thread the wire and a small frill above it.

4. Take a fairly deep hem at the bottom—this will make the curtain hang better—and slip stitch it neatly by hand. The bottom hem must be the same depth on all the curtains.

Pelmets

This is a simple method of making pelmets which looks expensive and costs little.

1. Measure the length of the pelmet rail along the front and round the ends.

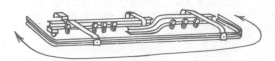

2. Cut a piece of material to this length, allowing for turnings.

3 If you have a patterned material, cut it across rather than lengthways. Join if necessary, otherwise the design will be horizontal instead of vertical.

4. Cut a piece of lining the same size. Cut some stiffening too, if needed.

5. With the wrong sides outwards, sew these two pieces together at both ends and along one side. If you are using stiffening, lay this behind the lining and sew the three thicknesses together.

6. Turn inside out, tuck in the open edge and sew it together.

7. Attach Rufflette tape along the top of the strip, on the wrong side, ½ in. from the edge.

8. Slip in the hooks at intervals and fit the hooks over the pelmet rail.

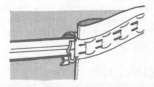

Pillowcases

The normal size is 18 in. wide by 28 in. long, with a folded flap of about 6½ in.

1. Cut a piece of material 1 ft. 7 in. wide by 5 ft. 4 in. long.

2. Take a 1-in. turning at one end and a small turning at the other.

3. Tack a line across the material 6½ in. from the small hem.

4. With the right side outside, fold the larger hem up as far as the line of tacking. Sew both sides with a french seam.

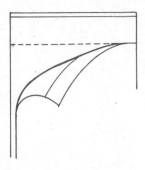

5. With the wrong side outwards, fold the flap back. Turn in the edges and hem down firmly each side.

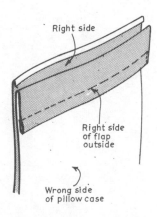

Right side

Right side of flap outside

Wrong side of pillow case

6. Turn inside out and press.

Bedspreads

On low divans, these look better hanging to floor level.

To get the best effect, allow a length of 9 ft.—6 ft. for the length of the bed, a drop at the foot and sufficient at the head to drape over the pillows.

If you have to join the material, the joins must go down the length of the bedspread and not across. They must be evenly spaced: either one down the centre or, if there are two, each an equal distance from the side edge.

Here are two simple methods:

PLAIN

1. For a 4 ft. 6 in. bed, allow two widths of 48 in. material. This will give a good drop either side. Any excess width must be either turned in or trimmed off an equal amount each side.

2. Do not cut a strip off one side only, or the seam will not be in the centre.

3. Allowing 9 ft. for the length, you will have to buy 2×9 ft. of 48-in. material, which is 6 yards.

4. Cut into two 3-yard lengths and join together.

5. If it is patterned material, or has a pile, make sure that the pattern matches and that the design or the pile face the same way.

6. If the sides need trimming off, do this next and then hem them down.

7. Take a good hem top and bottom, and blind hem the bottom one.

SOPHISTICATED STYLE THE EASY WAY

The top and the sides are cut separately and sewn together to fit over the bed like a box.

1. For the top, allow sufficient material to cover the top of the bed only without a drop, plus a further yard in length.

2. For the two sides and the foot, allow twice the distance round those three sides of the bed, plus a further two yards. The depth will be the space between the top of the bed and the floor, in which case you may be able to cut two or even three strips from a 48-in. width.

3. Bear in mind the general advice given earlier for joins and matching patterns.

4. Join the side pieces to make one length of material. Take a turning along one

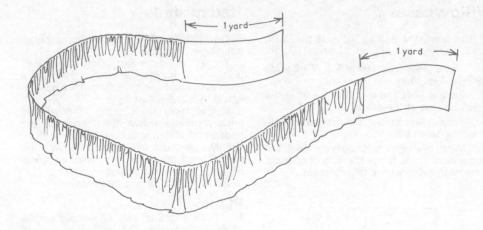

side which will form the hem.

5. Starting at a point one yard from the end, gather the unhemmed edge of the side piece to within one yard of the other end. This gathering can be done in sections.

6. Join the side to the main piece. Start at the head end, go down one side, across the bottom and back to the head at the other side. Turn the corners as in Section *Sewing a Straight Length of Material Around the Corner of Another Piece, Page* 342.

7. Turn and sew the hem at the top.

8. Sew cord or frilling over the seam, on the outside, from where the gathering starts on one side to where it ends the other.

9. When the bedspread is in place, the spare yard at the head end should be folded back, the pillows laid on top of it, and then folded back over the pillows again.

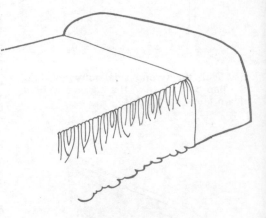

Make Do & Mend

Make-do-and-mend jobs are not the most exciting in a housewife's day, but they do give an immense feeling of satisfaction when they are finished. A good job of mending well done is the equivalent of getting a new article for nothing, with a consequent feeling of pride in the achievement. To say nothing of the fact that such a job is sometimes just plain necessary.

Patching

The same principle will apply to whatever you are patching: sheets, pillowcases, knees of trousers, elbows of shirts or anything made of a woven fabric.

1. Cut out the torn part to make a neat square or oblong hole.

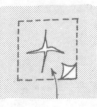

2. Cut an odd piece of matching material, the same shape as the hole but bigger.

3. Lay this piece over the hole on the wrong side of the article so that it overlaps the hole all the way round.

4. Pin it in place.

5. Turn in the patch all the way round and hem it down to the original article.

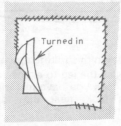

Turned in

6. Turn to the right side of the article. Tuck in the edge of the hole neatly. Hem it down to the patch all the way round.

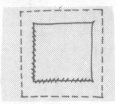

Turning cuffs

1. Unpick one cuff with a seam ripper, noting how it was put on in the first place.

2. Pull out all the loose pieces of cotton, turn the cuff round so that the outside is now facing inwards, and pin it in place.

3. Sew it on again just as it had been sewn before.

4. Leave the second cuff until you are satisfied the first one is correct.

5. Keep an eye on the second cuff to make sure the one you are working on looks as good.

This only applies to linked cuffs. It is not possible to turn buttonholed cuffs but they can be shortened, thus losing sight of the worn edge:

1. Unpick the side seams with a seam ripper for a depth of about 1 in. from the edge.

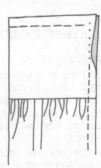

2. With the wrong side of the cuff facing you, turn the worn edge over about a quarter of an inch.

3. Pin it along the fold.

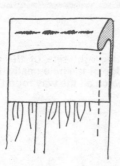

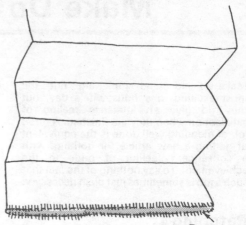

Frayed end of trouser leg

4. Tuck the now bulging inner side of the cuff under, about ½ in. below the worn line so that the inside of the cuff is the same length as the outside.

5. Slip stitch along this tuck very neatly so that the stitches do not show on the outside. Re-sew the side seams.

3. Press flat.

4. Working on the outside of the trousers, take a tuck in the leg by bringing the second line of tacking up to meet the top one. The fold thus made will be the top of the new turn-up.

This does very well for childrens' clothes and it is certainly good enough for playing in.

Frayed trouser bottoms

WITH TURN-UPS

Bear in mind here that you don't want to alter the length of the trouser leg.

1. Unpick the inside hem of the trouser leg and unfold it to lay out flat. Pick out loose pieces of cotton and brush out fluff. Do not press at this stage.

2. While the creases are still obvious, make a line of tacking stitches along each one of them. Also make a line round the trouser leg at the point to which the turn-up previously reached.

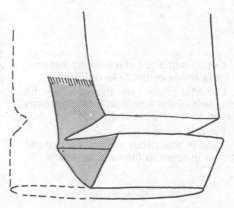

5. Tack down this fold temporarily.

6. Turn back the leg to expose the lower fold of the tuck you have just made. Sew round this tuck, near the edge, with running stitches.

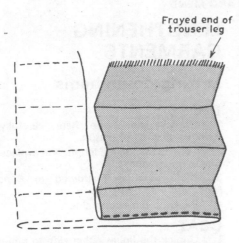

Frayed end of trouser leg

unpick the side seams to the point at which you propose to re-fold the bottoms.

3. Secure the unpicked seams at this point by hand sewing a few stitches.

4. Press out flat.

5. Turn in the bottoms about ½ in. higher than they were before (or less if you can get away with it). Slip stitch the hem on the inside.

6. If the trousers taper, the unpicked side seams on the inside will not meet. So hem each one down separately, very lightly, so that nothing shows on the outside.

7. Working on the right side of the material again fold in the bottom of the leg along the third line of tacking stitches and tack along the fold.

8. Turn the leg inside out. Cut off the excess turning as far back as the first line of tacking.

9. Oversew or blanket stitch the cut edge. Blind hem it to the outer piece.

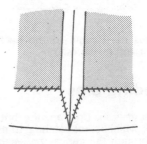

7. Press.

Sewing on buttons

TO FINE MATERIALS

1. Secure the sewing cotton to the material with a few neat little stitches where you wish to put the button.

2. Pass the cotton over and under, through the holes in the button until it is reasonably secure, bearing in mind that you must never sew a button on too tightly. If the button wobbles about, so much the better.

3. Wind the cotton round the threads between the button and the material about ten times.

4. Pass the needle and cotton to the back of the garment and fasten off neatly.

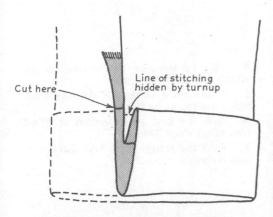

Cut here

Line of stitching hidden by turnup

10. At the seam, lightly catch the new turn-up to the leg.

11. Press very lightly before removing the tacking. Press again more firmly after the tacking has been removed.

WITHOUT TURN-UPS

You cannot help shortening these a little.

1. Unpick the hem carefully.

2. If the trousers are tapering, also

TO THICK MATERIALS

1. Always allow a 'stalk' between the button and the garment to permit the thickness of the overlapping material to lie flat under the button without puckering.

2. Secure the sewing cotton in the usual way, but as you pass the cotton over and under and through the holes, hold the button about $\frac{1}{4}$ in. away from the garment. When you have finished going over and under, the button should be hanging very loosely.

3. Wind the cotton round and round the threads between the button and the garment, and up and down as well, until the button stands quite firmly like a daisy on a stalk.

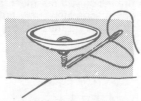

4. Pass the needle to the back of the garment and fasten off.

Mending zips

1. About 1 in. up from the bottom, on the side which is not catching in the slider, slash through the canvas between two of the teeth with a razor blade.

● *You must use a razor blade—scissors do not make a clean enough cut.*

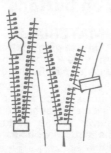

2. Bring the slider right down to the bottom and run it up again. The teeth will lock beyond the point where you cut the canvas.

3. With a needle and stout thread sew, over and over again, across the zip just above where it begins to lock, to form a buffer beyond which the slider cannot go.

● *The zip will now be about an inch shorter than it was before.*

LENGTHENING GARMENTS

Letting down hems

DRESS

1. Unpick the entire hem carefully. Remove all ends of cotton.

2. Turn up to required length. Pin in place. Check for evenness.

3. Blind hem as instructed in *Blind Hemming, Page 345.*

4. Press on the wrong side.

COAT

1. Unpick the lining either side to about 6 in. above the hem.

2. Completely unpick the hem and the facing at the sides.

3. Remove all ends of cotton. Open out and press flat.

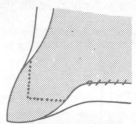

4. Fold up the hem to the new length all the way across and pin.

5. Check for evenness. Make sure both fronts are the same length.

6. Sew the hem as instructed in *Blind Hemming, Page 345.*

7. Fold the facing back into place and sew it down.

8. Sew the lining back into place.

9. Press on the wrong side.

False hems

This method is used when the existing hem is insufficient to allow a good turning after lengthening.

COAT

1. Work as **1, 2** and **3** for **Coat** on Page 358

2. For the false piece, cut a strip 3½ in. deep and long enough to go round the bottom of the coat from outer edge to outer edge, from a near matching material.

3. Sew the false piece to the *outside* of the coat from edge to edge.

4. Turn it back with the fold immediately above the sewing line.

5. Oversew the cut edge and blind hem as in *Blind Hemming, Page* 345

6. Finish off as **8** and **9** for **Coat** on Page 358

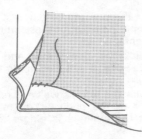

Here is an alternative, neater method for thick materials:

1. Work as **1, 2** and **3** for **Coat** on Page 358

2. Cut the false piece to fit the coat from front fold to front fold, instead of from the outer edges.

3. Sew on the false piece as in **3** above but only between the front folds—do not attach it to the facing.

4. As **4** and **5** above.

5. After folding the facing back into place, turn in the bottom edge and sew it down.

6. Slip stitch the facing and press.

● *This method avoids too much bulk at the hem line.*

DRESS

1. Unpick existing hem. Pick out pieces of cotton and press flat.

2. Cut a strip of matching material about 3½ in. wide and long enough to lie flat round the hem of the dress after it has been joined.

3. Join the two ends on the wrong side, and press flat.

4. Lay the right side of the false piece to the right side of the dress, edge to edge at the bottom, and sew it.

5. Turn the false piece to the inside and fold immediately above the sewing line.

6. Oversew the raw edge of the false piece and blind hem as in *Blind Hemming, Page* 345

7. Press on the wrong side.

Letting in pieces

There are a few other interesting ways of lengthening garments, particularly childrens' dresses:

1. Let in a piece at the waist. Either unpick the waist seam, or cut a waistless dress round the middle. Sew in a strip of toning or contrasting material.

2. Let a band into the skirt, either of contrasting material or braid.

3. For children, sew a frill round the bottom.

SHORTENING GARMENTS

Coat

1. Unpick the hem, lining and facing as for lengthening.

2. Press out flat.

3. If necessary, cut off a strip and oversew the cut edge. You can if you wish, provided the hem will not be too deep, manage without cutting to take advantage of the existing bound or sewn edge.

4. Turn up to the required length. Match for evenness and finish off as for lengthening.

5. Turn up the lining so that it does not show under the coat.

Dress

1. Unpick the hem, lay out flat and press.
2. Cut away surplus length if the hem is likely to be too wide.
3. Oversew the raw edge.
4. Turn up the hem to required length, check length and evenness.
5. Blind hem as in *Blind Hemming, Page* 345
6. Press on the wrong side.

TWO VARIATIONS FOR CHILDREN'S DRESSES:
● *Take a tuck or tucks round the skirt. Or:*
● *Cut a wide strip out of the skirt. Insert in its place a narrower piece of braid.*

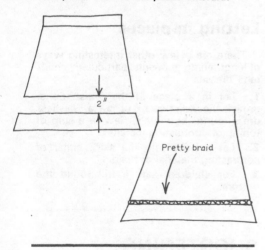

2"

Pretty braid

LETTING OUT GARMENTS

When a garment is tight across the shoulders try re-setting the sleeves.

1. Check how much seam allowance has been left round the inside of the armhole.

2. If there is ½ in. or more on both the sleeve and armhole, carefully unpick the seam and remove the sleeves.

3. Pull out loose threads. Press flat.

4. Re-set the sleeves. Sew them in again, leaving a smaller seam allowance. Sew right round twice for extra strength (you will have had to sew very near the edge).

5. If the seam is already near the edge do not try this. The result would not last very long.

Tight bodice

1. Unpick the darts—this may be sufficient—or:
2. Alter the position of buttons, if open at the front. If neither of these alternatives is sufficient:
3. Unpick the side seams and re-sew nearer the edge. If you have to do this you must:
4. Unpick the skirt as well and re-sew to line up with the bodice. You may now find that the armhole is bigger than the sleeve. If it is:
5. Unpick each of the four seams at the armhole for about 2 in.
6. Insert a small diamond shaped piece of material. Sew each side of the diamond to one of the four pieces of material.

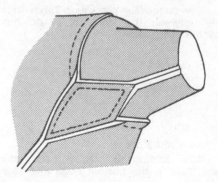

Tight skirt

1. Unpick the darts and make smaller ones, or:
2. Unpick the side seams and re-sew as

near to the edge as you need or dare.

3. This may necessitate altering the bodice to the same extent at the waist and re-sewing it to line up with the skirt.

TIGHT SKIRT WITH WAISTBAND

1. For a skirt with a waistband, follow the procedure above, but remove the waistband first.

2. If you have to alter the side seams, remove the zip and re-set it to keep a smooth hip line.

3. Make sure the darts are even in size and quantity: i.e., are one either side or two either side of centre.

4. Replace the zip first and the waistband last.

Tight waist (dress)

1. Unpick the waist seam. Remove the zip if there is one.

2. Alter the darts and/or the side seams as for bodice and skirt above. Replace the zip.

3. Make sure all the darts match up and re-join.

Tight trousers

The easiest way for a non-tailor is to insert a V at the back.

1. According to how many inches too small the trousers are, cut a V-shaped piece of near matching material with the bottom edge of the triangle 1 in. longer than this.

2. Unpick the centre back seam of the trousers to the same depth as the V.

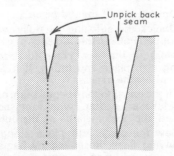

Unpick back seam

3. Sew in the V piece with the point of the triangle downwards.

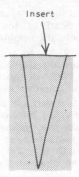

Insert

4. Face the insert with a piece of lining cut to the same size. Sew the lining to the outside, turn it to the inside and hem it down all the way round.

TAKING IN LOOSE GARMENTS

Shoulders

1. Unpick shoulder seams.

2. Make matching darts on the front and back bodice, or extend the existing darts or make additional darts.

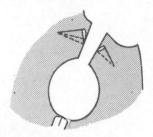

3. Re-sew shoulder seam.

Bodice

1. If there is a front opening—and providing it does not spoil the shape of the garment—alter the position of the buttons.

2. Unpick the waist seam.

3. Extend all the darts a little in width and length, and try on.

4. If this is insufficient, take in the two seams a little. Start at the waist and gradually taper into the original seam near the armhole.

5. Before re-sewing the bodice to the skirt, adjust the waist of the skirt so that the two pieces fit together seam to seam.

● *If you alter the dart on the left, you must alter the dart on the right, and vice versa. Otherwise the garment will be lop-sided. The same applies to the side seams. But you can alter the darts at the back and not the ones at the front, and vice versa.*

Skirt

1. Try extending the darts lengthways.

2. If not sufficient, unpick at the waist and extend the width of the darts as well.

3. If further adjustment is needed, unpick the side seam and re-sew slightly farther in than previously.

4. Before re-sewing the bodice to the skirt, make any necessary adjustments to the waist edge of the bodice so that the two pieces fit seam to seam.

Waist

DRESS
1. Unpick and work in the same order as you would for tightening *(see Tight Waist (Dress))*. This time, increase the size of the darts, make extra darts or take in the side seams.

SKIRT
1. Work in the same order as you would for tightening.

2. Take in each time instead of letting out.

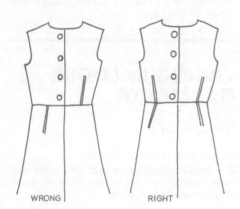

WRONG   RIGHT

BRAS

When the elastic in your bra has stretched to uselessness but the rest of it is still good, buy a new piece of elastic to put in the back. Bra-backs are sold in all haberdashery departments and come in several sizes, i.e., $1\frac{1}{2}$ in, 2 in. and so on.

1. Do not cut off the old piece.

2. Unpick the stitching carefully with a seam ripper. Pull out the odd ends of cotton.

3. Measure the new piece for size by pinning it in place and fitting. If it is too long, cut off the excess.

4. Fit the end into the opened seam on the bra. Make sure that, when the bra is fastened, the hooks will be on the outside.

5. Sew the piece into place along the old sewing lines. If sewing by hand, go over the seams twice for extra strength.

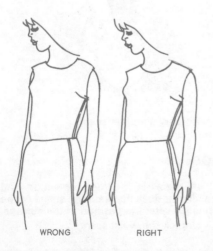

WRONG   RIGHT

ELASTIC IN BRIEFS

1. Measure the elastic round the waist first. It should just fit without being stretched. Allow a 1-in. overlap for joining the two ends.
2. Remove the old elastic from the garment.
3. If you have a bodkin, thread the elastic through it. Or fasten a small safety pin to one end of the elastic.
4. Thread the bodkin or safety pin through the inlet and right round until it comes out again. While doing so, hold the other end of elastic or pin it down to the garment.
5. When the elastic has been threaded and you have both ends firmly in your hand, overlap them for 1 in. and sew the two ends together very firmly.

FRAYED PLEATS AND VENTS

Pleats and vents in straight skirts are inclined to burst open at the top. If they do:
1. Make a 'clock' at the top of the opening.
2. Use your sewing cotton double.
3. Starting in the centre, immediately above the opening, work a satin stitch triangle on the right of the seam. Keep the centre line straight and the outer edge sloping towards the seam.

4. Make an identical satin stitch pad on the left of the seam.
5. Make two more pads one on either side of the seam. This time have the apex of the triangle in the centre and the bottom edge straight.

DARNING

● *For a hole in a woolly garment, use darning wool.*
● *For a hole in cotton socks or pants, use two strands of cotton.*

1. Start above the hole and just to the right. Make a line of running stitches to just below the hole.
2. Work back up with another row of running stitches. Work down again with another row. Continue; gradually working nearer to the hole.
3. When you get to the hole, make running stitches on either side of it so that the cotton or wool is lying across it. DO NOT TUG.
4. Keep working like this until you get to the other side of the hole. Then do a few more rows for strength.

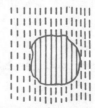

5. Turn the sewing round. Work in the same way at right angles to the previous lines of stitching.
6. To close in the hole, put the needle under the first strand and over the next, under and over right the way across, with a few running stitches to finish off.

7. On the next row, go under the strand you went over before.

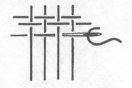

8. Make a few more rows of running stitches after you have finished weaving over the hole.

SHIRT SLEEVES

Shortening Shirt Sleeves

1. Take a tuck around the upper part of the sleeve.
2. Turn the sleeve inside out.
3. Feed the lower sleeve back through the upper sleeve until you have what looks like a short sleeve.
4. Sew round neatly about 1 in. in from the fold.

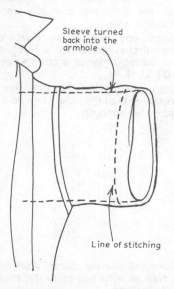

Sleeve turned back into the armhole

Line of stitching

Sometimes the shortened sleeve of a shirt or blouse has to be let out again for a growing child. To allow for this:

1. Take two small tucks in the sleeve,

one round the top, as above, and one at the cuff. This is done in the same manner by turning the cuff back towards the outside and sewing round on the inside.

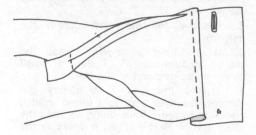

2. As the child grows, let out first one tuck and then the other.

INVISIBLE MENDING

This should be done professionally, but as an emergency measure, on all fabrics except very fine ones, you can do a fairly neat job with human hair.

1. Replace frayed edges and tidy up the tear as much as possible.
2. Sew backwards and forwards across the tear with a piece of hair taking care not to pucker the material.
3. Try a brunette for dark materials and a blonde for the paler shades.

SHEETS

By removing the worn centre and using the unworn sides, an old sheet can be kept in service for a long time.

1. Cut the whole sheet right down the middle, lengthways.
2. Cut away from each inside edge, from hem to hem, as much as you need to remove of the very thin parts so that you have only firm material left. The inner edges must be straight and will become the side edges when you have finished.
3. Join the two original outer edges together with a run and fell seam, then hem the two new outer edges. Work all the time on the wrong side.

Index

Prepared by Dennis J. Nisbet, Member, Society of Indexers.

G

H

Printed by Garrod and Lofthouse International Limited.